JOHN CALVIN

JOHN CALVIN
A Sixteenth-Century Portrait

William J. Bouwsma

OXFORD UNIVERSITY PRESS
New York   Oxford

Oxford University Press

Oxford   New York   Toronto
Delhi   Bombay   Calcutta   Madras   Karachi
Petaling Jaya   Singapore   Hong Kong   Tokyo
Nairobi   Dar es Salaam   Cape Town
Melbourne   Auckland

and associated companies in
Berlin   Ibadan

Copyright © 1988 by Oxford University Press, Inc.

First published in 1988 by Oxford University Press, Inc.,
200 Madison Avenue, New York, New York 10016

First issued as an Oxford University Press paperback, 1989

Oxford is a registered trademark of Oxford University Press

Library of Congress Cataloging-in-Publication Data

Bouwsma, William James, 1923-
John Calvin : a sixteenth-century portrait.

Bibliography: p.   Includes Index.
1. Calvin, Jean, 1509-1564.   2. Sixteenth century.   I. Title.
BX9418.B715   1988   284'.2'0924   87-12338
ISBN 0-19-504394-4
ISBN 0-19-505951-4 (PBK)

Frontispiece photo courtesy of the H. H. Meeter Center for Calvin Studies,
Calvin College and Seminary, Grand Rapids, Michigan.

2 4 6 8 10 9 7 5 3 1

Printed in the United States of America

ACKNOWLEDGMENTS

Among those who have helped me with this book, I owe a particular debt to the late M. Howard Rienstra, Director of the Meeter Center for Calvin Studies at Calvin College, for constant encouragement in a project about which I often felt anxious. He, Jill Raitt of the University of Missouri, and my Berkeley colleagues Henry F. May and Randolph Starn read the entire manuscript and gave me numerous suggestions for its improvement. Some of my deepest and most general obligations can be discerned from my notes; on particular matters I am grateful, among others, to Svetlana Alpers, Natalie Davis, Charles Garside, Thomas Laqueur, Sheldon Rothblatt, and Richard Webster. Marion Battles of the Meeter Center helped in various important ways.

My secretary, Dorothy Shannon, not only relieved me of many of the tasks of preparing the manuscript for publication but gave me constant moral support. Jeanne Rutenburg, my research assistant, has helped me in a myriad of routine tasks; in addition, her extensive knowledge of the patristic and medieval exegetical tradition has given me confidence in the individuality of Calvin's exegesis even when it was dependent on those who had gone before him. In determining the significance of a figure who saw himself as, first and last, a biblical theologian, this was of major importance. Although few of her findings are directly visible in my text, she has contributed more to this book than I can adequately acknowledge. But I am grateful above all to my wife, Beverly Bouwsma. She not only endured the usual trials of the spouse of a scholar in travail; she also read my work at various stages, lightened prose that was sometimes unreadably dense, and, most important, made me feel, when I felt discouraged, that I could complete this study.

A Humanities Fellowship from the University of California at Berkeley gave me a year of freedom to begin my work on this book, and the Berkeley History Department and College of Letters and Science were generous in giving me leave to write it. I feel particular gratitude, however, to the National Humanities Center, which awarded me a two-year Mellon Senior Fellowship, and to its Director Charles Blitzer, its Assistant Director, Kent Mulliken, and its exceedingly gracious and helpful staff for providing an ideal environment and ideal resources for completing my work.

I have incorporated into this book material from various pieces previously published: "Calvin and the Renaissance Crisis of Knowing," *Calvin Theological Journal*, 17 (1982), 190–211; "John Calvin's Anxiety," *Proceedings of the American Philosophical Society*, 128 (1984), 252–256; "The Quest for the Historical Calvin," *Archiv für Reformationsgeschichte*, 77 (1986), 47–58; "Scripture, Ecumenism, and Spirituality: The Hard Case of John Calvin," *CICA Annual* (1986), 30–44; and "The Spirituality of John Calvin," *Christian Spirituality: High Middle Ages and Reformation*, ed. Jill Raitt and John Meyendorff (New York: Crossroads Press, 1987), vol. 17 of *World Spirituality: An Encyclopedic History of the Religious Quest*.

May 1987   W. J. B.
Berkeley, California

CONTENTS

Contents

To Beverly
and to John, Philip, Paul, and Sarah
for a better understanding of ourselves

INTRODUCTION

The Quest for the Historical Calvin

Calvinism has been widely credited—or blamed—for much that is thought to characterize the modern world: for capitalism and modern science, for the discipline and rationalization of the complex societies of the West, for the revolutionary spirit and democracy, for secularization and social activism, for individualism, utilitarianism, and empiricism.[1] What John Calvin thought is by no means necessarily identical with what is meant by the "Calvinism" to which these large consequences have been attributed. He is nevertheless implicated in the supposed achievements of the movement that bears his name, if only because of the propensity of many "Calvinists" to invoke the authority of Calvin to legitimate their own ways of life and thought.[2] It is accordingly remarkable that Calvin himself is now one of the least known among the great figures of his century. Machiavelli and Thomas More, Erasmus and Rabelais, Michelangelo and Copernicus, Cervantes, Montaigne, and Shakespeare, all Calvin's near contemporaries, are variously admired and vividly alive for us;[3] but Calvin is virtually unknown, except perhaps as a reminder of the crimes and follies of the past.

The causes of Calvin's present obscurity are complex, but one among them has been his neglect, with a few honorable exceptions, by secular historians. Whether they have been intimidated by the mass of specialized Calvin scholarship,[4] persuaded by their own secularism of the irrelevance of religious discourse to real life (and therefore also of the irrelevance of real life to theological discourse), or simply dissuaded from seeking to make Calvin's acquaintance by the forbidding persona that has been imposed on him, they seem tacitly to have acquiesced in the notion that knowing him could not add much to our understanding of the past. They have accordingly left Calvin to theologians and Calvin specialists whose interest in the historical Calvin has been at best marginal.[5]

A further element in the obscurity of Calvin is suggested by the gigantic statue, erected by his followers and familiar to every visitor to Geneva, at the Reformers' Wall behind the University. Unlike the human Calvin, the

1

statue is difficult to forget, as of course it was intended to be; it is, after all, a memorial. But it is a good deal more than that. For here Calvin stands, more than twice as large as life, stylized beyond recognition, stony, rigid, immobile, and—except for his slightly abstracted disapproval of whatever we might imagine him to be contemplating—impassive. Drained of his humanity, this *man*, who was singularly eloquent about the universality of human frailty and who, in his own life, was constantly looking within himself for reminders that no human being is ever free from the struggle with sin and weakness, has been converted into a strangely ambiguous icon in order to create an impression and to stimulate a degree of veneration about which his own views might be interesting to hear.[6]

As depicted here, Calvin is also a notable illustration of the paradoxical tendency of Protestantism, in whose origins a repudiation of the possibility of holy men in this world had been prominent, to make saints of its own founding fathers; this icon of Calvin, however appropriate it may have seemed to its creators in the early twentieth century, would have been familiar, substantially if not stylistically, to the sixteenth. But the Calvin of latter-day Geneva also meets the need for ancestral legitimation on the part of followers for whom the living Calvin, with all of his characteristically sixteenth-century ambiguities, hesitations, and contradictions—in a word, his finiteness and humanity—was hardly convenient.[7] The Calvin with whom most of us are acquainted is chiefly an artifact of later Calvinism. He demonstrates our very human tendency to invent the fathers we need, even if it means making very sure that they cannot rise up to contradict us.[8]

The result is apparent in studies of Calvin almost to the present day. Biographies of Calvin, however responsible their scholarship, remain quasi-hagiographical; and studies of Calvin's thought continue to be shaped by the assumption that theological discourse should be immune from the scrutiny to which other kinds of discourse are subjected. It is commonly treated ahistorically and assumed to be free from the confusion, the incoherence, the contradictions, and the other marks of human frailty that we are free to recognize and may feel challenged to explain in other areas of human expression;[9] and its real meaning is assumed always to be its overt and intended meaning. Calvin is thus widely perceived as a dispassionate systematizer, and therefore—again the icon looms in the background—"not so much a personality as a mind."[10] Among treatments of Calvin, exceptions to these observations are rare, and some of the exceptions might be described as ahistorical exercises in demonography rather than hagiography.[11]

A kind of secular analogue to the systematization of Calvin as theologian has been the attempt, equally ahistorical, to identify him with particular traditions of philosophical discourse, especially Platonism or Stoicism. Although labels of this kind have some plausibility, they are of little use for understanding figures of the sixteenth century, when intellectual purity of the kind they imply was rarely possible. Calvin's age was utterly eclectic, in ways of which it was no more than half aware; and so was he. This is why, it seems to me, the identification of Calvin's "sources" is an exercise unlikely to yield major returns.[12] Like other cultivated men of his time, he was open to so much that the important question is less what he read than why he preferred and made a part of himself some works and authors rather than others. This book is, accordingly, not a study of Calvin's sources, although from time to time, for the sake of perspective, I have identified secular contemporaries with whom his thought had affinities.

But the limitations of traditional approaches to Calvin have not been the only obstacles to understanding him historically. He also suffers as a result of the tendency of historians to shy away from major figures in cultural history; great artists, writers and thinkers are left, for the most part, to specialists who rarely ask a historian's questions.[13] Complex texts, as Dominick LaCapra has remarked, are rarely analyzed as historical artifacts.[14]

To reestablish the connection between Calvin's texts and the sixteenth-century thinker to whom they owe their existence, we can profitably ponder an observation about philosophy by William James, a figure who may have a better, if a subtler, claim to be considered one of Calvin's spiritual sons than many who have thought of themselves as Calvinists. "What the system claims to be," James declared of philosophy in one of his most influential works, "is a picture of the great universe of God. What it is—and oh so flagrantly—is the revelation of how intensely odd the personal flavor of some fellow creature is."[15] I believe that one of the basic tasks of humanistic scholarship is to discover the personal, and therefore historical, flavor that constitutes the humanity of all cultural artifacts.

Recent developments in Calvin studies have made the recovery of a historical Calvin increasingly practical. Thanks largely to Heiko Oberman and his students, the tendency of earlier Reformation scholarship to emphasize the inspired originality of the Reformation has given way to recognition of its embeddedness in the spirituality of the later Middle Ages.[16] More particularly, the cliché that made "humanist" and "Reformer" into antithetical categories is fading, so that growing recognition that Calvin's formation and culture were those of a Renaissance humanist can now help us understand Calvin the Reformer. In addition, historians not primarily concerned directly with Calvin (and therefore, perhaps, able to look at him freshly) have for some time been making at least passing observations about him that nag at the mind: for example, Hans Baron's recognition of the affinities between Calvin's political attitudes and the civic conceptions of the Italian Renaissance republics; Michael Walzer's suggestion that even Calvin's theological achievement was essentially political in its concern to balance opposing impulses; Hugh Trevor-Roper's observations about the depth and durability of Calvin's Erasmianism; and Robert Kingdon's interest in relating Genevan developments generally to the ethos and social institutions of the later medieval town.[17] Works focused directly on Calvin from a historical rather than a particular confessional perspective are also beginning to appear.[18]

This book, then, tries to interpret Calvin as a figure of his time: as a representative French intellectual, an evangelical humanist and therefore a rhetorician, and an exile. It is not directly concerned with Calvin's theology, though it may suggest novel ways of looking at that subject. I have conceived of it as a portrait rather than biography, not only because the general shape of Calvin's life has long been familiar, but above all because I am persuaded—this was a tragedy for a man who attached such value to personal progress—that, except for showing increasingly the abrasions wrought by troubles and time, Calvin made little advance over the years in those matters that troubled him most.[19] Unlike Saint Augustine, whose life, both outwardly and inwardly, was a genuine pilgrimage, so that to understand what he wrote one must, so to speak, catch him on the wing, Calvin was still wrestling as inconclusively with the same inner demons at the end of his life as when he first arrived in Geneva. The evidence on which my portrait is based is drawn indiscriminately from every period in his life for which data are available, and the portrait itself is relatively static.[20]

This is not, however, primarily a psychological study. I have thought it necessary to explore Calvin's complex personality as deeply as the (chiefly) indirect evidence permits; a good portrait, I assume, suggests psychological depths. But my book is not simply a portrait; it is a *sixteenth-century* portrait. I am less interested in Calvin's inner life for its own sake than in using it to illuminate the momentous cultural crisis central to his century, which was at the heart of the Renaissance as well as of the Reformation and as crucial for Catholic Europe as for the peoples that separated from the Roman church. The model for this book, in purpose if not in form, is Lucien Febvre's treatment of Rabelais in his *Problème de l'incroyance au XVIe siècle*. It is no longer so true as when Febvre wrote that great book, thanks largely to Febvre himself, that the "entire century must be rethought."[21] But my book, like his, is as much concerned to scrutinize the man in order to understand the time as to scrutinize the time in order to understand the man. That the relation between man and time was close is suggested by Calvin's large following. As Philippe Ariès has remarked, a novel theological position can establish itself only if it is "very close to" as well as "slightly different from the general feeling of its age." "If it were very different," Ariès continued, "it would not even be conceivable by its author, or understandable by the elite any more than by the masses. If it were no different at all, it would pass unnoticed."[22]

I do not conceive of the sixteenth century quite as Febvre did. For him, sixteenth-century culture lacked those resources which in the next century would be adequate to support such harmonies as the genial Rabelais seemed to foreshadow and, I suspect, Febvre loved. For me, the century was tense, driven, fundamentally incoherent, and riven by insoluble conflicts that were all the more serious because they were as much within as between individuals and parties.[23] Calvin, I think, provides an even better means of entry to the century, conceived in these terms, than Rabelais, though this is partly because he resembled Rabelais more than either he or Rabelais could have appreciated. This is why I present my cultural portrait of Calvin as a kind of dialogue between antithetical impulses, and Calvin's thought as an effort to balance between them. "Balance," however, suggests political accommodation rather than reconciliation; and Calvin's success, like that of most political compromises, was tenuous and unstable. His limited success in meeting his own needs, however, paradoxically provides much of the explanation for the success of Calvinism as a movement.

The approach by way of tensions and contradictions makes it clear that I cannot accept the received version of Calvin as a systematic thinker. I do not believe that Calvin even aspired to the construction of a system, as the term "system" is commonly understood; as a biblical theologian, he despised what passed for systematic theology in his own time. He sought, like other humanists, to develop as effective a pedagogy as possible, and this meant arranging what he had to communicate in the most readily apprehensible and effective manner;[24] the urgency of the crisis of his time required it. Beyond this, the intellectual and cultural resources available to thinkers of the sixteenth century made the production of "systematic thought" almost inconceivable, a circumstance that students of Calvin's thought have not always kept in mind.[25] A systematic Calvin would be an anachronism; there are no "systematic" thinkers of any significance in the sixteenth century. Its achievements were of another kind that, I suspect, Calvin himself valued more.

Immediately, to be sure, Calvin seems difficult to know. Luther could not avoid conveying much about himself even in treatises, commentaries, and sermons; but Calvin rarely employed the first person singular, and even when he did so the identity of his "I" is often problematic.[26] His reticence was partly deliberate. Aiming to be as much as possible a transparent medium of the Gospel, he strove to exclude himself, on principle, from his public discourse. But his reticence was also a function of a withdrawn and scholarly temperament.[27] There was a deeper truth than he was perhaps aware of when he remarked that before his entry into public life his "one great object" had been "to live in seclusion without being known."[28]

Nevertheless, I think that Calvin reveals a great deal about himself to those who have learned his oblique modes of communication. His need to hide himself discloses a crucial element in his personality. He also revealed himself by the manner, tone, and imagery of his communication, which sometime seem to undermine its substance. He disclosed himself, too, in broad, protective generalities whose truth is less than obvious. Every Christian, or every human being, he may assert, has had such and such an experience, is convinced of this or that. But if we ask how he can know this, the answer may often be that he was thinking of himself. He may also reveal himself through remarks that in context seem unexpected, gratuitous or even irrelevant; on such occasions Calvin's persona seems suddenly to drop, and a very human self to peep through. If we keep these principles in mind, it may be possible to read Calvin as Kant said we should read Plato: "to understand him better than he understood himself."[29]

I

THE MAN AND
THE TIMES

1

A Sixteenth-Century Life

I have called this book a portrait rather than a biography because I think that in what mattered most to him, Calvin developed little between his break with the church that had nurtured him and his death some thirty years later. Although his career was filled with accomplishment, his inner life showed few signs of the progress which he associated with godliness; he was still wrestling at the end of his life with the self-doubt, confusions, and contradictory impulses that had been with him from the beginning. His deep uneasiness, although it may have goaded him to feats of exertion, made the myriad problems with which he had to contend unusually abrasive. It also helps to explain the troubling contrast revealed in actual portraits of him between his young manhood and his old age. In a likeness painted when he was about thirty, his face, handsome, sensitive, and fastidious, is grave but tranquil and open. Later portraits are strikingly different. Calvin's face has become worn and wrinkled, and the clear eyes of his youth are glazed with fatigue and revulsion. The present chapter will sketch the external events that lead up to and link the two portraits; the following chapter, the inner turmoil that underlies Calvin's thought.

Calvin was born on July 10, 1509, in Noyon, a small episcopal town in Picardy, France, the youngest of four (or possibly five) children, all boys. His father held a position of some responsibility in the service of the cathedral chapter. His mother, the daughter of a town notable, died four or five years after Calvin's birth, and his father soon remarried. Shortly after, young Calvin was sent from his father's house to that of the Montmors, a neighboring noble family, where he received some of his earliest education.

Intending his son for the priesthood, Calvin's father dispatched him to the University of Paris when he was about twelve, then the normal age for beginning higher education. Here Calvin finished the arts course and took a master's degree; and, like many other students of his generation, he was attracted to the novel evangelical humanism and the eclectic spirituality of Erasmus and Jacques Lefèvre d'Etaples. But before young Calvin had

9

reached the age of twenty, his father decided that he should become a lawyer rather than a priest. Between 1528 and 1533, therefore, Calvin worked on a law degree in the schools of Bourges and Orléans, and was *licencié* in the law. Meanwhile he continued his humanistic studies, and in 1532 he published an edition, with a learned commentary, of Seneca's essay on clemency. His father, excommunicated in a dispute with the cathedral chapter, had died the year before.

Most students of Calvin have passed quickly over the earlier part of his life because of the significance attributed to his supposed "conversion" to "Protestantism." But religious conversion is a more problematic conception than is ordinarily recognized. It is as much a cultural artifact as an individual experience, and in Christianity it commonly corresponds to the archetypal conversions of Paul and Augustine, the latter not altogether independent of the former. Both were identified with an event, located more or less precisely in time, effecting a sharp break with the past. Life before conversion, from this standpoint, is irrelevant except as preparation for this break or as a stimulus to repentance; life afterward is made new.[1] As a badge of spiritual authority, a conversion of this kind is often an unexamined assumption of religious biography.

The evidence for a "conversion" corresponding to this model in Calvin's life is negligible.[2] It consists almost entirely of a single passage in the preface to his commentary on the Psalms, written in 1557, nearly thirty years after the supposed event, to which, during this long interval, he had never before directly referred. His silence may not itself be decisive; Calvin was generally reticent about himself. But the passage seems to me almost useless as evidence for what it is commonly taken to demonstrate. Calvin wrote:

> God drew me from obscure and lowly beginnings and conferred on me that most honorable office of herald and minister of the Gospel. My father had intended me for theology from my early childhood. But when he reflected that the career of the law proved everywhere very lucrative for its practitioners, the prospect suddenly made him change his mind. And so it happened that I was called away from the study of philosophy and set to learning law. Although, out of obedience to my father's wishes, I tried my best to work hard, yet God at last turned my course in another direction by the secret rein of his providence. What happened first was that by an unexpected conversion he tamed to teachableness a mind too stubborn for its years—for I was so strongly devoted to the superstitions of the papacy that nothing less could draw me from such depths of mire. And so this mere taste of true godliness that I received set me on fire with such a desire to progress that I pursued the rest of my studies more coolly, although I did not give them up altogether. Before a year had slipped by anybody who longed for a purer doctrine kept on coming to learn from me, still a beginner, a raw recruit.[3]

By "conversion" Calvin meant only a shift and quickening of his interests. He said nothing about any *belief* that would later be associated with him, indeed nothing incompatible with the evangelical humanism of a whole generation of students at Paris, most of whom remained faithful to Rome in spite of their antagonism to what they commonly described as "superstitions" in the church. All we can be sure of, from this account, is that much later in his life, Calvin believed that at this time he became more open— "teachable" is his word. There is nothing here that would suggest what would subsequently be called "Protestantism," a word unknown before 1529.[4]

What is probably more to the point is that Calvin attached little or no significance to "conversion" as a precise event in his many discussions of the Christian life and the way of salvation. Indeed, he was inclined to minimize the importance even of the conversion of Paul.[5] He also had reservations about a far more famous sixteenth-century conversion that was already assuming mythical proportions among Lutherans. Calvin paid tribute to Luther's role in launching a reformation in the Church—not *the* Reformation—but at the same time he emphasized the gradual development in Luther's understanding of the content of reformation and the incompleteness of Luther's work:

> We remember with amazement how deep was the abyss of ignorance and how horrible the darkness of the papacy. It was a great miracle of God that Luther and those who worked with him at the beginning in restoring the pure truth were able to emerge from it little by little. Some claim to be scandalized because these good personages did not see everything at once and did not finish and polish such a difficult work. It is as though they were accusing us of not seeing the sun shine as fully at dawn as at midday.[6]

Calvin always emphasized the gradualness rather than the suddenness of conversion and the difficulty of making progress in the Christian life. "We are converted," he said, "little by little to God, and by stages."[7] In any case the new direction taken by Calvin after his flight from Paris in 1535 should not be exaggerated. The experiences of childhood and youth were significant for Calvin's entire life, as they are for most human beings. So were the spiritual currents to which he was exposed in the old church; Calvinism was the creation of a devout sixteenth-century French Catholic.

Calvin's relationship with his parents seems to me worth more attention than it has generally received. The death of his mother when he was a small child and his subsequent exclusion from his father's household may have begun in him a sense of homelessness that would be later deepened by exile; he grieved for his motherland all his life. The loss of mother and home may also have been an element in what seem to me his undeniably ambiguous feelings about his father, a matter of particular moment for one whose thought depended so heavily on the understanding of fatherhood. Sixteenth-century sons did not commonly denounce their fathers, nor did Calvin express directly any antagonism to his. But although he later spoke with affection of the Montmor family in which he was placed,[8] he never expressed himself warmly about his father. On the contrary: the coldness with which

he reported his father's imminent death in a letter to a friend made it seem
little more than an unwelcome interruption to the cultivation of his friends.
"I promised on leaving that I would return soon," he wrote, "and I have
been on tenterhooks about this for some time. For when I was considering
returning to you, my father's illness delayed me. When the doctors gave
hope of his recovery, I only wanted you; and this longing, strong before,
increased as the days passed. Meanwhile this drags on day after day until no
hope of his survival remains; his death is certain. Whatever happens, I will
see you again."[9] We have already seen, in passing, Calvin's unflattering
explanation of his father's decision to make him a lawyer rather than a
priest. Years later he insisted that a child's obedience to his father is required by divine decree, but he said nothing of any more tender bond.[10] We
are on delicate ground here, but I do not see how any account of Calvin as a
human being can ignore such basic experiences. Later chapters will suggest
how they reverberated throughout his maturity.

Calvin's spiritual formation at the University of Paris was also of permanent importance for him. Whatever may be said of his "conversion," it did
not obliterate but built on his evangelical humanism. The philological training he first received in Paris was crucial to his biblicism. Even during his first
years at the Collège de Montaigu, hardly a humanist academy, he improved
his Latin. But, as has often been the case with good students, the more
important part of his Paris education seems to have been informal. He
sought out like-minded fellow students and congenial mentors.[11] He studied
Latin with Mathurin Cordier, to whom he dedicated his commentary on
Ephesians a decade later, calling him "an instructor sent to me by God." To
Cordier, he said, he owed his understanding of "the true method of learning." His legal studies, which he seems to have pursued in a rather leisurely
way, continued, rather than interrupted, his formation as a humanist, for the
mos gallicus to which he was introduced at Orléans depended heavily on
humanistic philology. He also began to learn Greek, in Orléans and Bourges,
from Melchior Wolmar, to whom he dedicated his commentary on Second
Corinthians. Meanwhile he returned at intervals to Paris, where, with François Vatable, he began the study of Hebrew at what would eventually become the Collège Royale. He would later deepen his knowledge of that
language under Sebastien Munster at Basel.

Latin, Greek, Hebrew: these were the "three languages" in the scholarly
and educational program of Christian reform inspired by Lefèvre and Erasmus. Led by Guillaume Budé and protected by the king's sister, Marguerite
d'Angoulême, it had taken root among Paris intellectuals during the generation before Calvin's arrival.[12] The reformism of Paris had been nourished by
Italian humanism, which, combining literary classicism and philology,
pointed, under the slogan "*ad fontes*," to the study of the Greek and Latin
Fathers and the Bible in its original languages. Like Italian humanists, Paris
reformers looked to the ancient church as a model for contemporary reform.
Having not yet heard of "Protestantism," indisposed to see Luther as a
"heretic," and as Gallicans unimpressed by his condemnation in Rome,

they were also eagerly reading Luther's works during Calvin's first years at the University.

Indeed, following Erasmus, they made a point of their commitment to the Roman church; as loyal Catholics, they aimed to reform it, not to destroy it. A letter from Erasmus to Albert of Brandenburg in 1519 suggests what troubled the circles young Calvin frequented. In this letter Erasmus was careful to excuse the papacy from responsibility for the abuses he attacked; he blamed others. "The world," he declared, "is bowed under the burden of human regulations, of the opinions and dogmas of the scholastics, of the tyranny of the friars." He blamed the friars for seeking "deliberately to ensnare the consciences of men," and for beginning "boldly to disregard Christ and to preach only their own novel and even shameless doctrines." Among these doctrines he singled out as particularly obnoxious those connected with indulgences.

He found the consequences infinitely deplorable: "the gospel teachings have gradually lost all their force; and it was bound to happen, as matters continued to slide from bad to worse, that eventually the spark of Christian piety would be completely extinguished which could have rekindled the flame of charity."[13] Both Lefèvre and Erasmus added to this reformist concern an emphasis on the Bible as the basis for renewing the church; above all, as Lefèvre emphasized, the Bible provided "the only truth that saves."[14]

Among the most enthusiastic followers of Erasmus in Paris, and one of those truest to the Erasmian spirit in Calvin's time, was François Rabelais.[15] Much later in his life, Calvin included Rabelais, though without revealing any knowledge of *Gargantua et Pantagruel*, among a group of French humanists, mostly old Erasmians, whom he attacked in very general terms for pride, vanity, and scorning the Gospel.[16] Except for their refusal to abandon the papal church, there was little in the reformism of Erasmus and Rabelais that did not become a permanent part of Calvin's reform program.[17]

Between 1527 and 1534, at any rate, and in a more general sense all his life, Calvin inhabited the Erasmian world of thought and breathed its spiritual atmosphere; he remained in major ways always a humanist of the late Renaissance.[18] He never condemned humanism in general, and only occasionally individual humanists for particular shortcomings. Unlike Luther, he rarely attacked Erasmus. Most of his associates during his exile had been influenced by both Lefèvre and Erasmus.

With his talent for rapidly digesting whatever interested him, Calvin, in Paris, quickly acquired a broad acquaintance with classical literature, and he studied works of such leading Italian humanists as Lorenzo Valla.[19] In his Seneca commentary he openly identified himself with the humanist movement by paying his respects to Budé as the "first ornament and pillar of literature" and to Erasmus as its "second ornament," although at the same time he displayed a kind of sophomoric satisfaction at having discovered in Seneca "things which have escaped the notice of even Erasmus, though he sweated twice in this arena, which have now for the first time been noticed by me," a point he was scoring "without any ill-will."[20] His emotional investment in this work is apparent in the anxiety with which, writing from Orléans, where he was finishing his legal studies, he begged a friend in Paris to "write as soon as you can and let me know with what favor or coldness it has been received."[21] He also retained all his life a belief in his own talent for writing poetry.[22] But of all the branches of humanist learning, Latin oratory made the deepest impression on him. He acquired a thorough familiarity with both Cicero and Quintilian; and while he was studying law at Bourges, he lectured on rhetoric at a local Augustinian convent. The rhetorical culture of Renaissance humanism left a profound mark on every aspect of Calvin's mature thought.

Lefèvre and Erasmus also guided his patristic and biblical studies to the end of his life, and he continued to venerate them. Beza recorded his visit to Lefèvre, cordially received, probably early in 1534 after he had decided to break with the old church. There is no record of his having visited the aged Erasmus, with whom he coincided in Basel for much of 1535; but it can hardly be an accident that he employed in the last French version of the *Institutes* the description of the Gospel particularly associated with Erasmus: "Christian philosophy."[23]

Although a good deal of what follows is intended to describe Calvin's Erasmianism in greater depth, there are also major respects in which he was not an Erasmian. The differences between Calvin and Erasmus seem to me, however, temperamental rather than substantial. Where Erasmus, following his beloved Lucian, and Rabelais, following Erasmus, ridiculed the abuses they detested, Calvin acrimoniously attacked them. He saw nothing but irreligion in Lucian.[24]

The durability of Calvin's humanism, and the importance he attached to it as a resource for the Gospel, are implicit in one of the major achievements of his last years, the establishment of an academy in Geneva for the training of leaders for the Genevan church and state. This institution had been foreshadowed in the Ecclesiastical Ordinances of 1541, in which, after describing the duties of those entrusted with the teaching of sacred doctrine, Calvin declared that, since such instruction is useless without "the languages and humanities," a college should be established to prepare both for the ministry and for political responsibility.[25] His academy was a typical Erasmian "trilingual" institution. Its students were first thoroughly grounded in Latin grammar and rhetoric by the study of Virgil, Cicero, and other classical authors, and in the fourth year they began Greek. They learned history from Livy and Xenophon and dialectic from the arguments of Cicero rather than from medieval textbooks. This curriculum prepared students, like bachelors of arts in the Scholastic curriculum, for professional training in theology, law, or medicine.

Humanistic studies also continued to be central, for Calvin, in theology. Future Calvinist ministers learned Hebrew by studying the Old Testament, perfected their Greek and Latin by further analysis of classical authors, went more deeply into history, and learned physics from Aristotle. Calvin's ideal for both pastors and secular rulers resembled Quintilian's generally educated orator, the ideal of humanist educators everywhere.[26]

Late in 1533 Calvin's years in Paris came to an abrupt end when royal policy became less tolerant of a movement that, if not obviously heretical, seemed to threaten the peace. His close friend Nicolas Cop, rector of the University, expressed in a public sermon, on which Calvin had probably collaborated, beliefs widely shared among evangelical humanists. Immediately afterward Cop and Calvin fled from Paris.[27] Cop went to Basel. Calvin, although he did not leave France immediately, moved about for over a year, stopping briefly in Noyon to renounce benefices his father had arranged for him in better days (a gesture consistent with Erasmian Catholicism), before making up his mind to follow Cop. Although Basel had instituted Protestant worship, it was a relatively tolerant international publishing center. Erasmus was more comfortable there than in Catholic Freiburg.

Cop's address provides us with an opportunity to look at something very close to Calvin's position at the time of his departure from France. The discourse opened on an Erasmian note of appreciation for "the Christian philosophy," a philosophy, as Cop had said, "divinely given to man by Christ to show forth the true and surest felicity," a philosophy that "eclipses the wisdom of the world." To bring it to mankind, "God had willed to become man." This philosophy "pardons sins by the grace of God alone," promises to Christians the Holy Spirit that "sanctifies the hearts of all, and brings eternal life." The discourse was notably christocentric. It represents Christ as "the intercessor with the Father" and "the glory of the Father"; we should therefore "pray that he may flow into our souls and delight to shower us with the dew of his spiritual grace."

Cop went on to contrast Gospel and Law in a way characteristic of evangelical humanism. The Law, he declared, "threatens, burdens, promises no benevolence," but "the Gospel acts without threats, it does not coerce by precepts but rather teaches us the supreme good will of God toward us." From here Cop proceeded to attack salvation by works. God's benefits come to us "not because of our virtues or value but through the grace of God alone." "Who could be so obtuse," Cop asked, "as to think and assert that eternal life is a repayment for our good deeds, or that our good deeds are worthy of eternal life?" Other concerns Calvin would later express also appear here, including his identification of sin with a torpor from which God alone can arouse us: "He does not allow us to drowse long in darkness but rouses us from our deep sleep." Cop reached a climax with an assertion of the obligation of Christians, in spite of persecution, to proclaim these truths publicly:

Why then do we conceal the truth rather than speak it out boldly? Is it right to please men rather than God, to fear those who can destroy the body but not the soul? Oh the ingratitude of mankind, which will not bear the slightest affliction in the name of him who died for the sins of all, him whose blood has freed us from eternal death and the shackles of Satan! The world and the wicked are wont to label as heretics, imposters, seducers and evil-speakers those who strive purely and sincerely to penetrate the minds of believers with the Gospel. . . . But happy and blessed are they who endure all this with composure, giving thanks to God in the midst of affliction and bravely bearing calamities. . . . Onward, then, oh Christian men. With our every muscle let us strive to attain this great bliss.

It was time, then, for Calvin, as a Christian man, to move onward. This did not necessarily mean, even yet, a break with the Roman church. What it did mean was something else almost as serious; it required Calvin to go into exile, like so many other figures not only of the Reformation but also of the Italian Renaissance.[28] For the rest of his life he was compelled to live among strangers with all those "feelings of privation and unworthiness," in Thomas Greene's phrase, that come from rejection by one's own community. Besides leaving him with loneliness and regret, exile exposed him to temptations he could not altogether resist: a sense of his own superiority to others less courageous or decisive than himself and a contempt for compromise that was sometimes at odds with his strong political instincts.[29]

Calvin, quite simply, loved his native country. At times he injected patriotic sentiments into his works. "Love of country, country, which is, so to speak, our common mother," he remarked, "is naturally planted in us,"[30] or again, "His native soil is sweet to everyone, and it is sweet to dwell among one's own people."[31] Like most of his friends in Paris, he was a Gallican; even in the final version of the *Institutes*, he noted with pride how ancient Gaul had "reverenced the bishop of Rome to the point of obeying him only in so far as it pleased."[32] He always paid particular attention to events in France, dispatching missionaries there[33] and lamenting the afflictions of his persecuted French followers.[34] His remarks on the pain of exile have a personal ring. "Exile is in itself sorrowful," he declared, "and the sweetness of their native soil binds all human beings to it."[35] It is "a wretched safety when men cannot otherwise make provision for it than by inflicting a voluntary exile on themselves."[36] He must often have thought of Ovid's words: "I shall leave the city, shall flee, go into exile, endure my loss as best I can with miserable, cruel patience."[37]

Calvin did not hesitate to call on his correspondents in France to join him in exile, citing the example of Abram's willingness "to renounce his kindred and his father's house" without any promise of present reward. But even his letters exhorting others to join him reflect his sense of the harshness of exile. As he wrote a French noble, candidly if not altogether persuasively: "Be forewarned that you will not enter an earthly paradise where you may rejoice in God without molestation: you will find a people rude enough; you will have trials vexatious enough. Do not expect to improve your condition except in so far that, having been released from miserable bondage of body and of soul, you will have leave to serve God purely."[38] It seems likely that Calvin's own experience of exile contributed to his understanding of the Gospel as a haven for the dispossessed, a refuge for those quite literally alienated.

Calvin had now reached an age that he would look back on as the most vigorous and productive time of life. In the decade between twenty-five and thirty-five, he declared, a man "bears his fruit," he is "in full vigor as an adviser and in doing what is suitable in human life." At this age "a man can be useful."[39] His own concern to be useful was also thoroughly Erasmian; Erasmus had described his own activity as intended always "to serve some useful purpose."[40] Calvin always believed that even his scholarship was justified only by its utility. "In all your studies," he wrote to a fellow pastor, "you must be careful that they are not for your amusement, but for the service of the church of Christ. Those who seek in scholarship nothing more than an honored occupation with which to beguile the tedium of idleness I would compare with those who pass their lives looking at paintings."[41]

But he was still uncertain, in early 1535, about his "calling"; indeed, still an Erasmian, he was probably vague about his beliefs. To clarify these matters, following perhaps a remark of Augustine about making progress through writing, Calvin, whose life so far had been devoted to study, began studiously to write. He started by composing a preface to his cousin Pierre Olivétan's French translation of the Bible, the first of his writings to express hostility to the papacy as the source of corruption in the church; and then he undertook to explore his religious views in what emerged as the first edition of his *Institutes of the Christian Religion*. This was finished by the end of the summer of 1535 and published in Basel the following March.

Institutio, the word Calvin chose for his title, is generally translated as "Institutes." But the term is complex; it can signify "instruction," "manual," or "summary" (which may suggest a medieval *summa*), or all three at once. Calvin, whose diction was unusually precise, may have aimed to preserve the ambiguity of the term.[42] Reminiscent of both the *De institutione christiana* of Lactantius and Quintilian's *Institutio oratoria*, the word would have been particularly evocative to a humanist. It had also been used by Erasmus in several titles.[43]

In later editions, in which he expanded and reorganized the work, Calvin came to see his *Institutio* more precisely as a textbook in theology, but the first edition served two rather different purposes. The address to the French king with which it opens suggests that it was intended in part to end the persecution in France of those with beliefs like his own; the work is thus a kind of apologia.[44] This purpose also helps to explain its moderate tone, which contrasts with the growing bitterness of later editions. But this moderation also suggests the degree to which Calvin, in writing the work, was still exploring his own position. It represented a solidification and deeply personal appropriation of the christocentric evangelical humanism of Cop's sermon in Paris. It was a long step forward in a direction already decided on by a young French Catholic.[45]

But the question of Calvin's usefulness was still not altogether answered; and, restless and uncertain, he left Basel, made a brief trip to Italy, returned to Basel, risked a trip to Paris to straighten out his personal affairs, and then headed for Strasbourg, presumably to make the acquaintance of the reformers of that city and perhaps of other French refugees. But the military situation forced him into a fateful detour to the south, through Geneva, where the question of what he was to do with his life was not so much resolved as taken out of his hands. Disheartened by exile and unsure of his next step, young Calvin was now, perhaps, unusually vulnerable to authoritative direction by an older man. This may explain his inconsequential visit (if it in fact took place) to Lefèvre; but Lefèvre had refused to leave the old church.

Luther had been a great influence on the *Institutes*,[46] and Calvin both acknowledged him as the father of the movement with which he had now identified himself and admired his theological insight. He always preferred Luther to Zwingli.[47] Long after the rift between them, Calvin was ready to pay him tribute. "I have often said," Calvin declared, "that even though he were to call me a devil, I would nevertheless hold him in such honor that I would acknowledge him to be a distinguished servant of God."[48] Luther also seemed to him an alien figure, however, perhaps because much of what he wrote was in an alien language. But above all, as Calvin wrote to Bucer in 1538, although he was "perfectly convinced of Luther's piety," he was repelled by his "craving for victory," his "haughty manner and abusive language," his "ignorance and most gross delusions," his "insolent fury," the same failings that had repelled Erasmus.[49] Calvin was also critical of Luther's scholarship. He thought him, as an expositor, careless about "propriety of expression or historical context" and satisfied—for Calvin this was not enough—when he could "draw out fruitful doctrine."[50] Like Zwingli, Calvin did not consider Luther the only early Reformer; he was "not the only one in the church of God to be looked up to."[51]

But in Guillaume Farel, the leader of the Genevan Reformation, twenty years older than himself, who had also been shaped by the evangelical humanism of France, he found the authority and direction he yearned for. The sources differ slightly on how they came together. According to Calvin, he had intended only to pass one night anonymously in Geneva, but his presence had been betrayed, against his wishes, to Farel. This, however, was in a document intended to give readers a more general impression of his self-effacement than is suggested, for example, by his anxiety about the reception of his Seneca commentary. It suggests that he wanted to represent his encounter with Farel as a case—a humanist stereotype—of the scholar drawn against his will into an active life for which he was temperamentally unsuited.[52] Beza, who must have heard Calvin speak about the episode and who could also hardly have been unaware of this account, put it rather differently. According to Beza, when Calvin passed through Geneva, he paid a visit to Farel and to Pierre Viret, who was working with him, "as good men are wont to do to each other."[53] Calvin, at least before the struggles of a lifetime had worn him down, was a genial man with a talent for friendship.[54]

What then occurred, at any rate, can best be told in Calvin's own words:

> Farel, who burned with an extraordinary zeal to advance the gospel, immediately strained every nerve to detain me. And after having learned that my heart was set upon devoting myself to private studies, for which I wished to keep myself free from other pursuits, and finding that he gained nothing by entreaties, he proceeded to utter an imprecation that God would curse my retirement and the tranquility of the studies which I sought, if I should withdraw and refuse to give assistance when the necessity was so urgent. By this imprecation I was so stricken with terror that I desisted from the journey I had undertaken.[55]

Calvin had been detained in Geneva by the "fearful denunciation" of an older man whose relationship with himself he would later see as analogous to that of Paul with his "beloved child" Timothy.[56] This would not be his last encounter with an older man upon whom he could project his need for paternal authority, combined at last with affection.

The relations between fathers and sons, even spiritual fathers and sons, do not always proceed smoothly, however, especially when the son has reason to distrust his father; and Calvin's ambivalence emerged on several occasions when he criticized Farel. His resentment at being frightened into remaining in Geneva may be inferred from a letter to Bucer attacking Farel's irascibility, although he admitted that it was necessary, "with such a great instrument of Christ, somehow to excuse his excessive vehemence."[57] Calvin was also incensed, as though it recalled to him earlier paternal treachery, by Farel's intention, at the age of 69, to marry a much younger woman. Calvin recognized that he could not prevent this alliance, "since the sole reason for objecting is the inequality of age." He professed to be worried that so unsuitable an alliance for Farel might kill him.[58]

Farel indeed needed help in Geneva, then a sizable city of some 10,000. Its religious reformation was precarious; the Genevans had chiefly aimed at consummating a political revolt against Savoy, whose duke controlled the bishopric of Geneva and through it the town. But since the main support for Geneva came from Protestant Bern, political liberation depended on religious change;[59] and it is doubtful that many Genevans favored more than local control of a church that would otherwise remain much the same. The passionate Farel's frustration at the inertia and the obstacles to more fundamental reform interposed by the Genevans must have been considerable.

Two aspects of the situation were especially difficult. One was that the leaders of evangelical reform in Geneva, in the absence of significant local sentiment for it, were mostly French; and the tension between French exiles, for whom reform would justify their sacrifices, and native Genevans, who had hardly intended to trade the lordship of Savoy for the dictation of foreign ministers, would persist and even intensify during Calvin's residence. The position of the reformers was also made difficult by the control over the Genevan church exercised by the town council. This control included the appointment of clergy; when Calvin's situation in Geneva had, by the end of 1536, been clarified in his own mind and he was willing formally to become a preacher and pastor, this was accomplished not through a ceremony of ordination but by action by the town council.[60]

The subordination of church to city fathers in Geneva was similar to the situation in other towns that had broken with Rome. In Geneva, as elsewhere, the town council reserved to itself the ultimate discipline of excommunication. The inability of the reformers, because of this, to enforce directly their authority over church members particularly troubled Calvin. What he and Farel wanted is suggested by the case of a man who, according to Calvin, thought himself worthy of receiving communion, although he "had absented himself from preaching for a whole month and was busily occupied in the public forum, so to speak, of gambling and dissipation." To make matters worse, "a rumor of his fornication was also whispered about." In spite of this, the man "would have broken through to that most holy sacrament, if I had not blocked his way." This wretch had joked about the matter with the person who had conveyed to him Calvin's objections to his participation in the Lord's Supper, saying that "he left confession to the papists." Calvin had replied "that there was also, nevertheless, a kind of christian confession."[61]

The town council resisted the unwelcome pressures of Calvin and Farel, and it found allies among Anabaptists who had taken up residence in Geneva, where the religious atmosphere, still largely undefined, promised a freedom threatened by Calvin's activism. Supported by the Anabaptists and hostile to the demand that the power of excommunication be transferred to the ministers, the magistrates expelled Calvin and Farel from Geneva in May of 1538.[62] This new exile, with its implication of personal failure, was even more disheartening than Calvin's flight from France, which had been undertaken in a somewhat positive spirit. As he reviewed his experience in Geneva, he was filled with an anxiety that was increased by the possibility, kept open by his supporters in the town, that he might be invited to return to a community that suited him so little. He was also still ambivalent toward political responsibility. That he both dreaded and was attracted by it is suggested in a letter written a few months after his expulsion. "I fear above all things returning to the charge from which I have been delivered," he confided, "as I consider all the perplexities by which I was surrounded all the time I was there." He doubted his vocation: "While I was then conscious of the calling of God which held me bound and by which I consoled myself, now, on the contrary, I am afraid of tempting him if I resume a burden that, as I have come to know, is unbearable for me."[63]

Once again, however, weakened by failure, Calvin found himself under the influence of an older man. This was Martin Bucer, the leader of the evangelical church in Strasbourg, only slightly younger than Farel, with whom Calvin had already been in correspondence before leaving France.[64] After their expulsion from Geneva, Calvin and Farel had appealed unsuccessfully for support to Bern, and to an assembly representing the various evangelical churches in Zürich, before taking refuge in Basel. Shortly thereafter Bucer invited Calvin to Strasbourg as pastor to a congregation of French refugees. He remained in Strasbourg for three years, during which, in addition to his pastoral duties, he lectured on the New Testament in the Strasbourg academy. He was happier in Strasbourg than he had been in Geneva, probably happier than he would ever be again, in spite of the fact that his sense of exile must have been more intense in a town that spoke an alien language. The church in Strasbourg was already organized and reasonably under the control of Bucer and his fellow pastors, Wolfgang Capito and Matthew Zell; here Calvin was respected and appreciated, and he was able to work out a better balance between his scholarly impulses and his duties to the evangelical community than he was ever able to do in Geneva.[65]

He accomplished a great deal in Strasbourg. Here he wrote, and from here he published, his commentary on Romans, first presented as lectures in Latin to an audience, mostly German-speaking, of relatively mature ministerial candidates.[66] Here too he prepared, and probably wrote much of, the second, considerably enlarged edition of the *Institutes*. He also composed his reply to the letter in which Cardinal Sadoleto had sought to persuade the Genevans to return to the old church; Geneva was evidently still much on his mind. Within the town he again confronted a considerable Anabaptist minority.[67] He may also have had a polemical encounter with the Jewish controversialist Josel of Rosheim; Josel reported that among those who attacked him in Strasbourg was one who delivered "a violent, angry, and menacing" harangue.[68] From here, in addition, he traveled to the colloquies of Haguenau, Worms, and Ratisbon, where he disputed with Catholic theologians and broadened his acquaintance with Protestants. Calvin was busy in Strasbourg, but in describing all he had to do there in a letter to Farel, he seems to be boasting as much as complaining. After describing how he had revised twenty leaves of a manuscript for a waiting messenger, probably for the new edition of the *Institutes*, he wrote that, "in addition, there were lecturing and preaching to be done, four letters had to be written, some disputes had to be settled, and more than ten interruptions had to be dealt with."[69]

But hovering over all this accomplishment was Martin Bucer. Calvin found in Bucer, once again, the paternal authority and guidance for which he yearned. Indeed, Calvin compared Bucer to Farel. "That most excellent servant of Christ, Martin Bucer," he reported, "employing a kind of remonstrance and protestation like that to which Farel had recourse before, drew me back to a new post." Bucer had held before him the example of Jonah's punishment for refusing the call of the Lord."[70] "Don't think,"

Bucer had written him in connection with his plans after the expulsion from Geneva, "that you can leave the ministry even for a short time without offending God, if another ministry is offered you."[71] As long as Bucer was alive he felt more secure. When Bucer died in 1551, though Calvin had not seen him since his exile to England in 1549, he was desolate. "The grief I have felt at the death of Bucer increases my anxiety and fear," he wrote to Viret.[72] But again, as with Farel, Calvin's feelings about Bucer were mixed. He criticized him for equivocation, for revising his views to suit his theological opponents, and for his administrative decisions, though always persuading himself that he did so only with Bucer's good in mind. "I love and cherish him so much," he assured Bullinger, "that I freely admonish him as often as seems proper." But he was also ambivalent about Bucer. "I should do grave harm to the church of God if I either hated or scorned him," he wrote, as though this were a genuine possibility.[73]

He learned a great deal from Bucer's Augustinian theology and from his exegetical practice. "I have particularly copied Bucer, that man of holy memory, outstanding doctor in the church of God," he wrote in the preface to his commentary on the synoptic gospels, "whom I judge to have pursued a line of work in this field which is beyond reproach." He paid tribute to Bucer's "profound learning, abundant knowledge, keenness of intellect, wide reading, and many other varied excellences in which he is surpassed by hardly anyone. No one in our time has been more precise or diligent in interpreting scripture than he."[74] Much in his order of worship was borrowed from Bucer; he mentioned this in his deathbed farewell to the ministers of Geneva.[75] Discussion with Bucer and others in Strasbourg may also have strengthened Calvin's hostility to the authority of town councils over churches. Bucer and his colleagues had recently lost a struggle with their own council.

But Bucer's influence over Calvin also extended to two major decisions affecting his personal life. The first was Calvin's marriage, in which Bucer took upon himself the responsibility, customarily a father's, for providing Calvin with a wife. Bucer's motive may have been partly practical; Calvin had been compelled to take lodgers into his house in Strasbourg and needed help with its management: for an unsentimental age a sufficient reason in itself for marriage. But since Bucer had himself been one of the first reformers to marry, it may be assumed that, like Luther, he was acquainted with the emotional satisfactions of marriage and applied his experience, like a good pastor, to Calvin's case. Calvin himself, who probably knew little about feminine companionship, had small interest in changing his condition. "I have never taken a wife," he wrote, "and I do not know if I shall ever marry." But he acknowledged that marriage might be practical: "If I did so, it would be to free myself from trivial worries so that I could devote myself to the Lord."[76] His reflections about the matter otherwise were rather theoretical, even priggish, and certainly naive. To Farel he wrote, "I am none of those insane lovers who embrace even vices, once they have been overcome by a fine figure. The only beauty that attracts me is this: if she is modest, accommodating, not haughty, frugal, patient, and there is hope she will be concerned about my health."[77] These righteous abstractions may have disguised a good deal of anxiety; and although Bucer seemed to him right in principle, Calvin was in no hurry to marry and rejected the first choices of his friend. In the end he chose, perhaps without assistance, a member of his congregation, Idelette de Bure, a widow who brought with her two children from a previous marriage.[78] They were married in August of 1540. This, given the early loss of his mother and his inexperience with women, may have reassured him.

Calvin's union with Idelette de Bure proved to be far more than a *mariage de convenance*. She bore him at least three children, but none survived infancy.[79] Like his contemporaries in an age of high infant mortality, Calvin could not afford to be sentimental about children whose acquaintance he had never made, and he was compelled to satisfy his paternal instincts elsewhere. François Hotman was only one among many who, having left authoritarian fathers and an oppressive fatherland behind, looked to Calvin as an adopted father.[80] Calvin himself boasted that he had "in christendom ten thousand children."[81]

The depth of Calvin's grief on the death of his wife in 1549 suggests how important the marriage had been for him. To Viret he wrote a singularly personal letter:

> Although the death of my wife has been bitterly painful to me, yet I restrain my grief as well as I can. . . . You know well enough how tender, or rather soft, my mind is. Had I not exercised a powerful self-control, therefore, I could not have borne up so long. And truly mine is no common grief. I have been bereaved of the best companion of my life, who, if any severe hardship had occurred, would have been my willing partner, not only in exile and poverty but even in death. As long as she lived she was the faithful helper of my ministry. From her I never felt even the slightest hindrance. During the whole course of her illness she was more anxious about her children than about herself. Since I was afraid that she might torment herself needlessly by repressing her worry, three days before her death I took occasion to mention that I would not neglect my duties [to her children]. She spoke up at once: "I have already committed them to God."[82]

Years later Calvin remembered his own grief in consoling a correspondent for a similar loss. "How deep a wound the death of your excellent wife has inflicted on you I judge from my own feelings," he wrote, "for I recollect how difficult it was for me seven years ago to overcome a similar sorrow."[83] He did not remarry, explaining to his congregation that he doubted whether a woman would be happy with him and that, without a wife, he would be more free to serve God.[84] The insertion of so sensitive a statement into a sermon suggests that he may have been under some pressure to marry again, a step that, for whatever reason, he was indisposed to take.

Bucer's role in Calvin's return to Geneva was clearer than in arranging his marriage, and met, perhaps, with greater resistance. Calvin was aware that a group in Geneva was actively at work to recall its exiled pastors, and the prospect of returning filled him with alarm; his language, when he thought of it, became uncharacteristically extravagant, even blasphemous. "Rather would I submit to a hundred other deaths," he wrote, "than to that cross on which one must perish daily a thousand times."[85] He represented Geneva to Farel, in highly contorted words, as "a great abyss" in which he would be "completely swallowed up." In Strasbourg he had his "own struggles," but these "only keep me in training, they do not bury me."[86] When he was finally invited to return, he wrote, "I was thrown for two days into such perplexity and trouble of mind that I was scarcely half myself." Whenever he remembered his misery in Geneva, he "could not but shudder with all my heart" at the thought of returning. He doubted his effectiveness if compelled once more to lead the Genevan church, since in Strasbourg he had "somehow become oblivious of the arts required to guide and direct the multitude." He distrusted his own feelings on the matter and yearned for guidance by others, who might be "safe and prudent guides," lest, relying on his own instincts, he make the wrong decision.[87]

He meant that he was prepared to accept Bucer's judgment, and Bucer told him to go back. On September 2, 1541, Calvin accordingly returned to Geneva, where he continued to look to Bucer for paternal guidance, encouragement, and, above all, approval. Six weeks later Calvin wrote to him, "Until I shall have confessed that I can bear no more, do not doubt that I am performing faithfully what I have promised you. And if in any way I do not match your expectation, you know that I am under your power. Admonish, chastise, do all those things that a father may do to his son."[88]

Calvin's dread of returning to Geneva was more than justified by the long ordeal that followed. He was, to be sure, more mature, and both more cautious and more determined to have his way. He proposed to reduce Geneva to order. "It is only when we live in accordance with the rule of God that our life is set in order," he declared a decade later; "apart from this ordering, there is nothing in human life but confusion."[89] But now, having been invited back by the town council, he could, up to a point, dictate his own terms. His first concern was to set the Genevan church to rights in accordance with the principle that "the church cannot stand firm unless a government is constituted as prescribed to us by the Word of God and observed in the early church."[90] The council complied with this demand and in November enacted Calvin's *Ecclesiastical Ordinances*, which spelled out what he believed necessary for a well-ordered church. These regulations vested the administration of the church in four groups of officers: pastors, teachers, elders, and deacons, generally specifying the duties of each, and establishing a "consistory," made up of the pastors and elders, to bring every aspect of Genevan life under God's law.

There was probably also a personal element in Calvin's concern to order Geneva. A righteous community administered by city "fathers" would be a good father writ large. At the same time, as a *home*, nurturing as well as ordering and protecting, it might represent the mother he could scarcely remember. Exile could also be justified by the creation in another place of something better than—and therefore a reproach to—what he had left behind.

The acceptance of the *Ecclesiastical Ordinances* was, for Calvin, only a beginning; it represented no more than "a form of discipline such as these disjointed times permitted," and because the lusts of the world "cannot bear to submit to the rule of Christ," the danger of rebellion was still great. "Unclean spirits" that could tolerate no discipline were still seeking "any sort of pretext to overthrow the authority of the church."[91] The support of the town council was unreliable. It continued "in a tumult for no reason" and was incapable of initiative even "in a good and praiseworthy cause." None of its members could be trusted; they were "so childish that they are frightened by a silly shake of the head."[92] Even his brother pastors gave him difficulties. "Now," he wrote, "I begin to learn again what it is to live in Geneva. I am surrounded by unbelievable thorns. For the past two months there has been serious strife among my colleagues." He accused two among them of perjury.[93]

There were two major causes of friction between Calvin and Geneva. One was the continuing unwillingness of the Genevans to submit to the discipline he thought necessary. This reluctance found expression in an anonymous note of protest attached to the pulpit of one of the Genevan churches. It called the attention of the authorities to the fact "that people did not wish to have so many masters" and that the ministers "had now gone far enough in their course of censure."[94] A letter exhorted the council not to be "ruled by the voice or the will of one man, for you see that men have many and divers opinions: each one wants to be governed as he likes."[95] Resistance also found expression in "daily clamors" of protest against actions of the consistory that interrupted the sermons of the ministers.[96]

Calvin's other major difficulty with the Genevans was caused by religious refugees, especially from France, who entered the town in increasing numbers. He welcomed them as brethren; their company doubtless made him feel more at home. They also helped to vindicate his own exile; this may have been an element in his encouragement of other French Protestants to emigrate.[97] He found in Scripture support for the obligation "to be kind and dutiful to fugitives and exiles, and especially to believers who are banished for their confession of the Word." No duty, he concluded, could be "more pleasing or acceptable to God."[98] But Genevans were increasingly unhappy over the arrival of outsiders, many of whom threatened to become permanent residents and so to upset the existing power structure. Genevans also blamed the *émigrés* for raising the cost of living.[99]

Calvin's frustration at the constant resistance to his policies overflowed into his exegetical pronouncements; Satan was at work in Geneva as well as in the world outside:

I say nothing of fire and sword and exiles and all the furious attacks of our enemies. I say nothing of slanders and other such vexations. How many things there are within that are far worse! Ambitious men openly attack us. Epicureans and Lucianists mock at us, impudent men insult us, hypocrites rage against us, those who are wise after the flesh do us harm, indirectly, and we are harassed in many different ways on every side. It is in short a great miracle that, weighed down by the burden of such a heavy and dangerous office, any one of us should persevere.[100]

He often felt isolated. "The crushing effect of a general though false consensus against us," he confessed, "is a hard temptation and one almost impossible to resist."[101] He could only console himself that "greater commotions had been stirred up against Moses and the prophets, although they had to govern the people of God."[102] This might suggest that Calvin considered the Genevans a people of some other ruler.

Meanwhile the refractory Genevans were only one among the burdens of which he repeatedly complained. To Bucer, when he had been back in Geneva scarcely six weeks, he was already writing, "I am entangled in so many troublesome affairs that I am almost beside myself."[103] "You can scarcely believe what a burden of troublesome business I am weighed down and oppressed by here," he wrote Melanchthon; and again, "In addition to the immense troubles by which I am so sorely consumed, there is almost no day on which some new pain or anxiety does not come."[104] He often felt overwhelmed. "The wisest servants of God," he noted, "sometimes weaken in the middle of the course, especially when the road is rough and obstructed and the way more painful than expected. How much more, then, should we ask God that he never withdraw the aid of his power among the various conflicts that harass us, but rather that he instill us continually with new strength in proportion to the violence of our conflicts."[105] His weariness made him feel especially close to the apostle Paul, who had not only been "attacked by his avowed enemies but was no less vexed by evils at home." Paul had seen "how weak many, indeed all of his people were" and "by what varied devices Satan disordered everything." "How few were prudent, how few sincere, how few constant; and on the other hand how many are hypocrites, ambitious, troublesome!" Calvin exclaimed. "Among such difficulties, God's servants can only tremble and suffer great anguish, all the more since they must swallow many things in silence for the peace of the churches."[106]

The clergy, in such a desperate situation, were sheep among wolves, endangered on every side, struggling desperately to perform their duties, needing the wisdom of the serpent to survive.[107] Any conscientious minister, Calvin charged, would "surely be loaded with much abuse and called contentious, morose, a disturber of the peace."[108] "None are more exposed to slanders and insults than ministers, wicked men find many occasions to blame them, they never avoid a thousand criticisms, as soon as any charge is made against ministers of the word it is believed as surely and firmly as if it had been already proved."[109]

Such trials imposed harsh demands on the clergy, for which they were often unprepared. Calvin was undoubtedly drawing on his own experience in warning candidates for the ministry of what they faced:

> Today hardly one in a hundred considers how difficult and arduous it is faithfully to discharge the office of pastor. Hence many are led into it as something trivial and not serious. Afterwards experience teaches them too late how foolishly they aspired to the unknown. Others think themselves endowed with great skill and diligence, and promise themselves great things from their talent, learning, and judgment; but afterwards they experience too late how limited their equipment is, or their powers fail them at the outset. Others, while knowing there will be many serious battles, have no fear, as though they were born for contention, and assume an iron front. Still others who want to be ministers are mercenaries. We know indeed that God's servants are wretched in the eyes of the world and of common sense, for they must make war on the passions of all and thus displease men in order to please God.[110]

Calvin's anxiety over the situation in Geneva reached a climax early in the decade of the 1550s, when the political power of his opponents was increasing and the town council resisted with renewed vigor the right of the ministers to excommunicate. "You cannot believe how much I am displeased with the present state of our republic," Calvin wrote early in 1551.[111] A year later he complained again, "Our fellow citizens occasion us much concern; the disorder of this republic is so great that the church of God is tossed about like Noah's ark in the waters of the deluge."[112] The situation was still unchanged in 1553: his enemies still strove "to overthrow the whole order and condition of the republic."[113] He blamed the opposition less on licentiousness itself, as this could be controlled by appropriate institutions, than on men who, seeking power for themselves, encouraged it.[114] The confrontation between Calvin and his adversaries may help to explain the trial and execution of Servetus, which occurred when tensions in Geneva were at their height; each side needed to demonstrate its zeal for orthodoxy. But it was the town council that insisted on burning Servetus; Calvin, as his apologists have often pointed out, although responsible for Servetus's arrest and prosecution, favored a less brutal mode of execution.[115]

The situation remained tense until May of 1555 when, chiefly because the problem within Geneva became entwined with other issues, Calvin's opponents overreached themselves and the tide turned in his favor.[116] His position in Geneva was henceforth reasonably secure, although he seems to have had some difficulty in persuading himself that this was so. "Besides open contentions," he wrote Farel, "you will not believe how many ambushes and clandestine intrigues Satan daily directs against us. So, though public order is tranquil, not everyone can enjoy repose." There were still "many hidden enemies at home, some of them eager to come out in the open."[117] Calvin did not accept Genevan citizenship until 1559.

Coping with his opponents in Geneva was, however, only one, although perhaps the most wearisome, of the tasks that wore Calvin down. He was engaged on many fronts. It is unnecessary to review these here in any detail, but they should be kept in mind because they help to explain his mounting sense of harassment. He had constantly to negotiate with other Protestant leaders to obtain support for his position in Geneva or to hold them together in a common front. He also had to keep a close watch on the international situation, which he professed at times to find impenetrable:

> In matters so confused I not only pass no judgment but I do not even dare to inquire about the consequences. For as often as I have begun the attempt, I have been immediately so overwhelmed by obscurity that I think nothing better than to keep my eyes closed to the world and fix them on God alone. . . . I sigh anxiously night and day, but as much as I can I repel all the needless thoughts that steal into my mind from time to time. . . . It is something that I do not indulge a prurient nature. I occupy myself in considering things already settled. Matters that arise each day I connect with earlier ones. Reflecting on these things furnishes me, I confess, with grounds for both hope and fear. But because I am entangled in so many conflicting considerations, I restrain myself from saying or doing anything rash and inappropriate.[118]

In other moods, especially when the Gospel was at stake, Calvin could be emphatic enough. He emphasized the danger of the Turks to Europe.[119] He knew that the free cities of Germany provided fertile ground for evangelical religion. "There is no doubt about the cities," he wrote; "they all wish us tranquility, and most of them aspire to the Gospel."[120] He followed closely, with a mixture of hope and apprehension, ecclesiastical developments in England, deploring the religious policies of Henry VIII but encouraging Bucer's hopes that the English would "strive for the purity of Christianity, until everything there is visibly regulated according to the one and only rule of Christ."[121] The death of Edward VI troubled him, but the accession of Elizabeth cheered him again.[122] He encouraged rulers to promote the Gospel in the dedications of his commentaries: the Canonical Epistles to Edward VI, Isaiah to Elizabeth, Hebrews to the King of Poland.

His commentaries occupied, indeed, the largest share of his time after his return to Geneva. "I have destined the rest of my life," he wrote in 1551, "if leisure and freedom are granted me, chiefly to this study," hoping thereby to provide, as he explained with excessive modesty, "a ready entrance to the meaning for the not utterly lazy reader."[123] He presented the commentaries as lectures, without notes and with only a Bible to refer to, at least several afternoons a week to audiences consisting mainly of young pastors and students, mostly French. Because some of his audience were not French-speaking, the lectures were in Latin. He analyzed in great detail one book of Scripture at a time, beginning with the New Testament and eventually moving to the Old.[124] The immense learning that went into their preparation was largely concealed, but Calvin tacitly engaged, as he lectured, in a dialogue both with the Fathers and contemporary exegetes, including Erasmus, Bucer, Bullinger, and Melanchthon.[125]

Except in the case of some (perhaps all) of his New Testament commentaries, Calvin did not have the leisure to prepare written texts of his lectures. They were taken down by amanuenses. Calvin described how this worked: "I do not have much time for writing, but [a secretary] takes everything down as I dictate and afterwards arranges it at home. I read it over, and if anywhere he has not understood my meaning, I restore it." [126] Eventually, several secretaries took down Calvin's words and met afterward to prepare a master copy. He did not, however, always find time to review the text. His commentary on Hosea (at least) was released for publication without reworking, though not without his permission. Other commentaries bear engaging marks of their origins in the informal remarks with which he ended particular lectures: "I cannot now proceed farther, for the clock is striking," or "No lecture tomorrow because consistory meets." [127]

In addition to the commentaries, Calvin composed various theological polemics and prepared the later revised and enlarged editions of the *Institutes* in both Latin and French. If the first edition was written primarily for himself, later editions were more clearly intended for others. "The duty of those who have received from God fuller light than others," he announced in the preface to the last French edition, "is to help simple people and lend them a hand to guide them to all of what God meant to teach us in his word." But, as the epistle to the final Latin version indicated, he had another audience in mind as well: he aimed "to prepare and instruct candidates in sacred theology to read the divine word so that they may be able both to have easy access to it and to advance in it without stumbling."

In addition to these administrative and scholarly tasks, Calvin had heavy pastoral duties. He preached regularly and often: on the Old Testament on weekdays at six in the morning (seven in winter), every other week; on the New Testament on Sunday mornings; and on the Psalms on Sunday afternoons. During his lifetime he preached, on this schedule, some 4,000 sermons after his return to Geneva: more than 170 sermons a year. The importance he attached to his preaching is suggested by the fact that, in reviewing the accomplishments of his lifetime on his deathbed, he mentioned his sermons ahead of his writings. [128] He also performed other duties. In the single decade after 1550, he performed some 270 weddings and 50 baptisms. [129] His services were in demand, too, as a marriage broker; this might involve, among other tasks, determining whether a prospective bridegroom with an unwholesome past was free of venereal disease. [130] The seriousness with which he took his responsibility in administering communion, as in everything else, helps to explain the importance he attached to excommunication. The possibility of some negligence on his part, he confessed, haunted him whenever the Lord's Supper had to be distributed because of his ignorance about the spiritual condition of communicants. The power to excommunicate might at least protect a few of these from eternal damnation. [131]

Calvin, then, was a driven man, driven by external demands but above all by powerful impulses within himself. We might now call him an overachiever; he was never satisfied with his own performance, always contrasting the petty done with the undone vast. As a young man he was already lamenting his "habitual sloth." [132] To Bullinger he confessed (thinking perhaps of Farel and Bucer) that "others, by their importunity, shake me free of my torpor," complaining again of his weariness: "I am so exhausted by constant writing that often, almost broken by fatigue, I hate writing letters." [133] Self-accusation for his deficiencies in energy and achievement still figured prominently in his last will and testament, in which he reviewed his ministry. "Alas," he declared, "the will I have had, and the zeal, if it can be called that, have been so cold and sluggish that I feel deficient in everything and everywhere. If it were not for [God's] infinite goodness, all the affection I have had [from him] would be nothing but smoke. Truly, even the grace of forgiveness he has given me only renders me all the more guilty, so that my only recourse can be this, that being the father of mercy, he will show himself the father of so miserable a sinner." [134] The tensions he felt about the limits to his energy may explain the headaches about which he sometimes complained. "About midnight," he wrote to a friend, "I was seized with a severe headache such as is all too familiar to me." [135]

He thought much, not only about weakness and fatigue, but also about aging, illness, and death. He sought to impress on his congregation, because he felt that no one could sufficiently realize its truth, that life consists in growing older:

> If we consider it well, when a man rises up in the morning he could not walk a step, he could not take a meal, he could not turn his hand without constantly growing older; his life grows shorter. We ought therefore to recognize that, with the blink of an eye, our life is escaping from us and flowing away. This is what it means to be consumed night and morning. . . . It means that all one's strength is ebbing and that there is no vigor in us to keep us in a stable condition, but that we are always tending towards death, that it is approaching us, and that we must come to it.[136]

From this perspective, as he wrote one of his French correspondents when he was beset by a host of ailments that he must have known would shortly end his own life, illnesses are "messages of death" from which "we should learn to have one foot raised to depart when it shall please God." [137] He followed closely his own bodily decline, a personal *memento mori*. "Well, it is true," he observed, "that I see my body decaying. If any strength remains, it declines from day to day, and I contemplate death without having to seek it ten leagues away." [138]

His last letters, as he continued to drive himself, are full of clinical detail but strangely devoid of such theological reflection on his own behalf as he offered for the consolation of others. It was rather as though he were trying to impose some kind of order on the horror of his physical disintegration by the precision and detachment of his observations. Even dying had, for Calvin, to be put to use, as in the description of his singularly complex pathology that he prepared for the medical faculty of Montpellier. His ailments included, by his own account, arthritis, kidney stones, unspecified intestinal disorders, hemorrhoids, bleeding from the stomach, fever, muscle cramps, nephritis, and gout.[139]

He died on May 27, 1564, worn out by his physical ailments and by the multitude of external problems and pressures that pressed in upon him in Geneva. But it is possible that the tensions and conflicts within himself were even more erosive: notably, as this account of his life may already have hinted, the tension between the trust that had found expression in Cop's address of 1534 and the insecurity that was both hidden and revealed in his need to control himself and his environment. This tension and the complex anxieties with which it was associated are the subject of the next chapter.

2

Calvin's Anxiety

All human beings may be anxious; some, individually, in groups, and from time to time, are more anxious than others. Calvin was a singularly anxious man and, as a reformer, fearful and troubled. For all their similarities, he differed in this respect from the genial Erasmus; in Calvin, Erasmianism played a kind of counterpoint to a more somber vision of human existence. His anxiety drove him through his career of strenuous and distinguished accomplishment, and it found expression in his thought in ways of which he could scarcely have been conscious. But Calvin was also unusually sensitive to anxiety, that of others as well as his own. He brooded over it, and much of what he had to say was consciously intended to soothe a peculiarly anxious generation. Whatever its private sources, nothing bound Calvin more closely to his time than his anxiety. He offers the historian, therefore, a unique opportunity to study the inner turmoil of a peculiarly troubled age.[1]

He noted the symptoms of anxiety in himself. Even in Strasbourg, he observed, he was "inclined when seething with anger or stirred up by some great anxiety to lose control and eat too greedily."[2] He was also aware of the anxiety at the center of his life's work: he recognized in himself a terrible self-concern hardly consistent with the security he attributed to faith. "The thought repeatedly recurs to me," he once confessed, in what was both a flash of insight and a unique burst of self-revelation for one so skilled in self-concealment, "that I am in danger of being unjust to God's mercy by laboring with so much anxiety to assert it, as if it were doubtful or obscure."[3]

Similar worries surrounded the more active dimensions of his career; he was troubled by his tendency to rely too much on his considerable political skills. In thinking about Joshua he brooded over the propriety of worldly calculation in doing the Lord's work. "Are we to approve of his prudence," Calvin asked, "or are we to condemn [Joshua] for too much anxiety because, without consulting God, he was so concerned to take precautions against danger?" He could only resolve the question by suggesting the possibility of omissions from the biblical text which would have revealed either that Joshua had consulted God before sending out spies to reconnoitre Jericho, or that God had directed him to do so.[4] In the same work, one of his last, composed when he knew he had not long to live, he also hinted at his anxiety about the future of the Genevan church that he had worked so strenuously to establish. "It is not strange," he reflected, "that today the authority of God's servants, whom he has furnished with excellent and wonderful gifts, protects and preserves the church. But once they are dead, a sad deterioration will promptly begin, and impiety now hidden will erupt without restraint."[5]

But Calvin's anxiety also operated at deeper levels. It found radical expression in his ambivalence about the order of nature. He clung, at times with frantic tenacity, to the conception of a natural order that had traditionally helped human beings to feel comfortable in the world. But this conception was also antithetical to his deep sense of the incomprehensibility of God and the contingency of the world. There were, as we will see, psychologically and culturally not one but (at least) two Calvins.

He often attacked those who sought to understand nature as an intelligible order, denouncing the "madness" of "philosophers who weave themselves veils out of mediate and proximate causes, lest they be forced to acknowledge the hand of God openly at work."[6] He saw all natural events as, in principle, discrete and even miraculous, though on some matters provisional generalization might be possible. Both the integrity of the universe and the survival of mankind were, for Calvin, directly and constantly dependent on God's mysterious will.

His anxiety can thus be interpreted partly as the penalty of a view of reality implicit in much contemporary philosophy.[7] But such views, for Calvin, were not primarily philosophical; there is awe as well as terror in his accounts of the turbulence of nature. When God "suddenly changes the face of the sky by rain, or thunder, or tempests," he observed, perhaps recalling his own sensations during Alpine storms, "those who were before insensible must necessarily be awakened, for unexpected changes best display the presence of God."[8] Thunderstorms especially frightened him, for "when God thunders from heaven, there is a sudden change that not only disturbs the air but also terrifies our souls."[9] Storms over water also impressed him; in these "God seems to want to shake the world and overturn what was otherwise unassailable, for even the rocks tremble when the sea is violently agitated." The violence of the sea, he asserted, using an expression that came often into his mind as though it corresponded to a sensation he knew well, is "so frightening that one's hair stands up on one's head."[10] The possibility of death by water seemed to him, indeed, implicit in the arrangement assigned in traditional physics to the elements; because water is lighter, it ought totally to cover the earth. Only the power of God—though, he reminded himself, this could be depended on—restrains water from submerging the whole earth.[11] The survival of the human race from moment to moment thus depends on God's keeping the seas under an *unnatural* control.[12] It occurred to him too that "when the sun and moon rise up, they can destroy the whole earth," for "when so great a body, indeed a body almost immeasurable, hangs over our heads and rolls on so swiftly, who would not tremble?"[13] The anxieties of the century, it appears, did not always reinforce the traditional cosmology.

Calvin's distrust of the world also appears in his treatment of human affairs, where his attachment to traditional conceptions of order is even more transparent. It is particularly significant in one so committed to *scriptura sola* that he tended to employ, in his treatment of sin, a vocabulary not only of good and evil but also of order and disorder, concepts alien to biblical discourse. "Since the fall of the first man, we see nothing but frightful confusion," he may say;[14] or, "We throw heaven and earth into confusion by our sins, for if we were rightly disposed to obey God, all the elements would certainly serve us, and we would discern an almost angelic harmony in the world."[15] Sin, from this standpoint, is frightful largely because it gives rise to chaos.

With its implication of irregularity and unpredictability, this pointed to the unreliability of the future. Calvin, for all practical purposes, shared the belief that "there is only confusion here below" for which he reprimanded those who thought events subject to fortune.[16] The world, for him, is an uncertain place in which "we cannot be otherwise than constantly anxious and confused."[17] Again employing meteorological imagery, he warned that we should not be deceived by those fleeting moments "when we can sun ourselves under a serene and peaceful sky, for every day this life is exposed to sudden storms."[18] It is "useful" to know that there is "nothing certain or permanent in this life." In the rise and fall of kings and nations, "God shows as in a mirror the frequent and sudden changes in the world which ought to awaken us from our torpor so that none of us will dare to promise himself another day, or even another hour, or another moment."[19]

But the notion that what ails the world is confusion had much practical value for Calvin. Confusion, unlike sin, can be remedied, at least symbolically, by various ordering devices at human disposal. Thus, when Calvin associated disorder with obscurity,[20] he could conceive of correcting it by sharpening the contours of the various entities composing the world; once one thing has been clearly distinguished, physically or conceptually, from others, it can be assigned its proper place in the order of things.[21] Descartes was not the first European, or even the first Frenchman, who craved clear and distinct ideas. Calvin's concern about such matters is one source of his famous clarity of style; he stabilized the meanings of words, as Higman has pointed out, but therefore also the structures of the universe he inhabited, by such linguistic devices as frugality in the use of adjectives.[22]

Thus he abominated "mixture," one of the most pejorative terms in his vocabulary; mixture in any area of experience suggested to him disorder and unintelligibility. He had absorbed deeply not only the traditional concern for cosmic purity of a culture that had restricted mixture to the sublunary realm but also various Old Testament prohibitions. Mixture, for Calvin, connoted "adulteration" or "promiscuity," but it also set off in him deep emotional and metaphysical reverberations. He repeatedly warned against "mixing together things totally different."[23] "When water is mixed with fire," he observed, "both perish."[24] He abominated the papacy above all because it had, as he believed, mixed human invention with divine ordination, earthly with heavenly things. *Scriptura sola* was intended precisely to prevent such mixture.[25]

The positive corollary of Calvin's loathing of mixture was his approval of boundaries, which separate one thing from another. He attributed boundaries to God himself: God had established the boundaries between peoples, which should therefore remain within the space assigned them, a painful thought for an exile.[26] "Just as there are in a military camp separate lines for each platoon and section," Calvin observed, "men are placed on the earth so that each nation may be content with its own boundaries." In this manner, he concluded, "God, by his providence, reduces to order that which is confused."[27] He sometimes conceived of Scripture itself as a God-given system of boundaries imposed on human existence; he admired Paul because, in spite of his anxiety, Paul had restrained himself from "leaping over the boundaries of God's word." The escape of Joshua's two spies from Jericho in a basket obscurely troubled him, "seeing that it is criminal to leap over walls."[29] He approved of land surveys because they ensure that "each one has his rights and things are not confused."[30] But he disliked Gothic churches because their walls were opened up by broad windows.[31]

The distinctions enforced by such devices as walls, boundaries, and linguistic categories were useful to Calvin to order particularly sensitive areas of life such as sex. "It is disgraceful for men to become effeminate," he asserted, "and also for women to affect manliness in their dress and gestures."[32] Paul's injunction to women to cover their heads in worship and men to bare theirs provoked him to insist on preserving the outward marks of sexual identity; the alternative could only be a rapid descent into "such confusion that everything is permitted."[33] He attacked men for what seemed to him feminine habits, such as complaining;[34] and he could not endure women who resembled "lansquenets" [German mercenary soldiers] and aspired to fire an arquebus "as boldly as a man." Such women were "monsters so scandalous that one ought not only to spit at meeting one but pick up some piece of filth to throw at them for so audaciously perverting the order of nature."[35]

Calvin would have liked to incorporate everything in heaven and earth into his philosophy; this would have eliminated all the unknown dangers that provoke anxiety. For this purpose he depended particularly on antitheses defined by conceptual boundaries.[36] He tended to feel uneasy if he could not organize his understanding of the world by dividing phenomena neatly into antithetical categories: black and white, darkness and light. But the reductionism implicit in such categorization also severely limited his perceptions and above all his imagination. Fortunately he was too intelligent to practice it consistently.

One of his favorite antitheses was the dichotomy between we and they, insiders and outsiders, compatriots and aliens, which, theologically disguised, was an element in his insistence that God predestined some human beings to damnation as well as to salvation. It was reassuring to him that "the boundaries dividing the reprobate from the elect can never be crossed." [37] There was a problem for him here; he was well aware that this distinction was one to which no human being could have access. It therefore had no practical significance, and he customarily discouraged speculation about it. But his anxiety about the maintenance of this boundary was sometimes too intense to be suppressed, and he occasionally implied that he knew personally a fair number of the reprobate.

From the language of disorder released by the collapse of boundaries, Calvin slipped easily into a language of impurity and pollution that expresses his anxiety even more vividly. "All human desires are evil," he wrote, "and we charge them with sin, not as they are natural but because they are disordered; and we affirm that they are inordinate because nothing pure or sincere can proceed from a corrupted and polluted nature." [38] He could treat almost any case of sin as "pollution," even the sin of Judas. [39] He deliberately made his own, in doing so, biblical language, which he recognized as figurative. The Bible often employs it, he observed, "because sins resemble filth or uncleanness as they pollute us and make us loathsome in the sight of God." [40] But what was clearly metaphorical in Scripture took on, for Calvin, a special quality of numinous and personal revulsion; pollution, always contagious, posed directly the fatal danger of mixture. "Nothing is more infectious than association with the ungodly," Calvin warned, "for, since we are inclined to vice, it cannot be but that, when we frequent corruption, the contagion spreads more widely. Hence the utmost zeal and caution must be employed, lest the impious with whom we come in contact should infect us by their vicious behavior, especially where there is danger of idolatry, towards which each of us is inclined." [41] His fear of impurity justifies the characterization of Calvin as a puritan; in this way, at least, he points to Puritanism.

An almost obsessive pollution imagery, inconsistent with much else in his understanding of the human condition, pervaded Calvin's discourse. "We take nothing from the womb but pure filth [*meras sordes*]," he charged. "The seething spring of sin is so deep and abundant that vices are always bubbling up from it to bespatter and stain what is otherwise pure. . . . We should remember that we are not guilty of one offense only but are buried in innumerable impurities. . . . all human works, if judged according to their own worth, are nothing but filth and defilement. . . . they are always spattered and befouled with many stains. . . . it is certain that there is no one who is not covered with infinite filth." [42] Evil-doers, as "filth and ordure," ought to be for us "like a stench, too strong to bear," making "the whole world stink." [43] Among his particular enemies Eck was a purveyor of "rotten filth," the doctrines of Rome were "stinking excrement," the Nicodemites had "polluted themselves with all the filthy things of the papacy." [44]

Calvin may have been more fastidious than Luther (or for that matter Thomas More), but he did not altogether avoid their scatological imagery.[45]

But Calvin, so anxious himself, was also remarkably sensitive to the anxiety of others, with which he doubtless had much pastoral experience. He saw anxiety everywhere, in episodes recorded in Scripture, the study of which occupied so much of his mature life, and among his contemporaries. He brooded about the place of anxiety in human existence, and he wrote about it, sensitively, compassionately, and at length. A vocabulary of anxiety pervades his discourse; it includes not only *anxietas* and its equivalent *solicitudo* in Latin, but in French, *angoisse, destresse, frayeur, solicitude,* and even *perplexité*.[46] He generally treated it as a perennial and abominable affliction of sinful humanity, though he was also aware of its uses.

He had much to say on the subject. He thought anxiety universal. "Before men decline into old age, even in the very bloom of youth," he observed, "they are involved in many troubles, and they cannot escape from the cares, weariness, sorrows, fears, griefs, inconveniences, and anxieties to which mortal life is subject."[47] Amid the many uncertainties of life, "we cannot be otherwise than continuously anxious and disturbed."[48] "We know by daily experience how various are the numerous and uncertain cares that distract our minds."[49] "We are always fearful for ourselves in this life,"[50] although the terrors of darkness are especially upsetting: "If anything happens in the daytime, we ask what it is and are not so frightened; but if there is a noise at night, terror seizes on all our senses."[51]

Calvin's observations were sometimes accompanied by particular insights, sometimes acute. He saw human existence as a perpetual crisis, in the classical sense, of anxious indecision: "The old adage that the life of men is like being at the point where two roads meet," he declared, "refers not only to the general course of life but to individual actions. For no sooner do we undertake the least thing than we are pulled hither and yon, and we mix together opposing counsels as though tossed by a storm."[52] We are all too easily terrified, he noted: "We all know the slight causes from which horror often seizes our minds, and when we begin to tremble nothing can calm our tumult and agitation."[53] We tend also to magnify danger; "in the smallest matters we imagine lions and dragons and believe ourselves exposed to slaughter."[54]

He reflected on the consequences of anxiety. "Those who are extremely anxious," he noted, "wear themselves out and become in a sense their own executioners."[55] It is "an aggravation worse than murder when we are consumed within by trepidation as by a lingering death."[56] Anxiety paralyzes the mind: "we can often escape from lesser evils, but when we are oppressed by anxieties, we can, in our despair, neither see nor judge."[57] There were times when Calvin could only imagine happiness negatively, as freedom from anxiety. "The most important thing in a blessed life," he asserted, "is to be always tranquil and at peace, terrorized by no one."[58]

He located anxiety in particular areas of human activity such as politics.

He knew how anxious princes are; however attractive their lives may appear, "we do not see what torments harass them within."[59] He also attributed to anxiety those breaches of a legitimate politics that some publicists now justified on the basis of reason of state. "When every prince fears his neighbors," Calvin pointed out, "he is so apprehensive that he does not hesitate to cover the earth with human blood."[60] Nor did he consider such anxiety unrealistic; political existence is indeed insecure. We may rely "on human power and the alliances of kings," but "whenever the Lord pleases, those who were formerly on our side will in a minute be turned against us to our ruin; and remedies we thought useful to us will be our ruin."[61] Nations are as insecure as princes. "One people becomes great and powerful: well, God reduces it to nothing. Another expands and extends its boundaries very far, and then God crushes it."[62] It is folly, Calvin thought, to "promise ourselves a lasting and tranquil condition." He recalled that many had considered the Turks mythical beings, or at worst a remote reality, but the Turks had easily demonstrated how genuine and formidable an enemy they were.[63] He attributed much private crime to anxiety, which led individuals to anticipate the injuries they feared from others by attacking first.[64]

He saw too how deeply anxiety suffused material life. "No one," he remarked, "is hungrier or more in want than unbelievers whose peace is destroyed by care for possessions."[65] He attributed envy to anxiety. "Our covetousness," he warned, "is an insatiable abyss unless it is restrained, and the best way to hold it in check is for us to desire nothing more than the needs of this life demand. But we transgress this limit because our anxiety exceeds the needs of a thousand lives."[66] He mimicked, in the pulpit, a greedy man's excuses: "Oh, I don't know what will become of me, for I will get old and I will need help. So many accidents happen to me, I ought to have at least enough to support my needs; and then I have children, and I don't want to leave them poor."[67] He deplored the fact that even Christians who happily confide their souls to God are less willing to entrust him with their bodies; "still troubled about the flesh, still worried about what they shall eat, what they shall wear, unless they have on hand abundance of wine, grain and oil, they tremble with apprehension."[68] He also noted the connection between anxiety and work. "We know," he remarked, "how anxiously some people labor, both that their own circumstances should not be reduced and that they may leave their whole fortune to their children."[69] Anxiety is the root of avarice and usury.[70]

Calvin observed, too, how anxiety surrounded households and nuclear families. He sounded much like Leon Battista Alberti's worried uncles in the *Libri della famiglia*, perhaps because he too had read Seneca. "If anyone is responsible for a large household," Calvin warned, "he must apply himself day and night, with anxious care, lest anything go wrong through his carelessness, inexperience, or negligence."[71] The care of children, he knew, is a particular occasion for anxiety; the more fond parents are of their children, he observed, "the more careful and fearful they are for them."[72]

Calvin must also have had personal experience with the anxiety underlying the "curiosity" he often denounced, the craving to know more, and with greater certainty, than is appropriate to the human condition, which usually arises "from idleness and distrust."[73] Among common folk this "perverse disease" led to astrology and the "mere craziness" of fortunetelling; to magic, necromancy and soothsaying; to "gaping after new revelations" and to "similar frauds, which the world avidly receives and snatches at with an insane violence." "Nothing displeases God more," Calvin thought, than when men "greedily overstep their boundaries to inquire into the truth" in such ways.[74]

Such forbidden knowledge was related to anxiety by its motive: access to the future in order to ward off its dangers. Calvin understood that anxiety is rooted in dread about what might lie ahead. Although we are tranquil today, he remarked, "doubt might steal into our minds about what will happen tomorrow and make us continually anxious."[75] Anxiety is thus closely related to the awareness of change, which almost universally seemed dangerous to the men of his time. As Calvin remarked, "We are perturbed and tremble at the least change."[76] "We must struggle," he observed, "not only with the affliction of present evils, but also with the fear and anxiety with which impending dangers may harass us."[77]

Although he used "fear" and "anxiety" interchangeably, he was aware of the distinction between concrete dangers against which provision can be made and the dread of the unknown to which a more precise use of these words now points. So he differentiated between "trouble" and "anxiety" as they manifest themselves in families. "Trouble," he declared, "has its source in sad matters such as the death of children, parents, or a spouse; quarrels and petty differences that come of faultfinding; the delinquencies of children; the difficulty of bringing up a family; and similar things," that is, from clearly identifiable problems. But anxieties are revealed in the hysterical vivacity, resulting from an awareness of the transitoriness of happiness, which is likely to surround "happy things such as pranks at weddings, joking, and other things that occupy the minds of married people." This suggested, alas, the impossibility of genuine relief from anxiety; even the most joyful moments in life are flawed by the inability totally to obliterate from our minds the dark though undefined possibilities of the future.[78]

Calvin recognized the danger, both practical and spiritual, in anxiety about the future; ultimately it betrays lack of faith. The anxious "do not concede the care of the world to God."[79] We forget God in the terrible self-concern that impels us "to secure the successful outcome of events."[80] Such "audacious impiety" is also futile, as "God, by a look, overcomes all the undertakings or preparations of the world."[81] Calvin's own disapproval of worldly anxiety put him profoundly at odds with that practical rationality of the modern world to which Calvinism is sometimes supposed to have contributed. Yet his knowledge of such anxiety and its power in his own time may reflect some oblique intimation of the transformation of Western culture that lay ahead.

But for every human being, beyond the future, beyond the limits of time, lurk the uncertainties surrounding death; this is why, in some ultimate sense, all anxiety is about death, which may either redeem all previous suffering or obliterate all previous happiness. Death is therefore not just one among the various matters about which human beings may be anxious; it is qualitatively different. Death and judgment are finally what every twinge of a more mundane anxiety is about. The fear that brings into focus particular dangers, and anxiety as a response to danger in general, are fused in the confrontation with death and judgment, for what is dimly apprehended by anxiety is here seen face to face, becomes specific, takes on a terrifying identity so that at last it too can be feared. All of this Calvin understood, and anxiety is the subjective link between his perception of the human condition and his doctrine. He gave particular attention, therefore, to the distress of contemporaries about death, judgment, and ultimate destiny, in passages whose intensity suggests his personal acquaintance with such anxiety. The anxiety of the sinner for Calvin makes Christianity at once plausible and necessary.

He argued—this was one of his objections to Stoicism—that the fear of death is inevitable. "For a man to flee and shudder at death" was for him "a natural disposition that can never be fully controlled," and "no one willingly hurries toward it." [82] We are all horrified at the sight of a corpse, he thought, because it reminds us that "the same annihilation will swallow us as it does the brute beasts." [83] But death, as God's punishment for sin, is also *unnatural*, and thus especially fearful. As more than physiological collapse, indeed as "the curse of God," Calvin warned, it should produce "an astonishing horror in which there is more of misery than in death by itself." [84] Calvin shared and intensified the unusual terror of death that afflicted the later Middle Ages.[86] All change, all variety, all confusion reminded him of it, and he thought the absence of terror like his own not admirable or enviable but obtuse and inhuman, no more than devilish pride. Those who are indifferent to death "see the whole earth mixed together in confused variety and its individual elements, so to speak, tossed hither and yon; and yet, as if they did not belong to the human race, they imagine that they will remain always the same, liable to no changes." [87]

The enormous variety among possible causes of death made a deep impression on him. "If we look upwards," he asked, "how many deaths hang over us from that direction? If we inspect the ground, how many poisons? How many wild and ferocious beasts? How many serpents? How many swords, pitfalls, stumbling blocks, precipices, buildings collapsing, stones and spears thrown? In short we cannot move one step without meeting ten deaths." [88] The theme stimulated him to a singularly concentrated expression of *memento mori*. "Our body is the receptacle of a thousand diseases" so that our lives are "enveloped in death." We cannot freeze or sweat without danger. On a ship "you are one step from death"; on a horse, "if a foot slips your life is in danger''; if you walk the city streets, every roof tile threatens your life; a weapon, your own or a friend's, means harm; wild beasts wait to destroy you; any garden may harbor a snake; your house may catch fire or fall on your head; your land may be barren and threaten famine; poison, treachery, robbery, violence of every kind surround you. "Amidst these difficulties," he concluded, "must not man be most miserable, since, but half alive when in life, he weakly draws his anxious and languid breath as though he had a sword perpetually at his neck?"[89]

It especially troubled Calvin, and was crucial to his indictment of the Roman church, that even those who called themselves Christians feared death. "The majority, on hearing the name of death" he observed, "are not merely terrified but nearly paralyzed, as though they had never heard a single word about Christ."[90] It was "intolerable that there should not be in Christian hearts a light of piety sufficient to overcome and suppress that fear, whatever it is, by a greater consolation."[91]

He considered death fearful above all, however, because of the judgment that follows, its terrors already anticipated by conscience. "The conscience," Calvin wrote, "cannot bear the weight of iniquity without turning toward a consideration of God's judgment. But God's judgment cannot be felt without evoking the dread of death."[92] So these three were linked in a kind of terrible triad of attritional subjectivity: the fear of death, the torments of a guilty conscience, and apprehension of judgment.

He exploited once again the powerful image of maritime disturbance to convey the experience of a guilty conscience:

> The metaphor of the sea is elegant and very well fitted to describe the uneasiness of the wicked, for in itself the sea is troubled. Though it is not driven by the wind or agitated by frightful tempests, its billows carry on mutual war and dash against each other with terrible violence. In the same manner wicked men are disturbed by inner distress which originates in their spirits. They are terrified and confused by conscience, which is the most agonizing of all torments and the most cruel of all executioners. The furies agitate and pursue the wicked, not with burning torches, as in fables, but with anguish of conscience and torment of deceit. For everyone is distressed by his own deceit, and his own terror grows; everyone is driven to madness by his own wickedness; he is terrified by his own evil thoughts and by conscience.[93]

Conscience, then, leads a sinner to picture himself before the divine tribunal. Calvin imagined Everyman recalling this desperate situation: "Whenever I descended into myself, or raised my mind to thee, extreme terror seized me—terror which no expiations nor satisfactions could cure. And the more closely I examined myself, the sharper the stings with which my conscience was pricked, so that the only solace which remained to me was to delude myself by obliviousness."[94] He was as well acquainted as the young Luther with the terrible God of judgment; he knew, at close hand, the terror such a God inspired and thought it justified:

If the judgments of God are so dreadful on this earth, how dreadful will he be when he shall come at last to judge the world! All the instances of punishment that now inspire fear or terror are nothing more than preludes for that final vengeance which he will thunder against the reprobate. Many things which he seems to overlook he purposely reserves and delays till that last day. And if the ungodly are not able to bear these chastisements, how much less will they be capable of enduring his glorious and inconceivable majesty when he shall ascend that awful tribunal before which the angels themselves tremble![95]

Indeed, Calvin's terrible imagination could go further. The greatest of all evils, he suggested, must be "when, oppressed by the hand of God, the sinner feels he has to do with a judge whose wrath and severity contain innumerable deaths beyond eternal death."[96] Behind the judgment to which death exposes us, then, await further deaths beyond our ability to conceive.

At times he hinted at an even deeper terror. In his powerful but murky sermons on Job, he allowed himself to consider the hypothesis, tantalizing though impossible, that a person might have obeyed God's law fully and be "justified according to the justice that is known and understood." Would he then, Calvin asked himself, be fully acceptable to the Father? His answer was that even this would be impossible, for "there is a higher justice in God by which he could condemn the angels." Nothing, not even the most perfect of his creatures could "suffice or satisfy." "We should know," Calvin concluded, "that when God judges us according to his law, although we discern no evil or vice in ourselves, we will nevertheless not be just."[97] For Calvin there appears, then, to be a kind of satisfaction owed by creature to Creator that is neither moral nor possible. He saw guilt in creatureliness itself, guilt shared even by human beings created in God's image before the Fall, guilt toward the Father even on the part of his good children, guilt in *existing*. This numinous guilt was so intense in Calvin that it drove even this ferocious enemy of Scholastic speculation to discuss openly matters so far beyond human knowing. Usually he managed to avoid such thoughts.

Although the anxiety that chiefly concerned Calvin was existential, a condition of human existence under sin that could be relieved only by God's mercy, he also recognized that anxiety might have a historical dimension. It fluctuated, even among Christians, according to the way in which God's mercy was believed to work. Calvin was convinced that the anxiety of Christians had been recently intensified by papal teachings and practices.

Central to the heightening of religious anxiety was, he believed, an emphasis on works in the way of salvation: no one who believes he must appease so righteous a God by his own works can be confident of the outcome: "Our consciences cannot but be vexed and disquieted with perpetual unrest so long as we look for protection from works."[98] Such a belief can only ensure that we "will always be troubled and always tremble," and remain "in wretched anxiety all our life."[99] The horror of the doctrine was made concrete in the multitude of ecclesiastical prescriptions, "grievously decreed under pain of eternal death" and imposed "with the greatest severity as necessary for salvation," many of them "extremely difficult to observe," and, "if heaped up together, impossible, so great is the pile." "How then," Calvin asked, "can they who are so burdened escape being perplexed and tortured by extreme anguish and terror?"[100]

Among particular sources of this distress the most aggravating, both doctrinally and as a practical problem, was the obligation to confess and receive absolution for every sin as a condition of acceptability to God. The burdens of the confessional figured centrally among the original complaints of the Reformers against the papal church, but Calvin's denunciation of the confessional was certainly among the most empathetic:

> The souls of those who have been affected with some awareness of God are most cruelly torn by this butchery. First they called themselves to account and divided sins into arms, branches, twigs, and leaves, according to their formulas. They then weighed the qualities, quantities, and circumstances; and so the matter pressed forward a bit. But when they had progressed farther, and sky and sea were on every side, there was no port or anchorage. The more they had crossed over, the greater was the mass ever looming before their eyes, indeed it rose up like high mountains; nor did any hope of escape appear, even after long detours. And so they were stuck between the victim and the knife. And at last no other outcome but despair was found. Then these cruel butchers, to relieve the wounds they had inflicted, applied certain remedies, asserting that each man should do what lay in his power. But again new anxieties crept in. Indeed, new tortures flayed helpless souls: "I have not spent enough time"; "I have not duly devoted myself to it"; "I have overlooked many things out of negligence, and the forgetfulness that has come about from my carelessness is inexcusable!" Still other medicines that alleviated this sort of pain were applied. Repent of your negligence; provided it is not utterly careless it will be forgiven. But all these things cannot cover the wound, and are less an alleviation of the evil than poisons disguised with honey in order not to cause offense at the first taste because of their harshness but to penetrate deep within before they are felt. Therefore that dreadful voice always presses and resounds in the ears: "Confess all your sins." And this terror cannot be allayed except by a sure consolation. Here let my readers consider how it is possible to reckon up all the acts of an entire year and to gather up what sins they have committed each day. For experience convinces each one that, when we have at evening to examine the transgressions of only a single day, the memory is confused; so great is the multitude and variety of them that press upon us.[101]

Calvin was outraged by the doctrinal "mixture" he discerned in the papal church. The papacy had promiscuously jumbled together sinful human inventions with God's holy will. "In the papacy," he charged, "each has undertaken to add his bit and portion, and laws have been piled on top of laws. And why? For it seemed that plainly walking in the word of God was inadequate and that it would be better still to introduce a mixture." The result was the total destruction of the Gospel: "whatever they advance of their own is not only superfluous and useless but only spoils it all, like pouring sour wine into good."[102] All those "services by which the Roman church proposed to promote the salvation of those in its care only deepened the anxiety that brought Calvin and others to challenge its authority.[103]

Yet, in spite of the terrible suffering to which anxiety gives rise, Calvin considered it necessary to make this world go round. Anxiety, the mother of prudence, is essential to human survival. Scripture by no means forbids "care and concern about our worldly affairs" but only excessive care that might lead to neglect of the needs of others.[104] Anxiety alerts us to danger. We are all, Calvin thought, like small children who, "if they were not afraid, would run about in every direction. But if they feel some fear, you can't make them leave their mothers' laps. Even little chicks do not gather under the wings of their mothers unless they are troubled and afraid. We are so lacking in sense that if we did not know we were in danger, we would behave like straying animals."[105] He particularly defended the value of anxiety to families: a father should be "solicitous for his wife and children."[106]

But anxiety had also a part to play, for Calvin, in the spiritual life. It is the means by which the law prepares for the gospel: by threatening punishment the law stimulates an anxiety that inhibits sin and promotes repentance. "All who have at any time groped about in ignorance of God," Calvin wrote, "will admit that the bridle of the law restrained them in some fear and reverence toward God until, regenerated by the Spirit, they began wholeheartedly to love him." So we must "anxiously attend to God's threats."[107] Fear is also "like a bridle"; without it we would all be excessively self-confident and inclined to sloth and pride.[108] He emphasized passages in Scripture that he thought, by inspiring terror, "useful to be known, for our worldly security needs sharp stimulants by which we may be driven to fear the Lord."[109] He was approaching, though he avoided the term, the Scholastic doctrine of attrition, according to which a crude fear of punishment is the first step toward reconciliation with God. But he also had something more subtle in mind; the conception suggested a way of reclaiming for Christanity what the Stoics considered the two great obstacles to human happiness: fear and hope. In choosing instead to insist on their utility, Calvin also pointed out their interdependence. They may seem contrary affections, "but experience shows that hope truly reigns where fear occupies part of the heart. For hope does not operate in a tranquil mind, nay it is almost dormant. But it exerts its power where it uplifts a spirit worn down by cares, soothes it when troubled by grief, and supports it when it is stricken by terror."[110] Hope, one of the theological virtues, thus depends on anxiety. The insight anticipated the modern insight that anxiety is evidence of the life of the spirit.[111]

Some anxiety was thus, for Calvin, also useful in later stages of the Christian life. It obviously stimulated theological reflection in his own case, as in that of other sixteenth-century Christians. More generally it promotes vigilance, Calvin thought, against the wiles of the devil.[112] It is salutary, too, as discipline. Faith "pacifies and quiets the minds of the pious so that they wait patiently for God," but it is also necessary "for patience itself to be exercised in solicitous expectation until the Lord fulfills what he has promised." [113]

At the same time Calvin, like any experienced spiritual director, knew the dangers of anxiety. "The fear that arouses faith is not bad in itself," he observed, but it must not "get out of control." [114] Although lack of faith may be "the mother of all immoderate cares," [115] the reverse can also be true. This was illustrated, for Calvin, by Zedekiah's inability to respond to the assurance of God's protection "because fear so occupied his mind that there was no entrance for the promise." He drew from this tragedy the lesson that there is none of us "whom many cares do not disturb and many fears perplex." Happily "God succors us when he sees us oppressed by anxious thoughts." [116]

But if anxiety, like anything else, is for Calvin reprehensible when carried to excess, some kinds of anxiety, especially when its useful work is done, seemed to him intrinsically bad, above all anxiety about the dependability of God's mercy. The persistence of such concern in the elect could only be interpreted as a sign of defective faith and an obstacle to its growth. "We can only worship God properly with tranquil minds," Calvin pointed out. "Those who are troubled by anxiety, who debate with themselves whether they find him friendly or hostile, whether he welcomes their service or rejects it, those in a word who are wavering between hope and fear, may trouble themselves anxiously about honoring God but never submit to him sincerely or from the heart. Their trepidation and anxiety make him abhorrent to them; indeed, if it were possible, they would wish his majesty to be blotted from their consciousness." [117] The goal of the Christian life prominently included the relief of anxiety. "We know," Calvin declared (an introduction he commonly employed for assertions to which he could endure no contradiction), "that freedom from fear, from the torment and anxiety of every care, is *the most desirable of all goods*, for inner peace of mind surpasses all the good things that we can conceive." [118] This seems again a curiously negative, almost Stoic, conception of beatitude; and it was hardly Calvin's only statement on the *summum bonum*. That he could express himself in this way suggests again, however, the depth and irrepressibility of his own anxiety.

The alternatives open to Calvin in coping with anxiety, both his own and that of his age, are suggested by two of his favorite images for describing situations of extreme spiritual discomfort. The images are of an abyss (in Calvin's Latin, usually *abyssus* but occasionally *vorago* or *gurges*) and a labyrinth (*labyrinthum* but also *ambages*). These images also enable us to penetrate somewhat more deeply into Calvin's experience of anxiety; they point to the contrasting strategies with which he dealt with it; and they help to identify tensions and contradictions in his thought. In this way they suggest the sources of his anxiety in the cultural dilemmas of the age. That it had cultural as well as personal origins gives to Calvin's distress large historical resonance.

"Abyss," a term Calvin found especially useful, has a complex history in Western discourse. For the Greeks it signified the chaos opposing and surrounding the cosmos, constantly threatening its annihilation. The abyss was the unbounded, the infinite in the negative sense of non-finite, the absence of form, meaninglessness, nonbeing.[119] Having no boundaries, it is unintelligible. The Latin Fathers indentified hell with the abyss, but as later Christian speculation associated infinity with God, "abyss" began to acquire a more positive significance. Savonarola united its positive and negative possibilities in his meditation on the Psalm *Miserere mei Deus*, composed as he awaited execution: "The abyss of God's mercy is greater than the abyss of misery."[120]

Calvin, though not necessarily distinguishing them, was aware of all these possibilities. He could refer, for example, to "an abyss of God's goodness";[121] God's will, God's judgments, God's governance of the universe were all "an abyss."[122] Usually, however, he meant the term to express his own horror and to induce horror in others. He often referred to hell as "the abyss": so the wicked will be "thrown into the abyss, even into hell".[123] He insisted that only the Lord can "deliver us from the abyss of death,"[124] and in his will he thanked God for drawing him out of the "abyss of idolatry."[125] But sometimes a more classical note crept into his usage, so that "abyss" is made to suggest boundlessness as well as divine retribution. So covetousness is "an insatiable abyss," wickedness an "abyss."[126] He took a further step toward classical usage by associating "abyss" with chaos; he could speak of "an abyss of confusion," and he illustrated the violence of a storm by suggesting that "the sea threatens to *abysm* the land."[127]

The abyss was thus a symbol of Calvin's horror of the unlimited. It signified the absence of boundaries and the unintelligibility of things, the void, nothingness, disintegration of the self. One consequence of God's punishment of sin, as he imagined it, would be the loss of "form or semblance or anything whatsoever."[128] A curious comment on Jeremiah's prophecy that the corpses of the Israelites would "fall like dung upon the open field" points in the same direction. Calvin noted that such material "excites nausea by its sight and odor"; the prophet had intended to convey here, therefore, "a sense both of fetor and of visible deformity," that is, of decay and disintegration.[129] Excrement, for Calvin, was not simply matter out of place;[130] as an image of formlessness, that is of chaos, it stirred up his deepest horror of nonbeing.

"Labyrinth" set off, for Calvin, quite different, though hardly more comfortable, reverberations. If "abyss" brought into focus his dread of disintegration and nonbeing, "labyrinth" suggested the anxiety implicit in the powerlessness of human beings to extricate themselves from a self-centered alienation from God. "As the kingdom of God is a kingdom of light," he declared, "all who are alienated from him must necessarily be blind and wander in a labyrinth. . . . the whole life of man is a ruinous labyrinth of wanderings until he has been converted to Christ."[131] He used the notion of entrapment in a labyrinth to convey the sensations accompanying acute uncertainty and indecision in the face of the future; it was peculiarly appropriate to describe anxiety. "Among so many uncertainties," Calvin exclaimed, "we can only be full of anxiety and fear. Wherever men turn, therefore, a labyrinth of evils surrounds them." [132] But, because we cannot escape this misery, "labyrinth" had, in addition, claustrophobic overtones; a labyrinth was a kind of dark prison in which human beings grope frantically for an exit they cannot find. "When they follow their own imaginings," they only entangle themselves more deeply in "a terrible labyrinth." [133] The Latin root of *anxietas*—*angustia*, literally the sensation of being compressed and suffocated—hints at what Calvin was trying to convey by "labyrinth," and on at least one occasion he made the association explicit. "When a lesser evil presses [*urget*] upon us," he said, "we look around and hope for some way to get out [*exitum aliquem*]; but when we are oppressed [*oppressi*] by greater anxieties [*angustiis*], in our despair we can neither see nor think. For this reason Isaiah says that the Israelites grope in a labyrinth [*labyrinthum*] into which they have been cast." [134]

The suggestion of claustrophobia in passages like these is confirmed by the curious associations set off in Calvin's mind by the story of Noah's "confinement" in the ark, in which he drew on, and yet made his own, both the just Noah of Chrysostom and the persecuted Noah of Luther. [135] Calvin found it "stupefying" to consider that "Noah and his household lived for ten months in a fetid heap of animal droppings, in which he could hardly breathe." "Should we not marvel equally," he continued, as another claustrophobic image occurred to him, "that a fetus, shut up in its mother's womb, lives in filth that would suffocate the strongest man in half an hour?" [136] Calvin's Latin seems to exploit here, perhaps unconsciously, the similarity of *fetor* and *fetus*, and he may have been disturbed, on reflection, by the almost Manichean revulsion he had here revealed toward human physicality. In the *Institutes* he suppressed the association of filth with the uterus in favor of another that was, however, equally claustrophobic. Now the ark became "a sort of grave" for the living Noah. But Calvin continued to represent Noah's enforced proximity to the droppings of animals as his greatest tribulation. [137] It seems not to have occurred to him that Noah might have taken measures to minimize the problem, a possibility at least as admissible as the projection of his own anxiety, and perhaps his own olfactory sensitivity, onto Noah.

Calvin associated anxiety, then, with two rather different, indeed almost diametrically opposite sensations: with a kind of vertigo and disorientation in which his own identity and sense of direction were endangered, but also with a feeling that the whole of reality was pressing in on him from all directions, crushing out his life and breath. [138] But the presence of these two kinds of anxiety in Calvin, the anxiety of the void and the anxiety of constriction, of nothing at all and too much, of freedom and oppression, the abyss and the labyrinth, also impelled him toward two rather different modes of relief. The analysis of Calvin's anxiety thus provides a key for identifying opposing impulses in his thought, and also for identifying its conflicts and contradictions. One side of Calvin was concerned to relieve the fear of the abyss by means of cultural constructions, boundary systems, and patterns of control that might help him to recover his sense of direction. In a historical situation in which all such constructions were losing their plausibility, Calvin struggled, in a way characteristic of the later medieval culture that Johan Huizinga so brilliantly described, to shore them up. This gave to much of his thought a profoundly traditional and conservative quality. But another side of him aimed precisely to relieve the pressures with which such human constructions, systems, and patterns constrained and threatened to suffocate him.

The two impulses were not necessarily equal. Calvin seems to me to have been more disturbed, and at a deeper level, by the abyss than by the labyrinth. He associated the labyrinth primarily with the papal church he sought to leave behind, its theology, and the cultural assumptions of his past, whereas the abyss conjured up a more personal terror. It represented the direction in which he was advancing and therefore that unknown future whose indeterminate horrors usually seem more frightening than the remembered and finite troubles of the past. In the end, however, Calvin needed somehow to strike a balance between the two sides of himself, with their contrary discomforts and contrasting modes of relief. It will be a central argument of this book that his thought reflects a brave and ingenious, though not wholly successful, effort of a lifetime comfortably to combine them.

3

A World Out of Joint

Europeans during the later Middle Ages were at once increasingly sensitive to the failings of their world and increasingly anxious. Each tendency worked on the other, and it is therefore difficult to determine whether Calvin saw so much to censure because he was anxious or was anxious because so much was wrong. What is indisputable is the intensity of his moralism and his insistence on the universal obligation of human beings not only to conform to the will of God themselves but to reform a deviant world. He could hear God saying, "It is necessary that I be obeyed, in everything and by everyone, or I shall renounce you."[1] Calvin's nervous moralism sometimes recalls that of the monk Pelagius as the Roman Empire was collapsing.[2]

His moralism found expression in his characteristic vocabulary of order and disorder, purity and contamination. He equated contempt for "the sacred name of God" with the total overthrow of order.[3] "It is true," he preached, "that confusion is constantly increasing. . . . We must recognize that we are the cause of all the disorders in the world. . . . If everyone would try to repress vices and iniquities and if, when there is evil, everyone tried to avoid it, God would certainly bless that response and we would have a desirable order among ourselves." But alas, everyone "heaps wood on the fire," and it is no wonder that "things are so mixed up, that there is neither any bottom or boundary, as in an abyss."[4] He saw God's law as a narrow path; only if we stay within its boundaries, straying neither to the right nor to the left, will we be safe.[5]

But the problem was not, for Calvin, simply individual; every sin not only offends God but threatens the community. His anxiety on this point often brought him close to the sects. "When crime is left unpunished," he insisted, "it pollutes the whole country."[6] Hence the search for and denunciation of wickedness is a universal obligation: to God but also to others. The struggle with sin must begin with oneself,[7] but "no one should be prevented by his own sins from correcting those of others and, if necessary, punishing them."[8] God requires that sin should be expunged from the world.

Calvin's emphasis on obedience to this divine mandate had a negative corollary in his distrust of liberty, even of that Christian liberty which Luther so valued. He could not openly reject it; sometimes he sounded much like Luther on the subject. But it made him uncomfortable. He thought it more likely that people would "seek the license of the flesh than the liberty of the Spirit."[9] "Today," he observed, "the doctrine of the Gospel does not reduce all to obedience"; instead "many rush toward a more unrestrained license."[10]

Even his enunciation of the general principles governing Christian behavior suggests a yearning for precise regulation. "Even though the freedom of believers in external matters is not to be restricted to a fixed formula," he wrote, "yet it is surely subject to this law: to indulge oneself as little as possible; but, on the contrary, with unflagging effort of mind to insist upon cutting off all show of superfluous wealth, not to mention licentiousness, and diligently to guard against turning helps into hindrances."[11] He could turn even scriptural texts explicitly authorizing liberty into a warning against it.[12] He thought popery itself preferable to freedom. Indeed, it would be better "for the devil to rule mankind under any sort of government than that they should live idly, without any law, without any rule."[13]

As these passages imply, Calvin tended to equate righteousness with control, sin with unrestraint. "The Lord," he asserted, "cannot endure excess, and it is absolutely necessary that it be severely punished."[14] It is characteristic of the godless "always to run to extremes."[15] Noting how often "an excessive word escapes our lips," he especially deplored speech "unrestrained by calculation, fear, or prudence."[16] "We all see," he told his congregation, "how volatile men are in speaking, so that sometimes, before we have conceived a thing, it is spoken. He who can control himself so that no word leaves him that is not controlled and well regulated shows that he is endowed with a singular grace."[17] Nor did he appreciate spontaneity of mind: thoughts too, must be protected from the devil.[18]

He thought a degree of reserve especially appropriate in dealing with God, commending Jeremiah's caution regarding prayer. "If he had immediately rushed into prayer," Calvin reflected, "he might, in the first impulse of his fervor, have disputed with God; for such is the character of man when he suddenly addresses God that he boils over beyond all measure." Jeremiah had done right, then, "to place boundaries around himself, almost surrounding himself with barriers, so that he could not allow himself more liberty than was proper." Recognition of God's power had made Jeremiah "moderate and humble, so that he could control all those erratic perceptions with which men ordinarily titillate themselves."[19] Boundaries could protect from internal as well as external dangers.

Calvin's insistence on restraint even (or perhaps especially) in religion was accompanied by a distrust of what he often called "zeal" that would have been reassuring to a philosopher of the Enlightenment. Scripture provided him with numerous lessons in the need to control this dangerous impulse. The troubles of the church in Philippi reminded him that "we must take care lest any immoderation or excessive harshness creep in under color of zeal.''[20] An exhortation of Paul to Timothy induced him to remark that ''nothing is more difficult, once we grow warm, than to control our fervor.''[21] All zeal not controlled by the Holy Spirit ''erupts into furious insanity'' and provides ''a marvelous cover for all kinds of crimes.''[22] What was wanted was not zeal but that ''we should always prudently consider what the Lord commands us, lest our fervor boil over without reason or restraint.''[23] Faith produces humility and obedience; zeal expresses only a vain self-confidence.[24] Calvin's emphasis here suggests not only dismay at sectarian disorder but the presence of tendencies toward ''zeal'' within himself, especially that ''ferocious beast'' of his anger, which was one of his own worst vices.[25] Another excess he recognized in himself was grief, which, uncontrolled, ''drives out reason and humanity'' and signifies rebellion against God's will.[26]

He denounced with particular harshness sins associated with unrestraint. First among these was self-love, which manifests itself as ambition and pride in social relations: the primary sin for moralists of the earlier Middle Ages. ''We all rush into self-love with such blindness,'' Calvin wrote, ''that each of us seems to himself to be justly proud and despises all others''; and, ''as if exempt from the common lot, we aspire to tower above the rest and haughtily and savagely abuse everybody else, or at least look down on him as an inferior.'' We must ''tear from our inward parts this most deadly pestilence of love of strife and love of self.''[27] ''No one,'' he remarked, in another of the generalizations with which he commonly disguised his own self-examination, ''willingly yields to others, but each cherishes within himself a secret hope of being first.''[28] Ambition is the ''mother of the many evils in human society, especially in the church.''[29]

He also recognized the malignant sensitivity engendered by pride. ''If any man disapproves of us or of anything we do or say,'' he observed, ''we are immediately offended, without considering whether the judgment is right. If anyone examines himself, he will find this seed of pride in himself.''[30] By preventing us from acknowledging the truth in criticism of ourselves, pride protects us from recognizing our other sins. This, for Calvin, was a prime example of how one sin can open the way for or reinforce others. Every sin weakens the system of controls within the self.

Greed, with which moralists of the high Middle Ages had tended to replace pride as the worst of sins,[31] was for Calvin like pride in this respect; greed leads to wealth and so to other excesses. ''Luxury follows immediately on plenty,'' he argued, and encourages human beings to ''grow wanton in their lusts and intoxicate themselves with pleasures.''[32] Wealth leads to ''pride, pomps, scorn of God, cruelty, frauds, and everything of the kind; and then it brings bodily delights and pleasures, so that man is wholly brutalized.''[33] Even too much food brings general moral decay. It ''tempts us to give reins to our lusts''; those who ''enjoy splendid and well-supplied dinner tables will hardly be able to keep themselves from excesses.'' Wealth collaborates with pride when spent on ''elegant and ornate dress.'' This is not displeasing to God in itself, he hastened to add, remembering perhaps that social order depends on such external signs, but "those with an appetite for splendid dress will gradually go farther with additional luxuries."[34] "If the servants of God have a choice," therefore, "nothing is safer than to eliminate whatever they can of magnificence."[35] The social consequences of greed were even more deplorable, for Calvin, than its corruption of the greedy. He considered it "a major plague ruling the world that men have a mad and insatiable lust for possessions."[36] The rich, he thought, "are almost grieved if the sun shines on the poor."[37]

Sex was for Calvin another area susceptible to excess. He condemned the excuse for sexual freedom, disseminated in the popular *Roman de la Rose* and *Decameron*, that it is "natural." For Calvin the issue is not nature in general but appropriateness to human nature;[38] only sexual relations ordered and controlled by marriage are permissible to human beings.[39] He denounced dancing because he thought it a prelude to fornication, and he defended the euphemism "to sleep with" because bolder language might incite sin.[40] He was harsh in his condemnation of adultery, another sin with large ramifications. His anxiety about it could distort his exegesis; Christ's leniency toward the woman taken in adultery worried him because it might be seen to excuse it, "throwing open the door for any kind of treachery, for poison, and murder, and robbery."[41] Indeed, he defended Joseph's initial impulse, on observing what could only be interpreted as evidence of her adultery, to divorce the pregnant Mary. Joseph, Calvin remarked, "was not of such a soft and effeminate mind as to shelter a crime under his wing on the pretext of compassion."[42] From time to time he also condemned the polygamy of the Hebrew patriarchs.[43]

Drunkenness revolted him as "a shameful abuse" of a "noble and most precious gift of God."[44] He recognized the despair that often causes it, but as another kind of excess he could not view it with sympathy. Men drink, Calvin observed, "to bury reflection" lest it disturb their repose.[45] When men drink too much wine, a "very healthy food," it "enervates them, beclouds their minds, and, almost stupefying their senses, makes them inert."[46] Drunkenness too can lead to other sins; hence the proverb that "pride is born from drunkenness."[47]

But Calvin less often attacked specific sins than particular groups of sinners that seemed to him unusually difficult to control, for example young men, whose "shameful wantonness" and "unbridled desires" make them especially ebullient, and who are also easily angered and "rush at things more boldly and rashly."[48] When it treats social categories, his moralism merges into social commentary that enables us to see his world through his eyes.

The disorderly proclivities conventionally associated with women made him particularly anxious. Desirous of the power of men and even more ambitious for domination, though with less aptitude for it, women, for Calvin, constantly threatened the boundary between the sexes. "It seems to them," he charged, "that, if they do not have entire mastery, if one does not believe them about everything, if all their advice is not taken, one does them an injury and disdains them."[49] He also blamed women for many of the sins of men, especially for tempting them sexually with their own "lawless desires."[50] "Husbands are often corrupted by their wives," he asserted. "There have been too many examples of how men, otherwise inclined to behave virtuously, have been debauched and turned from the right way by women."[51] "A lascivious woman," he charged, "is worse than all the adulterers she captivates with her enticements. When a youth is not deceived and the devil does not apply the fagot, he can remain chaste and pure; but when a shameless and wanton woman entices him, it is all over with him."[52] He blamed Bathsheba for David's fall from grace: not simply for bathing, "but she ought to have been more discreet; she should have thought how not to be seen."[53] Women always seemed to him potentially wanton, even in old age; he was scandalized that a woman of seventy still "sought the delights of the bridal bed."[54]

He also railed against other supposed feminine weaknesses. Although he thought women "chargeable with many vices," he believed them "above all inflamed with a mad eagerness for fine clothes."[55] He mimicked an envious lady from his pulpit: "Oh! that one has a pretty petticoat of such and such cloth, and that one over there such a collar made in such a way, she wears it every day, not just on holidays. And there is one who has so well made a dress, and she is of lower rank than I, and don't I deserve as much as the others?"[56]

Other expressions of feminine vanity attracted his notice. "Fashionable ladies," he observed, "hardly venture to expose themselves to the sun's rays for fear of being sunburned."[57] Isaiah's catalogue of female adornments aroused in him a mixture of alarm and condescension. "It would be too impudent," he exclaimed, "to claim that what women contrive, going beyond nature in their silly vanity, is necessary for covering the body."[58] Young girls were especially prone to such vices; they "are more eager than they ought to be in curling their hair and in other aspects of dress."[59] It seemed to him that at weddings the dress of brides was "deliberately contrived to subvert all modesty."[60] He also disapproved of women who, in their concern to wear clothes well, "even turn away from food and cheat nature so that they may dress more elegantly and richly." Others, for the same reason, refused to nurse their infants.[61]

Calvin's acceptance of large anti-feminist generalities is apparent, finally, in his insistence on the frivolity and mental incompetence of women. He assailed them for gossip and loquacity. "Talkativeness is a disease among women," he asserted, noting their inability to keep secrets, a vice that "old age usually makes worse."[62] Nor was he impressed by feminine piety. "There are foolish little women," he observed, "who run from altar to altar and then do nothing but sigh or mutter till the middle of the day. By this pretext [of piety], they free themselves from all domestic duties. On returning home, if everything is not to their liking, they take offense, disturb the whole household with senseless cries, and sometimes come to blows."[63]

Women, he believed, are also unusually likely to be taken in by religious impostors.[64] The warmth of some of this abuse suggests both the importance and the precariousness, for an anxious man, of the subordination of women.

He was also particularly inclined to attack the great and powerful, those who were responsible for social control but did it badly. Their behavior had larger practical and exemplary importance than that of others. "When God strikes these high and proud heads," he remarked, "the little folk must take this as an opportunity to tremble and abase themselves."[65] Like Petrarch, he saw in contemporary princes material not for history, which aims to praise great and noble deeds, but for satire, which exposes vice.[66]

Although he occasionally dedicated his works to princes, rulers in all ages seemed to him competitive, greedy, and unscrupulous; he was as realistic as Machiavelli, if less accepting, about political behavior. "It is the universal spectacle," he wrote, "that no monarch should appear to lag behind his neighbors in craftiness, industry, resource, or audacity in extending his boundaries by any means; that no state or republic yields its reputation for cunning and general trickery to any other; that no individual in his dedication to self-seeking fall down in any branch of the evil arts."[67] Like others before him, he located the central problem of politics in the arbitrariness and willfulness of rulers, who endanger the world by doing as they please; they may be able to control others, but no human agency can control them. "They know no limit to their power," he complained, "and the stronger they are, the less restrained."[68] They ignore existing law, wishing "their own fancies to be taken as laws, their own decrees to be sacred and definitive. But by following their own pleasure, they often decree what is iniquitous and unreasonable."[69] Rejecting all restraint, they were, for Calvin, almost without exception, in a precise sense *tyrants*.[70] "Blinded by pride and presumption" and "inebriated by good fortune," they were self-indulgent, perfidious in their relations with each other, especially as regards respect for treaties, bloodthirsty, and indifferent to the slaughter in their wars of subjects whom, in peacetime, they flayed and devoured.[71] Again Calvin was sounding an Erasmian note.

He did not always confine himself to generalities. "France and Spain boast today," he remarked contemptuously in connection with their extended conflict, "that they are governed by mighty princes; but they feel to their cost how little advantage they derive from their bewitchment by this deceitful appearance of honor."[72] He attacked Henry VIII of England, though only after Henry's death, for the hypocrisy of his religious establishment, in which he had "duplicated the tyranny of the Roman pontiff." "He was," Calvin concluded, "a monster."[73]

As this suggests, he viewed with particular distaste the impiety and religious policies of rulers. He was especially sensitive to the subordination of religion to politics. "Nothing is more difficult," he observed, "than to persuade tyrants to submit to the power of God." A prince may formally confess to rule by divine favor, but in his heart he attributes his position to his own valor or his good fortune, his troops, his wisdom, and his wealth.

"Kings admit that the people are subject to God's power," but not themselves. Such "tyrants," Calvin concluded, "usually shut God up in heaven, thinking him content with his own happiness and indifferent to mingling in the affairs of men." Religion to kings "is nothing but a pretext."[74] Calvin was unimpressed by the great churches built by rulers, testimony only to "ambition and vainglory."

He particularly abhorred the abuse of religion for legitimation and social control and was revolted by its hypocrisy. "Today," he noted, "rulers, in presenting their titles, describe themselves as kings, dukes, and counts by the grace of God; but how many falsely use God's name only to claim supreme power for themselves! What is the value of that phrase 'by the grace of God' but to avoid acknowledging any superior at all?"[75] If kings can "retain the people in obedience and duty, any kind of worship and any way of worshipping God is the same to them."[76] Calvin and Machiavelli were alike in their realism; but what Machiavelli was prepared to accept for its utility, Calvin hoped to abolish.

It was hardly likely, given his view of princes, that Calvin would have thought well of the courtiers and counsellors with whom they surrounded themselves, or the lesser magistrates whom they appointed. The fact that these important personages of the second rank were often so unworthy was a further item in his indictment of princes. Far from attempting to restrain their masters, they encouraged their worst impulses.

The basic sin of courtiers and counsellors was indifference both to the true interests of their princes and to the common good; they sought only to serve themselves. Courtiers "refuse to be contented, but, in one way or another, one will acquire some lordship or an income of fifteen thousand francs, another twenty thousand, another thirty, another fifty; they must always be climbing to great titles and great honors. And at whose expense? That of the poor people, who will be skinned and preyed on and robbed on every side. And yet they will keep their mouths shut when Monsieur speaks."[77] Such lords are hypocrites and liars, "avaricious and rapacious, cruel and perfidious," "panderers, buffoons, and flatterers," "so inflated with pride that they think it disgraceful to mingle with the common people."[78] As counsellors, when they "discuss the affairs of the whole world and decide the fates of kingdoms, they see themselves as possessing all the power of God," whereas in fact they mock him "more shamelessly than buffoons in taverns."[79] Calvin sounded like Thomas More's Hythloday on the superiority of private to public life dominated by such men. *Utopia*, indeed, may have been on his mind when he discussed the evils of politics. He pointed, by way of illustration, to More's own wretched end, well deserved because of his hostility to the Gospel.[80]

Sometimes Calvin attacked the entire ruling class, courtiers and magistrates together. "We know," he declared, "the subterfuges under cover of which courtiers and magistrates dare shamelessly to mock God."[81] The misbehavior of judges especially troubled him. "Hardly any scandal is more offensive or more disturbing," he asserted, "than when magistrates are public examples of the worst conduct; no one dares even to murmur against them and most almost applaud."[82] Magistrates, instead of setting a good example, were commonly corrupt. "We see it every day," Calvin observed: "Godless judges take little trouble to get at the truth when it is buried by fraud and malice. Instead, unless they fear getting into trouble, they seem to collaborate with treacherous rogues."[83]

Nor, as he attacked the powerful, did he neglect the rich, a group that included great merchants. Among their delinquencies he included a giddy interest, arising from ambition, in changing fashions of dress.[84] But this sort of conspicuous consumption was, for Calvin, only one symptom of a general heartlessness toward the poor. The rich lacked compassion. Men who had enough to feed a hundred allowed their neighbors to die of hunger; they would snatch the sun from the sky for their own enjoyment, if they could, leaving the poor in the dark. In their greed for land, they forgot that, in the end, they would need only six feet of earth.[85] When the rich see a poor man going under, "they hurry like hunters to fall on him."[86] Calvin bitterly denounced the contemporary movement to enclose common lands. It is "madness," he charged, to "drive away from the land those whom God has placed on it along with us, and to whom he has assigned it as their abode."[87]

But he particularly criticized mercantile wealth. He approved of Isaiah's association of commerce with harlotry because, though it is "useful and necessary to a commonwealth," it is too often marked by fraud and dishonesty.[88] He thought guile so widespread in trade that "those are generally considered blessed who are most effective in weaving schemes of deception."[89] He attacked particular commercial practices: overcharging and misrepresentation as theft; falsification of weights and measures, which undermines the confidence on which human relations depend.[90] He also knew that buyers are as greedy as sellers. The seller "sets the price at twice what is fair," and the buyer "tries to bring the price down by his resistance."[91]

He had also noted an ambivalence in merchants that played an ironic counterpoint to their greed. They were oddly susceptible to deception by appearances; not only did they allow themselves to be cheated by the very tricks they practiced on others, but they also "somehow enjoy it." Moreover, they were strangely sensitive to criticism and flattered pastors who were lenient toward their sins. "This happens everywhere," he remarked, "but it is more common in rich commercial cities."

Such cities, filled with "luxury, pride, vanity, pleasure, insatiable greed, and self-seeking," seemed to him generally vicious,[92] especially the greatest trading centers of the day: Venice, whose merchants "think themselves equal to princes and above all other men except kings"; and Antwerp, where, he had been told, even shopkeepers "do not worry about expenses that even the wealthiest of the nobility could not support."[93] He was also aware of a connection between social change and political disorder. "We know," he asserted, "that riches and power always produce arrogance and a perverse confidence in men. Wars are not contrived in hamlets and villages;

but the great cities collect the wood and kindle the fire, and the fire then spreads and sweeps over the whole land."[94]

But, though he attacked the great above all, Calvin was not sentimental about the lower orders. This was partly because he believed that true Christians are a small minority in every social group,[95] but his position found support in his own experience. Geneva, doubtless confirming prejudices he had imbibed elsewhere, had shown him "the fierce passions of the common people, as a result of which the most frightful disorder inevitably follows if everyone is allowed to do as he pleases."[96] He was aware that poverty, too, has its temptations: the temptation to murmur against God, or to steal from one's neighbor. Neverthless he was convinced that the rich are in greater spiritual danger. He compared the life of the poor, in a haunting application of one of his favorite images, to sailing in a little boat on a small stream at little risk, whereas life for the rich is like being in a ship storm-tossed on the open sea.

He denounced, too, general evils that human wickedness had released. War, especially as civil conflict seemed imminent in France, troubled him deeply, although he was less optimistic than Erasmus about abolishing it, as "the lust for domination has ruled mankind in every age."[97] He believed defensive wars and wars for God's honor justifiable.[98] Implicit in his dependence on the power of the state to discipline human behavior was also some degree of acceptance of political violence, for he recognized, like Augustine, its role in the construction of states. "From the beginning," he remarked, "he who exercised himself most in robbery and pillage was the one who most enlarged his borders and became the greatest."[99] Nevertheless he deplored the fact that wars are generally initiated by the greed or ambition of rulers, and conducted by soldiers out of the basest of motives.[100] Whatever their causes, they "open the gate to robbery, pillage, arson, slaughter, rape, and every violence," for soldiers are so brutalized by combat that they no longer recognize God's image in each other.[101] There was little difference in how nations conducted war, although Spaniards, "making plunder their chief object, more readily spare the lives of men and are not so bloodthirsty as the Germans or the English, who think of nothing but slaying the enemy."[102]

In a time when aristocratic groups still idealized war, Calvin, like Erasmus, aimed to demythologize it. He denounced "the loftiness of mind that many consider a heroic disposition." The supposed "prowess" of men valiant in war in fact reduces them to the level of cats and dogs.[103] "Nothing is more desirable than peace for the happiest life," he declared, "for amidst the tumults of war an abundance of all things is worth nothing, for it is corrupted and perishes."[104]

A second general evil resulting from sin was luxury, which Calvin attacked, in his most Stoic moods, as a symptom of decline from an original simplicity whose merits he took for granted. He may have been thinking of the chateaux in the Loire Valley in denouncing, though recognizing their beauty, the construction of magnificent palaces "which surpass the order of

nature.''[105] The embellishment of walls with paintings, another kind of luxury, gave him similar uneasiness; this practice too aimed, he thought, at
changing "the simple nature of things.''[106]

The underlying problem posed by luxury, for Calvin, is the constant tendency of the human race to deteriorate in the presence of a bounty good in
itself. "When men enjoy abundance," Calvin believed, "they become lux-
urious and abuse it by intemperance.''[107] This tendency can be observed in
daily life; for example, at a banquet, where people are usually offered more
than they need, the company is always tempted "to eat and drink beyond
their ordinary portion.''[108] At the same time Calvin recognized the cir-
cularity in this problem. Experience shows, he observed, "how difficult it is
to be moderate when affluence surrounds us, for luxury follows immediately
on plenty.''[109]

The third general evil, even more important to Calvin, was hypocrisy, a
favorite target of earlier humanist moralists:[110] hypocrisy within the church,
as we will see, but also the hypocrisy that disguises self-interest as friendship. His outrage at hypocrisy reflected his appreciation of friendship.
"When we are dealing with our friends," he observed, "our hearts are glad-
dened, all our feelings can be expressed, nothing is hidden; and our minds
open out and display themselves freely. So the tongue is free and unin-
hibited, and it does not cleave to the roof of the mouth nor bring forth with
difficulty faltering syllables from the back of the throat, the usual case when
the mind is in a less happy condition.''[111] Friends were especially valuable in
times of personal distress: "Nothing is more welcome in grief than to have
friends near us to show us kindness, to share our sorrow, and to offer such
consolations as are possible.''[112] In friendship, in an otherwise predatory
social world, one could still find genuine love and trust. "At least some
shame remains among men," he reflected, "when they have to do with their
close friends. For although they may be otherwise wholly addicted to profit
and indulge in falsehoods, they retain some sense of fairness and shame
inhibits their wickedness when they deal with friends.''[113] His outrage at the
abuse of friendship was correspondingly strong.[114] He thought "open depravity" far less reprehensible than "the craftiness of the fox, which insinuates and cajoles in order to do harm.''[115]

Hypocrisy had already stimulated some of the most passionate lines in
his Seneca commentary. "Are there not also in our own age," he asked in
connection with Seneca's discussion of this vice, " 'monsters of men, drip-
ping with inner vices,' yet putting forth the outward appearance and mask of
uprightness? Yet *they shall melt like wax*' when '*truth, the daughter of
time*,' shall reveal herself. Let them sell as they will sad-faced shows of piety
to the public, the time will come when he who has sold smoke will perish by
smoke.''[116] He found hypocrites in many places, among them, like Erasmus,
at funerals, recalling on this subject, the old proverb that "the mourning of
the heir is laughter under a mask." "Although minds are sometimes pierced
by genuine grief," he observed, "an affected display of pious sorrow, with
abundant tears for everybody to see, does something for those who would

weep more sparingly in the absence of witnesses."[117] He was especially offended by the hypocritical abuse of language. "As those who propose to act truthfully with their neighbors freely open their whole heart," he remarked, "so treacherous and deceitful persons keep a part of their feelings hidden and cover themselves with dissimulation so that nothing certain can be concluded from their speech." How often, he noted, men "pretending friendship treacherously deceive the good by professing one thing with their tongues while entertaining something very different in their hearts." Our speech, he concluded, "must be sincere."[118]

The world was indeed in a deplorable condition, but the grimmest element in its plight was, for Calvin, the state of the church, which was "deprived of all worldly protection and lying under the feet of enemies who abound in all things and are armed with fearful power."[119] The church had become a den of thieves, its government "disordered, without law and restraint, unlike, indeed alien to Christ's institution, degenerated from the ancient ordinances and customs of the church, and contrary to nature and reason."[120] It exhibited all the evils of the secular world but, especially unbecoming in the church, they were there even more conspicuous. Wickedness in the church also aggravated wickedness elsewhere, as the church should be the first line of defense against it. Thus, although Calvin was prepared to denounce sin wherever he found it, he felt a particular duty to attack it in the church, where everything was so "mixed up," with "almost no order left," that the survival of the faith seemed almost hopeless.[121]

Calvin sometimes represented ambition as the root of all evils within as well as outside the church, "the mother of all errors, all disturbances and sects." The church, he charged, had always "been afflicted by the disease of lust for rule." This was why men had abandoned "the love of justice," humanity was "altogether extinct," and "brothers contend against each other, raging as it were against their own bowels." But here too ambition shaded off into greed and luxury, the outward and visible signs, perhaps, of inner vice. The papacy had sought "not only to lay hands on villages and castles, but to carry off vast provinces and finally to seize whole kingdoms." Those whose lives "ought to have been a singular example of frugality, modesty, continence, and humility" aspired to "rival the magnificence of princes in number of retainers, splendor of buildings, elegance of apparel, and banquets."[122]

Sometimes Calvin attacked first the greed of the church, moving from there to other evils. Greed, he declared, caused injustice, as when avaricious clergy misappropriated funds intended to relieve the poor.[123] The papists could calmly ignore the most abominable blasphemies "as long as these did not diminish their incomes."[124] "Abounding in luxury, adorning themselves with gold and jewels," they "think only of gold and silver and are so dazzled by inanities of this kind that they cannot raise their minds to heaven."[125] Greed then inflamed ambition, to the detriment of doctrine: "The golden vessels and costly vestments that swell the pride of the papists serve only pomp and ambition and corrupt the pure teaching mission of the church."[126]

Calvin was less interested in the supposed sexual offenses of the clergy. He described Rome, to be sure, as "a fetid and abominable brothel,"[127] and he played on the sexual anxieties underlying lay anticlericalism by describing how the pretense of celibacy pandered to clerical lust. "These 'chaste' fellows," he wrote, "keep their beds empty of one woman so that they can invade the beds of all the married folk." "Priests and monks provide for themselves where they can," he went on, noting the convenience of the confessional for seduction. Things had come to such a pass that "those who are content with having private whores in their houses without running around are considered chaste and modest."[128] But sexual irregularities seemed to him in some degree excusable because celibacy, being contrary to nature, leads to acts against nature. The rash vow of celibacy had been punished "first by the secret fires of lust and then by horrible and filthy practices."[129]

As with secular society, Calvin chiefly attacked the higher clergy, especially popes. He saw them, like secular princes, as essentially lawless: tyrants in the same sense. Claiming to stand above all earthly authority, "they allow no jurisdiction on earth to control or restrain their lust." A pope "exempts himself from all judgments and wishes to rule tyrannically." He "regards his own whim as law," an attitude "surely so unbecoming and so foreign to ecclesiastical order that it can in no way be endured. For it is utterly abhorrent not only to piety but also to humanity."[130] Indeed, papal tyranny is worse than secular tyranny because it is "raised up against the spiritual kingdom of Christ, over souls rather than bodies."[131] The worst exercise of this tyranny, for Calvin, was the claim of the papacy to dominion over Scripture itself, a blasphemous and diabolical assertion that undermined confidence in the promise of the Gospel.[132] But Calvin also abominated the effort of the papacy to tyrannize over bodies by its intrusion into politics. He thought the justification for its political claims spurious; Lorenzo Valla, he noted, had shown up the alleged Donation of Constantine as "fabulous and ridiculous."[133] The imposing claims, the huge wealth, and the enormous power of the papacy had, however, dazzled many poor souls; the papacy remained the greatest obstacle to reform.[134]

But the pope, like secular princes, was also the presiding officer of a corrupt establishment whose lesser members collaborated willingly with him. Calvin denounced them collectively, considerably exaggerating as he did so the effectiveness of the papal monarchy:

> The Roman Priest, a Heliogabalus, rages against Christ with his red and bloody cohorts and horned beasts, fetching from all sides, from the filth of his foul clergy, his allies, all of whom sup their food from the same pot, though it is not equally dainty. Many other hungry fellows also run up to offer their help. Most of the judges are accustomed to gratify their appetites at these sumptuous banquets and to fight for the kitchen and the kettle; and besides this the haunts of the monks and the dens of the Sorbonne send forth their gluttons who add fuel to the flame.[135]

First among this malignant crew was the episcopate, which, Calvin believed, had originated to serve the pastoral and teaching needs of the church but had degenerated, like the papacy, into an instrument of domination.[136] Bishops considered their sees only as sources of "revenues and vain insignia such as a miter and an episcopal ring and similar nonsense." Although they thought themselves semi-divine, they were so ignorant that "many peasants and artisans who have never tasted letters" could "speak better of the general principles of their faith than these haughty prelates in all their splendor."[137] They were "impious and perfidious men who dare to oppose God in his own name" and "wolves occupying the place of pastors."[138]

Monks represented, for Calvin, idleness and parasitism;[139] they were also notable examples of pride and hypocrisy.[140] But, as with bishops, he was above all offended, like Erasmus, by their ignorance, both in sacred and liberal studies. "There is no monastery," he charged, "that is not more inhospitable to all good studies than the dwelling of cyclops; monks would rather swallow the whole of Scripture than be forced to hear one lecture on it."[141]

> They are all completely unlearned asses, though because of their long robes they have a reputation for learning. If one of them has even tasted fine literature, he spreads out his feathers, proud as a peacock, his fame spreads wonderfully, and he is worshipped by his fellows. The old proverb holds that ignorance is bold, but the extraordinarily insolent pride of monks arises from the fact that they measure themselves only by themselves. Since in their cloisters there is nothing but barbarism, it is no wonder if the one-eyed man is king in the country of the blind.[142]

Calvin singled out the friars for special attention. "They flatter the people," he charged, "and at the same time they prop up the whole papal system." The pope had heaped on them honors and privileges because "they prop up his tyranny and lick his throne like dogs, while he and his mitered bishops consume the richest plunder."[143]

The substitution of domination for learning in the church had trivialized the Gospel. Sermons, Calvin charged, consisted of "little but old wives' tales and fictions, all equally frivolous." The schools "resounded with brawling questions, but Scripture was seldom mentioned."[144] Ignorance had led to indulgences, a "monster" that "daily runs more riotously and lecherously abroad. . . . The fact that indulgences have so long remained untouched and have had a lasting impunity in their unrestrained and furious license, can truly serve as a proof of how deeply men were immersed for centuries in a deep night of errors."[145]

Calvin also denounced in the clergy the general evils he discerned in lay society, notably hypocrisy. Here his Erasmianism is again conspicuous. Although his language was more violent than that of Erasmus, he meant by hypocrisy in the church what Erasmus had attacked as externalism. "Hypocrites are always mocking God with their nonsense," he asserted, "and they think him very cruel if he is not satisfied with external display."[146] He distrusted such display. "Those who have fallen away from true faith," he charged, "are far more ostentatious than the faithful."[147] The external embellishments of worship with which men commonly demonstrated their piety, such as "painted panels, statues, buildings of fine stone, gold, jewels, and costly vestments," seemed to him only "childish trifles."[148]

A hypocrite was also, for Calvin, a person who professed Christianity but did not "live justly and innocently" with his neighbors and was not "ready to aid them promptly and cheerfully whenever necessary." In short, faith without works is hypocrisy.[149] Hypocrites "pretend to worship God by many ceremonies" while permitting themselves "every cruelty, robbery, and fraud."[150] They fast and hear mass daily "to atone for frauds and villainies" as they plot further crimes.[151]

At its most general level, Calvin understood by hypocrisy "all methods of appeasing God or of obtaining his favor contrived and invented by man."[152] Hypocrites "wish for peace with God provided it is on their own terms; but because they cannot surrender wholly to God, they wander off and try to attract God to themselves."[153] The most flagrant vehicle of hypocrisy, for Calvin, was thus justification by works. It included any effort to obligate God, as when "one builds a splendid church, adorns it with rich furnishings, and provides income for saying masses," thinking that thereby "he holds all the keys of the kingdom of heaven so that he can push in even against God's will." Pilgrimages were, on the same grounds, also hypocritical; pilgrims, "if they sweat, think that every step ought to be reckoned to their account by God, and that God would be unjust unless he approved of what is offered him at such trouble."[154] In attacking as hypocrisy what the milder Erasmus had called superstition, Calvin seems to have departed from normal usage, in which hypocrisy involves deliberate deception.

As the addition of human invention to religion, hypocrisy of this kind was also mixture, and of a peculiarly abominable kind. Calvin could convey its horror only with the imagery of fecal and sexual contamination. Hypocrites, he wrote, "sluggishly lie in their own filth because they are confident that they can perform their duty toward God by ridiculous acts of expiation."[155] The papacy, as the ultimate source of hypocrisy, is a "Helen" with whom the enemies of truth "defile themselves in spiritual fornication."[156]

Worst of all, hypocrisy was for Calvin a failure in seriousness. When they encounter the Scriptures, he observed, hypocrites "flatter themselves by pretending that God does not mean what he says but wants to frighten them, as children are frightened by bugbears."[157] But the situation of such persons is far different from what they suppose. "Sated and intoxicated by an empty confidence in their own righteousness," he charged, "hypocrites never reflect on what Christ's mission was on earth. They do not recognize into what a labyrinth of evils the human race has been plunged, the dreadful wrath of God and the curse hanging over all, the confused heap of vices. So, insensitive to the miseries of mankind, they do not think about a remedy.

Untroubled, they will not endure being brought to live more orderly lives, and they are offended at being considered sinners."[158]

Nor did Calvin locate hypocrisy only in the Roman church. "We too," he lamented, "are but few in number, but how mixed! How many today profess the Gospel in whom there is nothing firm, nothing sincere!"[159] Even among those who presented themselves for the Lord's Supper he saw "a filthy mixture" of hypocrites: "indiscriminately, wicked and openly impious men impudently push in."[160] Coping with hypocrites was one of his own worst trials. He was almost certainly speaking from his own experience in Geneva when he remarked that "nothing more torments faithful minsters of the church than when there is no way to correct evils, when they are forced to endure hypocrites whose wickedness they know, when they cannot keep out of the church many harmful pests or even prevent them from spreading their poison by secret arts."[161]

One of the worst expressions of hypocrisy, for Calvin, was the subordination of religion to politics. Entire populations, he was horrified to observe, had learned so little of "true religion in the school of God" that they easily accepted religious arrangements imposed by their rulers. Having "taken no root in the truths of God," they "bend at every moment in the least breeze, as leaves are moved by the wind among the trees," seeing in the edict of a king "no mere wind" but an irresistibly "violent tempest."[162]

There was also, however, a special temporal dimension to Calvin's dark vision of the contemporary world. The evils by which he was surrounded on every side convinced him that his own time represented a low point in human history. The world he inhabited was endangered not only chronically and in general by the universal sinfulness of fallen humanity but acutely, immediately, and perhaps uniquely. This sense of living in a peculiarly endangered time gave his complaints and his call for reform a peculiar urgency.

One element in this attitude was his Erasmian conviction that learning had reached a kind of nadir, not only among the monks but everywhere in the European ruling classes. "Barbarism has so prevailed in the world," he declared, "that it is almost disgraceful for nobles to be reckoned among the learned and literate. The highest boast of the nobility has been to have no learning whatsoever. Indeed they glory in not being 'clerks,' as the learned are commonly called; and if nobles are educated in letters, it is only that they might acquire bishoprics and abbeys."[163]

The clerical establishment from which he had detached himself had also touched bottom. If, as he recognized, the corruption of Rome had remoter origins, its delinquencies had become acute chiefly during the last two centuries, during which—again he echoed Erasmus and a succession of humanist reformers going back to Petrarch—" popes have engaged in nothing but battles, bloodshed, slaughter of armies, sacking of some cities, destruction of others, massacres of nations, and devastation of kingdoms, solely to seize other men's dominions."[164] He specifically indicted contemporary popes: "Leo was cruel, Clement was bloody, Paul is ferocious."[165] The religion of these popes consisted of a "secret theology" of which the first article is that "there is no God," the second that "everything written and taught about Christ is falsehood and deceit," the third that "the doctrines of a life to come and of a final resurrection are mere fables."[166] The bishops of his time were "plunged in the darkness of gross ignorance and lost in their pleasures as well as in sloth." There was "no more intelligence in these animals than in oxen or asses."[167] The church resembled the sinful Jewish establishment at the time of the prophets,[168] a comparision which suggests that Calvin saw himself as a latter-day Isaiah or Jeremiah.

It also troubled him that his beloved France, once the best, was now the worst among the nations of the earth, though he could not quite bring himself to blame his fellow countrymen directly; France had been contaminated by others. "We have been gradually infected, I know not how," he explained, "by the vices of those with whom we associate and are familiar. And since by nature we are more likely to emulate their vices than their virtues, we easily accustom ourselves to corruptions and in this way, in a short time, the contagion spreads from one to another." He was especially troubled by the results of French contact with Islam, whose conquests in Europe had brought "only filthiness and defilement."[169]

Like the prophets, Calvin was particularly distressed by what he perceived as a steady erosion of the sense of community, visible at every level of society. Contemporary princes, he believed, were unusually lacking in consideration for their peoples, and wars were longer and more brutal.[170] Alms in this "unhappy age" were only given "contemptuously."[171] Young people had lost that deference to their elders on which social order depends, and they rejected all correction.[172] Sexual offenses, "rapes, adulteries, incests, and seductions," were more common than ever before.[173] "How monstrous," he exclaimed, "that the world should have been overshadowed by such dense clouds for the last three or four centuries, so that it could not see clearly" how to obey Christ's commandment to love our enemies![174] Everything was in "shameful confusion"; everywhere he saw only "perfidy, cruelty, plots, frauds, violence, injustice, shamelessness," while the poor "groan under their oppression and the innocent are arrogantly and outrageously harassed." God seemed asleep.[175] Never had the human race been in such distress: "justice destroyed in cities, spouses accusing each other, parents complaining of their children, in short all bewailing their condition."[176]

Of fundamental significance for him was the peculiar religious ignorance and growing unbelief, the fault of the papal church, that seemed to him characteristic of his time. Many people did not know "what the teaching of the Gospel is, nor why they confess that Jesus Christ is their Redeemer, having not been taught where they should base the hope of their salvation."[177] Far worse was widespread "atheism," which he located especially "at the courts of kings and princes, among judges, protonotaries and others of the round bonnet; among gentlemen, treasurers and great merchants." His world swarmed with "Epicureans" who had "entirely discarded their religion and sneered angrily at the whole teaching of our faith as 'fairy tales.'"[178] A "vast number of men who never embraced the faith sincerely" were "stampeding like brute beasts into the madness of the Epicureans." Because of this hypocritical crew, "the light which has been kindled may soon be put out, and God may leave a pure understanding of the Gospel to few."[179] "Epicureans" were worse than papists, and it alarmed him that these men, who respected no religion and behaved as they pleased, shared his dim view of the old church. It could at least be said for the papal church that it had maintained control over its members. "I am far more worried today by the fury of the Epicureans than of the papists," he confessed. "I cannot but be tortured and anxious when I see this diabolical conspiracy extinguishing all fear and worship of God, rooting out the remembrance of Christ, or exposing it to the jeers of the rabble. It is worse than if a whole country were on fire at once."[180]

Such wickedness explained, for Calvin, the recent disasters of Christendom. "How many are the distresses with which Europe has been afflicted for the past thirty or forty years!" he exclaimed; "how numerous are the chastisements by which she has been called to repentance!"[181] He compared the tribulations of his own time to those which had destroyed the Roman Empire; now as then, "the complaint circulates far and wide that we have clearly been born in a most unhappy age, and very few do not droop under so great a burden."[182] He was impatient with those who wondered why there had been "so many wars, so many plagues, so many crop failures, so many disasters and calamities, as if the true cause were not obvious."[183]

But what gave Calvin particular cause for anxiety was the imminence of divine punishment far more serious than anything the world had yet experienced. For human beings were not repenting for their sins. On the contrary: "luxury increases daily, lawless passions are inflamed, and human beings continue in their crimes and profligacy more shameless than ever."[184] So far God had restrained his anger at the wickedness of mankind and the loathsome confusion of things. But when the time was ripe he would assuredly "display and unleash" his power and bring the world into conformity with his will.[185] Clearly, for Calvin, there was much to be anxious about: enough, certainly, to propel even this reclusive intellectual into the active life.

II

THE LABYRINTH

4

Cosmic Inheritances

Calvin did not doubt that the world needed setting to rights, but it was never entirely clear to him how this should be done. The two cultures, Hellenistic and Hebraic, which Europeans had inherited from antiquity and combined more or less comfortably in earlier centuries suggested strategies of reform as different as their assumptions about God, the world, and the human personality. The great crisis of Western culture we call "the Renaissance" included, among its other innovations, a growing awareness of these differences; and Calvin himself, as we will see, made some progress toward recognizing them. But he was also typical of his century in that large areas of his thought were untouched by its novelties. Unusually anxious, he also clung to traditional certainties because he preferred the familiar dangers of the labyrinth to an abyss of doubt.

Much in his culture I will call, for want of a better label, "traditional." The traditional mode of culture formation converted the chaotic data impinging on human consciousness into a cosmos by various techniques of containment and definition. It made the universe finite and intelligible by giving it a boundary that guaranteed its integrity and defined a space within which everything in existence could be located and given a local habitation and a name. It dealt with human problems by rational analysis, discipline, and control. Confidence in the adequacy of these devices to order the world and invest it with meaning had been dissolving since the end of the thirteenth century, and their erosion had been an element in the growing anxiety of the waning Middle Ages. The effort to renew them had the disadvantage, however, of increasing the anxiety of the labyrinth.[1]

Fundamental to traditional culture was a confidence that the human mind is capable of knowing what exists as it really is: as God might know it, so to speak. This epistemological optimism found expression in the notion that, in the act of knowing, the mind is united and becomes identical with what is known.[2] Aristotle had said this directly: "The act of knowing is the same as the thing known."[3] In this conception of knowing, the role of the knower is

69

passive; the active role in the union of knower and known is played by the object, which impresses itself on the mind. This conception might be contrasted with the modern notion of thinking *about* a thing, a notion that assumes a distinction between thought and its object and recognizes the possibility of wide discrepancies between them.

The traditional conception was also absolutist and authoritarian. If our knowledge is of things themselves as they really are, there should be, in principle, no disagreement. Difference of opinion in matters of knowledge could only be construed as resulting from deficiency of mind or from perversity; a difference of opinion stubbornly maintained would, from this standpoint, be wicked. In any case the truth about things, especially in important matters, must be made to prevail. This position could lead to charges of heresy not only in religion but also in natural science or even history.

In another respect, too, the traditional conception was optimistic: in its assumption that language, properly used, is an utterly translucent medium for dealing with things. In traditional culture, words are taken to refer directly to things, whether to things already in the mind because they are known, or to external things. Seneca had made *vox sequitur rem* a commonplace,[4] and the point was applied by some thinkers to construct etymologies deriving words from the things to which they bore the relationship Socrates had described, perhaps only playfully, in the *Cratylus*.[5] The notion of concepts in the mind as "things" also suggests the idealism bound up with this culture. The noblest things were understood to be those farthest removed from the vagaries of sense: abstractions from sense experience, generalizations from particulars, and—best of all—entities (like those in mathematics) that can be dealt with entirely apart from sense. In this view, the human mind can be united with the highest realities of all.

Knowing, in traditional culture, was also generally thought analogous to, perhaps even a rarefied kind of, *seeing*.[6] In the background of this identification of knowing with seeing was the special respect for sight expressed by Aristotle[7] and regularly repeated thereafter; and this bias in favor of the visible had shaped much in medieval theology and spirituality. So Nicholas of Lyra, in the *Glossa ordinaria*, had pointed out that "I see" may be taken as standing, in general, for the exercise of all the senses.[8] This emphasis on the visual lurks, perhaps, behind medieval insistence on a visible church and the visibility of the sacraments. It is apparent also in the use of images, in the words of a thirteenth-century monk, John of Genoa, "to excite feelings of devotion, these being aroused more effectively by things seen than by things heard."[9] Because, by analogy, the highest kind of intellection was conceived as a process in which the eye of the mind beholds its object by the light of reason, Thomas Aquinas and Dante could represent ultimate religious experience as a beatific *vision*.

The belief in sight as the most secure foundation for knowing had other implications. The fact that the eye can look up and discern in the motions of the heavenly bodies a regularity and order absent from our lower world encouraged a tendency to see in the heavens a unique expression of the wisdom built into the universe by its Creator. One saw there a single, bounded, finite, and intelligible system organized as a hierarchy of spherical bodies, each in its own orbit, never colliding with one another, circling at varying distances around the earth in utterly regular and predictable motions. From this regularity observers inferred the existence of a "law" of nature to which the heavenly bodies are "obedient." Their obedience also implies that they are not just inert matter but spiritual beings, and as such able to transmit influences from the higher reaches of the cosmos to the earth. Astrology, the science of these influences, is therefore an expression of the unity and coherence of the system. Finally, the perfect order, the beauty, and the purity of the system were thought to convey much about its Maker and pointed to the possibility of a natural theology in which the "book of nature" complements revelation in Scripture.

Seeing also served important human purposes. Plato's Timaeus had argued that the eye is the organ of greatest utility to mankind, and astronomy the source of all philosophy, that most valuable gift of the gods. This meant that by looking to the heavens, we have access to an ultimate and utterly reliable wisdom applicable to earthly uses.[10] Cicero reflected this notion in the proposition "that the immortal gods implanted souls in human bodies so as to have beings who would care for the earth and who, while contemplating the celestial order, would imitate it in the moderation and consistency of their lives."[11]

But looking upward is also a function of erect posture, and much was also made to depend, in traditional knowing, on this peculiarity of human beings. In this view *uprightness*—the ambiguity of the term is also significant—distinguishes humans from other animals. It gives visible expression to the dignity and glory of the human species and even to the presence in humans of a "divine spark" that enables them to commune directly with heavenly divinity by means of their own highest faculties, those located, naturally, in the head. God's image and likeness in human beings were thus identified with human intelligence; and since this, however damaged, had evidently survived the Fall, it could be plausibly argued that the original image-likeness of mankind to God persists. The implications of this view for theology were of special importance. It reinforced the belief that human beings can know God as he is, unhampered by the limitations of the human condition; and it implied that theology is a science, devised by God and communicated in his books of nature and Scripture, that presents truths from his perspective. For this reason human knowledge, and notably theological knowledge, can claim a *certitude* that reflects its divine origin. For the understanding of Scripture this position notably precluded any awareness of what we now call the hermeneutical problem.

The dependence of this culture on a traditional cosmology helps to explain why the new astronomy of Copernicus and Galileo was resisted with such ferocity. The intelligible order displayed by the old science had been a source of comfort, and its subversion was tantamount to casting the human race adrift on an uncharted sea. But the attack on traditional culture could hardly have been effective had its foundations not been already massively eroded. Calvin participated in its erosion, but even as he did so he also clung to it.

He was not a philosopher, and he did not often make explicit, much less examine, the traditional assumptions that underlay his thought. He implied, rather than stated, the competence of the human mind to know the world in a traditional sense.[12] Nor did he reflect on the relationship of language and the realities to which it refers, although he repeated familiar commonplaces about *verba* and *res*. It was intolerable, he thought, "for men to seize on bare signs and neglect the truth of things."[13] Paul, he noted, had defended himself against trumped-up charges by confronting "words with the thing."[14]

But he often seemed much impressed by the special value of sight. He compared the eyes to guides that, in this life, "lead the other senses hither and yon."[15] He noted too, transforming the rhetorical sequence on which he was commenting into an epistemological pronouncement, how Isaiah had, among the senses, "put in the first place *sight*, which produces *certain knowledge*."[16] The use of "to see" for "to understand" came readily to Calvin; he compared Scripture to a painting in which we *see* sin and its punishment.[17]

He also followed the traditional scheme in its movement from sight, through the study of the heavens, to a grasp of the divine order governing the universe; and this order remained for him that of the old astronomy. Whether he thought that, to be appreciated as a manifestation of God's wisdom, the universe must be intelligible, or because he associated infinity with God, he insisted on the finiteness of the universe. "However widely the circuit of the heavens extends," he wrote, "it still has some limit."[18] He opposed Copernicanism, warning his followers against those who asserted "that the sun does not move and that it is the earth that moves and turns." Such persons were motivated by "a spirit of bitterness, contradiction, and faultfinding"; possessed by the devil, they aimed "to pervert the order of nature."[19]

Astronomy, Calvin insisted, "unfolds the admirable wisdom of God"[20] by displaying the wonderful order of the heavens, which are so cunningly arranged that nothing is "nearer the earth nor farther from it than is useful for preserving order"; and, "in this vast expanse, nothing is incoherent or deformed."[21] The sun is admirable for the speed, quietness, and regularity of its course.[22] The various entities in the heavens are also clearly distinguished from one another by the principles of hierarchy and subordination. The "innumerable multitude of stars" is "ordered like an army in all its ranks."[23] The heavenly bodies, in short, are infallibly obedient to natural laws imposed by God. "Eclipses and other observations" clearly prove that the stars are above the planets and that each planet has its own orbit. "The sun, moon, and stars," he concluded, "are not mixed confusedly together, but each has its assigned position and dwelling place."[24]

First among the signs "of divinity in man," therefore, Calvin listed "the nimbleness with which the soul surveys heaven and earth."[25] The "atheism" of "Epicureans" was nowhere more offensive to him than in their refusal to recognize the order of the cosmos: "Their philosophy imagined the sun to be two feet thick and the world to consist of atoms, and by such trifling they sought to destroy the wonderful craftsmanship visible in the architecture of the world."[26]

The order of the heavens was, for Calvin, deeply consoling. "On earth," he declared, "there often appears dreadful confusion, and the works of God, so far as we can understand them, appear mutually discordant; but whoever raises his eyes to heaven will see the greatest harmony."[27] But this advantage was purchased at a cost of which Calvin was hardly conscious. It introduced into his thought pagan impulses that would at other times give him trouble. Both Aristotle's unmoved mover and the spirituality of the heavenly bodies lurk behind Calvin's observation that "God, when he revolves the world, remains consistent, so that what we call changes or turnings produce no variation in himself, but each revolution is coordinated with all the others." He also slipped once into claiming that the heavens are "eternal and exempt from alteration."[28] Another problem was implicit in the order of the sublunary world. Calvin accepted the arrangement of the four elements according to weight. Earth, as heaviest, should be at the bottom; "the waters are lighter and, since they flow together, they are not so firm; air is consequently above the waters; and fire is still higher."[29] But he failed to notice that the "confusion" of elements which allows some land to protrude above the waters is necessary for human survival.[30] Still another problem lurked in his belief in the dynamic relationship of the heavenly bodies to existence on earth, which found expression in a cautious defense of astrology. "That art is indeed worthy of praise," he observed, "were men to preserve moderation."[31] At the very least God used the heavenly bodies as "signs" of impending good or evil "fortune."[32]

Conceptions of cosmic order also helped to shape Calvin's conception of the end of time. "The confusion of things revealed in the world today," he declared, "will not last forever, for the Lord, by his coming, will summon the world again to order."[33] In God's kingdom the whole world will be subjected "to order and to his government."[34] Calvin was conflating, unaware of its influence on his thought, classical cosmology with Christian eschatology.[35]

All this wonderful knowledge derived from observing the heavens depended, however, on the erect stature of human beings that enables them to look up; and Calvin more than once cited the familiar lines of Ovid describing this unique human attribute. "Men," he insisted, "are by nature shaped to contemplate the heavens and so to know their author."[36] "As we travel through the world," he proclaimed, "we ought always to erect our minds and senses to heaven."[37]

The natural laws that keep the heavenly bodies harmonious also provided Calvin, in a traditional way, with his model for order in human affairs. He began with a basic Aristotelian principle: "Man is a social animal, and all [human beings] naturally desire relationships with one another."[38] It has also been "implanted in us by nature that all human beings should willingly endeavor to assist each other."[39] Nature dictates subordination in society just as in the heavens. "Those who cannot submit themselves to the magistrates, who rebel against their fathers and mothers, who cannot bear the yoke of masters or mistresses," Calvin argued, "sufficiently show that they cannot join with anyone who does not reverse the whole order of nature and jumble heaven and earth, as people say."[40] On the one hand, subordination and hierarchy are antidotes to mixture in society; confusion in the ranks of society, on the other hand, "signifies a dreadful vengeance of God."[41] The responsibility of social superiors for the welfare of those below them is a corollary of social subordination; their beneficent influence should shape the lower reaches of society much as the heavenly bodies influence the lower parts of the cosmos. "Anyone who has been established above others," Calvin warned, "ought diligently to aim at improving them."[42] Those who have "a more honorable rank" must accept "a greater burden."[43]

Calvin's emphasis on the importance of social differentiation for the maintenance of order is one source of his doctrine of the calling. The calling to which every human being has been assigned by God was for him a kind of earthly equivalent of the orbit of a heavenly body. He emphasized its distinctness, and the obligation of each person to remain within his own calling for the sake of order. "Those who rudely interfere in the business of others cause great disturbance," he pointed out, "and are a trouble to themselves and others. The best way, therefore, to maintain a peaceful life is when each one is intent on the duties of his own calling, carries out the commands that the Lord has given, and devotes himself to these tasks: when the farmer is busy with the work of cultivation, the workman carries on his trade, and in this way each keeps within his proper limits. As soon as men turn aside from this, everything is thrown into confusion and disorder.[44] God "values above all the obedience with which we follow our calling."[45] Callings stabilized the social order.

Calvin's doctrine of the calling also reduced the uncertainty of social existence by limiting its mobility:

> The Lord commands each of us, in all the actions of life, to consider his calling. For he knows with what restlessness human nature seethes, with what inconstancy it is driven, and how greedy it is to embrace different things at once. Therefore, lest our folly and temerity mix everything up, he has ordained duties for everyone in his particular way of life. And lest anyone dare to leap over the boundaries assigned him, he has called these ways of life "callings." Every individual's way of life is therefore like a post assigned by the Lord so that he will not spend his whole life wandering about in uncertainty.[46]

The calling was thus the source of large subjective benefits.

There are divinely instituted laws, then, for human as well as for physical nature, though for Calvin, as for other natural-law thinkers, these laws work differently in the two realms. "God," he explained, "silently subjects his insensate creation to his will by a secret inclination," but "he teaches explicitly to men endowed with intelligence, so that they may obey him intelligently and with consent." [47] Natural law in human affairs is prescriptive, not descriptive.

This conception assumed the capacity of the human mind to grasp the laws of nature, and Calvin acknowledged that such a capacity had survived the Fall. "God wished men to retain some ability to discriminate between justice and injustice," he admitted, although he immediately qualified this by observing that "their minds are darkened with dense clouds so that they are repeatedly deceived." [48] But in matters pertaining to "the right conduct of life," the human mind still has some acuteness.[49] In society one can see that God "declares openly, every day, his clemency to the godly and his severity to the wicked and criminal." [50]

That "pagans have a law without [written] law" and "are by no means lacking in the knowledge of right and equity" proved, he believed, the universality of an innate law of nature.[51] All human beings abhor incest, adultery, theft, and murder; all nations respect ambassadors[52] and agree that "wars should not be undertaken suddenly" and "arms should not be taken up except for legitimate causes." [53] The law of nature also condemns ingratitude, dictates that "merit deserves reward," and requires "good faith in commercial transactions and contracts." [54] That the distinction between good and evil is rooted in nature explains too why lechers, thieves, and drunkards, without knowing Scripture, tend to hide from the light.[55] The Golden Rule is itself a law of nature.[56] Indeed, the written law in Scripture is "nothing but a witness to the law of nature by which God recalls to our memories what has been inscribed in our hearts." [57] When Calvin evaluated the behavior of the ancients in the light of this law, he was relatively generous. He "did not so dissent from the common judgment," he wrote, "as to contend that there is no difference between the justice, moderation, and equity of Titus and Trajan, and the madness, intemperance, and savagery of Caligula or Nero or Domitian, or between the obscene lusts of Tiberius and the continence of Vespasian." [58]

On rare occasions he seemed almost sympathetic to the pagan belief that to know the good—from nature—is sufficient to do the good. "By nature," he remarked, "we are all drawn to seek the good, but false imaginings pull us this way and that." [59] He hinted, too, at an innate natural innocence corrupted by social experience. If, he had noticed, little children "wish to eat or drink together, each one will take his own portion, and they will be in agreement. . . . Who teaches them that? I do not know what instinct of nature." [60] He also yearned for the laws governing human society to be as changeless as those governing the heavenly bodies; the immutable laws of the Medes and the Persians stimulated him to reflect that "when laws are variable, many persons inevitably suffer injury, for no private right will be secure unless the law is universal; and in addition where laws can be made and remade, caprice replaces justice."[61]

Laws, for Calvin, then, give access to the *principles* of social control. But the good order of society also depends on *institutions*. Calvin's social and political universe was ordered by three major institutions, related more or less hierarchically, which, he believed, had been essentially unchanged since the world began. First came the family, above that the polity, and over all the church.[62] All three had been established by God to enforce in human society the principles of order visible in the cosmos, beginning with that "distinction of ranks" without which "a multitude resembles a maimed or lacerated body in which nothing can be seen but dreadful confusion."[63]

Order in the family begins, for Calvin, with the subordination of wives to husbands, because every man, both through God's holy ordination and as a "privilege of nature," is superior to every woman.[64] He elaborated on this superiority. "From where," he asked, "come industry and all the arts and sciences? From where comes work? From where all the things that are most excellent and that we most value? It is certain that all come from men." It is "the law of nature" that a woman should "serve her husband and give him honor and reverence."[65] Women, Calvin insisted, "by the ordinary law of nature are born to obey, for all wise men have always rejected government by women as an unnatural monstrosity." God did not create "two heads of equal power but added to the man an inferior as helper";[66] a wife is to her husband "as body to head."[67] He was disturbed by the thought of women in power or active in public life. "How indecorous it would be," he exclaimed, "for her who is subject to one member to be placed over the whole body! There is no doubt that wherever natural propriety has been respected, women in every age have been excluded from public administration."[68] Lest anyone be misled by the example of Priscilla, who had been permitted to teach in the apostolic church, he explained carefully that she had "carried out this instruction privately, within the walls of her own home, so that she would not weaken the order prescribed by God and nature."[69] Because the principal virtue of a woman is modesty and the eyes of a modest woman are downcast, he may have thought that a woman is not, in the nature of things, competent to inspect the heavens.[70] His need to explain that God had honored woman by this arrangement and his agreement with Solomon that a "conscientious wife is her husband's crown" may suggest some concern about the practical consequences of these views.[71]

He was under no illusion about how well this arrangement usually worked, and he did not always blame women for disorder in the household. He thought men no more inclined to fulfill their responsibilities than women. "How rarely do you find a man who willingly undertakes the burden of governing a wife," he exclaimed, "for it is a business that involves countless vexations! How reluctantly does a wife submit to the yoke!"[72] But he was clear enough about how things ought to go. The husband should treat his wife well, and she, content in her inferior role, should not "behave impatiently." He also insisted that a woman's place is in the home. "A woman does well," he told his congregation, "when she keeps house, makes her bed, sweeps, boils the pot, takes care of her children."[73] Housework is "a sacrifice acceptable to God."[74] Women should not gad about; Dinah was raped because, "having left her father's house, she wandered about more freely than was proper."[75] Women who excel in nondomestic activity "sometimes make that an excuse for arrogance and disobedience toward their husbands."[76]

Marriage also requires submission, by both partners, to its own natural laws, especially that of monogamy. On this point the example of the Old Testament patriarchs was to be avoided. The multiple marriages of Jacob were a reminder that men are "not free to overturn the law of marriage, divinely consecrated from the beginning, by a depraved custom."[77] Calvin thought even divorce preferable to polygamy.[78]

Parental, especially paternal, control over children also seemed to him a law of nature. Nature dictated their early discipline, as the training of domestic animals suggested. "It is good for us to be formed from childhood to bear the yoke," he observed. "If a horse is left free in the fields and not in due time tamed, he will hardly ever endure to be pacified, he will always be refractory. Oxen also will never be brought to bear the yoke if they are placed under it only in the sixth or eighth year. We know by experience that it is the same with men."[79] Nor did parental authority end, for Calvin, when children reach maturity, for "the claims of nature are never altogether extinguished; indeed older people, since God has commissioned them, ought to rule, or at least to advise, as long as they can."[80] But parental control also had a deeper basis: because God is called "father," we ought to recognize, as we cannot in mothers, "something divine in every father."[81] Ham's disrespect toward his father reminded Calvin that fathers are, "next to God, most deeply to be reverenced; and even if there were no books or sermons, nature itself continuously dictates this lesson to us." He described filial piety as the "mother of all virtues."[82]

He proposed to bring up boys and girls somewhat differently, in accordance with their different natures and callings. With both, of course, the father, though generally tolerant and flexible, should be prepared when necessary "to use severity and to temper mildness with rigor,"[83] but sons were more likely to require the father "to play the part of an angry person" and to correct "with harsh words or even with the rod."[84] Daughters, however, presented special dangers. Fathers should keep them "under strict discipline if they wish to save them from all dishonor," and they must not be allowed "to go too boldly into public assemblies and excite the desire of young men."[85] A father also has the responsibility to arrange a suitable marriage for a daughter, for "though girls often reject marriage through shame or ignorance of themselves, they are still sensual and likely to be led astray." Fathers must therefore consider what is best "so that their prudence may correct inexperience or perverse desire."[86] Calvin was strongly opposed to the free choice of marriage partners by children. "It would be altogether unreasonable," he asserted, "for young men and women to seek spouses for themselves out of desire." It is in accordance with "the common order of things" that young men "should not be joined in marriage except with the consent of parents and that young women should not marry except with those to whom they are given." [87]

In the end, of course, as in treating the relations of husband and wife, Calvin was sufficiently politic to recognize that parents should deal tactfully with their children: "This middle position is a just rule, that children suffer themselves to be directed by their parents, and that parents not drag their children unwillingly into something, but use their power only to promote their children's welfare." [88] Children, nevertheless, like wives, must be controlled.

Residues of cosmological thinking are less evident in Calvin's treatment of the political and ecclesiastical institutions with which he was more actively engaged. They too required control, but he provided for it in radically different ways that will be examined elsewhere in this book. Cosmological themes had, however, a large influence on his conception of the human personality.

This was a subject fraught with difficulty, especially for a thinker of the sixteenth century who aimed above all for fidelity to Scripture. Calvin's basic problem was that he had inherited what he took to be an objective and scientific description of personality but which was in fact an artifact of ancient culture loaded with cosmic reference and fundamentally antithetical to the anthropology of the Bible. Above all it left no room for that literally central element in biblical anthropology, the "heart."

Calvin recognized, and noted with approval, that philosophers had described human being as a microcosm, though he evaded the deeper implications of this conception. It meant only, he argued, that a human being is "full of countless miracles" and therefore "proof of the glory of God." [89] That cosmological habits of thought deeply influenced him is apparent, however, in his view of the personality as a hierarchy of discrete faculties reflecting the hierarchical structure of the universe. [90]

Among these faculties the highest constituted the soul. Every thinker of Calvin's time was aware of the obscurity of the soul; Aristotle had described it as "one of the most difficult things in the world." [91] Calvin may not have been altogether satisfied with his own account of the matter; this is suggested by his defensive suggestion, after one effort to deal with it, that "some give a different interpretation; but all sensible people will, I hope, readily agree with me." [92] Fundamental to his position was the proposition that the soul (*anima*) is "the principal part of man"; [93] he always treated it with special honor. His difficulties began when he tried to characterize it further; the result was a series of vague, various, and often incompatible passages. [94] He was clear, at any rate, that the soul is the life of the body, "animating all its parts and rendering its organs fit and useful for their actions"; it is therefore present in a fetus from the moment of conception. [95] But he was unable to proceed with much assurance beyond this. Sometimes he identified it with "intelligence and reason," sometimes with the affections, sometimes with the will.[96] At other times he shifted out of this philosophical mode altogether and identified it with the heart.[97] Sometimes he combined these possibilities. It occurred to him that intelligence and heart together constitute the soul, but again that perhaps these are identical. This suggests an effort to assimilate the anomalous heart into an alien classical anthropology by intellectualizing it.[98]

There were other difficulties. Usually Calvin analyzed human being simply into soul and body, which corresponded to the superior and inferior realms of the cosmos; when he did this, he often made little distinction between "soul" (*anima*) and "spirit" (*animus*),[99] from which we may perhaps infer that he was uncertain about both. He sometimes identified spirit, like soul, with intellect.[100] Occasionally, however, like Erasmus in the *Enchiridion*, he employed a tripartite Neoplatonic anthropology in which "as the soul gives life to man" and corresponds to the realm of nature, the spirit, responding to the Holy Spirit, represents "supernatural life in man."[101]

He was clear, however, about the distinction between soul, whatever its composition, and body: however closely connected, soul and body are distinct "substances."[102] The soul "inhabits" the body, like a guest or (occasionally) a prisoner.[103] The distinction also figured prominently in his reflections on immortality. "Soul," he asserted, "denotes the immortal spirit that dwells in the body."[104]

The esteem for intelligence in the cosmological model of the personality was also reflected in Calvin's identification of God's "image and likeness" in human being. He could not deny that some "sparks" of the divine image are discernible in every part of human being, "even in the body itself."[105] But he preferred to identify God's image with "intelligence and reason," because in them he could sense "a spark of the Spirit of God." "It is a sign of his image and likeness," he proclaimed, "when he has made us reasonable creatures. God imprinted his image on men by giving them intelligence and discretion; they have prudence; a great many are acute, have wisdom and skill."[106] "The mind of man is [God's] true image."[107]

The intellect, therefore, is "leader and governor" of the soul;[108] and like other humanists, Calvin celebrated its powers. Those who refuse to acknowledge its competence and condemn it "to perpetual blindness," he charged, "not only go against the divine word but also run contrary to the experience of common sense."[109] It is their mental powers that make human beings "more noble and more exquisite than the animals, the trees, or the fruits of the earth."[110] "Manifold indeed," he wrote, echoing Cicero's *De natura deorum*, "is the nimbleness of the soul with which it surveys heaven and earth, joins past to future, retains in memory things heard long before, nay pictures to itself whatever it pleases. Manifold also is the skill with which it devises things incredible and is the mother of so many marvelous devices. These are unfailing signs of divinity in man."[111] But above all, "reason and judgment" are able to control and order the lower faculties of the personality. "God has given us reason and judgment," he insisted, "to combat our passions."[112] In sum, we display the image of God "insofar as

we have intelligence and reason, discriminate between good and evil, and
have some order, some regulation."[113]

Notably missing from Calvin's discussion of the higher faculties of the
personality, however, are imagination and creativity. Under the pejorative
label "fantasy" *(fantasia, fantasie),* he attacked them. For Calvin only God
can create. "Since he is the only true God," he argued, "it follows that the
inventions of men are utterly insane and therefore deceptions and mockings
of the devil to deceive mankind."[114] He was thinking here of those inventions of their own with which the papists had corrupted true religion,[115]
but in the background of his thought on this matter was a traditional esthetic
in which art is limited to the imitation of nature.

The "affections," or more pejoratively the "passions," as in much of
classical thought, hardly seemed to Calvin to participate in the nobility of the
soul. Often clashing with one other, they endanger its harmony[116] and constantly threaten "to drag us from the right path."[117] Always tending to excess, they resist control by the higher faculties of the soul. Boundless in their
demands, rebellious against God, they are "vicious and perverse because
they burst out and endure no restraint."[118] Like the Furies, they make us
worse than beasts. They are "so many soldiers of Satan, resisting the righteousness of God and obstructing and disturbing his reign."[119]

Lowest of all is the body, the primary source of human wickedness, and
Calvin suggested that God had displayed his own disdain for it by creating it
from the dust in order to keep us humble.[120] It is the body, he wrote, that
prevents us from recognizing God as the source of order in human affairs.
The body also brought into focus his dread of pollution.[121] At times, then,
the body seemed to him not only the prison of the soul but worse: "carrion,
dirt, and corruption," full of a "stinking infection" that defiles the rest of the
personality.[122] Thoughts of the body, especially when associated with sexuality, could produce in his rhetoric sudden reversals in which he would
switch within a single paragraph from wonder at the miracle of human procreation to a sense of the body as "ordure and contagion" and of the pro-
creative act as "a shameful thing one dares not mention."[123] This
conventional and unbiblical attitude to the body may have had deep roots in
Calvin's own feelings. "There is something so unaccountably shameful in
the nakedness of man," he remarked, "that scarcely anyone dares to look
upon himself, even when no witness is present."[124] This attitude also gave
him theological difficulties. Although professing to believe in the resurrection of the body, he complained about the tendency of Christians to be more
impressed by this carnal event than by the raising of the soul.[125]

Calvin used this hierarchical model, as theologians had done at least
since Augustine, to describe unfallen humanity. "In the mind," he declared
of Adam, "the light of right intelligence flourished and ruled, uprightness
accompanied it, all the senses were obedient to reason, and the body corresponded to this order."[126] The Fall, in this perspective, signified the collapse of "the legitimate order of nature."[127] Here, however, was a further
problem for Calvin. Conceiving of sin as the result of the disorder of fac-

ulties ordered by nature and of salvation as the restoration of right order to the personality, this conception carried with it optimistic overtones of its classical origins hardly consistent with the doctrine of original sin. It was doubtless possible to interpret the conception in such a way as to safeguard in theory a religion of grace. But in practice the value it attached to the supposedly higher faculties of human beings encouraged belief in the possibility of reform by strengthening the mind through education and by moral effort.

The cosmological model of order was spatial, and it allowed little place to time and change. Even the movement of the heavenly bodies, being circular, did not imply change, which was confined to the lowly earth. The immutability of the cosmos elsewhere was, however, a major element in its attraction, perhaps especially for an anxious man like Calvin. He was comforted by "the consistency of the heavens, eternal and exempt from all change." [128] He dreaded change as a sign of God's displeasure: "almost any change is injurious," [129] and we are properly "terrified by almost anything new and sudden." [130] Deliberate pursuit of novelty is therefore one of the worst evidences of human wickedness, at best a failing of "weak minds" likely to be exploited by evil men. [131] His abhorrence of change found expression even in his final moments. "I pray you, make no change, no innovation," he pleaded on his deathbed. "People often ask for novelties. I do not desire for my own sake, out of ambition, that what I have established should endure and that people should retain it without wishing for something better, but because all changes are dangerous and sometimes hurtful." [132] Change to Calvin, as to all the followers of Petrarch, represented estrangement and loss: the loss of peace but also the loss of continuity, community, and cultural context. [133]

He opposed novelty above all in the church, which suggests why he was so insistent, like the great eleventh-century reformer Hildebrand, that he taught nothing of his own but only "the doctrine of the living God and of Christ." [134] Knowing that the "Lord keeps the same even course, so that he may retain us throughout our lives in what we have learned," should "bridle" our desire for novelty and ensure prudence in our reforms. Innovation, Calvin repeatedly argued, had come only from the papacy. [135]

His ideal for society and the human condition often seems as static as his ancient model. He yearned for peace, which he associated with "deliverance and exemption from every doubt and care." He thought "nothing more desirable than peace." [136] Conflict, however, alarmed him as much as Erasmus. "We see," he declared, "what an atrocious evil contention is. Once it has fermented, it produces such violent emotions that even the most prudent of men lose control of themselves." People imagine they desire peace, but "everyone disturbs it by his insane lusts." [137] There is no peace here below: "nothing is certain, and one need only turn his hand to produce change." [138]

The cosmological vision that supported Calvin's hatred of change and love of peace had a large influence on his perception of the past. The imperfection implicit in all change contributed to his understanding of history as decline. "The world," he lamented, "always deteriorates and becomes gradually more vicious and corrupt; the world grows worse as it becomes older." [139] This vision of the past is implicit in the violent and destructive figures he employed in speaking generally of change. "Even if the air is calm in one direction or another," he warned, "at any moment some change could suddenly occur. A storm is always gathering even when the sky is tranquil, and so it also happens in human affairs. Since this is the way it is, no condition on earth can last." [140]

Rome, contemporary as well as ancient, provided him, like so many others before and after, with the most decisive illustration of the inevitability of decline. He recognized the superiority of the Roman Empire to other empires, [141] but this, for him, only intensified the significance of its decay. "Where now is the majesty of the Roman Empire?" he asked. "Where is the excellence of the people that ruled the entire world?" [142] Once a glorious republic, then corrupted into the worst of the four monarchies, Rome had sunk lower and lower. "Where now," he asked again, "is the liberty of Rome? Where is the beauty of that illustrious republic? May not Rome now justly be called the workshop of iniquity and every kind of crime?" [143]

Occasionally, mingling moralism and nostalgia, he sounded like a Stoic idealizing the Golden Age. He thought that the human race had once enjoyed far better health; this accounted for the longevity of the patriarchs. But by the time of Moses, "the vigor of the entire human race" was already much diminished, and human beings survived to the age of seventy only with "trouble and distress." [144] Modern armies, again, were markedly inferior to those of antiquity, which had been "far more tolerant of heat, exertion, and hunger," as well as "careless of those luxuries that have today corrupted our soldiers." [145]

Calvin was troubled above all by what he perceived as a steady moral decline. He believed that friends had been more loyal in the past; [146] and, in another echo of Erasmus, that "inns have today replaced [private] hospitality." [147] Forgetting now their polygamy, he contrasted the chastity of the age of the patriarchs with modern license, which had now reached such a pass "that husbands are forced to hear in silence of the dissolute conduct of their wives with strangers." [148] Moral decline had also been accompanied by that of religion. When the human race was young, Calvin believed, all people worshipped one God; but in the course of time "they fabricated a multitude of Gods," "mixed up God himself with angels so that everything was confused," and even "transferred a part of divine worship to mortals." [149] The vision of history as decline also left open the possibility that the future holds in store events even more terrible than those in the past.

But in addition to viewing the past as prolonged decline, and without being aware of any incompatibility between the two conceptions, he discerned in history a cyclical pattern of decline and recovery. For Calvin, as for Machiavelli, good morals and institutions inevitably degenerate because of the unreliability of human nature; but the increasing intolerability of human existence regularly generates a movement of reform. This conception thus allowed for improvement, but only as return to a happier state that, in the nature of things, must eventually also pass away. Like others influenced by this conception, Calvin described it with the vocabulary of regression. Improvement in the human condition was *re*form, *re*birth, *re*storation, *re*stitution, *re*newal, or even *re*volution, a more obviously cosmological conception.[150]

Because he was convinced of the peculiar degradation of his own time, a cyclical conception of history thus suggested to Calvin not further decay—at least immediately—but imminent improvement. It might mean more than that; occasionally he attempted to combine classical cycles with the linear time of Judaism and Christianity. He hoped that, "the world having revolved through various cycles of disturbance, God may at last bring everything back to the purpose which he decreed."[151] The "cycles of disturbance" would eventually stop.

He found both in Scripture and in post-biblical history repeated cycles of renewal and decay, finding especially instructive the similarities among the time of Noah, the apostolic age, and his own time. Each had renewed the world after a long decline. This comforted him. Because history repeats itself, the renewal of equality and self-restraint after the flood, for example, gave him hope for his own generation.[152] He was also encouraged to learn how tribulations like his own had confirmed the faith of Paul, for "nothing happens to us now that was not experienced by the holy fathers"; they too had endured trouble, confusion, tyranny, hypocrisy, apostasy, and false teachers, and emerged victorious.[153] A cyclical conception of history promised success for the contemporary reform movement.

Calvin's cyclical approach to the past notably shaped his treatment of Christian antiquity. He admired the primitive age of the church as a kind of apogee in its history. "Is there any antiquity of the church," he asked, "either earlier or of higher authority than the days of the apostles?"[154] He contrasted the generosity of the primitive church with the greed of contemporary churchmen.[155] He noted its free election of pastors, he generally approved of the ancient councils, he contrasted ancient monasticism favorably with that of his own time even though he could not approve of it fully, and he thought that all antiquity had agreed with him on both the meaning and the administration of the Eucharist.[156] He also insisted that the Fathers would generally have sided with the Reformers against Rome.[157] He relied heavily on Chrysostom for the interpretation of Scripture,[158] and, in larger ways, on Augustine, "the best and most reliable witness of all antiquity," to whom "the godly by common consent justly attribute the greatest authority."[159] Unlike some Protestant leaders, he believed that the church had remained basically healthy "for about five hundred years" in both its teachings and its institutional practice.[160]

He discerned signs of deterioration, however, as early as the second century,[161] and he believed that by the time of Gregory the Great it had "much degenerated from its ancient purity."[162] From then on, its decline had been steady as a result of the penchant of the papacy for self-aggrandizement. Its corruption had also been accelerated by the papal alliance with the Carolingians, for Calvin a pact between thieves.[163] In the eleventh century the conflict between popes and emperors had pushed the process further, and from that time to the present the popes had not ceased, "now by fraud, now by treachery, now by weapons of war, to invade other men's domains." For two centuries they had "so troubled Christendom in the effort to hold or increase papal authority that they have nearly destroyed it."[164] This was the vision of medieval history of Machiavelli and Guicciardini.

The result had been a gathering religious crisis. The negligence of a power-hungry papacy had allowed Satan to raise up "innumerable follies which, in their monstrous absurdity," Calvin charged, "outdid the superstitions of all the Gentiles."[165] The consequence had been a "fearful defection of the whole world," in which "the truth of the Gospel gradually vanished and the treasure of salvation was taken away."[166] The writings of the Fathers, already imperfect, were now "utterly defiled by dirty hands"; patristic theology had given way to a new theology that "contaminated God's Holy Word with sophistic subtleties and the squabbles of dialecticians."[167] Calvin's perception of the disarray of his own world, described in the previous chapter, was thus embedded in a larger historical vision that was ultimately cosmological.

Since Calvin's conviction of the decline of the church was embedded in a cyclical conception of history, his historical vision also incorporated the Renaissance conception of the Middle Ages as a dark interval between two ages of light. For although his explanation for the decline of true religion was moral and political, the most serious result of that decline had been doctrinal; it was thus an expression of the more general decline of learning that had accompanied the rise of papal power. Indeed, Calvin argued that ignorance had been partly responsible for the rise of papal monarchy: other bishops had been too unlearned to resist the claims of the bishop of Rome.[168] "Those who have any tolerable knowledge of history are aware," he wrote, "of both the ignorance and the ferocity of those times. This indeed is in accordance with the common observation that the most ignorant governors are always the most imperious." "What a deep night of errors men were immersed in for several ages!" Calvin exclaimed.[169] But, after medieval darkness, light was returning. "The church will always rise up again and be restored to her pristine and flourishing condition," he insisted;[170] and "such a restoration of religion has been effected in our time."[171] But what was happening was literally a *re*formation; nothing new had occurred, no radical change had taken place. As Calvin so publicly informed Sadoleto, "All we attempted has been to renew that ancient form of the church."[172]

The attachment of a cyclical conception of history to the career of the church, a conception closely associated with a Stoic reliance on moral self-discipline as the source of order in human affairs, was itself, though he was unaware of it, a "mixture" of the kind he abhorred. For, as Saint Augustine had recognized, Christianity is not concerned with immediate historical crises; for Augustine only the wicked walk in circles, and intervals of relative order secured by various human techniques of social control, even by moral rigor, are not of any religious significance. Calvin was here conflating, without realizing it, two quite distinct types of crisis. One was the immediate crisis of his own time; and the anxiety that this crisis aroused in him turned him into a reformer. But Calvin associated this historical crisis with that basic and perennial "crisis," independent of the ebb and flow of human affairs, inherent in the fallen human condition itself: a crisis that demanded more radical remedies than his reformist zeal could provide.

He seems at least obscurely to have recognized the problem here, and he tried to establish a connection between the historical and existential crises, and thus to reduce the tension within himself between a powerful traditional moralism and his theology of grace. He did this by locating the cause for the peculiarly sinful behavior he professed to see in his own time in a faithlessness for which he could finally blame the papal church. Because human beings lacked faith, as he characteristically put it, the world had become "troubled and confused, justice had been destroyed in cities, spouses were complaining of each other and parents of their children: in short all were bewailing their condition." [173] He attributed the decline of faith to papal ambition, which had adopted as its instrument the substitution of superstitions and human traditions for the Gospel. His argument appears somewhat circular here; he could—and would—do better.

The cosmological inheritances reviewed in this chapter had been a traditional resource for the management and reduction of anxiety. But Calvin's anxiety could not finally be soothed by this kind of thought. When pushed to extremes, indeed, the cosmological model proved claustrophobic; it intensified rather than reduced anxiety, so that, in desperate cases like his, the greater the struggle with anxiety, the more anxiety grew. The cosmological mode of thought was nevertheless of enduring importance for Calvin, and it was the basis for the moralism treated in the next chapter.

5

Restoring Order

The last two chapters have described Calvin's anxiety about the deficiencies of the world, his terrible sense of urgency for bringing it into conformity with God's will, and the cosmological model for its reform. Because, in the cosmos, order was thought to depend on the control of lower entities by higher, the model meant that in individual human beings, the mind should control all lower faculties, and that in society, peoples should be controlled by rulers, women by men, and children by parents. It also meant that in the church, clergy should control laity. God, of course, controls everything. Calvin's term for the control that orders the world is "moderation" (*moderatio*). God, as governor of all things, employs moderation, which is the foundation of order.[1] Calvin often described it as a "bridle" (*frenum*).

Moderation, or "temperance," had been one of the four cardinal virtues of antiquity. To Aristotle it signified a mean between extremes; Horace called it golden (*aurea mediocritas*). Erasmians valued it; Erasmus himself had condemned Luther for immoderation,[1] and Rabelais praised the ancients because they "held that moderation [*mediocrement*] was golden, that is to say precious, universally praised and everywhere welcome." The Bible showed, he believed, "that the prayers of those who prayed moderately were never unanswered."[3]

This seems gentler than Calvin's conception; Calvin's emphasis was not on the balance and harmony achieved through moderation but on the dangers of spontaneity and the fragility of control. This is why, unlike Luther, he had little to say about the freedom, much about the servitude of a Christian. He praised religion because it prohibited "wandering freely"; godliness "keeps itself within proper limits."[4] Christianity, he thought, acts to "restrain and bridle" the mind and "make it captive."[5] He described love itself as a "bridle for retaining men in check and preventing them from lapsing into ferocity."[6] Only those whom "God has not retained as his servants" have no bridle.[7]

Even the most benign of human impulses, Calvin warned, are always threatening to escape control. He feared the consequences of zeal, even his own zeal, in the service of the Lord. "Whithersoever the Lord calls us," he urged, "we must energetically run; but anyone who goes too far will at length experience the unhappy result of exceeding his limits." [8] The wrath of Moses against Pharaoh troubled him, perhaps because it reminded him of his own irascibility. "By nature we are too much inclined to impetuous passions," he reflected; "we must diligently beware lest our indignation get out of control." Zeal weakens the ability of the faithful "sufficiently to restrain themselves or contain themselves within limits." [9]

A moderate zeal is nevertheless necessary to grapple with the disorders of the world; and if some reformers had too much, Erasmians, he thought, had too little; they were too much inclined to appease "the enemies of God" with flattery. "Let us," he pleaded, "avoiding their coldness, their sloth, insist with the greatest fervor on the glory of God." [10] He recalled with distaste a witticism of Erasmus at the expense of Capito: Erasmus "could not deny that Wolfgang Capito was a holy man who labored with the purest motives to reform the church. But he was convinced that it is as useless for the ministers of Christ to struggle to correct the wickedness of the world as to reverse the flow of rivers. Like other lazy philosophers, attacking all of us [genuine reformers] in the person of one man, he charged us with a careless zeal." [11]

Otherwise, however, his devotion to moderation allied Calvin with Erasmianism. Like Rabelais he found moderation in Scripture as well as philosophy: the Holy Spirit "teaches the observance of moderation"; [12] and Christ, because his passions "never exceeded their proper bounds" and were as different from ours "as pure water flowing in a gentle course differs from turbid and muddy froth," was a perfect model of moderation. [13] God's grace is also a force for moderation; once we have recognized its presence in ourselves, "nothing so well confines us in modesty and humility." [14]

Like Erasmus, Calvin sometimes suggests the optimism implicit in an ethic of control. Ancient philosophers had not minimized its difficulties, but they had generally believed virtue possible through heroic effort, at least for some. Calvin sometimes sounded this note. Like many others before him, he was moved by the "noble answer" of Socrates to his wife, "who, having one day lamented in prison that he was condemned wrongfully, received from him this reply, 'What then—would you rather that I should have suffered death for my offenses?' " The virtue of Socrates, he thought, should encourage others to preserve a moderation that, "the more difficult it is, the more strenuous should be our efforts to attain it." [15]

Calvin continued to insist on the power of reason for moderation. "In dumb animals," he observed, "only the instinct of nature rules; reason should control men and restrain their appetites." [16] Paul had enjoined young men to temperance, "for temperance, as Plato teaches, cures the whole mind of man." Paul had meant, then, "Let them be well ordered and obedient to reason." [17] At the very least, every human being knows the difference between right and wrong. "No one is so ignorant," he insisted, "that he does not distinguish between justice and injustice and cannot calculate how to regulate his life." [18] In this perspective, "a good and righteous life depends on our being ruled by the light of intelligence, folly is the root of all wickedness"; and "a sound mind" is "the beginning of the integrity and uprightness of life." [19] A sinner becomes righteous again by "opening the eyes of the mind." [20] This comes close to saying that to know the good is to do the good. Such notions could lead Calvin into ingenuous and uncharacteristically obtuse pronouncements. "Whoever considers seriously the reason for marriage," he declared, "cannot but love his wife." [21]

There are similar implications in Calvin's identification of the soul with the mind. "There are two primary endowments of the soul," he declared. "The first is its capacity to reason, the other to judge and choose. The soul of man excels first in intelligence or reason, then in judgment, on which choice and will depend." [22] He was not careful to state that this was how the soul functioned only before the Fall, nor are such passages altogether neutralized by recalling the limitations of sixteenth-century psychology or the fact that he was addressing Christians who had already some experience of sanctification. Emotionally, if not theologically, a large part of Calvin remained pagan.

A residual belief in self-reformation through human effort can also be detected, it seems to me, in the exasperation with which Calvin so often denounced sin. He gave off two messages, one explicit in the substance of his discourse, the other implicit in his tone, which was that of an outraged moralist who believed that the sinner might have avoided his sin had he only resisted with more determination. Calvin denounced this sinner, angrily, repeatedly, and obsessively, as though he could in this way compel him to change his ways. He could not dismiss, as a hopeless case, the failure of the higher to govern the lower faculties.

Because he attributed such powers to the higher faculties in the personality, it is not surprising that he attached an almost Stoic importance to self-control. Self-control, he believed, can balance between equal and opposite "lusts of the flesh," avoiding the excesses both of too little and too much, keeping the self "curbed." [23] Self-control is essential in every aspect of existence. It should regulate grief and joy, in which people always run to excess. [24] Courage should be moderated, for "we should learn to be bold by rule, not by temerity." [25] Even "the natural affection of a husband to a wife and of a father to a son must be checked and restrained" lest it distract from "our calling and what the Lord commands." [26]

He was well aware of the difficulty of self-control. "It is given to many to control their hands and feet," he observed, "but it is extremely hard to rule all the affections." [27] But difficulty only added to the need for exertion; we must "stretch all our nerves and strive to do right." [28] This meant, first, constant vigilance. "Each of us should watch himself closely, lest we be carried away by violent feeling," so that we can "bridle our affections before they become ungovernable." [29] The passions must be "repressed, bridled, and chained up; we must make every effort to beat down the impetuous frenzy in them." [30] Scripture supplied Calvin with examples of self-control, among them pious Hezekiah. [31]

"If we seek to exceed our limits," Calvin warned, "we manifestly tempt God." [32] But self-control keeps a human life "within bounds." [33] As boundary maintenance in the realm of ethics, it preserves the integrity of the self. Calvin's concern with self-control was first of all personal; it originated in his own dread of going out of control. He feared his own anger, even his own grief, which could so overwhelm him, as he once wrote to Farel, that he could "set no bounds to it." [34] He was anxious above all about what might happen if *John Calvin* let go, and he was often unable to admit that he might be helpless to deal with this possibility.

Moderation was for Calvin a panacea, often prescribed almost automatically, for a host of human problems; as a moralist he sometimes seems a more prosaic Polonius. "The righteous," he solemnly observed, "will manage their domestic affairs with prudence and discernment so that they will be neither too lavish nor sordidly parsimonious, but will aim in everything to combine frugality and economy without giving way to luxury." [35] In the pursuit of knowledge "we must employ discrimination and moderation, lest we desire to know more than God pleases to reveal." [36] In the management of grief "the faithful ought to consider their sorrows, but moderation should be observed." [37] We should be moderate in asserting our rights.[38] Death should be always on our minds "that it may accustom us to moderation." [39]

Calvin often thought of self-control simply as repression; thus, "all wantonness must be repressed so that we desire nothing but what is lawful, and also lest our appetites become excessive." [40] This attitude may explain his occasional ascetic impulses. "The life of the godly," he wrote, "ought to be tempered with frugality and sobriety, so that throughout its course a sort of perpetual fasting may appear." [41] Fasting, which he thought practiced too little by Protestants,[42] was for Calvin an archetype of Christian discipline: when human beings "eat only sparingly and lightly, out of necessity, content simply with black bread and water," they show their general acceptance of the need to "bridle themselves." [43]

The ability of human beings to reform themselves can be increased, he believed, by the force of public opinion. He regarded shame as "a bridle to repress our wicked and extravagant passions." [44] "There is hardly one in a hundred," he observed, "who is as steadfast as he ought to be when God alone is witness. But shame renders us courageous and constrains us to be constant," and thus "the vigor that is almost extinct in private is aroused in public." [45] Even death is sometimes more endurable than shame.[46] This is why "we cannot subject ourselves to the will of God if he takes away from us our kindred and friends." [47]

Other modes of restraint can also be useful. Private admonition serves, within the church, "like a bridle to restrain and tame those who rage against the teaching of Christ; or like a spur to arouse those little inclined; and also sometimes like a father's rod to chastise mildly and with the gentleness of Christ's Spirit those who have fallen away more seriously." [48] Misfortune can drive people to discipline themselves: for example, when God seems angry, a person who has plenty of food will restrict his diet.[49]

All of this suggests a typically humanist confidence in the value of education, not only to train the mind but also to inculcate virtue and shape character. Like other humanist pedagogues, Calvin had thought much about "the right method of teaching," which he believed should be "moderate," avoid "fallacies" and "futile questions," discourage "an immoderate itch to know more than is proper," and aim at "genuine edification."[50] Instruction should begin as early as possible,[51] and it should be administered with gentleness.

In spite of an occasional note of exasperation at slow learners, Calvin's educational views were strongly anti-authoritarian. "Those who take upon themselves responsibility for teaching and exhorting," he urged, "should not sit above and prescribe to others, but should join them and walk along with them as companions."[52] As a young man he had condemned "immoderate harshness" and "lash-loving executioners" in the classroom,[53] and he later suggested that by harsh treatment children can be "so intimidated as to be incapable of a liberal discipline."[54] A good teacher "should treat his pupils in such a way as always to encourage rather than discourage them. For nothing alienates us more from heeding instruction than to see that we are considered hopeless."[55] Good teaching should also be carefully accommodated to the capacities of one's pupils.[56]

The major impulse behind Calvin's interest in pedagogy was nevertheless his conviction that "moderation" can be internalized by the techniques of the new education. The first and most general of these is the right order of instruction. One should start "with general teaching and the more essential of the chief points as the foundation. Then there should follow reminders, exhortations, and whatever is needed for perseverance, confirmation, and progress."[57] Like Erasmus, Calvin also believed that morality should not be learned from personal experience, citing the proverb "that fools become wise too late." This meant, he explained, that fools "never obey good and sound advice while they may, but at length learn by their own misery and by experience, too late, that the precept they despised was true."[58]

Morality should be learned instead from the experience of others, especially as recorded in histories. This humanist principle followed the dictum of Quintilian that "as a rule history seems to repeat itself and the experience of the past is a valuable support to reason." Because history is filled with examples of both ethical and unethical behavior that can be made admirable or shameful by the art of the historian, history can teach ethics more effectively than philosophy itself.[59] Calvin adopted this perspective on the past. "Histories," he declared, "are a true school for learning how to order our lives." There had never been a time when it was more necessary to set out "examples of virtue for men to copy" and "to stimulate the idle and sluggish and dawdlers in the race."[60] History teaches most readily, of course—this was another truism of humanist historiography—"when outstanding virtue is seen in persons of high station, when they are praised to the skies in proper terms, and when the widest notice is taken, so that many may be stirred to follow their lead."[61]

Like other humanists, Calvin had also thought about what is involved in the imitation of others. He knew the importance, and the difficulty, of following the spirit as well as the form of an exemplar, "lest we enact the part of apes or actors."[62] For example, because Joseph's dominant trait was mildness, we should imitate him in that, not in his pretended severity to his brothers.[63] Beyond this, imitation too should be "moderate," controlled by decorum. "There is a general decorum that philosophers look upon as an aspect of moderation," Calvin remarked, "and everybody shares in that." But "there is also an individual appropriateness, because what is suitable for one person may be quite unsuitable for another. Therefore every individual ought to know [in choosing a model for imitation] what kind of character nature has given him."[64]

He was also prepared by his cyclical view of history to accept Quintilian's argument that the validity of imitating past behavior depends on the similarity of one age to another. To be useful, one's model must have lived in a time like one's own. This was not notably restrictive for Calvin, given his talent for discerning analogies between other times and his own. The time of David he thought particularly like his own. "Let the faithful today," he observed, "not be discouraged at the sight of the sad, most corrupt and utterly confused state of the world; but let them consider that they must endure it patiently, seeing that their condition is the same as that of David in the past." Because of this similarity, "we may learn from his example."[65] He valued the prophecies of Daniel for the same reason. "The similarity of the times," he explained, "makes these predictions adaptable to ourselves and fits them for our use."[66] He also discerned similarities between his own time and the times of Moses and Paul.

He was prepared to find examples anywhere, for "the histories of all past times" are "a true school on how to regulate our life."[67] But he preferred examples drawn from Scripture. Sacred history is superior, he argued, first because it lays down "general principles by which we may examine every other history" and thus "make use of it," and second because it displays more clearly than secular history "what should be imitated and what avoided."[68]

But he differed from secular historians in preferring negative to positive examples in the past. For the saints, he believed, "the histories of all times" are chiefly useful to display "those judgments and punishments of iniquity that the impious carelessly neglect."[69] He thought Scripture, especially the Old Testament, unusually valuable for identifying behavior that provokes God's wrath. A case in point was Sodom, whose people had gone through the whole Stoic cycle of sins from luxury and abundance through pride and cruelty, until finally they had succumbed to "strange lusts" and "uncontrolled passion."[70] The history of Israel, the elect nation of the Old Testament, provided the best "mirror" for the elect of Calvin's own time; it was a kind of painting "in which we can contemplate ourselves." But even its lessons were chiefly negative; God, Calvin insisted, will punish our sins as he punished theirs if we follow their example.[71]

He was thus by no means averse to the intensification of what medieval theologians had called "attrition"—fear of punishment—to impose order on the world. "It is said that men have the fear of God before their eyes," he observed, "when it rules their lives and, wherever they turn, it intervenes and restrains their lusts."[72] Thus, though he deplored it in others, he sometimes praised religion as an instrument of social control. It is "the best teacher of mutual equity among ourselves," he argued, "and where zeal for it is extinct, all regard for justice also perishes."[73]

His use of positive examples also differed somewhat from that of other humanists. Sometimes he sounded like them, though also like the biographers of saints. "The imitation of the saints will be useful in shaping life," he suggested, "if we learn from them sobriety, chastity, love, patience, temperance, contempt of the world, and other virtues."[74] At times he discerned a Stoic simplicity in a biblical figure such as Moses; hence Moses "should serve us today as an example and rule."[75] But his *exempla* more often illustrated the theological virtues and were indeed less likely to illustrate particular virtues than a general spiritual orientation. He emphasized Job's uprightness and sincerity, his resistance to temptation, his perseverance in obedience, and his fear of the Lord;[76] David's inwardness, the depth of his penitence, and his trust in God's help;[77] and Jeremiah's self-control in the midst of his anxieties.[78] In Scripture, Calvin wrote, "philosophers do not come before us skillfully disputing, peacefully in the shade, about the virtues; here the indefatigable constancy of holy men in the pursuit of piety invites us with a loud voice to imitate them."[79]

It was only a step from here to the *imitatio Christi,* which Calvin often prescribed to his followers, notwithstanding his rejection of the notion of Christ's righteousness as "only an example set before us to imitate."[80] As he prayed at the end of one of his lectures on Jeremiah, "Grant, Almighty God, that as thou hast been pleased to set before us an example of every perfection in thine only-begotten Son, we may study to form ourselves in imitation of him, and so to follow not only what he has prescribed, but also what he really performed."[81] Christ, he declared, "invites each member of his body to imitate him," and "only those who are his true imitators and are ready to run the same course can be considered his disciples."[82] Although we are not equal to him, the Gospel "commends to us the imitation of Christ; for although we will not catch up with him, we must nevertheless follow at a distance in his footsteps."[83] But again there are differences that may suggest the influence of the humanistic distinction between mechanical and spiritual imitation; for Calvin, we are to imitate not so much the particular actions of Christ as the general orientation of his spirituality; indeed Calvin worried lest ordinary Christians presume to follow Christ too precisely.[84] He wishes us to be like him, Calvin argued, in just two ways: in the "denial of ourselves and willing acceptance of the cross."[85] It is Christ's always moderate "zeal" that we are to imitate.[86] In the saints we are to imitate only those qualities in which they have imitated Christ so that their example will only "point to him."[87]

Calvin's biblical examples differed in still another respect from the examples cited by other humanist moralists. The latter generally elucidated a moralism intentionally woven into their works by the ancient historians, who assumed the provision of ethical examples to be a major purpose of historical composition. A humanist reading of an ancient historian is likely to seem, as a result, unexceptionable. But Calvin's moralistic readings of Scripture are often gratuitous and forced.

This was the result of two interrelated assumptions underlying his exegesis. The first was that a commentator should embroider the generally austere biblical account in order to strengthen its impact on a contemporary audience. So Calvin noted, in connection with the destruction of Sodom and Gomorrah, that the text had presented the matter "in very unostentatious language," and accordingly that "the atrocity of the case might well demand a more copious narration, expressed in tragic terms." It was accordingly his duty as a commentator to help others grasp, imaginatively as well as cognitively, "that horrible vengeance."[88] In addition, Calvin assumed that everything in Scripture is for our benefit; and where there was little else that seemed useful, he might at least find moral edification in a text. Exegesis was for Calvin not narrowly philological; it also called for a rhetoric that could enlist *copia* in the service of morality.

As a result he did not hesitate to appropriate from the exegetical tradition, perhaps occasionally even to invent, embellishments to biblical discourse. Thus he elaborated on the hatred and persecution of Noah by his contemporaries in order better to display Noah's heroic obedience to God.[89] He also discerned possibilities for edification in the most unlikely episodes. So the deception of hiding a silver cup in Benjamin's sack that led to Joseph's reconciliation with his brothers raised for Calvin the odd question why Joseph, "considering his great wealth," would not have preferred to drink from a golden cup. The question was a pretext for remarking on the admirable continence of Joseph's age, though at the same time it stimulated Calvin, not altogether consistently, to praise Joseph's temperance because, "in the midst of the greatest license, he was yet content with a moderate rather than a magnificent way of life."[90] Calvin also commended David for his immunity to a vice that especially exercised sixteenth-century moralists: the "accursed corruption of vengeance, that is so rooted in men that it seems to them a virtue."[91]

Here too, however, he was more likely to notice wickedness rather than righteousness. He regularly read into the biblical text his own distaste at the polygamy of the patriarchs. Polygamy had become a contemporary issue; Calvin noted the existence of contemporary sects—*"fantastiques"*—who practiced it. He refuted them by noting that God had said, "It is not good for man to be alone, let us make for him a helpmate like himself"; God had *not* said, "Let us make two or three wives."[92] He vigorously condemned the polygamy of his beloved David. David, he declared, "had violated and broken his marriage by his plurality of wives," and he interpreted the misfortunes of David's later life as punishment for this. David's six wives in Hebron had given him only six children, whereas "one woman by herself could have had a dozen, indeed as many as twenty."[93]

Such moralism often distorted his exegesis. Any hint of deception on the part of a biblical personage troubled him. As he remarked, "Those who hold what is called a dutiful lie to be altogether excusable do not sufficiently consider how precious truth is in the sight of God." He denounced, on this basis, the lies of the Hebrew midwives in Egypt, although the biblical text reports that they had found favor with God precisely *because* they had deceived Pharaoh.[94] Rebecca's deceit in procuring Isaac's paternal blessing for Jacob made him similarly uncomfortable. Her "crafty proceeding," he observed, "taints an act that was laudable in itself," though "the fault does not wholly deprive the deed of the merit of holy zeal." The lies of Rahab that led to the fall of Jericho troubled him too; he reconciled himself to her deceit only by reflecting that, although her conduct had not been spotless, it deserved some praise. "It often happens," he concluded, "that although the saints intend to stay on the right path, they deviate into circuitous courses."[95]

He feared that such morally ambiguous episodes as these might be taken as examples to be imitated, as he made clear in condemning the parents of the infant Moses for abandoning him in the bulrushes and so failing in the universal responsibility of parents to protect their children. "God," he believed, "has planted even in wild and brute beasts such an instinctive solicitude to protect and cherish their young that the mother often neglects her own life in their defense." It was therefore peculiarly reprehensible that human beings, "created in the image of God, should be carried by fear to such cruelty as to desert the children entrusted to their fidelity and protection." Such parents as these "might make the providence of God an excuse for idleness and sloth." Yet Calvin could not quite withhold his sympathy from the wretched couple; and, torn between his duty to render judgment and his considerable talent for empathy, he reflected that "we must not, after all, judge the father and mother as if they had lived in quiet times, for it is easy to imagine the bitter grief with which they contemplated the death of the child."[96]

His moralism also prevented him from sympathizing with the tribulations of biblical figures. He allowed himself to see in David's grief at the deaths of Saul and Jonathan little more than an example of "badly regulated passions." Here, he declared, "we see in a mirror a man who displays a disordered grief and has no moderation in him."[97] But his almost deliberate insensitivity is nowhere more in evidence than in his reading of the book of Job. It interested him deeply; he devoted one of his longest sermon sequences to it; and, baffled by its contrast between the faith and humanity of Job and the moralism of Job's friends, he hardly knew what to make of it. He finally came to the remarkable conclusion that Job's friends, although their "arguments and reasons" were good and their teachings "holy and useful,"

had mysteriously defended the wrong cause.[98] The indictment of Job by
Eliphaz the Temanite, though wrongly applied, seemed so persuasive to him
that it must have come from God himself.[99] Job, in contrast, though in the
right, had defended his position badly. Although he acknowledged himself a
sinner who deserved his afflictions, he had murmured against God and his
rhetoric had been reprehensible.[100]

Calvin's moralism thus all but prevented him from understanding this
poetic and paradoxical work. He was blind to its ironies. When Job responded to his self-righteous friends with "How harsh are the words of the
upright man!" Calvin could only remark, "By this, Job wishes to show that
when a man has a good conscience, he will remain firm without ever being
shaken by anything anyone says to him. . . . By this we are admonished to
walk uprightly before God and show clearly that there is no hypocrisy in
us." [101] It is hardly surprising, then, that Job's wish that he had never been
born, his longing for death, elicited no sympathy from Calvin; Job's "inexcusable excess," however unintentional, chiefly suggested to him rebellion
against God.[102]

Part of the explanation for Calvin's obtuseness may be that he was consciously struggling, as he read Job, with ambiguous feelings about his own
rhetorical gifts. What seemed to him culpable in the words of Job—although
the biblical text seems neutral on the matter—reminded him that, when men
blaspheme, they employ "something like a natural rhetoric, they are rhetoricians." When it comes to praising God, we can scarcely utter a word; but
when it comes to blasphemy, "there is nothing more elegant." In addition
Job lacked moderation: his discourse exemplified the tendency of men to
"have neither measure nor limit, so that their passions begin to boil
over." [103]

Something even more serious than such misreading also resulted from
Calvin's moralism. This was a loss of the openness to the complexity and
mystery of human existence that he could display elsewhere. The terrible
vision that caused the bones of Eliphaz the Temanite to shake and his hair to
stand up evoked from Calvin only a banal didacticism. "God," he explained, "is showing him that men should walk in humility. . . . men should
not just enjoy themselves, or puff themselves up for being righteous, for
being worthy; but they should know that there will be nothing but sin in them
when they find themselves in God's presence, that they will stand there in
confusion, that they will consider their corruptions, and that they will be
displeased at them." [104] Calvin's moralism could also lead him into a facile
view of calamity as punishment for sin. He reported complacently, in a letter
to Viret, the anecdotes with which he had illustrated a sermon on God's
vengeance against sinners:

A man during sermon-time on the Lord's day went into a wine shop to drink;
by accident he fell on his sword, which had slipped out of its sheath, and he
was carried off dying. Another man, last September, on the day when the
sacred Lord's Supper was administered, as he tried while drunk to sneak

secretly through a window looking for a whore, broke his bones in many places by a terrible fall. I concluded, "Till hell swallows you up with all your households, you will not have faith in God when he stretches forth his hand." I perceived that my zeal did not please many, because they are not willingly aroused from their lethargy.[105]

He could also sound like Job's friends in promising prosperity to the righteous. "Adversity," he asserted, "is a sign of God's absence, prosperity of his presence."[106] If we always obey God's commands, he assured his congregation without qualification, "he will give a good result to everything we do. . . . God will cause all our enterprises to prosper when our purpose is right and we attempt nothing except what he wills."[107] The relationship with God, in this view, is contractual. "Just as, in arranging marriages, contracts *[tabulae]* are drawn up," as Calvin put it, "so the spiritual marriage between us and the son of God is made binding by the Gospel as by a kind of contract. Let us preserve faith, love, obedience as agreed on by us; he on his side will be faithful to us."[108] This seems remarkably close to the old pagan formula *do ut des,* and on the same basis Calvin promised prosperity to kingdoms that had established true religion. As he wrote to the Duke of Somerset when his hopes for the church in England were highest, "The prosperity of kingdoms can be assured and those who guard them kept faithful only when he on whom they were founded and by whom they are preserved—the Son of God himself—rules over them. Thus there is no way for you more firmly to establish the kingdom of England than by banishing idols and setting up the true worship of God."[109]

The political (and religious) simplicity that this formula suggests is probably misleading; Calvin was not a simple man, especially about politics, and he probably knew that this was what Somerset expected to hear from him. He was more, though not entirely, convincing when he made the point negatively, as he often did. He could explain both disease and bad weather as punishment for sin;[110] and he observed in connection with the fifth commandment that disobedient children generally come to bad ends. "We see how many men of this sort perish either in battles or in quarrels," he wrote; "others are cast down in ways less common. Nearly all offer proof that the threat [in the commandment] is not in vain. Some people may escape punishment until extreme old age. Yet in this life they are bereft of God's blessing, and can only miserably pine away."[111]

He could be more particular. He attributed the execution of Thomas More to More's hostility to Protestantism, his persecution of "good men by fire and sword," and his vain desire for renown. "Do we need a more obvious example than this," Calvin asked, "of the judgments by which God punishes the pride of the impious, unbounded desire for glory, and blasphemous boastings?"[112] He could also justify providence on a larger scale. He attributed the fall of the Roman Empire to a voluptuousness made possible by the booty of conquest, here sounding unusually Stoic. "Before they penetrated into Greece," he explained, "the greatest moderation prevailed among [the Romans]; but no sooner had Asia been vanquished than they began to grow soft and effeminate; and when their eyes were dazzled by pictures, vases, gems, and draperies, and their nostrils enthralled by ointments and perfumes, all their senses were immediately overpowered and, by imitating the luxury of the East as representing a more refined culture, they began more and more to deteriorate in every kind of debauchery." Thus the Roman Empire had perished.[113] "God," he asserted, "poured such fury upon that nation that he made it a spectacle before the world." [114]

This facile moralism was in conflict with other important strands in Calvin's thought. Insofar as it implied the possibility of justifying God's ways to man, it was at odds with his nominalist conception of an incomprehensible God. It was also in tension with his conviction of the helplessness of the fallen human condition and the bondage of the will. Finally, it tended to make the church into an agency, one among others, of social control, to degrade it into something not altogether dissimilar from what he saw in the papal church.

His moralism, indeed, may have been an antidote to a danger, at least equally serious, from an opposite direction. It was commonly said in the eighteenth century that if you scratched a Calvinist, you would find an antinomian. Antinomianism, as an extreme expression of inwardness, may well have been attractive to Calvin; but for a person made so anxious by disorder of any kind, the suspicion of an antinomian impulse in himself must have been singularly terrifying. Perhaps this accounts for the harshness of his moralism and that of many of his followers. The antidotes to his moralism are the subject of later chapters.

6

Rational Religion

"If we wish to be his disciples," Calvin declared, "we must unlearn everything we have learned apart from Christ. For example, our own pure instruction in the faith began with forgetting and rejecting the whole instruction of the papacy." [1] This statement reveals much about Calvin himself. His plural pronoun was not only collective but editorial; "we" was an abstracted and slightly protective "I." He was not only saying that he considered a radical break with the religious past possible and necessary, but claiming that he had himself made such a break.

This was an illusion. Discontinuities, historical and biographical, are rarely as decisive as they seem to those involved; and Calvin's claim to have made so large a change reflected the limitations in his awareness of how far his understanding even of the Gospel depended on inherited assumptions he could not easily, or ever wholly, shake off, if only because he was largely unconscious of them. The Reformation slogan *scriptura sola* was intrinsically naive; and Calvin's claim that Scripture was his "only guide," and acquiescence in its "plain doctrines" his "constant rule of wisdom," could never have been more than an aspiration. [2] He had "forgotten" only a fraction of what he had learned under the papacy. Like other first-generation Protestants, he had acquired in the old church both his spiritual need and his criteria for "pure instruction in the faith."

Among the cultural baggage Calvin carried to Geneva were a conception of human being as a hierarchy of faculties governed by the mind and an assumption that the mind is adequate to grasp the world as it actually is. These beliefs inclined him toward an intellectualized Christianity that he never relinquished, even though he was moving at the same time toward another that was radically different. The intellectual element in his Christianity is the subject of the present chapter.

Fundamental to this kind of Christianity in Calvin was a conviction that all truth, having its source in God, is objectively *given*, that it is the same for all people in all times and places, and that it is self-consistent and intelligible.

This view was basic to his veneration for the liberal arts, gifts of God through which "all things necessary to be known" had been revealed to mankind.[3] He particularly valued philosophy as a "noble gift of God," though inferior to Scripture; philosophers in all ages, he believed, had been stimulated by God himself "that they might enlighten the world in knowledge of the truth."[4] God requires us to respect and use this gift:

When God opens our eyes, if we close them are we not worthy of condemnation for having perverted the order of nature? When God . . . wishes us to contemplate his works here before approaching him and participating in his image as we are intended to: if we profane all that and wish to know nothing, is it not manifestly to battle against our God to renounce the good that he wished to do us, yes, that which is the chief one and that most to be esteemed? . . . God has not put men in this world to deny them any intelligence, for he does not wish them to be like asses or horses, he has endowed them with reason and has wished them to understand.[5]

This belief justified his use of secular authors, according to the principle that "we are at liberty to borrow from any source anything that has come from God."[6] The opening sentence of the *Institutes* drew on Cicero's definition of philosophy,[7] and from time to time he relied on Plato, Aristotle, and other ancient philosophers. He was especially impressed by Plato's insight that all existence depends on God.[8] The elect too, Calvin observed, "obey the voice of reason."[9]

The primacy of intellect in the cosmic model of human being was reflected in Calvin's emphasis on doctrine and the odd exegesis to which his nervousness on the matter sometimes drove him. When Christ taught that men should be judged by their fruits, he argued, he did not mean their way of life but their teaching *(ratio docendi);* this, for Christians, "holds first place."[10] Again, he felt compelled to warn, lest the expulsion of the money changers from the temple be taken to mean that Christ put deeds ahead of beliefs, that it is "disorderly and perverse to correct faults before the remedy of doctrine has been applied."[11] He could even represent the Christian life, as though this made it easier to live, as the product of a syllogism: "We are God's creatures; ought we not, therefore, to give ourselves completely to his service? Surely we must. The reasoning is indisputable."[12] He also suggested that knowledge is the source of affect. "We must know," he claimed, "before we can love";[13] and "repentance and faith proceed from the truth taught."[14] These convictions were reflected in an emphasis on the Gospel as *doctrine*. Its importance was implied in Paul's warning to Timothy, Calvin argued, "not to depart from the form of teaching he had received"; because "the least deviation from doctrine is exceedingly harmful."[15] Doctrine, he pointed out, "is a great deal more precious than persons."[16] Such sentiments point to a tendency in Calvin to understand faith less as trust in God's promises than as intellectual assent to a body of propositions.

His intellectualism also nourished his objection to the papal doctrine of implicit faith, the belief that a simple believer might share "implictly," by his trust in the church, in the benefits of its teaching, though ignorant of the meaning of that teaching. Calvin admitted the value of implicit faith as preparation for informed faith. He recognized that much of Christian belief, "so long as we dwell as strangers in the world," can only be implicit, "not only because many things are as yet hidden from us, but because, surrounded by many clouds of errors, we do not comprehend everything." [17] But this is no excuse for failing to strive for the fullest possible understanding of the teachings of the faith. Without this, "God has spoken in vain through his prophets and apostles," for "there is no faith where there is no knowledge." [18] The "pious ignorance" of implicit faith causes us only to "wander through endless labyrinths." [19]

He had, though without giving the matter any systematic attention, various criteria for the validity of religious knowledge, which were in general the same as for the validity of other kinds of knowledge. It must be consistent both externally, with other kinds of truth, as truth "ever remains in agreement with itself," and internally, as "it is certain that the Spirit does not contradict itself." [20] This position seems to imply a distrust of paradox; it disposed Calvin to deny anything unusual even in the Incarnation. "If anyone says that it is strange to be told that our God has been a mortal," Calvin once wrote, "I reply that there is no absurdity in this, that God, who is immortal in his essence, should have inhabited our mortal flesh. . . . If men did not invent barbarous fancies to please themselves, there would be nothing here that one should find so strange." [21]

Inclined to associate knowing with seeing, Calvin also required religious truth to be clear and distinct, free of all ambiguity. Scripture, like spectacles, gives us "a clear view of the true God." [22] He insisted on this clarity. We may find Scripture "difficult and obscure," he acknowledged, but "this must be blamed on the dullness and slowness of our senses: blind and weak-sighted men must not accuse the sun because they cannot gaze upon it." [23] He sharply contrasted the saving knowledge of the elect with the "confused awareness" of the reprobate. This was one source of his objection to allegorical interpretation; it is "a trick of Satan" because it makes "the teaching of Scripture ambiguous and deprives it of all certainty and firmness." [24] Although he could hardly deny that Scripture is "a most rich and inexhaustible fountain of all wisdom," he could not endure the notion that it "brings forth multiple meanings." [25]

He also insisted that religious truth, if it is to be relied upon, must be immutable. This was his answer to "the imaginings of the fanatical and impious" that some parts of Scripture, though perhaps once edifying, are now irrelevant.[26] God, he argued, had provided a written law so that "it would not serve only one age but would retain its vigor and authority until the end of the world." [27] Only by meeting all these criteria of valid knowledge can the doctrines that constitute the faith of a Christian, for Calvin, possess the objective *certitude* on which subjective *certainty* depends.

From this standpoint the aim of exegesis is to provide "something certain," so that "whoever wishes to distinguish with certainty among the various doctrines by which the world is agitated can succeed without difficulty if he offers himself as a pupil to Christ, connects the Law and the Prophets with the Gospel, and makes use of this carpenter's rule to test all doctrines." Calvin was careful, to be sure, to emphasize the role, as well, of "the spirit of judgment and discretion," but his metaphor, in an evangelical context, is somewhat unsettling.[28] So is his description of the certainty of salvation as an *obligation* we owe to the honor of God, as though faith were a responsibility rather than a gift.[29] Calvin's concern for certainty sometimes suggests that the Lord speaks less to announce the Good News than to relieve doubt; the word of God, as he put it, provides a "certain and permanent support" for faith.[30] He had failed to find this in the papal church. Rome, he charged, considering Scripture a "wax nose" that could be twisted in any direction, "takes away every certainty."[31]

Calvin, this implies, was himself afflicted with serious doubts. This is also suggested by the harshness with which he treated those who disagreed with him; dissent made him anxious and impatient, and in this condition he was inclined to identify his own views with God's.[32] He feared those of his opponents, on the other hand, as a "powerful poison" that, "flowing insidiously into our minds, soon corrupts the whole life."[33] He favored death for heretics because error can do "far more evil than swords."[34] He was warm and sympathetic to those with whom he agreed; but when speaking of those who dissented from his own view, he used abstractions that relieved him of the need to recognize their humanity. They constituted "the mob," which could be dismissed as "ignorant and stupid" and consigned to destruction.[35] What he considered *human* constructions in religion particularly threatened his certainty. "I wish the sacred oracles to be treated so reverently," he asserted, "that no variation whatsoever can be introduced by the choice of men, and only what is certain is held in the mind."[36]

In his need for certainty Calvin was a man of his time; Luther too had required, "even in matters that are not necessary and external to Scripture, to be absolutely certain, for what is more miserable than uncertainty?"[37] But unlike Luther, Calvin, in dealing with his uncertainties, sought—at times—for proof and evidence. Indeed he was more traditional in this respect than Erasmus, who had attacked the theologians at the Sorbonne for taking as a *definition,* instead of recognizing it as a *eulogy,* the biblical description of faith as "the evidence of things unseen"; on the basis of this mistake they thought it necessary to seek proofs for the Gospel.[38] In his need for certainty, Calvin came close to this traditional project. "As faith is not content with a doubtful and changeable opinion," he wrote, "so is it not content with an obscure and confused conception but requires full and fixed certainty such as men are wont to have from things experienced and proved."[39]

In fact Calvin was fully prepared to exploit the resources of Scholastic discourse, with which he was well acquainted.[40] He respected the acuteness in its conceptual distinctions. As he noted in connection with the hard question of God's responsibility for human affairs, "distinctions concerning relative necessity and absolute necessity, likewise of consequent and consequence, were not recklessly invented in the schools."[41] He insisted that definition is basic to controversy; it is "the hinge and foundation of the whole argument."[42] He defended the use of a specialized professional vocabulary against those who insisted on limiting theological discourse to the language of Scripture; indeed, he used the old categories of form and substance. God's successive covenants with his people represented, for Calvin, changes in the form of belief while its substance remained the same.[43] This hardly makes him "the last of the Schoolmen"; like other humanists, he used Scholastic procedures when they were convenient or to score points. But they were also congenial to some part of his complex temperament.

His attraction to Scholastic modes of thought went even deeper. He was not prepared, like Lorenzo Valla,[44] to acknowledge that substantives are only human constructions without demonstrable reference to external reality; on the contrary, he relied heavily on substantives, adjectives transposed into nouns, such as "iniquity," or "corruption." He needed to believe in the concrete existence of some "thing" or "quality" corresponding to such words because this made plausible the replacement of the evil realities they denoted by good realities such as "sanctity," or "purity." An inherited philosophical and theological language sometimes required him to perceive the world as divided between antithetical categories. Linguistic habits helped him to sort the world into elect and reprobate. Language made him sometimes sound Manichean.[45]

He also played with the Scholastic *quaestio*[46] or resorted to simple syllogistic reasoning: "Let believers exercise themselves in constant meditation upon the benefits of God, that they may encourage and confirm hope for the future and always ponder in their mind this syllogism: God does not forsake the work which his own hands have begun, as the Prophet bears witness (Is. 64:8). We are the work of his hands. Therefore he will complete what he has begun in us."[47]

Calvin's intellectualism sometimes found expression in his treatment of theology as a rational quest. As he observed in connection with the incorporeality of the soul, "The more anyone endeavors to approach God, the more he proves himself endowed with reason."[48] He often appealed to such rational criteria as the principle of noncontradiction: God can turn darkness into light and light into darkness, he argued, "but if you require that light and darkness not differ, what else are you doing but perverting the order of God's wisdom?"[49] He applied what he called "contraries or opposites" to establish a point: "If one of the following assertions is advanced, the other is necessarily denied; if God is judge of the world, fortune has no place in its governance."[50]

Given his intellectualistic anthropology, his respect for valid method and argument, and his conviction that religious truths are accessible to human beings in nature, it is hardly surprising that Calvin was attracted to natural theology. There was nothing original or otherwise remarkable in his views about it; he repeated commonplaces long available, especially those of Cicero. What is notable is how often Calvin alluded to them and how important they were to him. What nature can teach, though this was for him by no means the whole of religion, seemed to him perennially valuable, by no means rendered irrelevant by the Fall. Even when he acknowledged its limitations, the exasperation in his tone implied that he thought anybody could, from nature, learn much about God if he tried hard enough. "The heavens have a common language for teaching all alike," he argued, "nor is there anything but carelessness to hinder even the most remote peoples from profiting, as it were, at the mouth of the one teacher."[51] Respect for the religious insights of the natural man, even after the Fall, is also implicit in Calvin's belief in the superiority of Greek religion to other expressions of ancient paganism.[52] The Greeks, who represented the gods with human figures, were less deluded than the Egyptians, who worshipped dogs, oxen, and even cats and herbs.[53] Degrees of natural insight imply, in principle, the validity of natural theology.

The value of nature for religious instruction pointed, for Calvin as for earlier natural theologians, to an innate religious instinct. "It has been usual in all ages," he noted, "for godless men, to whom religion is only a fable, to call upon God when compelled by necessity. Did they do so as a joke? By no means: they were brought to honor the name of God by a secret instinct of nature."[54] "There is naturally fixed in the hearts of all," he declared, "the conviction, which cannot be excised, that God must be worshipped."[55] The reluctance of Pilate to condemn Jesus demonstrated to him the persistence, even among the most corrupt, of "an innate sense of religion which does not allow them to rush about audaciously when divine things are involved."[56] Belonging to human nature as such, this religious instinct must also be universal. "Men were never such brutes," Calvin remarked, "but that they ascribed all excellence to God; whatever things are useful to men or are esteemed for excellence and dignity are treated as benefits of the gods even by profane writers."[57]

Calvin's natural theology, like that of others before him, was based largely on seeing. "We have been stationed here "as in a theater for contemplating the works of God," he proclaimed, "nor is there any work of God so minute that we should pass over it lightly, but all things ought to be carefully and diligently observed."[58] He also described the universe as a mirror "in which we can contemplate God, who is otherwise invisible."[59] Every human being is "formed to be a spectator of the created world and given eyes that he might be led to its author by contemplating so beautiful a representation."[60] This experience combined instruction with pleasure. "Let us not be ashamed," Calvin wrote, as though he feared his readers might be, "to receive a pious delight from the open and visible works of God in this most beautiful theater."[61] But we must avoid the pleasure alone: "It would be better to have our eyes put out than to enjoy these beautiful works of God if we did not profit from them by ascending to their author."[62]

He thought every aspect of external nature redolent with religious instruction; he did not exclude, as he wrote early in his career, the little singing birds, grasses and flowers, rivers and mountains.[63] He thought every human being, sinner though he might be, "a rare example of God's power, goodness, and wisdom," containing within himself "enough miracles to occupy our minds, if only we are not irked at paying attention to them."[64] Simply "because we exist," there is no need "to go beyond ourselves to comprehend God."[65] We also see God's skill in the exquisite workmanship of our bodies, "from the mouth and eyes down to the toenails." We should be able to discern in ourselves, body and soul, "a hundred revelations of God."[66] But we encounter him especially "in the extraordinary endowments of our minds" and "the agile motions of the soul, its noble faculties and rare talents."[67]

But Calvin based his natural theology, like the natural theologians of antiquity, above all on the heavenly bodies. "There is certainly nothing so obscure or contemptible in the lowest extremities of the earth," he agreed, "in which some evidence of the virtue and wisdom of God cannot be seen; but his image is engraved more clearly in the heavens."[68] It is "the symmetry and regulation" of the universe, amazing in view of its vastness and the speed of its motions, that particularly display the glory of God.[69] Astronomy, therefore, "may justly be called the alphabet of theology."[70] Calvin also believed that nature teaches the existence of angels, because pagans knew about them;[71] some awareness of eternal life and the resurrection, which are implied by the universality of burying the dead;[72] and the immortality of the soul.[73]

But he was especially concerned with what nature can teach about God, a subject on which we have a particular responsibility, "according to our capacity, to be diligent and to take pains to be good scholars."[74] What nature teaches above all is God's existence. Though "invisible in himself," his work "clearly declares its maker."[75] "How," Calvin asked, "can anyone who has enjoyed the sight of heaven and earth close his eyes and ignore their author, without being guilty of the gravest sin?"[76] The proof of God's existence from nature is so compelling, he thought, that however their gods might differ in detail, "no nation has ever been so barbarous that it did not worship some deity."[77] This meant, for him, that an honest atheism is impossible. Because there is "a seed of true religion planted in us by nature, we are forced, even against our will, to look up to that majesty which excels all things, nor is there anyone so insane that he wishes to cast God down from his throne."[78]

But he ran into difficulties when he tried to describe the God revealed by nature. He was uncertain how far or how deep natural knowledge of God could go. He often stated firmly that God displays himself to us only indirectly through his works, and that we cannot know his "essence."[79] Yet he often implied that we ought, after all, to be able to know God as he really is from nature. He could denounce at one moment the "curiosity and audacity" that impel us to "inquire into the eternal essence of God" and at the next express his confidence that we do, in nature, confront God's "essence."[80]

The supposed unity of truth also compelled Calvin to identify the God of the Bible, who is infinitely concerned for at least some of his human creatures, with the God of nature and reason, who does not obviously share this concern. This identification was problematic enough, but even nature and reason seem not to have given a consistent impression of the deity. Human beings have variously discerned in nature a rational and intelligible God whose wisdom is revealed in the order of the universe, an incomprehensible God whose power is revealed in the mystery of the universe, and a righteous God whose terrifying moral demands are revealed in the inexorable justice of providence.

In spite of these difficulties, the identification of the biblical God with the God of the philosophers had important consequences. One was a conception of God as immutable. This required that God's knowledge be immediate rather than discursive, and it also precluded his changing his mind.[81] This position gave Calvin major exegetical difficulties, since Scripture, taken literally, often appears to say the contrary. He solved this problem with the notion that in such cases divine revelation had been accommodated to the "rudeness" of those to whom it had first been committed. Because he, living in a more cultivated age, understood this, he was in a position to set matters straight. The prayer of the Psalmist, for example, that his enemies be "blotted from the book of life" should not be taken to imply that God might alter his decrees, for of course a decree of God "cannot be changed."[82] "When we make a decision," he told his congregation, "it can be changed; but it is not so with God, for what is in God is immutable."[83] He was not disturbed in this case by a certain affinity between this conception and Aristotle's unmoved mover, a notion that elsewhere he attacked. "From everlasting to everlasting thou art God," he explained, must be understood as meaning that, although God "subjects the world to various alterations, he remains himself at rest." "Although he subjects the world to many alterations," Calvin insisted, "he remains unmoved," in "settled and undisturbed tranquility."[84] This comforted him. "Were the world to change and perish a hundred times," he declared, "nothing could ever affect the immutability of God."[85] God represents "not variation but constancy."[86]

In another sense, too, Calvin's philosophical God could not be moved; he was without passions. Calvin was compelled, accordingly, to treat biblical references to God's anger or grief much as he treated texts describing God as changing his mind. "The word 'wrath,' " he explained, "stands, following a convention of Scripture, for God's retribution; for when God punishes, he has, as we imagine, the appearance of anger. Thus the word does not signify feeling in God."[87] Nor does God sorrow: "he remains forever like himself in celestial and happy respose."[88] Here again we can sense Calvin's dim view of the passions. He refrained, however, from denying God's ability to love.

This remote and immovable philosophical deity impinged on human existence chiefly as a judge; he displays himself "in his justice and equity."[89] God "is the fountain of all equity and uprightness; it is impossible for him to do anything that is not good and just."[90] To believe otherwise would be "shocking blasphemy."[91] If we entertained such a belief, "our minds would reel and at length give way."[92]

It needed "rare wisdom," nevertheless, to believe the God of the Old Testament "just in all his actions";[93] and those episodes in which the Old Testament God seemed impulsive and barbaric made Calvin uncomfortable. He repeatedly apologized for this God and tried to demonstrate that his apparent savagery was, properly considered, true justice. When God decreed that Moses, a figure to whom Calvin felt especially close, should die before entering the promised land, Calvin insisted on the seriousness of Moses's offense. Moses, he argued, "had attributed less power to God than was his due." His punishment was necessary, therefore, to make clear "how dear his glory is to God."[94] The slaughter of the people of Jericho, "without distinction of age or sex, including women and children, the aged and the decrepit," seemed to Calvin "an inhuman butchery," until he recalled that God had destroyed this people only after patiently enduring its iniquities for four centuries.[95] On similar grounds he persuaded himself that David's slaughter of the Jebusites was "not at all cruel, however severe it might appear."[96] He struggled against his repugnance at the extermination of the Midianites by reminding himself that God "always tempers the most severe punishments with the most perfect equity."[97] It also troubled him that children should be made to suffer for the sins of their fathers until he recalled that all human beings deserve death through original sin.[98]

It is unlikely, however, that these vague rationalizations altogether satisfied him, and he admitted that some cases were beyond him. He gave up trying to make sense of the wretched fate of the family of Achan, who had stolen silver and gold from the spoils of Jericho. "It seems harsh," he admitted, "indeed inhuman and barbarous for tender children who had nothing to do with the crime to be hurried off to a cruel execution, to be stoned and burned for the crime of their father." He could repeat to himself only "that although our reason dissents from the judgments of God, our presumption must be restrained by a pious modesty and sobriety, lest we blame what does not please us."[99] It would have been "a barbarous atrocity and a piece of inhuman arrogance to trample on the necks of kings and to hang their dead bodies on gibbets," he observed of Joshua's treatment of the Amorite kings, had it not been done at God's command: "That at which everyone would otherwise be horrified, they should reverently embrace as done by God."[100] There is a hint of Machiavellism in Calvin's argument that what is otherwise wicked is justifiable when done by God, the supreme ruler.

The intelligibility of God's justice pointed to the larger question of the intelligibility of providence, and on this matter, too, Calvin sometimes gives the impression of believing that human beings can understand much in God's mind. His admission that the fairness and rationality of God's governance "often escapes us"[101] implies that sometimes we can understand it; it suggests that providence is at least in principle intelligible. At any rate, although we ought to restrain our curiosity, it is "extremely useful" to contemplate the providence of God, especially in retrospect; for "when we connect the ends of things with their beginnings, that wonderful plan shines clearly." [102] Calvin demonstrated what this could mean in reflecting on the death of Luther. God sometimes removes good men from the world, he explained, in order to spare them the disasters with which he intends to punish their contemporaries. This was why Luther had been "snatched from the world" shortly before Germany was afflicted by calamitous wars. [103]

What we have been considering so far suggests that Calvin tended toward the scholasticism of the *antiqui,* with its relative confidence in the powers of human reason. But he was eclectic even in his rationalism; he was prepared to follow its negative as well as its positive impulses. "The light in which God dwells," he observed, "is *not without reason* called unapproachable, because it is overspread with darkness." [104] As a result Calvin also exhibited some of the traits of the nominalist *moderni,* who, by a more self-conscious reasoning, found reason inadequate to illuminate religious truth.

Nominalism has sometimes been represented as a biblically oriented reaction against Hellenic and Arab determinism. [105] But although the God of nominalism may be closer to the Bible in some respects than the God of High Scholasticism, he is also the end product of the long reaction, begun by the Greeks, of philosophy against mythology. The God of the Bible is infinitely concerned with the world and the destiny of the spiritual creatures whom he has placed within it. But the God of the nominalists was transcendent, unknowable, and chiefly concerned that his human creatures acknowledge and pay tribute to his glory. This God too was a philosophical construction. [106]

Calvin's tendency to assume God's intelligibility was counterbalanced, therefore, by his insistence on God's transcendence and a nominalist conviction that the first duty of man is to glorify his Creator. This conviction was expressed in the first article of his catechism of 1537: "We are all created for this end, that we should know the majesty of our Creator and that, having known him, we should hold him above all things in esteem and honor him with all fear, love, and reverence." [107] "The true definition of piety," he repeated, "is when the true God is entirely reverenced, so that he alone is exalted and that no creature obscures his majesty." [108] The study of his "high and magnificent works" should impel us to glorify God and to exclaim, "Lord, how great is your power! Lord, how great is your virtue! How great is your goodness, justice, and wisdom"! [109] There is also a negative corollary of the glorification of God: the humiliation of man. "God does not receive his full due," for Calvin, "until all mortals are reduced to nothing." [110] This may suggest that his insistence on the weakness and sinfulness of human beings was not simply a reflection of his realism; it was the necessary obverse of the glorification of God.

So unshakable was Calvin's veneration for everything "reason" connoted that he continued, even when he emphasized God's transcendence and incomprehensibility, to represent him as an intellectual being. What may appear chaotic and meaningless to us, he insisted, is nevertheless "governed by his inestimable wisdom." [111] However incomprehensible his ways may appear, they are nevertheless infused with "the best reason." [112] He may seem inconsistent to us, but in fact he is "never inconsistent nor unlike himself." [113]

This insistence on the reasonableness of God was reflected in Calvin's denial of the rhetorical art of Scripture; a reasonable God could hardly communicate in a medium so suspect. Artificial, long-winded, and deceptive, the preserve of flatterers and hypocrites, rhetoric, to Calvin the philosopher, was all too human and ambiguous. Rhetoricians "talk pretentiously," he asserted, "but only to receive loud applause or to affect the minds of men with vain fear or joy." [114] The appeal of rhetoric to the lower faculties of the personality made it seem inappropriate for divine communication.

In his reluctance to acknowledge the rhetorical power of Scripture, Calvin was in good company. To the ancient fathers he admired, the style of Scripture had seemed very different from what they had been taught to admire by classical rhetoricians, and they contrasted the "spiritual communication" of the Bible with the worldly style of human oratory. They were also unprepared by their own rhetorical training to recognize the techniques by which Scripture obtained its effects. They insisted that, composed for the most part by simple men, its style is humble. [115]

Calvin often identified himself with this judgment. "Our hearts are more firmly grounded," he asserted, "when we reflect that we are captivated with admiration for Scripture more by grandeur of subject than by grace of language." God had chosen to express "the sublime mysteries of the Kingdom of Heaven" in "mean and lowly words" to make clear that its power does not come from "eloquence alone." "Since such uncultivated and almost rude simplicity inspires greater reverence for itself than any eloquence," he asked, "what ought one to conclude except that the force of the truth of Sacred Scripture is manifestly too powerful to need the art of words?" [116]

He was especially concerned that the New Testament should be seen to display truth naked and unadorned. "God," Calvin argued, "has arranged that the Gospel should be stripped of any support from eloquence." [117] That the Evangelists "recount their history in a humble and lowly style" proves that, being "rude, uneducated men," they must have been inspired by the Holy Spirit. [118] "The height [Paul] reaches, the profundities he reveals, the strength he exhibits," come not from rhetoric but from the truths he conveys. [119] The Holy Spirit to be sure, has its own eloquence, but it is "intrinsic" rather than "borrowed." It does not "swell with ostentation nor fill the air with empty chatter, but is substantial and efficacious and has more of sincerity than refinement." This kind of eloquence "is not in conflict with the simplicity of the Gospel, which, without scorning it, not only yields and submits to it but serves it as a handmaiden serves her mistress." [120] He saw in Paul a determined adversary of rhetoric. Paul's disclaimer of "subtle arguments" he construed as a rejection not only of human philosophizing, "which, by its insinuating allurements," gives "the appearance of an acuteness that attracts the minds of men," but also of "persuasion," with the "meretricious flattery by which it wins over the minds of its hearers." He contrasted both these dubious enterprises with the irresistible word of the Lord, which, by its vehemence, "compels our obedience." [121]

But in spite of his effort to make sense of the universe and to tie it all together in a single tidy package, Calvin remained anxious. What we have so far seen of his culture was no more than a brave and determined, but in the end largely unsuccessful, effort to find comfort in the universe by traditional means. Indeed, the more fully he articulated his orderly universe, the more he worried over the permeability of boundaries, the collapse of categories, contamination and impurity; and the more he felt trapped. He could move, for relief, only in the opposite direction, toward freedom. The result is the subject of the next five chapters.

III

THE OPENING

7

Humanism

The failure of the philosophical culture to relieve Calvin's anxiety compelled him to turn for relief in another direction. In Renaissance humanism and its assumptions about the human personality and the possibilities of knowledge, he found a way to extricate himself from the labyrinth of philosophy. His humanism was thus not merely peripheral or auxiliary to his achievement, as has commonly been supposed. It was crucial to his thought. It constantly challenged his traditional culture, and Calvinism had its origins in his struggle to come to terms with the double legacy of philosophy and humanism. Much of Calvin's genius lay in the skill—which, however, was that of a humanist—that enabled him to contain, and sometimes to conceal, the tensions and contradictions in his thought. This is what makes his achievement so characteristic of his time.

Humanism too had deep roots. It was descended from the ancient rhetorical tradition, which had contested the pretensions of philosophy at least since the confrontation between Socrates and Protagoras. Protagoras, the best known of the Sophists, had doubted the capacity of human beings to achieve the certainties that philosophers aimed at. He believed that human knowledge consists at best only of useful or probable opinion; and he conceived of language not as a mirror of reality but simply as a conventional instrument for human communication. This position had been converted into a more systematic pedagogy by Isocrates, transmitted to Rome by Greek teachers of rhetoric, and made available to the Renaissance in the treatises of Cicero and Quintilian. The Latin church fathers, most of them rhetoricians, gave the rhetorical tradition a measure of respectability in the Renaissance.

The practical value of rhetoric had been rediscovered by the ruling groups of the Italian city-states in the fourteenth and fifteenth centuries. Because the abstract discourse of Scholastic philosophy seemed irrelevant to the needs of the bustling modern world, Renaissance humanists rejected Scholastic education, which depended primarily on logic, the art of organizing truth into rationally intelligible systems of thought, and turned instead to rhetoric, the art of persuasion. They looked for inspiration not to the philosophers of antiquity but to its orators, poets, and historians. Their preference for persuasion over rational conviction was associated with a view of human being as passionate, active, and social rather than intellectual. Accordingly they saw language less as a medium for conveying truth about the world than as an essential ingredient of life in society through its ability to move the feelings and stimulate the will to act. Rhetoric, in the words of Coluccio Salutati, can "inspire souls and set hearts afire." [1]

For humanists, in short, language was power. "What could be more important," Salutati had asked, "than to control the motions of the mind, to turn your hearer where you will, and to lead him back to the place from which you moved him, pleasantly and with love?" [2] We tend, in our time, to belittle rhetoric by attaching to it the adjective "mere," but this too is an oblique tribute to its power; we fear its capacity to manipulate and mislead. In Calvin's time, although its dangers were not ignored (indeed humanists, Calvin among them, often denounced rhetoric—rhetorically), men emphasized its capacity to inspire, to persuade, and to lead. Against the stifling claims of order and conformity, rhetoric represented freedom, innovation, and accomplishment.

Lay humanists in Renaissance Italy proposed to exploit the energies of persuasive language to reform the world. The religious interests of many of them suggest, too, that the rhetorical tradition had deep affinities with the biblical world of thought and feeling; humanism was closely intertwined with movements to revitalize Christianity by returning to the Bible. It inspired the evangelical Catholicism of Erasmus and Lefèvre d'Etaples as well as much in Protestantism. If Calvin's traditional culture put him on the side of Socrates and Athens, his humanism allied him with Protagoras and Jerusalem. It supplied the dynamic element in his thought, constantly challenging his philosophical culture.

Calvin's humanism is apparent, on the most superficial level, in his love of the classics. The youthful enthusiasm that had nourished his Seneca commentary continued to find expression in the classical allusions that abound in the works of his maturity. He could only hint at his pleasure in studying the Bible by comparing it to his delight in the classics. "Read Demosthenes or Cicero," he suggested, "read Plato, Aristotle, or others of that crew [*cohorte*]: they will, I admit, allure you, delight you, move you, enrapture you in wonderful measure. Then betake yourself to that sacred reading." [3] His division of classical authors here into two groups is significant: he mentions first the orators of Greece and Rome; the philosophers come second. His reliance on pagan literature in the *Institutes* and elsewhere is also revealing. He could probably not have avoided treating in places the views of philosophers; they were commonly invoked in theological discourse. But he was under no such obligation to cite, as he regularly did, Cicero and Quintilian, Homer and Virgil, Plutarch and Seneca, Horace, Juvenal, and Ovid, the authors most cherished by humanists. He did so not only because the readers whom he chiefly addressed loved these authors but because he loved them himself.

His study of Scripture, indeed, sometimes set off in him associations with the classics. He traced Paul's organic conception of the church back to Livy,[4] and the darkness at the moment of Christ's death reminded him that "the ancient poets, in their tragedies, imagine that the light of the sun is withdrawn from the earth when any abominable crime is committed, in order to show a portent of divine wrath."[5] This parallel did not trouble him, but another, between the sudden intervention that had transformed the despair of Abraham into joy and the *deus ex machina* of various pagan myths, did disturb him. He attributed the similarity to Satan, who, "by figments of this kind, has endeavored to obscure the wonderful and amazing interventions of God."[6]

But his humanism also went deeper; as early as his Seneca commentary Calvin, like a humanist, understood language as conventional. "It is usage rather than etymology or intrinsic meaning [*proprietas*]," he wrote, "that distinguishes one word from another,"[7] although he agreed with Quintilian in identifying proper usage as "the practice of educated men";[8] following the language of "the common people," he thought, would be "only barbarism."[9] Although he believed that it would be better "for words to be subject to things," he knew that in practice human beings "have power over names as well as things and may therefore apply words to things" as they please.[10] He was also untroubled by linguistic change; Moses, he noted, had described as " 'kings' those who hold the first place in a town or in any considerable assembly of men," although now the word is used quite differently.[11] Calvin, in short, recognized that language is a cultural artifact.

He repeated from time to time the humanist cliché that language is "the bond of human society."[12] God has put us into the world and given us speech, he remarked, "to communicate with each other."[13] The ability to speak, for Calvin, is basic to our dealing with each other humanly. "If there had been no language," he asked, "what could distinguish or differentiate men from brute beasts? They would all treat each other barbarously; there would be no humanity [*humanitas*] among them."[14] For him, as for the civic humanists of Italy, the point had large political significance. "We know," he remarked, "that commands are expressed orally; and in communication among men, he who rules proclaims by mouth what he wishes to be done."[15] A prince has "not only to rule the people by his decisions and authority but also to persuade them to obey." This requires rhetorical skill, for "doctrine stated generally does not move us."[16] The ancients had represented this truth by imagining gold chains in the mouth of Hercules, "by which he attracted the ears of the common people."[17]

Calvin was especially impressed by the capacity of language to convey feelings that we might otherwise conceal from one another in the "hidden and tortuous recesses of the heart." The tongue, its messenger, communicates what is stored there in what seemed to this reticent man a cause for wonder. It was always "a kind of miracle when, through the Lord's doing, one's tongue betrays his mind and inward feelings." From language, then, comes intimacy, "mutual support in charity," and "tender love and fraternity." [18] Speech, by the same token, combats loneliness. "Nothing is more disagreeable," he reflected, perhaps remembering his exile in Strasbourg, "than to wander among a people with whom we cannot communicate by language, the bond of society. Since language is, as it were, the image and mirror of the mind, those who lack the use of it are as strange to each other as the beasts of the forest." [19]

Effective communication, for Calvin as for other humanists, required more than fidelity to truth, the sole aim of philosophical discourse, which accordingly, refusing to make concessions to a general audience, employed a specialized vocabulary. A humanist, in contrast, recognized that the distance between one human being and another can be bridged only by the essential rhetorical virtue, decorum—that is, deliberate adaptation to one's audience for the sake of persuasion. Calvin held decorum in profound esteem. It was central to his pedagogy. "A wise teacher," he insisted, "accommodates himself to the understanding of those who must be taught. He begins with first principles in teaching the weak and ignorant and should not rise any higher than they can follow. In short he instills his teaching drop by drop, lest it overflow." [20] He also recognized its historical dimension; because audiences differ from age to age, rhetorical communication is not timeless but timely. "It would be a cold way of teaching," he observed, "if the teachers do not carefully consider the needs of the times and what is appropriate to the people, for in this matter nothing is more unbalanced than absolute balance." [21] His respect for decorum must also be taken into account in determining his meaning. He was often more concerned to sway a particular audience for particular purposes than to achieve the "absolute balance" of a detached and systematic theology. Since he was more concerned to effect a change in behavior than to state abstract truths, his denunciations of human wickedness are sometimes particularly unbalanced. This has led to the mistaken view that he thought God's image and likeness had been altogether obliterated by the Fall as well as to larger disagreements about what he believed. [22]

The failure of Job's friends to console him was, for Calvin, a warning of the consequences of neglecting decorum. Consolation, he pointed out, requires "a singular prudence," for "afflictions are like sicknesses; if a doctor used the same remedy for every sick person, how would that be? It is necessary in the first place to consider what people are like, and then how to deal with them." [23] We must persuade those we wish to console that "in some degree we are one with them." Truth like that so abrasively administered by Job's friends is only useful when it is "adapted in such a way as to have an effect on those who hear it." [24] They had neglected to consider "the person whom they addressed, for it is necessary to treat one individual differently from another." [25]

Calvin thought communication in figurative language particularly effective. "Although a figurative expression is less precise," he replied to one of his critics, "it expresses with greater significance and elegance what, said simply and without figure, would have less force and address. Hence figures are called the eyes of speech, not because they explain the matter more correctly than simple, proper language, but because they win attention by their propriety, arouse the mind by their luster, and by their lively similitude so represent what is said that it enters more effectively into the heart."[26] Decorum and figure seemed to him basic to *eloquence,* which he praised as a "special grace of God." It comes "from the Holy Spirit."[27] Rhetoric, indeed, had, for Calvin, some mysterious affinity with divinity. God's creation of the world was a magnificent expression of his rhetoric. God, as Calvin, put it, had by his spoken word compelled "the empty and formless matter of the world called chaos to shine with an admirable fitness [*decore*] and beauty." The creation is marked throughout by the decorum of the Master Rhetorician.[28] Calvin wrote these words when European writers were discovering that human beings can create imaginary worlds out of language.[29]

But *persuasio,* in the rhetorical tradition, merged almost imperceptibly with philological scholarship: *eruditio.*[30] The two interests were connected by the historical perspective of the Renaissance, a product of the concern of decorum with appropriateness to the times. Italian humanists, to develop their persuasive skills, imitated the most eloquent writers of antiquity. But, as Petrarch had already recognized, their world differed markedly from that of antiquity; and they concluded that, to make effective use of what they could learn from the ancients, they needed to understand these differences.[31] This task led them to an imaginative reconstruction of the ancient world through its literature. The result was a theory of imitation based on a distinction between what is perennially valuable in ancient culture—its essence or spirit—which they might hope to capture in their own discourse, and its time-bound accidents that it would be ridiculous, as they often put it, to "ape."[32] This view of imitation converted many humanists into *érudits* and a few into historians as it stimulated in them an awareness of change and reflection on its causes and structure.

Because antiquity had chiefly to be studied in texts, *eruditio* required mastery of the three languages of scholarship, Latin, Greek, and Hebrew. For Calvin, as for his master Erasmus, competence in these languages was essential for the study of Christian as well as of pagan literature; and, like other humanists, he celebrated recent advances in philology. It disturbed him that there were still "great theologians" who "furiously" denounced language study "with as many insults as they can muster."[33] Ignorance of languages resulted, he believed, in mistakes in matters "easy and obvious to anyone."[34]

Most recent scholars have agreed that, for his time, Calvin was a distinguished textual scholar.[35] Proficient in all three languages, he relied on the best contemporary scholarship, notably that of Erasmus and Budé.[36] His youthful Seneca commentary corrected the spelling of earlier texts and revealed a special appreciation for the value of punctuation to clarify meaning; and he became increasingly sophisticated in the use of humanist historical-critical methods. Like other humanists, he castigated the mistakes of medieval scholars.[37] He criticized the imprecision of Roman historians,[38] and Xenophon for his "fables" and his betrayal of the "seriousness and fidelity of a historian" in praising Cyrus "like a rhetorician."[39] He criticized those who ignored such matters as "fickle spirits" who sinned "in seizing upon whatever first comes to hand, when they ought to proceed further, and in stubbornly clinging to one word, when they ought to compare many things together." Such "simple-minded" persons are "repeatedly deceived, for they do not apply themselves to a sound knowledge of anything."[40]

He applied the general principles of humanistic hermeneutics in his own scholarship. A major novelty of humanistic reading, based on seeing classical authors as human beings rather than vehicles of transcendent wisdom, was insistence that an interpreter of a text faithfully respect its author's intention. "Since it is almost [the expositor's] only task to unfold the mind of the writer whom he has undertaken to expound," Calvin wrote, "he misses his mark, or at least strays outside his limits, insofar as he leads his readers away from the meaning of his author."[41] Of a work of Augustine, one of his favorite authors, he remarked, "If I am twisting it into another meaning than Augustine's, let them not only rail at me as usual but spit in my face."[42] He also insisted on understanding works as wholes and in the context of an author's general purpose. "When passages of Scripture are seized on rashly and no attention is given to context," he observed, "it is not to be wondered at that errors often arise."[43] As Erasmus had recommended, he clarified obscure passages by comparing them with others,[44] and he was unusual for his time in citing sources by work as well as author.[45] Attention to such matters made him even more acute than Erasmus in distinguishing between authentic works of Augustine and those falsely bearing his name.[46] He did not hesitate to criticize, on the basis of his own arithmetic, the chronology, attributed to Berosus, of the period after the flood.[47]

With the novel resources of Renaissance *eruditio,* Calvin, in his *Institutes* and commentaries, was laying the foundations for a biblical criticism at once learned, responsible, and reverent. He blamed both sectaries and papists for their obscurantism in the face of the new scholarship. The former were those "fickle" and "simple-minded" ones mentioned above who seize "on whatever first comes to hand where they ought to proceed further" and stubbornly cling to one word where they ought to compare many things together." Their simple- mindedness was "repeatedly deceived."[48] Papists, to their shame, still clung to the Vulgate "when the writings of Valla, Faber [Lefèvre d'Etaples] and Erasmus, which are in everybody's hands, point the finger, even to children, at how it is corrupted in innumerable places." Because "the Hebrew or Greek original often exposes their ignorance in citing Scripture, checks their presumption, and so keeps down their thrasonic boasting," they dismissed "those who have spent much time and labor in the study of languages seeking the genuine sense of Scripture from the sources."[49] Calvin thought it important, even for the laity, "to know how Holy Scripture uses words. . . . we cannot at all understand the doctrine of

God if we do not know the procedure it employs and its style and language."[50] He cited the ancients who, "though unacquainted with languages, notably Hebrew, always recognized that nothing is better than to consult the original for the true and genuine meaning."[51]

He was also deeply aware of his membership in a community of Protestant exegetes, all indebted to Erasmus.[52] He did not respect them equally. He admired Bucer, "that man of holy memory, outstanding doctor in the church of God, whom I judge to have pursued a line of work in this field which is beyond reproach."[53] He thought Zwingli's exposition "apt and ready" but too free. About Luther he was equivocal; he often followed Luther but criticized him as "satisfied when he could draw out a fruitful doctrine" and insufficiently careful either with facts or manner of expression.[54] He admired the diligence of Oecolampadius but thought him superficial; Melanchthon, he noted, had only touched on major points; Bullinger was too verbose.[55]

The slogan *ad fontes* had led these scholars back to the exegetical tradition of the church, of which Calvin was generally respectful. "Since in this life we cannot hope to achieve a permanent agreement in our understanding of every passage of Scripture, however desirable that would be," he wrote, "we must not be carried away by the lust for novelty, nor be pushed into scurrility or impelled by hatred or titillated by ambition, but only do what is necessary and depart from the opinions of earlier exegetes only when it is beneficial."[56] He probably consulted the *Glossa Ordinaria,* Nicholas of Lyra, and other medieval commentators, generally deriding them but finding in them information regarding Jewish interpretation.[57] But above all he turned for guidance, though always with discrimination, to the Fathers. Their "godliness, learning, and sanctity," he wrote, "have secured them such great authority that we should not despise anything they have produced."[58] He especially approved of Chrysostom, long a favorite of humanist students of Scripture because of his simple, literal-historical approach to the text.[59] He included Cyprian, Ambrose, Gregory, and Bernard, along with Augustine, among those who had at least intended to "build upon Christ."[60] Much in his own exegesis applied what he had learned from them, although whatever he found in earlier writers he made his own.

His humanistic erudition is evident in many particular observations about Scripture. He knew that biblical language follows principles of its own, beginning with the peculiarities of Hebrew word order.[61] He recognized the importance of knowing the idioms of other languages. He thought that the habit among some ancient peoples of considering all blood relations as "brethren" relevant to biblical references to the "brothers" of Jesus.[62] He knew too that biblical numbers are not to be taken literally: "thrice," for example, "stands for frequent repetition," and "ten signifies many."[63]

He was also aware that the biblical texts had been assembled and transmitted by fallible human beings over many centuries, and he recognized the relevance of this circumstance to their interpretation. The earliest materials in the Scriptures, he noted, had been passed down orally, "over a long suc-

cession of years," before being put into writing.[64] The prophetic books also
had a complex history. Originating as shapeless collections of prophecies,
Calvin believed, they had undergone a series of later reworkings.[65] There
were similar problems with the New Testament, including the possibility of
copyists' errors. Calvin noted anomalous material that might have originated
as the marginal note of a scribe;[66] and that, because a passage in the Fourth
Gospel had been unknown in antiquity, "some conjecture it was introduced
from elsewhere." He accepted it, but because it had long been received in
the Latin church and contained nothing "unworthy of the Holy Spirit."[67]
He knew too that the division of the biblical text into verses, and at least in
some instances into chapters, was arbitrary and in some cases misleading.[68]

Sometimes so desperate for "certitude," he could, indeed, be sur-
prisingly relaxed about the problems with which this *eruditio* confronted
him. He tolerated some ambiguity in Scripture. "It is possible," he could
say, "to expound this passage in four different ways. Everyone may use his
own judgment."[69] "In a doubtful case," he remarked concerning the au-
thorship of particular psalms, "everyone is free to choose the most likely
conjecture."[70] The variety of human minds is such, he suggested, that we
tend to be pleased by different things; and this implies that, even in the
interpretation of Scripture, "each may use his own judgment, provided no
one tries to force all others to obey his own rules."[71] He refused to conjecture whether the devil had actually lifted Christ to the pinnacle of the temple,
only remarking that, "since the matter is uncertain and it is permissible to
admit ignorance without harm, I prefer to suspend judgment."[72] In spite of
his insistence that Scripture must always be useful, he also admitted that he
was quite incapable of determining how this might be so for some passages,
for example genealogies. The names of some of Noah's descendants seemed
instructive, but he thought others too obscure to tell us "anything certain."[73] Against the claim of the Roman church to have settled the matter,
he denied, with no sign of distress, the existence of a fixed New Testament
canon.[74]

He could also correct mistakes in Scripture. He believed that Matthew,
in describing the journey of the magi, had improperly labeled as a star what
must really have been a comet.[75] Indeed, he came close to the irony of that
latter-day Calvinist Pierre Bayle when he professed to accept as historical
fact the darkness that covered the earth at the crucifixion and, having done
so, noted that "the scribes and priests and a large part of the people calmly
ignored and, their eyes closed, were unaware of, this darkening of the sun."
This, he observed piously, "ought to strike us with horror at their monstrous
madness; they must have been more stupid than the insensible beasts." He
doubted, in any event, that the eclipse had been seen everywhere on earth.[76]

The openness to which some of these passages attest was accompanied
at times by hints of relativism and tolerance of human variety that suggest
Montaigne. Calvin liked to depict Asia and Europe, East and West, as polar
opposites, their contrasts a revelation of the wide range of human behavior.
"We must observe the difference between oriental nations, which abound in

various ceremonies," he asserted, "and ours, which behave more simply."[77] One aspect of Asian ceremonialism particularly interested him: its expression of grief by rending garments and tearing hair, which, Calvin dryly observed, "would be a trifle excessive among us, but each nation has its customs." "The Italians and other Western nations," he noted, "allow the hair and beard to grow when they are in mourning; hence the phrase *to lengthen the beard.*"[78] He thought it important to recognize such differences because what is suited to Asians might be inappropriate to Europeans. Thus if we wished to imitate them, "we would behave like apes or actors on the stage."[79]

More commonly, Calvin emphasized the differences between one time and another. He was prepared to take indirect, if not open, issue with Paul's belief that long hair for men is contrary to nature, explaining that Paul meant by nature "what was then accepted by agreement and custom, at least among the Greeks."[80] He was also concerned lest David's nap on the fateful afternoon before he saw Bathsheba should be reckoned against him as part of his sin. "As far as his sleeping is concerned," he said, "it is not to be condemned, as it might seem to some people who have not been accustomed to the way of life that prevailed then, and have thought that David is here caught in great intemperance." The siesta was only an ancient custom, not a sin.[81] So too there was nothing reprehensible in David's dancing before the ark. Although some dancing is "dissolute and lascivious," David was simply conforming to a custom of the time. "We must all by nature make merry," Calvin observed tolerantly; "there is no one who is not given to it."[82]

But the deepest mark of his humanism was his recognition that the Bible is throughout a rhetorical document and a work of interpretation. So, he wrote of the Gospels, "because bare history would not be enough, indeed would be of no value for salvation, the Evangelists do not simply narrate that Christ was born, died, and conquered death, but at the same time they explain for what purpose he was born, died, and rose again, and what benefit thence comes to us."[83] The Evangelists were not annalists but artists.

Calvin was little troubled, therefore, by discrepancies among their accounts; indeed he was scrupulous to identify them. The authors of the Gospels, he explained, had not written "in such a way as always to preserve the exact order of events, but rather to bring everything together so as to place before us a kind of mirror or screen on which the most useful things of Christ could be known."[84] He argued, indeed, that the differences among the Gospels, given their general agreement, increased their credibility; their differences proved that there had been no collusion among their authors.[85] The differences also freed him to vary, for pedagogical purposes, the order in his own presentation. "Since the Evangelists transfer units of Christ's teaching here and there to different places as the occasion demands," he explained, "we need feel no compunction about rearranging them."[86] Nor did it disturb him that the biblical narrative contains inaccuracies and instances of carelessness on the part of its human authors. "It is well known," he observed, "that the Evangelists were not sufficiently careful with their time sequences, nor even bothered about the details of what was done or said."[87] To Calvin the notion of verbal inerrancy would have suggested willful blindness.

Eruditio was indeed, for Calvin, always the handmaiden of *persuasio;* it explained, above all, the persuasiveness of the Scriptures. His learning compelled him to recognize their eloquence, and this recognition illuminated their purposes and therefore their meaning. The traditional view that denied this eloquence, he argued, was based on ignorance; "Moses and several of the prophets are no less eloquent and polished in their Hebrew language than the Greeks and Latins, whether orators or philosophers, are in theirs."[88] He deeply admired the poetry of the prophetic books,[89] and he could even discern humor in Scripture; a Pauline play on words suggested to him that the Holy Spirit "has not always avoided pleasantries and jests," though he hastened to add that it always avoided scurrility.[90] He analyzed biblical rhetoric as other humanists anlyzed secular classics. "Hebrew writers," he might point out, "customarily use *interrogatio* when they wish emphatically to deny something; among them it is elegant, although for the Greeks and Latins it would be tasteless."[91] The language with which Amnon referred to Tamar exemplified, for him, the subtlety of Hebrew; it enabled Amnon to conceal his incestuous desire for Tamar, perhaps first of all from himself, by referring to her as "the sister of his brother Absalom, as though she were not his own sister."[92]

Above all, Calvin called attention to the tropes that made Scripture eloquent. Often, to be sure, he insisted on sticking to what he called "the natural sense."[93] At times he argued for this in such absolute terms that he came close to contradicting his own appreciation for figurative language. "The true sense of Scripture," he might say, "is that which is natural [*germanus*] and simple." Hence we should "not only ignore as doubtful, but vigorously reject as deadly corruptions, those fictitious readings that lead us away from the literal sense."[94] In such passages, however, like other humanists, he was chiefly attacking the allegorical excesses of some medieval exegesis. "Allegories," he wrote, "ought not to go beyond the limits set by the rule of Scripture, let alone suffice as the foundation for any doctrines."[95] Allegorizing was too likely to degenerate into "playing games with the sacred Word of God, like tossing a ball back and forth."[96] Origen and his latter-day followers were the worst examples of this frivolity. Thinking "the literal sense too humble and mean," they had concluded "that beneath the shell of the letter lurk more sublime mysteries that cannot be exposed except by hammering out allegories."[97]

But otherwise Calvin cherished and regularly commented on figures of speech in Scripture. Christ himself, he noted, had used figures; in the parable of the seed, for example, he had taught more clearly and with "more energy and efficacy than by simple expression."[98] The use of figurative language in Scripture proved decisively, against the Schoolmen, its general propriety in religious discourse. Beyond this, Calvin believed, an awareness of biblical rhetoric can contribute to theological understanding. Recognition that in saying "This is my body," Christ was employing metonymy, for example, excludes both transubstantiation and the merely symbolic interpretation of the sacrament suggested by treating the words as metaphor.[99] Awareness that fire is a metaphor for God's wrath similarly avoids a crudely material conception of hell.[100] But above all, knowledge of biblical rhetoric explains its power. If the prophets "had spoken without figures and simply narrated the things with which they were concerned," he observed, "their speech would have been frigid and would not have penetrated spirits."[101]

Like earlier commentators in the tradition of Augustine's *De doctrina christiana,* therefore, Calvin regularly identified metaphor, allegory, personification, metonymy, synecdoche, and other tropes. He recognized that light is a common Scriptural metaphor for "whatever pertains to full happiness," darkness a metaphor for "death and misery of every kind."[102] Jeremiah's figure of Rachel grieving for her children seemed to him a peculiarly vivid way of saying that the land would be desolate. "Rhetoricians," he observed in this connection, "rank personification very high, and Cicero, when he wants to teach the greatest splendor of oratory, says that nothing touches an audience more than to raise the dead from below." Jeremiah, "though not taught in the schools of the rhetoricians," had been taught this device by the Holy Spirit "so that he might penetrate more effectively into the hearts of the people."[103]

He was also sensitive to the voices of biblical writers, and, as Petrarch had recognized in the case of classical authors, was aware that these were shaped by the circumstances of their lives. He identified Jeremiah as a man "from a pastoral town" who "had been from his boyhood among shepherds." This explained, he thought, peculiarities in Jeremiah's expression, "for education in large measure forms the speech of men."[104] In the New Testament the Fourth Gospel was his favorite partly because of its "greater vivacity, strength, and power."[105] Paul's abrupt and "passionate outbursts" exemplified, for Calvin, the way in which feelings tend to find expression in broken words in which "the seething of the mind almost chokes the throat."[106] Calvin, in short, recognized that full appreciation of the Bible depends on reading it as literature.

This sensitivity to the literary virtues of Scripture is also revealed by the intensity of his own responses to it and his empathy with biblical personages. Where the text told stories, he retold them, dramatizing the feelings and exploring the motives of their protagonists. When Mary rebuked the boy Jesus for his truancy, Calvin apologized for her. "The weariness of three days was in that complaint," he explained.[107] The distress of the Hebrew spies hidden in the house of Rahab reminded him of anxieties he associated with a labyrinth. Once the gates of the city were closed, "their exit barred," with no hope of escape, the wretched men were trapped; they could only "call upon God."[108] He had to learn "from experience," like Moses, that the people entrusted to his care had closed the door against God and that they were a "very heavy rock" for him to move. He knew empathetically that Moses would "willingly have withdrawn and turned his back" but could never reject "the burden of his vocation." [109] He brought to the interpretation of Scripture the experiences and feelings of his own bitter life.

But his rhetorical Christianity is most profoundly apparent in his emphasis on Scripture as everywhere accommodated by God's decorum to human comprehension: God speaks to us of things "according to our capacity for understanding them, not according to what they are." [110] Taking into account "the diversity of times" and "diverse ways of learning," the Holy Spirit always "accommodates itself to our infirmity." [111] This had strong egalitarian implications; it means that God "wants not only to instruct learned clergy [*les grands clercs*] and people who are very subtle and have been trained in school, but wishes to accommodate to even the roughest common people [*les plus rudes idiots qui soyent*]." [112]

Calvin distinguished, however, several rather different audiences for Scripture, and therefore different modes of accommodation. God had spoken through Moses and the prophets to an ancient and primitive people, and Christ had addressed his own contemporaries. But at the same time both the Jewish and Christian Scriptures have been accommodated to peoples of later, more advanced ages.

The communication of God's word to its first rude audience, for Calvin, explained many otherwise puzzling biblical texts, especially those which seemed to deal with natural phenomena in unscientific ways. Such passages should be interpreted figuratively, figures being, Calvin thought, appropriate to the earliest stages of human culture,[113] although the limits of his historicism are suggested by his inability to believe that such respected figures in the early history of the Jews as Moses and David could themselves have been simple men, whatever the character of their time. He perceived them as skilled orators, at least as cultivated as himself, who had deliberately condescended to the rudeness of their people. Moses, he explained, "did not speak acutely or in a philosophical way, but popularly, so that even the most uncultivated might understand." He had "deliberately abstained from subtle disputations that might smack of the schools and deeper learning." This explains why "he did not treat the stars scientifically, like a philosopher." [114] David, in describing the sun as emerging from a tent, was not trying to teach "the secrets of astronomy" to "the rude and unlearned" but had deliberately chosen "a homely style." [115] Calvin's sensitivity to "differences of times" implied that what is right for one age in the history of the church might be rejected by another. On this ground he thought "foolish" the continuance of the Jewish use of musical instruments in worship. He also considered perpetuation of the polity of the apostolic church generally inappropriate.[116] But he did not make explicit the most radical implication of this view: that the improvement of the church might take another form than return to origins.

He also noted repeatedly how Christ had accommodated his teaching to his own contemporaries. Although he did not equate the culture of this audience with that of the early Jews, he emphasized its simplicity in order to bring out the condescension of Christ's discourse. "In order to be more easily understood by the simple, he borrowed a way of speaking then customary among his people." [117] He "adapted his replies to those with whom he conversed. . . . The person of the speaker and the question itself" could determine the Lord's reply.[118] Sometimes he spoke imprecisely to "accommodate himself to his listeners." [119] At other times he used proverbs "then in common use," as Calvin often did in his own sermons.[120] In general, Calvin observed, Scripture employs, for the sake of simple folk, metaphors that, taken literally, are misleading. To deepen reverence, it sometimes speaks of God "in heaven," although "God is by no means contained in heaven," which is his creation and "bears the mark and impression of his glory and majesty." Scripture uses imagery to teach us, when we think of God, "to imagine nothing earthly" and "to adore him in all humility." [121] In recognizing the decorum of Scripture, Calvin revealed a flexibility in exegesis not always conspicuous among his followers.

But God also accommodates his word to human beings in all ages, including the wisest and most cultivated. Otherwise it would be "impossible for God to make us feel his power [*vertu*] without annihilating and destroying us [*nous abysmer du tout*]." [122] If God "wished to speak his own language," Calvin asked, "would mortal creatures have been able to bear it? Alas, no. How then has he spoken to us in Holy Scripture? He has stammered [*bagaye*]." He has presented himself "like a nurse who will not speak to a child in the same way as to a man but keeps in mind the child's capacity." [123] God must "descend to us so that we may mount to him." [124]

Calvin's belief in God's accommodation of his word to human weakness in every age was central to his understanding of the Incarnation, as it had been for Valla and Erasmus. He believed, with Irenaeus, "that the Father, himself infinite, becomes finite in the Son, for he has accommodated himself to our little measure lest our minds be overwhelmed by the immensity of his glory." [125] Like Valla and Erasmus, too, he rendered *Logos* as *sermo*, God's "speech"; *oratio* rather than *ratio*, rhetorical rather than philosophical discourse. "As 'speech' is said among men to be the image of the mind," Calvin observed, "so it is not inappropriate to apply this also to God and say that he expresses himself to us through his speech." [126] Rhetorical communication, he insisted repeatedly, is God's only way of revealing himself to human beings; we know nothing of God except through his revelation in Christ, who "represents and exhibits to us whatever is useful to be known about the Father."[127] This is why the sacrament in which Christ is present shows how "our merciful Lord, according to his infinite kindness, accommodates himself to our capacity." [128] In short, "whenever our mind seeks God, unless it meets Christ it will wander, restless and confused, until it wholly fails." [129]

Thus Calvin never forgot, in his devotion to *eruditio*, the importance of *persuasio;* not only his sermons but also his *Institutes* and commentaries aimed at persuasion. The *Institutes* is not logically ordered; it consists of a series of overlapping topics generally following the order of the Apostles' Creed. This organization allowed Calvin the flexibility for a variety of persuasive strategies. His hortatory letter to the King of France establishes at the outset the rhetorical character of the work, and the text is throughout a complex mixture of demonstration, advocacy, and apologetics. As Quirinus Breen pointed out, the *Institutes* exploits numerous rhetorical devices in order to teach, to move, and to delight.[130] Calvin's preliminary and, as the work grew, increasingly implausible claim to brevity was itself a conventional rhetorical move, intended here to suggest a contrast with Scholastic prolixity.[131]

Nor were Calvin's biblical commentaries simply works of erudition. They interpreted the text, to be sure, and often supplied information, philological, historical, geographical, or literary, drawn from his wide reading. But various responsibilities of an expositor of Scripture also called for persuasion. He was expected not only to elucidate its meaning but to adduce its relevance to a contemporary audience: as Calvin put it, "to apply to present use whatever instruction could be gathered from these divine compositions."[132] Because in Hebrew, as he knew, it was "the fashion to express in a word what might have been extended at length,"[133] he found it necessary at times to heighten its message with Erasmian *copia*. The destruction of Sodom, a catastrophe so laconically described in Scripture, called, Calvin thought, for "far more dignity of expression in tragic words." It was not enough for Moses simply to narrate "a judgment of God that no words would be sufficiently vehement to describe, and then leave the subject to the meditation of his readers";[134] and Calvin took it on himself to remedy this defect. He also supplemented biblical narrative with persuasive "discourses," chiefly moral.

A central principle of humanist hermeneutics also made his commentaries rhetorical. Faithful exposition required a commentator, above all else, to identify the general conceptions [*loci*] underlying a text, to unify his commentary by showing the relation of particular passages to its main themes, and so constantly to reiterate its essential message.[135] As a vehicle of general *interpretation,* a commentary was thus inevitably persuasive as well as demonstrative.

The significance of the message also precluded dispassionate presentation, and Calvin was prepared to introduce, into his commentaries and *Institutes* alike, anything that might increase their impact: digression, repetition, embellishment, amplification, and passages of great emotional intensity. He would have considered the coolness and detachment of mere scholarship profoundly unsuited to his purposes; he aspired—to use his own language—to be hot, not cool. He wanted all his discourse to be as powerful as possible. But this requirement applied above all to his sermons.

Calvin never forgot that the effect of a sermon depends on a collaboration between preacher and Holy Spirit. But he also attached great importance to natural talent and human training; effective preaching required "a combination of the right understanding of Scripture" and "a special gift for explaining it."[136] He thought it "not enough for a man to be eminent in profound learning if he has no talent for teaching [i.e., preaching]. There are many who, either because of defective speaking or insufficient mental ability, or because they are not sufficiently in touch with ordinary people, keep their knowledge shut up within themselves. Such people ought, as the saying goes, to sing to themselves and the muses—and go and do something else." [137] Yet his apologetic tone in discussing "eloquence" in the pulpit sometimes suggests persistent doubts of its propriety. If it is not to "contravene the simplicity of the Gospel," it must "not only submit and willingly subordinate itself [to the Gospel] but also serve it, as a maidservant her mistress." Yet when it does so, it is—the mixed figure is a bit jarring—"like a trumpet" that compels human beings to listen. [138]

The awesomeness of responsibility for the salvation of souls and the urgency of the task make decorum especially important in preaching. "The doctors of the church should be taught by long meditation so that, as need arises," Calvin believed, "they may minister doctrine to the church from God's word, as from a storehouse, wisely and aptly accommodating the teaching to the grasp of each individual." [139] A preacher must "pay attention to the persons to whom the teaching is addressed," continually reminding himself, "I am not at all here for myself alone. . . . If I were content with feeding only myself and had no regard for you and your capacities for making use of the teaching I bring, what would be the sense of that?" [140] Preaching, like consolation, is medicinal: "It is as if one went to a doctor and asked him for a remedy for an illness, and he discoursed of his art in general and argued about it, and the poor sick man meanwhile died. . . . It is necessary to adapt the medicine to those who need it." [141]

But Calvin's concern to combine responsible and scholarly interpretation—*eruditio*—with a discourse that would move the hearts of his listeners—*persuasio*—was not altogether successful. A sermon that is itself, like Calvin's sermons, a close consideration of a sequence of biblical verses can hardly fail to keep any rhetorical flight short and close to the ground. There are eloquent passages in Calvin's sermons, but fearful perhaps of losing control over himself and relying on Scripture as a bridle, he composed few eloquent sermons.

But if *persuasio* was not decisive for the form of Calvin's exegetical and theological discourse, it had profound implications for the substance of that discourse. Rhetorical culture rested on assumptions about the human condition, the possibilities of knowledge, human experience of the world, and the organization of life that were in sharp contrast to those on which Calvin's traditional culture rested. These matters will be treated in the remaining chapters.

IV

THE ABYSS

8

Being

Although Calvin continued to employ the vocabulary of an inherited philosophical culture and to rely on its strategies for the management of his anxiety, there were contrary pressures within himself that were nourished by other tendencies of sixteenth-century culture. A powerful impulse to let go contested his need to protect boundaries and prevent any aspect of his life from escaping control. The next four chapters, then, will deal with Calvin's attraction to conceptions, closely linked to his humanism, that promised escape from the labyrinth. The cost of this relief, however, was heavy; it left him precariously poised on the edge of the abyss.

Two areas of his thought provided openings toward this ambiguous freedom: his conception of the human personality and his understanding of what it means to know something. If his views on these matters examined in earlier chapters came chiefly from ancient philosophy, he found those to be considered now primarily in the Jewish and Christian Scriptures. Calvin is historically interesting as, among other things, a reminder of the dilemmas to which the combination of Hellenic and Hebraic strains in Western culture has periodically given rise.

Karl Barth noted that the sixteenth-century Reformers lacked an adequate (that is, fully biblical) understanding of the human personality.[1] This was clearly true of Calvin, but Barth's criticism also implies that it might have been otherwise, which seems unlikely: his observation would apply equally to almost all sixteenth-century thinkers—and most in later centuries. Our eclecticism even now is suggested by the easy currency of such a phrase as "the hearts and minds of the people," which combines elements from quite different anthropological models. But Calvin was sensitive to the difficulties in this combination; and without giving up the hierarchy of discrete faculties he had absorbed from "the philosophers,"[2] he struggled to come to terms with a conception of human being as a mysterious psychosomatic unity dependent on the "heart." Although he recognized the importance of the biblical heart, his effort to identify it with one or another of the

traditional faculties, as we have seen, suggests that he often failed to understand that it represented a radically different conception of the personality.
The result was considerable confusion. "In Scripture," as he once suggested, "*cor* sometimes signifies the seat of the affections. But here, as in
many other places, it means what they call the intellectual part of the soul."[3]
"The Hebrews," he declared on another occasion, "use this word for the
rational part of the soul, though properly it means the will or the appetitive
part of the soul, because it is the seat of the affections."[4]

But there were other times when, momentarily forgetting the philosophers, he recognized that the heart, as the spiritual center of the personality, belonged to a different cultural universe in which what is best is
located not at the top but at the center. "The seat of the law is not in the
brain but in the heart," he remarked, "so that, having been instructed in
heavenly teaching, we may be inwardly renewed."[5] From this perspective
he could confidently identify the heart with feeling: "In order to serve God
properly, our hearts must be given to him, since it does not suffice if we have
all the virtues that can possibly be imagined only externally. Affection must
come first."[6]

Through this understanding of the heart, Calvin was also moving toward,
though he never quite reached, a conception of the wholeness of human
being. In meditating on a prayer in which the Psalmist calls upon the Lord to
examine both his heart and his loins, Calvin remarked that "what some distinguish here is more subtle than solid, namely that 'heart' signifies the
higher affections, 'loins'—as they say—the sensual and more gross. For we
know that the Hebrews designated by the term 'reins' that which is most
secret in men. David, therefore, conscious of his uprightness, offers himself
wholly for God's examination."[7] But what impelled him most forcefully in
this direction was his need to come to terms with the Pauline distinction
between flesh and spirit. When he considered carefully the slippery vocabulary at his disposal, he was never in doubt that these terms signified not
faculties but orientations of the personality. "Under 'flesh'," he explained,
"is comprehended whatever men bring from the womb. 'Flesh' designates
men as they are born and as long as they retain their original disposition, for
they are wicked so that they neither know nor aspire to anything but what is
gross and earthly. Spirit, however, refers to what restores our corrupt
nature."[8]

"Spirit" could not, for Calvin, be strictly an anthropological conception;
it was not only a human potentiality but divinity at work, the effect of the
Holy Spirit, the source of regeneration. "Paul calls it 'life'," he explained,
"not only because it lives and flourishes in us, but also because it quickens
us by its energy until it destroys our mortal flesh and at last renews it completely. Conversely the word 'flesh' designates that more gross mass which
has not yet been purified by the Spirit of God from earthly stains, which
takes pleasure only in what is gross. It would otherwise be absurd to attribute blame for sin to the body. On the other hand the soul [*anima*] is so far
from being life that it does not, of itself, live."[9]

Calvin's thought on this matter was also indebted to his rhetorical training; he recognized the biblical "flesh" as metonymy, "a figure of speech,"
as he put it, "in which a part is taken for the whole." Understood in this
way, "the lower part includes the whole man." [10] "Flesh," therefore, can
signify not only the body "but at the same time the soul [*animam*] and also
its individual parts." On this point he attacked "popish theologizers" for
restricting the term to sensuality; "flesh," includes "our mind and reason
because they are carnal," indeed "all the affections of the heart." [11] So,
following Paul, he described heresy as a work of the flesh, "for what gives
rise to heresies but ambition, which does not lurk in the gross senses but
chiefly has its seat in the mind?" [12]

The tendency here to a holistic view of human being occasionally made
problematic, for Calvin, even his usual distinction between soul and body.
He was impressed by the biblical identification of the viscera as "the seat of
the feelings," [13] and his discussion of repression is almost gastroen-
terological. The more sinners are held back by "fright or shame," the more
"they dare neither execute what they have conceived in their minds nor
openly breathe forth the rage of their lust," he wrote, "the more strongly
they are inflamed; they burn and boil within and are ready to do anything or
burst forth anywhere." [14] A human being must be wholly renewed: "The
whole man is naturally flesh, until, by the grace of regeneration, he begins to
be spiritual." [15] Calvin recognized too the most radical implication of this
position: it ejects "reason from her throne and reduces her to nothing—that
reason to which philosophers attribute sovereignty and which they represent
as a most wise queen." [16] In this light it is possible for reason to "disagree
with itself, and some of its counsels to conflict with others like hostile armies." [17] By the same token the will can no longer be conceived as the obedient servant of reason; it is now, though not free, the capacity of the whole
person for choice.[18] The dethronement of reason helps to explain why Calvin, unlike most of his learned contemporaries, praised the manual equally
with the liberal arts; the abolition of hierarchy in the personality had implications for social hierarchy.[19]

But a wholeness defying analysis into discrete parts eludes full understanding, and Calvin also showed signs of an Augustinian awe before the
unfathomable depths of the personality. He tended to give an unflattering
interpretation to its obscurity. The "intricacies and secret depths in the
hearts of men" astonished him, but they also suggested "darkness and disorder," [20] and he generally drew from the mysteries of human being the banal lesson that the appearance of virtue is likely to be hypocrisy. Yet he also
proposed that, because "the recesses of hearts are so hidden," no human
being is qualified to judge another.[21] This sense of complexity hints at an
awareness, increasingly reflected in the art and literature of the Renaissance,
of the infinite possibilities of the human condition.

It can hardly be surprising, then, that much of Calvin's thought about
human being vigorously contested his reservations about the feelings and the
body. His positive regard for the feelings found expression in his frequent

attacks on Stoic *apatheia*. "We must reject that insane philosophy," he insisted, "that requires men to be utterly without feeling if they are deemed
wise. The Stoics of long ago must have been devoid of common sense in
taking away all feeling from a man." [22] He scorned Stoicism for requiring a
person to "cast off all human qualities" and, like a stone, be "affected
equally by adversity and prosperity, by sad times and happy ones," although he took comfort in the thought that no such monster had ever existed. The faithful, in contrast, "are not logs of wood, untouched by grief,
unafraid of danger, unhurt by poverty, untroubled by persecution";[23] and
Christ's feelings were an essential part of his humanity: he had "groaned and
wept both over his own and others' misfortunes." [24] "Those who claim that
the Son of God was immune from human passions do not seriously acknowledge him as a man," Calvin asserted; "within the capacity of a sane and
unspoiled nature, he was struck with fright and afflicted with anxiety." [25] To
feel anger, to grieve, to fear, to rejoice, to hope: none of these is contrary to
reason; all are proper to "our unfallen nature, implanted in us by God; we
cannot find fault with them without insulting God himself." [26] Calvin's own
sympathy went out even to "an unhappy little bird which, either for procreation or love for its little ones, forgetting its own life, chooses to endanger its
own life rather than to desert its eggs or its chicks." [27]

The feelings of the saints were to him as exemplary as their teaching. He
described David's distress as "a more effective stimulus to prayer [for us]
than if he had overcome his fear, grief and bitterness." [28] He admired even
the most passionate passages in the Pauline epistles, where, he noted, "the
more fervent emotions plunge impetuously on, without consideration or regard for anything but their object." [29] Every good pastor, Calvin believed,
should, like Paul, have a capacity for strong feeling.[30]

He also praised the body. Noting a tendency in himself to refer to it
"grossly," he apologized to his congregation for implying that it might be
intrinsically corrupt. "Our bodies," he emphasized, "are, in their essence,
good creations of God." [31] The body as well as the mind is fit to serve him.[32]
"From the top of the head to the soles of the feet," the body is a miracle
attesting to God's wisdom and power. He paid special tribute to fingernails,
"mirrors of God's providence, in which we see marvelous workmanship, for
they serve to put the hands to work, to strengthen them and to teach how to
bend the fingers and to hold what is necessary." [33] Care for the body's needs
is "obedience due to God," for "to deny what is necessary to support life is
no less alien to piety than it is inhuman." [34]

He was accordingly hostile to asceticism, and he attacked veneration of
John the Baptist as an ascetic. Matthew, he noted, "did not number among
the chief virtues of the Baptist" that he had taken up "a rude and austere
way of life, or that he rejected the ordinary decencies." [35] He called on human beings to rejoice because God has given them "a superabundance of
good things, in our drinking, and in our eating, and in everything." [36] We
should delight in the whole creation: "There is not one little blade of grass,

there is no color in this world that is not intended to make men rejoice." [37]
"Contempt of God's benefits" would be "profanation and sacrilege." [38]

Perhaps because in some moods he was attracted to it, Calvin explicitly dissociated himself from the venerable Augustinian formula *utor non frui*, which he associated with Stoicism. He thought refusal to *enjoy* God's gifts tantamount to rejecting his goodness. It is also unrealistic: no one can go through life without encountering much that gives pleasure, and consciences should not be troubled by an inability to resist pleasures God has intended for us. Christ, Calvin insisted, "allows God's temporal benefits to be used *and enjoyed as if they were not used.*" [39] We are put into this world "not only to be spectators in this beautiful theater but to enjoy the vast bounty and variety of good things which are displayed to us in it." [40] "Away, then," Calvin exclaimed, "with that inhuman philosophy which, while allowing only the necessary use of created things, not only malignantly deprives us of the lawful fruit of God's beneficence but cannot be practiced unless it robs a man of all his senses and degrades him to a block." [41] God intends for human beings "a life sweet, delightful, and lacking nothing"; [42] and his list of life's enjoyments probably reveals something of his own capacity for pleasure. It ranges over the entire sensorium and includes everything beautiful:

> Has the Lord clothed the flowers with the great beauty that greets our eyes and the sweetness of smell that is wafted upon our nostrils, and yet it is not permissible for our eyes to be pleased by that beauty, or our sense of smell by the sweetness of that odor? Did the Lord not distinguish colors, making some more lovely than others? Did he not endow gold and silver, ivory and marble, with a loveliness that renders them more precious than other metals or stones? Did he not, in short, render many things attractive to us, apart from their utility? [43]

He insisted that sculpture and painting are "gifts of God," [44] and he especially praised music. "Among other things fit to recreate man and give him pleasure," he wrote, "music is either first or one of the principal; and we must value it as a gift of God." [45]

He was equally positive about eating and drinking. It should give "inestimable joy to all pious men to know that all kinds of foods are put in their hands by the hand of the Lord, so that their use is blameless and legitimate." [46] Again he appreciated more than the utility of food. "Since it pleases God that we are in this world," he argued, "we should not at all abstain from drinking and from eating because of our troubles; this would be gratuitously making war on him. . . . God wishes that we should enjoy the good things he gives us for our nourishment." [47] From even frugal use of food and drink we discover that it "has savor as well as nourishment," and thus that God intends to "delight us with his delicacies." [48]

Calvin regularly accompanied passages of this kind with warnings against excess, especially in drinking wine. But in wine too he saw a precious gift of

God. "It is permissible to use wine," he argued, "not only for necessity, but also to make us merry." Christ's provision of an abundance of "most excellent wine" at the wedding in Cana was proof enough of its goodness.[49] Only two conditions should govern wine-drinking: first that it be moderate, "lest men forget themselves, drown their senses, and destroy their strength"; and second, that, "in making merry," they feel a livelier gratitude to God.[50]

Calvin's attitude to eating and drinking was partly connected with their social character. He worried, to be sure, about the excesses that marked some social gatherings, which were too often accompanied, as he remarked of Herod's birthday party, by "luxury, pride, unrestrained mirth, and other extravagances." But it was only the possibility of excess that troubled him: "It is not wrong in itself," he hastened to add, "to prepare a generous feast."[51] His insistence that "holy men" might properly invite their friends "to the enjoyment of feasting merrily together and thanking God" recalls a famous colloquy of Erasmus.[52]

His positive attitude toward sexuality had even larger implications, since fear of the unruly sexual instinct has been so closely connected with general distrust of the body. However much Calvin disapproved of contemporary license, he always assumed that sexual reproduction had been divinely instituted; their sexuality had been part of the original perfection of Adam and Eve.[53] "The generation of man," he observed, "is not unclean and vicious in itself, but is so as an accident arising from the Fall."[54]

Calvin's pronouncements about sex—and some other less direct evidence about his feelings—range from conventional approval of what is kept properly under control to hints of gratitude for genital pleasure. At times, in his vigorous and indignant rejection of celibacy, he expressed a confidence in the virtue of "nature" that suggests Lorenzo Valla or even Boccaccio. "It is tempting God," he wrote against the vow of celibacy, "to strive against the nature imparted by him, and to despise his present gifts as if they did not belong to us at all."[55] Calvin thought rejection of sexuality a sin that invited such retribution as the "bestial abominations" of the religious under the papacy.[56]

This position made him, like other Reformers, a strong advocate of marriage for all but a few whom God needs "to hold readier for his work." All others, in rejecting marriage, would "contend against God and the nature ordained by him"; we should "accommodate our mode of life to the measure of our ability."[57] Calvin sometimes justified marriage on the conventional and not altogether positive ground that it provides sexual relief. He advised any person who is unable to "tame lust" to "recognize that the Lord has imposed the necessity of marriage upon him."[58] But a more positive attitude is suggested by his reservations about the Pauline formula "better to marry than to burn." This formulation was "improper," he thought, "since legitimate marriage is in all respects honorable, whereas burning is very bad";[59] the Spirit "tells us that marriage is honorable for all."[60] Paul's description of the church as the bride of Christ, he pointed out, shows God's esteem for it.[61] He admitted the possibility of "uncontrolled excess" in marriage, but he was uncharacteristically lenient toward it. "Whatever sin or shame is in it," he declared, "is so covered by the goodness of marriage that it ceases to be sin, or at least to be so regarded by God," for "the intercourse of husband and wife is a pure thing, good and holy."[62]

He dealt with sexual attraction not only positively but with a touch of romantic feeling. He spoke of the "extremely tender love that a youth feels for a maiden in the flower of her age,"[63] and he interpreted a text referring to the "love of women" as signifying "a unique kind of love with which God has endowed both men and women, so that they may remain joined together for as long as they retain any drop of humanity."[64] But his participation in such feelings is most vividly conveyed by his empathy with biblical accounts of sexual attraction, as in the case of the complicated courtships of Jacob. Calvin defended Jacob's preference for Rachel over Leah, even though it violated his strong feelings about polygamy. "It is not to be considered altogether a fault," he argued, "that Jacob was inclined to love Rachel, whether because Leah was less beautiful, since only her tender eyes were pleasing, or because Rachel excelled her in the elegant shapeliness of every feature. For we see how naturally a secret kind of affection produces mutual love." He went on to adduce from this case a general principle: "Therefore he who shall be induced to choose a wife because of the elegance of her shape will not necessarily sin."[65] Nor had Calvin any difficulty in accepting the pleasure of sex; he noted approvingly that in the marital act God not only covers anything sinful "with the veil of holy marriage" but "allows husband and wife to give each other delight."[66]

He celebrated enthusiastically the miracle of human reproduction: "God needs no other orators to illustrate his power," he declared, "than infant children who are still at their mothers' breasts. They themselves are dumb, but the marvelous providence of God that shines in them speaks with eloquence and sonority. Anyone who considers how a fetus is begotten in the womb of its mother, is nourished there for nine months until it is brought forth into the light, and from the moment of birth finds ready food, must feel not only God's work in the world but also be carried away in admiration of him."[67] There was special poignancy, given the deaths in infancy of all his own children, in his sense of what children could add to a marriage. "Babies," he speculated, "must increase the love of the husband and wife; when God blesses a marriage with children, that must increase their mutual affection, so that they live together in greater concord."[68] Every aspect of human sexuality, for Calvin, was valuable and deeply moving.

His positive attitude to sex was accompanied by unusual sympathy for feminine sexuality. Like Luther he considered motherhood a calling,[69] and he paid warm tribute to it. "How incredible," he exclaimed, "the affection of a mother is for the infant whom she warms in her bosom and nurses and watches over with care, so that she passes sleepless nights, worries continually, and forgets herself!"[70] In a time when the sexuality of young women usually seemed dangerous to fathers and brothers, he treated it with respect. Persuading girls to enter convents before they were old enough to understand their own needs angered him; it imposed "a rule of perpetual celibacy on young women in the most ardent time of life."[71] Girls in that "tender and dangerous age" should be treated gently by their parents.[72] No girl, above all, should be married off without consulting her, or against her will.[73] He thought the marriage of young girls to older men "contrary to nature and reason."[74]

In spite of his insistence on the authority of men over women, husband over wife, in spite of the anti-feminine railing that crept into his sermons, he was well aware that the sexes are equal before God. He warned the men of his congregation against taking pride in their preeminence, which, in this context, he treated not as a law of nature but as an arbitrary disposition by God for the maintenance of practical order. Indeed, as far as "nature" is concerned, neither sex can claim superiority; husband and wife are "equal in bed,"[75] and no one can say "my father" without implying "my mother."[76]

Calvin also denied that women are created only for procreation. God, he insisted, intends her to be man's companion, not his inferior, in a marriage that "includes all the parts and usages of life."[77] Above all he asserted the spiritual equality of women. He rejected the common association of "flesh" with women, which implied that only men possess spiritual capacities.[78] Both sexes, for him, are created in the image of God,[79] and Christ "is the head of man and woman without any distinction."[80] It also follows that Eve can no more be blamed for the Fall than Adam; indeed, in what may seem an unexpected application of the double standard, Calvin tended to assign all responsibility for it to Adam.[81]

He insisted accordingly on the religious instruction of women as well as men,[82] and he paid tribute to women recently martyred, to whom God had given "a constancy more than virile."[83] Indeed, Calvin suggested that, in principle, nothing stands in the way of the assumption by women of the highest positions in the church. The fact that Jesus, after the resurrection, had appeared first to women led him to reflect that "for a short time he took the apostolic office away from men" and committed it to women.[84] It is hardly surprising, then, that he thought Paul's prohibition against the speaking of women in church, like covering their heads, a thing indifferent, to be resolved on practical grounds.[85]

The traditional conception of human being as a hierarchy of discrete faculties suggested a relatively mild view of sin; it posited the existence of higher powers within the personality capable of directing it toward the good and thus suggested that virtue is humanly attainable. Calvin recognize the paganism in the conception, blamed Origen for contaminating Christianity with it, and associated it with the papacy. "When one asks a pagan philosopher what justice is," Calvin asserted, "he will reply that it is a life wholly regulated by virtue. And this is also how the theologians of the papacy dispute."[86] From Christ's description of the eye as "the lamp of the body," they had inferred that "men possess reason and prudence with which to choose freely between good and evil."[87] Along with this freedom

they also taught that even if human beings "cannot aspire wholly to the good
. . . when they have done what is in them, the grace of God will not be
lacking"; in short, that they can earn God's grace.[88] Although they spoke
"in passing of faith in Christ and the grace of the Holy Spirit, it is quite clear
how much nearer they are to pagan philosophers than to Christ and his
apostles."[89]

Calvin's more unified conception of human being made this relatively
optimistic understanding of the human condition impossible. If the personality is not a hierarchy, the mind cannot rule over its lower faculties. This is
why, for Calvin, Plato had been wrong in claiming that to know the good is
enough to do the good.[90] In addition, if human being is an undifferentiated
unity, sin has vitiated every part of it. It cannot be identified with, much less
limited to, the body; and no privileged area of the personality can be depended on for salvation. This was what Calvin meant by "total depravity."
The attempt of the papists to "restrict original sin to the lower part of the
soul and the grosser appetites" was, he thought, a serious mistake. When
Adam fell, he did not merely succumb to a "lower appetite," but "unspeak-
able impiety occupied the very citadel of his mind and pride penetrated to
the depths of his heart." Whoever does not recognize that these supposedly
higher areas of the personality have also been wholly corrupted "knows
nothing of original sin."[91] Total depravity means, not that there is no capacity for good in human beings, but that no human activity is altogether
blameless. The best human work "is still always spotted and corrupted with
some impurity of the flesh and has, so to speak, some dregs mixed with it."
No deed even of the saints "does not deserve shame."[92]

Unable to dispense entirely with the old psychological vocabulary, Calvin sometimes turned the traditional anthropology literally on its head by
associating sin primarily with the supposedly higher faculties. It had come
into the world when Eve "shook off the bridle" and "her mind wandered
shamelessly and intemperately, drawing the body along into the same licentiousness."[93] "Once the mind is polluted, that is, the intelligence of men
spoiled," Calvin commented, "the rest is easily corrupted."[94] Reason was
thus fatally weakened; and, "overwhelmed by so many deceptions, subjected to so many errors, dashed against so many obstacles, caught in so
many difficulties," it could no longer guide us.[95]

So flawed a "faculty" as this, in any case, could not give adequate help
on fundamental questions of human destiny. Whatever the creation might
suggest about God, natural theology can hardly give any understanding of
sin, and it is silent on its remedy. On this crucial question the earth does not
speak, the fish are mute, even the stars tell us nothing, because the human
intellect is clouded by sin:[96]

> After man's rebellion our eyes, wherever they turn, encounter God's curse,
> [which] must overwhelm our souls with despair. For even if God wills to
> manifest his fatherly favor to us in many ways, yet we cannot, by contemplat-
> ing the universe, infer that he is Father. Rather, conscience presses us within

and shows in our sin just cause for his disowning us and not regarding or recognizing us as his sons. Dullness and ingratitude follow, for our minds, as they have been blinded, do not perceive what is true. And as all our senses have become perverted, we wickedly defraud God of his glory.[97]

Nor, for Calvin, can the mind, even when it comprehends the enormity of sin, move the will to reject it. The mind is "utterly useless."[98] David himself had fallen into sin; how then can "the carnal man, dominated by innumerable lusts, control himself by his free will?"[99]

Even the behavior of animals, who are at least governed by nature, reflects badly, Calvin thought, on that of humans. A beast, he observed, "will sleep as nature requires, it will drink, it will eat according to its nature. What will a man do? He will usually pay no attention to his nature in eating and drinking. We are insatiable pits, monsters in spite of nature." A human being "wishes to be considered a reasonable creature, having mastery over the brute beasts; but if he were to become worthy of such honor, he would have to be sent to school to the beasts, he has so perverted everything."[100]

What stands out in Calvin's treatment of human sinfulness is its comprehensiveness. It includes both actual sinning and the proclivity to sin: sinfulness as being literally full of potential sins. It afflicts every stage of life, including infancy; even the youngest child bears the "hidden seed" of Adam.[101] Every human being, from this standpoint, is at every moment on the verge of sinning, about to expose himself to its fatal consequences. This conviction at once expressed and intensified Calvin's anxiety. Boundaries and categories were useless for dealing with a problem of this magnitude, and he minimized conventional differentiations between more and less serious, mortal and venial sins.[102] The notion of particular sins was for him useful, for the most part, only to describe manifestations of sin, which differ from individual to individual, time to time, and place to place. "Human nature," he remarked, "universally contains the seed of all evils, but particular vices rule and are revealed in particular men." It may be, therefore, that "not all are bloodthirsty and cruel, not all are treacherous or scurrilous," but "one tends to cruelty, another to perfidy, another to lust, another to deceit, so that there is no one who does not exhibit something of the common wickedness." But "all of us are subject, by the same inward and secret spiritual impulse, to every moral ill."[103]

Anxiety, which is rooted in distrust of the future, is for Calvin also the source of sin. In a religious context it takes the form of faithlessness, inability to believe God's promises. "Unbelief," Calvin wrote, "is the wellspring and root of all evils."[104] For each of us sin begins at the moment when, "whatever God may promise, we cannot at all apply it to ourselves but, our eyes fixed on our nakedness, we sink down dazed by fear,"[105] overwhelmed by a self-centered anxiety, filled with "solicitude," a term, Calvin pointed out, that "is used for that anxiety which comes from distrust of divine power or help."[106] In this dreadful condition, human beings, fleeing from God, seek distraction or look for earthly security, and the result is the familiar range of particular sins. "Some are carried away by ambition, others are seized by avarice, others burn with lust"; but the only result is that each one "brings down on himself the wrath of God." [107] Most disturbing of all is that, in their self-concern, men fail to appreciate the seriousness of their condition. Having regard only to personal "profit or loss," they "change with every wind." Now they are "proud as lions," now "sleeping dogs"; now they are full of "uncontrollable pride," now of "flattery." We are all "too unstable," "light-minded," "inconstant"; we "follow anything that comes along." We are "rats in straw" and "there is no order among us." [108]

It was of the deepest urgency, to Calvin, for human beings to understand the gravity of this predicament. Much of his rhetoric was devoted to the thoroughly practical end of convincing his contemporaries of their sinfulness in all its depth and horror, and the impossibility of escaping from it by any devices of their own, in particular of the kind implied by the philosophical understanding of human being. "When we come before the presence of God," he wrote, "we must put away such amusements! For there we deal with a serious matter." God, he warned in language permeated with his own anxiety, can tolerate nothing "except what is in every part whole and complete and undefiled by any corruption." He imagined the terror of this encounter. "How," he asked, "shall we reply to the heavenly judge when he calls us to account?" He pieced together Old Testament passages to intensify the dreadfulness of this prospect: here we will have to do with a God "by whose brightness the stars are darkened, by whose strength the mountains are melted, by whose wrath the earth is shaken, whose wisdom catches the wise in their craftiness, beside whose purity all things are defiled, whose righteousness not even the angels can bear, who makes not the guilty man innocent, whose vengeance when once kindled penetrates to the depths of hell." [109] The tolerance of even the smallest sin by such a God is inconceivable, [110] indeed inconsistent with his nature. We must realize in all we do that "his eyes are on us," that "he may at last produce at his tribunal all the sayings and doings of men, yea, their thoughts also," and will then "render to everyone according to his ways, that he may gather the fruit of his own doings." [111] "The least offense that we commit," he warned his congregation, "already violates the majesty of God." [112]

Calvin's seriousness on this matter is indisputable. Nevertheless it should always be remembered, in assessing his intention, that he was a rhetorician, less concerned with the objective truth of his message than with its effect on his audience. His discourse was often calculatedly therapeutic and one-sided; especially on so momentous an issue as sin, he would have thought nothing more unbalanced than absolute balance. His first purpose, when he discussed this subject, was to bring sinners to repentance. But it was also important, to Calvin, as we have observed, for God to be glorified, and this required that man should be humiliated. He "cannot, without sacrilege, claim for himself even a crumb of righteousness, for just so much is plucked and taken away from the glory of God's righteousness." [113] This required man to be "stripped naked," as Calvin put it—Montaigne would echo this thought in the "Apologie de Raimond Sebond"—lest he attribute anything to himself.[114]

Failure to recognize the rhetorical element in Calvin's discourse has sometimes resulted in the mistaken view that he thought God's image and likeness in human being totally destroyed by sin,[115] and passages in his work can be found that might be taken to support this position. "Let us hold this as an undoubted truth which no siege engines can shake," he wrote, that "the mind of man has been so completely estranged from God's righteousness that it conceives, desires, and undertakes only that which is impious, perverted, foul, impure, and infamous," that "the heart is so steeped in the poison of sin that it can breathe out nothing but a loathsome stench," and that "if some men occasionally make a show of good, their minds nevertheless ever remain enveloped in hypocrisy and deceitful craft and their hearts bound by inner perversity."[116] In our relationship with God we are worse than infants, sick and frantic, in the grip of raging appetites that hurl us headlong to our ruin.[117] "Here lies the glory of our nature," Calvin exclaimed, "that the devil has his throne within us and inhabits us body and soul."[118] Even if we admit that some residues of God's image remained in Adam, "it was so corrupted that whatever remains is a frightful deformity," and what can be discerned of it in us is "so damaged and mutilated" that it may "truly be said to be destroyed."[119]

But in other passages Calvin expressed himself very differently. "The remains of God's image still shine forth in men," he proclaimed,[120] and again, to deter murder, "We ought to consider that God has created us all in his image, so that we are all of the same nature."[121] All men may be sinners, but we should always see in them "the image of God, to which we owe all honor and love."[122]

Calvin was doubtful, not about the persistence of God's image, but about the possible consequences of asserting it. His ambivalence on this matter and his sensitivity to his audience is vividly illustrated by the unsettling rhetorical shifts in his sermon on the opening verses of the Fourth Gospel, in which he began by celebrating the implications of the Incarnation for the status of God's human creatures in the universe:

God here makes known his power in us, the greatest and most excellent of all creatures. God wishes to be glorified both in heaven and earth, and in all of his works that we see; but a great deal more in man because he has imprinted his image in us, more than in all the rest. For he has not said of the sun, of the stars, nor of any other creature, however excellent it is, "I wish to make here a masterpiece which is in my image and likeness. . . . [The Evangelist] shows us that if men" contemplate the goodness of God everywhere they look, they must also consider it in their own persons. And since God has done us this honor of being glorified in us, so that even the pagans themselves have called man a little world because one sees in him a masterpiece that excels all others, we should recognize there the virtue and power of God. It is true that we can contemplate God in all his creatures, but when he manifests himself in man, then it is as though we were looking him in the face, whereas in viewing him in other creatures we see him obscurely and as if from the back. So when it is said that God is made visible in his creatures, in them we see, so to speak, his feet, his hands, and his back; but in man we see, so to speak, his face.

But then, as though it had occurred to him in mid-sermon that he was encouraging a damnable pride in his congregation by inviting them to admire God's image in themselves, he suddenly shifted out of his celebratory mode. His tone changed abruptly, as though he were seeking to undo any harm he had done. "But the light that God had put in man" he lamented, "is almost entirely extinguished. And in fact, if we judged according to what we can now see in mortal men, we would not much esteem the grace of God. For although man was created in the image of God, he has been disfigured by sin. What is it then that we see in men? We see there an image of God that is wholly deformed and spoiled, so much has the devil spoiled it by sin." But again, as though suspecting he had gone too far, he reversed himself again in an effort to balance between the truth and the consequences of proclaiming it:

> But even if men, following Satan's suggestion, have extinguished the light of God, it is nevertheless true that the devil has not been able, by his astuteness, to prevent the light of God from shining still in the midst of the shadows. . . . So one still always sees some light that God has left there, some spark from his lamp. . . . So [for example] there is some seed of religion in men, they have some remnant of their first creation; one sees still even in the most wicked and reprobate that there is some impression of the image of God.

But, now, as if even this might be too much, he backed off again and warned his congregation that they would only make themselves more inexcusable before God if they puffed themselves up by thoughts of his image in themselves.

In spite of all this, he still managed to end on a positive note. "Inasmuch as [sinners] have been unable to profit from [God's image and likenesss in themselves], their condemnation will be so much the more grievous and will have to be redoubled. This is therefore how it is: although our nature has thus been corrupted, we nevertheless still retain some spark of the grace that God had put into our father Adam, so that the proposition is true that the light shines in darkness." [123] These passages, however they differ in emphasis, make clear Calvin's commitment to the conviction, common among Renaissance humanists, of the significance of the creation of human beings in God's image and likeness. [124]

He was remarkable among humanists, nevertheless, for the clarity with which he grasped the significance of original sin. Above all he understood, as few before him had done, its implications for historical perspective. Augustine's insistence on the universality of sin had failed to shake the respect of most Christians for the superiority of antiquity, in virtue as well as wisdom. Medieval culture, both learned and popular, continued to revere the past, as it was represented by ancient culture, by custom, or by ancestral wisdom and example. But on the basis of his understanding of original sin, Calvin was prepared to reject, in principle as well as in particular cases, the superiority attributed to the past. This helped, paradoxically, to clear away a major obstacle to the idea of progress.

He fiercely and frequently attacked custom and tradition, veneration for which protected the abuses he associated with the papacy. "The world pretends to believe," he charged, "that whatever is customary is lawful; indeed, what generally prevails carries everything with it, like a violent flood." He deplored this, associating it generally with the tendency of human beings to "wicked imitation." [125] "When others precede us, we think the same course lawful for ourselves, especially when it is not just one or another who precedes us but the custom has been accepted by all. What in itself is manifestly wrong is covered by the specious veil of public consent." This, he agreed, was not "the fault of a single age," but "it flourishes today as much as or more than ever." [126] It was, he thought, doubly reprehensible when "sons, having embraced abominations received from their fathers, pass them down in turn to their children." [127] There is nothing sacred in custom; God's will always takes precedence over it. [128]

To attack custom and tradition was to repudiate the ways of one's fathers; Calvin recognized that, just as creation in God's image raises sons to the same spiritual level as fathers, original sin reduces fathers to the same level as sons. Thus, although Calvin continued to insist that God had endowed all fathers with authority, he vastly reduced its emotional force; Calvinist paternalism could never be more than arbitrary and mechanical. He was instrumental, therefore, in bringing into the moral and social universe a Copernican revolution even more disturbing than the disorder the new astronomy had recently introduced into the cosmos. Indeed, Calvin hinted at a connection between them. "Although the stains that bespatter the works of the saints are plainly visible, though to us they are only the slightest spots," he asked, "will they not offend God's eyes, before which not even the stars are pure?" *Sub specie Dei*, at any rate, the superlunary sphere was no longer immaculate. [129]

Seniority did not evoke any special veneration in this revolutionary Calvin; indeed, he had little respect for old age. Time, he thought, rarely improved the human character. Sometimes he repeated Aristotelian platitudes about the suspicion, meanness, and calculation of old men, whose larger capacity for self-control reflects declining vitality rather than virtue. [130] He represented all the stages of life as equally dismal: in infancy, lacking both intelligence and reason, we scarcely differ from animals; when we reach manhood, we boil with lusts; in old age we are weary of life, and a nuisance and trouble to others. [131] Without God's help, advancing years make us neither better nor wiser. In fact the opposite is more likely: we tend to regress rather than improve with time, and God bestows wisdom on young and old alike. "So all pride must be cast down; and the old, because they have lived

a long time and had long experience, should realize that they do not necessarily know the secrets of the Kingdom of Heaven." [132]

These accounts of the effects of aging may cast some light on his attitude
to his own father and, when introduced into his later sermons, may also have
been an oblique confession that he was aware of his own limitations as the
illness of his last decade wore him down. Old age, he suggested, "makes
men slower and more morose." [133] He found in the deeds of Moses and
Aaron, the octogenarian leaders of Israel, an opportunity for an oblique personal confession. Their accomplishments were remarkable, he suggested,
only in the light of "the natural slowness and coldness of advanced age." "I
do not agree," he added, "with the opinion of those who think that their
dignity was advanced by their age." Advancing years would normally have
made Moses and Aaron timid and their people anxious, "since they saw
their leaders not merely old but near the age of death." [134] "Old age is morose and difficult," he declared again, in what seems like a public apology,
"and the old tend to think that an injury is done them when they are
reproved." [135]

It was only a step further to rejecting the authority of forefathers in principle. Calvin was well aware of the force of ancestral example, and he deplored it. "How easy it is to slip into the imitation of one's predecessors!"
he exclaimed in disapproval. "Whatever gathers support seems lawful, and
age always commends itself as venerable, and close examples blind us, so
that whatever has been done by our forefathers is taken as virtue without
discrimination." [136] He attributed the habit of following ancestral ways to
the political religion of antiquity. The oracle of Apollo, he had learned from
Xenophon, had "pronounced that religion best for every city and people that
had been received from remotest antiquity." This, Calvin thought, was "a
wonderful deception of the devil, who did not wish to stir up the minds of
men to reflect on what is right, but kept them in that old lethargic belief that
the authority of your ancestors is sufficient for you." [137] "When sons follow
the example of their fathers," he insisted, "they [wrongly] think themselves
innocent." [138]

He applied these convictions to the vaunted superiority of antiquity.
"When you want to justify anything," he stated sweepingly, "you certainly
do not base it on antiquity." [139] He had begun as a young man, even before
his break with the Roman church, to reflect on the alleged virtues of the
ancients; his Seneca commentary had noted, like Augustine, "what those
splendid virtues of the pagans were which are always being rehearsed so
fulsomely." "Remove ambition," he continued, "and you will have no
haughty spirits, neither Platos, nor Catos, nor Scaevolas, nor Scipios, nor
Fabriciuses." [140] Much later he wrote, "If we diligently weigh everything
that impels profane men when they fight strenuously for good causes, we
will find ambition always to have been dominant." He did not deny that the
supposed virtues of the ancients were praiseworthy; they were gifts of God,
and for this reason "we are not afraid, in common speech, to call this man

naturally good, that one naturally depraved.''[141] But such language is not altogether correct. The greatest heroes of the pagan world,

> however admirable they may be regarded on account of their reputation for virtue, not only deserve no reward but rather punishment, because by the pollution of their hearts they defile God's good works. For even though they are God's instruments for the preservation of human society in righteousness, continence, friendship, temperance, fortitude, and prudence, yet they carry out these good works of God very badly. For they are restrained from evil-doing not by genuine zeal for good but either by mere ambition, or by self-love, or by some other perverse motive. Therefore, since by the very impurity of men's hearts these good works have been corrupted as from their source, they ought no more to be reckoned among virtues than the vices that commonly deceive on account of their affinity and likeness to virtue.[142]

Calvin's knowledge of classical antiquity was largely derived from works of history that, in the tradition of ancient historiography, dealt chiefly with military heroism; and he especially attacked the praise of military leaders for their supposed virtues.[143] He particularly detested Alexander the Great, whom he indicted for cruelty, envy and emulation, and a pride so vast that, though he was small of stature, the conquest of one world was insufficient to satisfy him. Alexander had displayed "neither prudence, or seriousness, or judgment, or any other virtue." He was Calvin's most extreme example of the refusal to recognize limits [*immoderatio*]. "Rashness seized the man; and even if he had not tasted wine, his ambition would have intoxicated him. Hence Alexander's whole life was inebriation, for in that man there was no moderation nor order."[144]

Calvin also loathed the ancient Romans, whom he criticized as though they were the forefathers of his enemies in modern Rome. They too had been insatiable tyrants. He had taken over, even as a young man, Augustine's dim view of the Roman conquests as "a great robbery."[145] Cruel, insatiable, and licentious, the Romans had "transferred to themselves the luxuries of almost the entire world, whatever was sumptuous and precious in Asia Minor, in Greece, in Macedonia, in all the islands, and even in greater Asia, and even this could not satisfy them."[146] The arrogance of the Romans was matched by their cruelty:

> There never was such an outrageous domination; wars begot wars, and in their greed for human blood they hardly spared their own. They were like an insatiable whirlpool that absorbed almost the whole world, and their pride crushed and trampled it under foot. Cruelty was added to pride so that all would look up to the Romans, and whoever won the favor of Rome by flattery could tyrannize over his own people. By these arts almost all Greece was destroyed. They well knew that many innocent people were indiscriminately killed in every city. That game delighted them, for they knew how easy it was to attract to themselves the might of the whole world where there was no strength or wisdom or power to oppose them.[147]

Like other Renaissance humanists Calvin noted with disfavor the decline of Rome from republic into monarchy. He described how the Caesars had usurped the liberty and authority of the Senate, concentrating all power in their own hands while craftily pretending to be no more than tribunes of the people. He also gave a republican interpretation to the fourth beast of the Apocalypse, which, in Daniel's vision, represented a kingdom, long associated with Rome, which would devour the whole earth. It reminded Calvin of how the Roman emperors had "dominated with acuteness and cunning instead of proceeding openly" and of how, "although they always asserted the consular power to be supreme in the republic, they could not restrain themselves but vomited out many insulting speeches." [148] God had fittingly punished the Romans by giving them increasingly shameful and infamous emperors. [149] Under such leadership republican institutions decayed. Senators, whom the Romans boasted were great as kings, were actually "thieves and tyrants" who rarely handed down justice; the empire itself was "a confused and monstrous mixture," "a mingling of impurities," "a dreadful pollution": all that Calvin most dreaded and abominated. [150]

Religion had inevitably decayed among so wicked a people. Whereas the Greeks, Calvin thought, had at least remained faithful to "the gods that had been handed down by their ancestors"—in this case a virtue—the Romans "dared, fearlessly and wantonly, to spit on all religions and, as far as they could, to introduce atheism." [151] He was particularly incensed by Cicero's observation that Judaism was "incompatible with the majesty of our Empire, the dignity of our name, and the institutions of our ancestors." [152] He also accused the Romans of the same cynical manipulation of religion for political ends as he discerned among contemporary rulers. "Truly," he asserted, "there was among them not even a superstitious fear of God; and although they boasted pompously of the piety both of themselves and their ancestors, anyone who carefully studies their writings will easily perceive what they really believed: they thought all gods ridiculous, and they abused the name and appearance of piety, in the interest of their own arrogance, to retain all their subjects in obedience." [153] The Romans were Calvin's most conspicuous example of the hypocritical exploitation of piety, and therefore also of the superficiality of pagan virtue. Again he followed Augustine: "Although there have often existed among unregenerate men remarkable examples of gentleness, faith, temperance, and generosity, it is nevertheless certain that they were only deceitful masks. Curtius and Fabricius were famous for courage, Cato for temperance, Scipio for courtesy and generosity, Fabius for endurance, but only in the sight of men, in public esteem. To God nothing is pure unless it proceeds from the source of all purity." [154]

A society that engendered such unseemly behavior, Calvin felt, could hardly have produced an adequate moral philosophy; and he was also a vigorous critic of ancient ethics. He attacked it for its lack of insight into the realities of the human condition; ancient philosophers had known nothing of "the corruption of nature originating in man's defection," as a result of which they "mistakenly confuse two very diverse states of man," that is, before and after the Fall. "They sought a whole building in a ruin, and a well knit structure in scattered fragments." [155] Their blindness to original sin was itself "remarkable as evidence of it." [156] From this obtuseness came other errors such as the praise of fortitude, which, more clearly scrutinized, discloses itself as "nothing but obstinacy or raging fury, as in fanatics [*phreneticis*]." [157] Like Petrarch, Calvin denounced the ancient cult of glory. [158]

The ethical teachings of the philosophers were also inadequate in practice. They "discoursed at their ease about the virtues" without any attention to the realities of moral struggle. [159] They could only *commend* virtue, a cold and useless mode of teaching. [160] On this point Calvin again sounded like Petrarch: although philosophers "argue admirably about avarice and generosity and in some measure demonstrate the difference between them, they never penetrate hearts." [161] Although they "have handed down many excellent precepts which they think contain righteousness, they could never bestow it on anybody. For who has obtained the capacity for living well from their rules? It is of little use to know what true righteousness is if we meanwhile lack it." [162] He noted that Brutus, who as a Stoic had said much to commend "the power and providence of God," could only complain, when defeated by Antony, that "fortune rules over human affairs." "The beliefs of all the impious," Calvin concluded, "fluctuate with changing events." [163] He contrasted philosophical exhortation with the passion of the Psalmist, who, "as if he had escaped from hell," proclaims victory out of the fullness of his heart. [164]

There was considerable precedent in the Christian past for rejecting the authority of pagan sages; there was less for the coolness Calvin sometimes expressed, which was related to his criticism of the pagans, toward the Fathers of Christian antiquity. Like the ancient sages, the church Fathers were only men, he pointed out; and although they had much of value to say, they were too concerned to come to terms with ancient philosophy and as a result "have left us a cold and dissembling theology." [165] It is therefore necessary to "decide prudently which among the fathers to imitate," remembering also that the Lord may, since their time, have "prescribed a different mode of behavior." [166] Indeed, all the practices of the ancient church must be examined critically. "I do not grant that that age was so free of all defect," Calvin asserted, "that whatever was done then must be taken as the rule." [167] He saw Christian antiquity as hardly a more reliable guide for the modern world than pagan antiquity. [168]

Spiritual fathers in the medieval church were, for Calvin, far less reliable. They had not only failed to correct the mistakes of antiquity but added to them offenses of their own. Patristic writings "that were marred with a few spots here and there" were "utterly defiled" when they fell into "these men's unwashed hands." [169] Theologians since antiquity had commonly justified their own errors by appealing to the Fathers; they should now "acknowledge both their own wickedness and that of the fathers." [170] All these fathers had collaborated in varying degrees in the deformation of the church that had required the reformation to which Calvin devoted his life.

This chapter has dealt with some of the implications of Calvin's conception of human being as both less and more than intellectual. Another set of implications concerned what the knowledge of a personality understood in this way can be like. The conclusions Calvin reached on this subject are the concern of the next chapter.

9

Knowing

By rejecting the traditional sovereignty of reason, a holistic conception of the human personality raised doubts about the capacity of human beings to know the world as it is. Calvin's conception of human being as both more and less than intellectual thus precipitated him into the middle of the general crisis about the nature and possibilities of knowledge, already apparent in the fourteenth century, that would end only with the philosophical and scientific movements of the seventeenth century.[1] Old certainties had been crumbling on all sides. Jean Gerson, the most influential theologian of the fifteenth century, had remarked on this. "Frequently opinions among doctors are not only different but contrary, at times because of temperaments, at times because of different circumstances," he wrote; "whence arises that comedy, 'So many heads, so many opinions.' "[2] Not everyone deplored this. Two generations before Calvin, the fiery Florentine preacher and reformer Girolamo Savonarola had found the works of the Greek skeptics so salutary that, according to a contemporary biographer, "shortly before his death he ordered that they be translated from Greek into Latin, since he loathed the ignorance of many people who boasted that they knew something."[3] Philosophy and theology in the universities had for some time been dominated by the nominalist *moderni*, skeptics about the capacity of human beings to grasp the essences of things. Rabelais's Gargantua described the disarray a growing skepticism had wrought in the schools:

> The world's got into a fine old mess since first I began to watch it. Now we've come to this, have we? So the most learned and cautious philosophers have all joined the thinking establishment of the Pyrrhonians, Aporrhetics, Skeptics, and Ephectics, have they? Good God be praised! Truly, from now on it will be easier to seize lions by the mane, horses by the hair, oxen by the horns, wild oxen by the muzzle, wolves by the tail, goats by the beard, and birds by the claw, than to catch philosophers of this kind by the words they speak.[4]

Lay humanists had early tended to skepticism. "Every truth that is grasped by reason can be made doubtful by a contrary reason," Salutati observed; "the more you know, the more truly you will know that you know nothing at all. For, to speak properly, what to us is knowledge is really only a kind of reasonable uncertainty." [5] Machiavelli thought that "in general men are deceived a great deal, though in particular things not so much"; [6] and Guicciardini was baffled by the complexity of things. "It is a great error," he declared, "to speak of the world generally and absolutely and, so to speak, by rule, because almost everything has distinctions and exceptions through the variety of circumstances, which cannot be evaluated by a single standard; and these distinctions and exceptions are not found written in books, but discretion must teach them." [7] He meant that the certainty attributed to knowledge transmitted in books was crumbling. Similar misgivings pervaded northern humanism. Cornelius Agrippa allegorized the story of the Fall into a lesson in skepticism. Adam, Agrippa suggested, represented faith, which had been led astray by reason in the shape of Eve, who had in turn been misled by sense experience in the guise of the serpent. [8] Albrecht Dürer mourned that "there is falsehood in our knowledge, and darkness is so firmly implanted in us that even our groping fails." [9] These troubled statements are not all of the same order, but they will serve to characterize the world Calvin inhabited.

Given the distrust of general propositions in much of this testimony, it is hardly surprising that the close connection between words and things had also become problematic. While nominalists distinguished between words or terms [*termini*], which are general, and things, which are particular, humanists were discovering that language serves many functions besides the communication of information about things, and indeed that some communication that *appears* to transmit knowledge really has quite a different purpose: persuasion, perhaps, or even deception.

For most thinkers, the disjunction between words and things was a cause for regret; it was linked with vapidity, pride, hypocrisy, and the general breakdown of communication. Thomas More had denounced his enemies for "gaye gloryouse wordes" that lacked meaning; [10] and Calvin's friend Melanchthon revealed his attachment to the comforting identification of words and things in his attack on "new and prodigious fancies and monstrous expressions by which, since they have no basis in reality, nothing can be understood." [11] But these protests only show that something had gone wrong.

From this perspective, philosophical discourse, especially as represented by Scholastic theology, seemed at best useless, at worst morally suspect, and usually misleading. All philosophers, declared the Spanish humanist Juan Luis Vives, explicitly including Plato and Aristotle, "refused to stick to this earth and to be contented with those things they could easily reach. . . . Unable to understand themselves, they tried to search and to pry into mysteries which by far exceed all human capacity. The less they knew, the more they boldly and arrogantly defined." [12] Melanchthon, like St. Augustine, dismissed philosophy as "a chaos of carnal dreams." [13] But the unreliability of philosophers, the wisest men of the past, only made more vivid the unreliability of all past knowing, all ancestral wisdom, all tradition, all custom. Many theologians had abandoned the effort to establish theology as a science in favor of a fideism at once authoritarian and obscurantist.

But because human existence is hardly tolerable under conditions of absolute doubt, Renaissance thinkers also began to experiment with ways of knowing traditionally rejected as unreliable; after all, if no knowledge is secure, it might at least be possible to recognize degrees of uncertainty and settle for maximum probability. From this standpoint the contingency of much human knowledge was no longer grounds for rejecting it out of hand. Now, for example, empirical knowledge, whether in the narrower sense of knowledge gained through the fallible senses or more broadly as everything we can learn through experience, acquired a respect not previously accorded it.[14] Popular proverbs, encapsulated collective experience, were increasingly cited.

Although the truth claims of such contingent knowledge remained ambiguous, it was often conspicuously useful; and a growing instrumentalism can also be discerned in Renaissance thought, a conviction that knowledge locked in the mind is worthless, that it has value only in the degree to which it can be put to work in the world. This too was reinforced by Quintilian.[15] For Vives "all our studies should be applied to the necessities of life, to the benefit of body and soul, to the cultivation and increase of piety." Study otherwise is not only vain but harmful.[16] For Melanchthon a true philosopher "takes a theory out of academic obscurity and makes it practically useful."[17] In his reading of Copernicus, Andreas Osiander suggested that we might adopt heliocentrism as a hypothesis because, whether true or false, it is useful to explain the phenomena.[18] Machiavelli's defense of religion on the ground not of its truth but of its social and political utility was an extreme example of this tendency.

Above all, teachings were esteemed for their ethical utility. Petrarch's great discourse on his own ignorance made the point with particular force. "What is the *use*," he asked, "of knowing what virtue is if it is not loved when known? What is the *use* of knowing sin if it is not abhorred when known?"[19] Although no one suggested that useless knowledge is not knowledge at all, its pursuit was regularly denounced as "curiosity." For Gerson curiosity meant rejecting "the more useful things" for others "less beneficial."[20] Petrarch thanked God, perhaps disingenuously, for having given him "sluggish and moderate gifts and a mind that does not saunter wantonly," in short for having spared him the temptation of curiosity.[21]

All these novel approaches to knowing had still another major result. Now it was no longer an essential criterion for the validity of knowledge that it fit coherently into a great system of thought and that it be consistent with all other knowledge. This criterion now seemed presumptuous, for it seemed to require of the human mind capacities only God could claim. It was also irrelevant to the human uses of knowledge, which retained all its utility even if it remained stubbornly discrete, incoherent, even contradictory and paradoxical. There might still be order among things; but this had now to be understood not as *the* order of things, which was God's affair, but *an* order imposed on a few things by some human beings for their own human, limited, and transient purposes. Such a conception opened up the possibility of many orders of things, as many as might be useful.

These changing attitudes to human knowing had influenced theology long before Calvin. Their general result was a humanization of theology based on a recognition of the limits of human understanding and an awareness that theology, however sublime its subject, is nevertheless a *human* enterprise, that it sees only darkly and uncertainly, not face to face. Erasmus, to whom Calvin owed so much, had known this. "Our fight," he wrote of Luther, "is not with the word of God, but with your vehement assertion, for the word of God does not contradict itself. Rather its human interpretations are at variance, one with another." [22]

Calvin's awareness that knowing had become a problem is basic to his thought; his bouts of dogmatism were symptomatic of the distress it caused him. [23] His concern with the problem of knowledge was embedded in his Renaissance vision of the past, with its division of history into three ages defined by the ebb and flow of human knowledge: antiquity had been enlightened; its learning had perished in a dark and intermediate age of barbarism and ignorance under the papacy; and now, at last, the light of learning had begun to glow again. Calvin exploited this scheme to justify religious reformation; as we have seen, he blamed the world's ignorance on the papacy and, like Erasmus, on its minions the monks. Popes, the primary agents of contemporary barbarism, had permitted "both themselves and others to be ignorant of and to neglect and scorn the true religion which is taught in the Scriptures and ought to be universally maintained." They had audaciously fabricated "new doctrines" and "iniquitous traditions" in place of Gospel truth. [24] That the claims of the old church to knowledge were false was Calvin's central complaint against the church in which he had received his first instruction. He aimed to replace ignorance and error with *truth*.

The importance of knowledge required him to consider the nature of religious truth in the *Institutes*. In its first two books he discussed what human beings can know and how they know it. The titles of these books announce this concern: "The Knowledge of God the Creator" and "The Knowledge of God the Redeemer in Christ." The first nine chapters of Book I constitute a kind of epistemological introduction to the work as a whole, as they consider the possibility and the processes of the knowledge of God before proceeding to its content. A major section of Book II is then concerned with what constitutes a specifically Christian knowledge. [25] Here and elsewhere Calvin reflected the general reservations of his age about the possibility of certain knowledge.

His doubts on this score were based on two considerations, not always clearly distinguished. One was largely philosophical. Human beings, for Calvin, are limited by their creatureliness and the incomprehensibility of a Creator whose will, the source of all things, is impenetrable. This meant that in principle, as creatures, human beings can claim nothing but a fragile and contingent knowledge of anything; certainty depends on God's grace. "Our members are naturally endowed with his gifts," Calvin declared, but "God keeps their use in his hand, so that what the ears hear and the eyes see must be ranked among his daily benefits; unless he quickened our sense at each moment all their power would soon vanish."[26] In addition the mind has been darkened by the Fall, which made "the very seat of reason" unreliable: "everything sound in our minds has been corrupted."[27]

Failure to remember these fundamental realities had resulted, Calvin believed, in serious mistakes about how and what we can know. One of these was basing claims to knowledge on ancient tradition, which tended "to inflate minds with pride and to render them more ferocious."[28] Antiquity, Calvin insisted, is irrelevant to truth; he ridiculed "counting up the number of ages an error has prevailed," as an argument in its favor.[29] The ancient fathers, he noted, had sometimes deviated from "the purity and precision of God's Word through weakness of the flesh or through ignorance; they had "mixed together hay with gold, straw with silver, wood with precious stones" and "often turned away from the right method of building."[30] Respect for antiquity had blinded posterity to their errors, which the papacy had exploited to establish its tyranny; and Christians had been "thrown into a labyrinth from which there is no exit."[31] Neither "the authority of the fathers or the practice of antiquity" could provide certainty.[32]

Nor, for certainties, did he consider reason much use. The human understanding is blind "on the highest matters,"[33] and it certainly cannot supply knowledge "of God, true righteousness, and the mysteries of the heavenly kingdom." Reason is lost in such things; to it they are "like a labyrinth."[34] We "are not led to God and do not even approach him by reason."[35] Scripture commonly employs the figure of smoke, Calvin noted, to convey the obscurity of divine things.[36]

Above all, for Calvin, reason cannot grasp the Gospel. For those most endowed with learning and intelligence, Christ crucified can only be "weakness and foolishness," the way of redemption a fable; wisdom is of no importance for faith.[37] It is futile, therefore, to try to support the Gospel with philosophy; even the ancient philosophers, the more they sought to approach God, only became more distant from him.[38] Calvin did not deny that "excellent sentiments" inspired by God himself could be found in the works of "philosophers and profane writers," but he thought these "radically contaminated," so that anything based on them is obscured by "a huge mass of errors."[39]

The limits of the human mind would appear, then, to make natural theology virtually impossible: nature, in this perspective, is for Calvin "nothing," God is "all," and in any case the heavens "are not transparent."[40] Nature can provide "nothing certain or solid or clear-cut"; its findings are so confused that it leads only to the worship of "an unknown God."[41] The proper response to nature, in any case, is emotional rather than intellectual; we are not so much to understand it as to appreciate it. Insofar as we can grasp the wonderful order of the heavens, Calvin thought, it should "ravish us with astonishment." The best we can conclude from inspecting it is that "God has made such a masterpiece that we should admire it, confessing that we cannot comprehend a thing so high and so profound and secret." [42]

In the absence of divine revelation, therefore, Calvin recommended, on religious matters, a deliberate agnosticism, a *docta ignorantia* that allows God to be wiser than we are. [43] "To be ignorant of things which it is neither possible nor lawful to know," he argued, "is to be learned." [44] He retold with approval Cicero's anecdote about Simonides who, when asked by Hiero the Tyrant what God is, requested a day to consider, asked for further delays as the question was repeated, and finally concluded that the question only became more baffling the longer he thought about it. "He wisely suspended judgment," Calvin concluded, "on a subject so obscure." [45] This comes close to the famous remark—so shocking to the pious—attributed to Protagoras: "About the gods I have no knowledge whether they exist or do not exist. There are many obstacles to such knowledge, for instance the obscurity of the subject and the shortness of human life." [46]

Calvin continued, to be sure, to insist on God's rationality. What appears chaotic and meaningless to us, he argued, is nevertheless "governed by his inestimable wisdom"; [47] however incomprehensible his ways may appear, they are nevertheless infused with "the best reason"; [48] and although God may seem variable to us, he is "never inconsistent nor unlike himself." [49] But God's rationality is impenetrable to his creatures. Whatever it is, it is nothing like human rationality, so imperfect and obscured by sin. Calvin had only limited respect, then, for the competence of the human mind in earthly matters, where, even in his most measured statements, he could describe it only as not altogether worthless. [50] It sometimes seemed to him a vast and unstable confusion, "entangled and intertwined like the branches of a tree," driven aimlessly "hither and thither" by every passing novelty. [51]

Believing the human mind incompetent to grasp even the Ten Commandments, he was critical of ancient moral philosophy. "If we want to measure our reason by God's law, the pattern of perfect righteousness," he declared, "we shall find in how many respects it is blind." It fails to comprehend at all the first table of the Law, and only imperfectly grasps the second. [52]

It is hardly surprising, then, that Calvin's attitude, not only to Scholasticism but to all philosophy, was less than positive. He most opposed it when it "contaminated" religion; he thought philosophers peculiarly tempted to attempt "to penetrate heaven." [53] Even when he was most generous about philosophy, he emphasized its limitations. "I do not deny," he wrote, "that one can read clever and apt reflections about God here and there in the philosophers, but these always betray a giddy imagination." [54] What even the best among them said of religion—Calvin probably meant Plato—"is not only frigid but empty." [55]

But he reserved his full scorn for speculative philosophy, of which Athens was his symbol as it had been for Tertullian. "There is no doubt," he asserted, "that God allowed the Athenians to fall into extreme folly so that they might demonstrate to every age that all the acuteness of the human mind, aided by learning and teaching, is only foolishness in relation to the Kingdom of God."[56] Philosophers were his "most potent example" of human weakness: "not one of them can be found who has not fallen away from solid knowledge into pointless and erroneous speculations. Most of them are sillier than old women."[57] Like Augustine he was particularly repelled by their inability to reach agreement. Among philosophers, he exclaimed, "how shameful is the diversity! Each one camouflages his utterances with his great wit and the grace of his art and knowledge, but if you look more closely, you will find only fleeting unrealities."[58] This came close to calling philosophy "mere rhetoric," a neat revenge for a rhetorician. "If anyone prefers it in a word," Calvin charged, "philosophy is nothing but persuasive speech that insinuates itself into the minds of men with fine and plausible arguments." He attributed this conception to Paul: "In my judgment, he means [by "philosophy"] whatever men invent out of themselves when they want to know something by their own understanding, and that not without a specious pretext of reason, in order that it might appear probable."[59]

His sharpest attacks on philosophy were directed against Scholasticism as the most flagrant example of the attempt of philosophers to storm heaven. He distinguished between more and less sound Schoolmen, but even the former—whom he chose not to mention by name—repelled him because of their "thorny subtleties."[60] He forgot the flirtations of the Fathers with philosophy when he imagined them standing in judgment on Scholasticism. "All the Fathers," he wrote, "detested with one heart the contamination of God's Holy Word by the subtleties of sophists and the squabbles of dialecticians [which] obscure the simplicity of Scripture with endless contentions and worse than sophistic brawls. . . . Why, if the Fathers were now brought back to life and heard such brawling art as these persons call speculative theology, there is nothing they would less suppose than that these folk were disputing about God!"[61] The Schoolmen, for Calvin, "malignantly converted prudence into cunning in order to construct for themselves profound cogitations with which shamelessly to insult God."[62]

His denunciations of Scholasticism recapitulated the attacks of generations of Renaissance humanists. Some of his charges were directed against the abstract intellectuality of Scholasticism and were closely related to his anthropology. In Scholastic discourse, Calvin charged, "vain men weary themselves with speculations which lack, so to speak, any practical value"; this was a peculiar "madness."[63] "Today," he charged, "sophists come to mock God with their sophistical subtleties."[64] He also attacked Scholastic discourse as incomprehensible. He reminded Sadoleto of this as one humanist to another: "Do you remember how it was when our [reformers] appeared, and what kind of teaching candidates for the ministry learned in the schools? You yourself know that it was mere sophistry, and sophistry so twisted, involved, tortuous, and puzzling, that Scholastic theology might well be described as a species of secret magic."[65] Such theology was only "babble" and "chatter"; its questions were "frivolous."[66]

The Schoolmen did not truly engage with the Gospel. "In the shady cloisters of the schools," Calvin wrote, "anyone can easily and readily prattle about the value of works in justifying men. But when we come into the presence of God we must put away such amusements! For there we deal with a serious matter, and do not engage in frivolous word battles."[67] The Schoolmen treated even repentance abstractly, having "never awakened from their brute stupor to feel a thousandth part, or even less, of their faults."[68] Sadoleto himself had "too indolent a theology, as is almost always the case with those who have never had experience in serious struggles of conscience."[69]

With such accusations Calvin mingled the equally serious charge of "curiosity," the immoderate pursuit of knowledge, to which we are "impelled by nature and therefore ask frivolous questions. To curiosity we add audacity and temerity, so that we do not hesitate to make assertions about unknown and hidden matters. From these two causes has been born a good part of Scholastic theology."[70] God "does not wish us to be too wise" but to exhibit "sobriety"; we must not seek to know more than "it pleases him to teach us." When he "is our teacher and we hear him speak, he is able to give us prudence and discretion to understand his teaching, and we cannot fail in that; but when our Lord keeps his mouth closed we must also keep our senses closed and hold them captive." He imagined himself questioning a wretch afflicted with the lust to know more than he should: "I wish to know this." "And why do you wish to know it?" "Because it pleases me." God had appeared "in a whirlwind and dark cloud" to discourage such curiosity.[71]

Behind the intellectual excesses of the Schoolmen, for Calvin, were pride and ambition, the "secret poison" that he discerned in "all who persistently quarrel over words."[72] The *quaestiones* "argued today in the schools of the Sorbonne" were only an "ostentatious display of intellectual sharpness." There "one question leads to another, for there is no end to them when everyone indulges his vanity in seeking to know more than he ought." Concocted from nothing, these questions produce "infinite quarrels." Once more he was reminded of the weather: "Just as dense clouds, when it is hot, are not dispersed without thunder, these thorny questions boil up into contentions."[73]

Calvin found much to reject in what had passed for knowledge; meanwhile he was formulating another conception of knowledge more appropriate to the conception of human being examined in the previous chapter. If the personality is conceived as a mysterious unity, knowing must be reconceived as a function of the whole, above all involving its "center," the heart. Unlike philosophical knowledge, a knowledge of the heart is not coldly objective but suffused with feeling. David, who "did not coldly philosophize about God's precepts but gave himself up to them with earnest affection," provided Calvin with an example of such knowledge.[74] This is what it means fully, with the whole of one's being, to know.

Faith, as knowledge, is thus, for Calvin, not simply "a common assent to the evangelical history"; it involves "the heart rather than the head and the affections rather than the understanding."[75] "What help is it," he asked, "to know a God with whom we have nothing to do? Our knowledge should serve first to teach us fear and reverence; secondly, with it as our guide and teacher, to seek every good from him" and "completely to trust in him."[76] By the same token, knowledge of Christ is not "a doctrine of the tongue but of life. It is not apprehended by the understanding and memory alone, as other disciplines are, but it is received only when it possesses the whole soul and finds a seat and resting place in the inmost affection of the heart. It must enter our heart and pass into our daily living and so transform us into itself that it may not be unfruitful for us."[77] Calvin was here chiefly concerned with the place of knowledge in the spiritual life, but his account suggests what we mean when we distinguish between ordinary knowing and "really knowing" in all areas of life.

The location of faith in the heart also suggests the inwardness of real knowledge, and it explains why Calvin preferred the ear to the eye as its receptor. Whereas the eye goes out to its object, the ear conveys what it receives into the heart. Calvin suggests, at times, a bias against visual experience. He thought it impossible to give visual representation to the spiritual; neither God nor the human spirit can be painted, he observed, conventionally associating attempts at such representation with idolatry and more specifically with the papacy.[78] We must rise above "what is revealed to our eyes."[79] The Christian life depends on "God's mouth"; because "mute visions are cold," he always *speaks* to us, and faith begins when we listen to his voice.[80] Thus we truly *see* only after we *hear*. This required him, he thought, to make the point that although a sacrament is an outward and visible sign, it is based on God's word.[81] All of this had practical implications for the work of the church; it suggested that preaching was far more important than the Roman church appeared to believe.[82] Indeed, Calvin thought oral instruction best in all teaching. "The living voice," he declared, "has a greater effect in exciting our attention, or at least teaches us more surely and with greater profit, than simply seeing things without oral instruction."[83]

His inwardness also stimulated in him a typically Renaissance esteem for learning from experience; he was resolved to be faithful to experience, "the father of prudence,"[84] wherever it might lead. Experience polishes "those who, by nature, are rough,"[85] and it "sinks deeper."[86] Like Erasmus, Calvin was fond of proverbs because they summarize common experience. He sprinkled his sermons with them. "Experience shows, and we have common proverbs about it," he might remark, that parents who fail to punish their children "send them to the gibbet."[87]

He also allowed experience a large part in religious life. There, he declared, "there are two kinds of knowledge: the knowledge of faith and what is called experimental knowledge,"[88] which work together. Thus, as he had argued at the beginning of the *Institutes*, "experimental knowledge," the experience of our own misery, turns us to God and so leads to faith.[89] His respect for experience is also related to his perception of God as power; for

God's wisdom is hidden from us, but we constantly experience his power. At the same time the affective knowledge of faith is the deepest of all experiences.

Because empirical knowledge is *affective*, it is also *effective*: with this insight Calvin clarified and strengthened the instrumentalism of Renaissance culture. The belief that knowledge is "for use" dissolved the boundary between the contemplative and active life; it brought biblical scholarship and theological reflection out of the study and into the world.[90] Calvin praised "the liberal arts and sciences" as "a most useful instrument not only for piety but for daily life."[91] This attitude was also an element in his distrust of "curiosity." "We are led by wild appetites," he charged, "to know things that are not useful, that cannot edify us either in faith or in the fear of God." God requires us "to learn in his school what is useful for constructing a holy life"; he "does not at all want us to be wise, to be speculative, to fly in the air, but to know how we must live."[92]

The antithesis of curiosity, a willful ignorance, was equally opposed to utility; for Calvin useful knowledge is in the middle between these two extremes. There were, he proclaimed, "two extreme vices in men":

> Those who want to be wise and intelligent give themselves up to much vain curiosity; they speculate, they bustle high and low and are insatiable, they desire to know this and that, they never rest because they are always working at vain and useless things. That is one very bad extreme, when men do not know their limit but flutter about and plunge into abysses so deep that they can never get out. On the other hand, those who do not want to torment themselves so, what are they doing? They become like brutes, as we see by experience, above all in the papacy. I ask you, do we not have there a fine mirror of that folly in men, that they think themselves well content with their plainness, wish to know nothing at all, and close the door to what ought to be common to all men? In short, for fear of being too curious they become like cows or other brute animals, without intelligence. And we see that those who do not know a word of Latin, speak Latin to make themselves more stupid, *Mitte arcana Dei*, that is, we shouldn't inquire into the secrets of God. This is how men always exceed their limits, not being able to keep to the mean.[93]

The most important knowledge of all, that which God imparts to his people, is for Calvin supremely and exclusively practical. Scripture contains nothing "that is not useful to us," nothing "but what is expedient."[94] It "keeps us under control and makes us walk in the fear and obedience of God; it makes us put all our trust in him so that we invoke him."[95] But Calvin's insistence on the unity of knowledge and practice was expressed above all in his insistence that faith—the most real type of knowledge—must find expression in works. Faith is not a thing that, "content with empty speculation, merely flits in the brain." It must "take root in the heart,"[96] and then it "affects the whole man with a hundred times more efficacy than the frigid exhortations of the philosophers."[97] Calvin objected to Catholicism because, as it seemed to him, its conception of faith as intellectual assent deprived it of efficacy. Papal theology was only "the bombast of the East Wind, which dries out what it touches and has no substance to feed and nourish poor souls." It offers "no more edification in the hope of the life of heaven or spiritual benefit than the demonstrations of Euclid": dryness of another kind. Its "chop logic," its "questions and quarrels, bear no fruit."[98]

All these tendencies in Calvin's thought—his reservations about the possibility of human knowledge, his detestation of speculation, his belief in knowledge as an experience of the whole personality, his emphasis on listening and inward appropriation, his empiricism, and his concern with the utility of knowledge—compelled him also, if not consistently, to adopt a remarkably human view of the theological enterprise. He understood, at least sometimes, that theology, as a human enterprise, does not state truths in an absolute sense, from God's standpoint. Its truths are as limited as the human beings who develop them. It may be that he did not himself immediately or fully recognize this. The first sentence in the first edition of the *Institutes* reads: "Almost the whole of sacred doctrine [*sacra doctrina*] consists of two parts: knowledge of God and of ourselves," a formula he had taken from Cicero. This rather absolute wording suggested that he held, in 1536, a traditional conception of theology as *God's* truth rather than ours. But the second edition, three years later, made an interesting change, as though something had troubled him about the earlier wording. Now, for "sacred doctrine," he substituted "our wisdom [*sapienta nostra*]," that is, the best sort of knowledge we limited creatures can manage.[99]

At any rate, Calvin's tendency to humanize theology shaped much of his discourse. It is apparent in his rejection of systematic theology, in the traditional sense of scientific discourse.[100] He knew that good teaching calls for orderly presentation, but this too is only a question of utility. The superiority of Scripture to philosophy derived in part from the fact that "the Spirit of God, because he taught without affectation, did not adhere so exactly or continuously to a methodical plan."[101] It would be "preposterous," he wrote of Moses and the prophets, "to reduce what they bring together to the rules of philosophy."[102] Calvin always aimed to be a biblical theologian in the humanist mode.

His repudiation of system was reflected positively in his recognition of the foolishness of Christianity. This gave him, I think, some difficulty, but not only because of the side of him that honored the intellect. He was by temperament *serious*; anxious about so much, he found it hard to take things lightly. He could not have written a *Praise of Folly*; it seems doubtful that he appreciated the seriousness behind Erasmus's lighter passages, much less that he could have enjoyed *Gargantua et Pantagruel*. He recognized that the Gospel must be folly to the wise, but his respect for wisdom made him uneasy with the texts that taught this. He worried, indeed, about what the biblical praise of folly might lead to. By "folly," he wrote,

we do not understand that men should be stupid, so that those taught good sciences must forget everything, and that those who have a good natural intelligence should brutalize themselves, as though none could be Christian unless he resembled a beast rather than a man. Christianity requires us to be children not in intelligence but in malice. The whole point is that no one should bring into the church of Jesus Christ a vain confidence in his own competence or knowledge, that no one should be inflated with pride or full of prejudice so as to reject what is proposed before having considered it.[103]

He took *seriously*, however, the paradox of the Gospel. He was less enthusiastic about it than Luther, but he agreed with Luther in principle; and he published a *Traité des scandales* in which he recognized the Gospel as the scandal of scandals: because it glorified not the magnificent and sublime but the humble and lowly. This was, perhaps, as close as he could come to an Erasmian playfulness. Jesus knew, he declared at the outset of this work, that "there are many things in the doctrine of the Gospel and its profession contrary to human understanding":

Many things are contained there that seem unreasonable to human judgment, even mad and deserving to be mocked. For it is said there that the Son of God, who is eternal life, put on our flesh, was made mortal man; that by his death we have acquired life; that in his damnation we are justified and in his curse we are saved. That is so contrary to our carnal sense that those who seem the most shrewd reject it utterly. Similarly, when the Gospel deprives us of any praise for our wisdom, virtue, and justice and leaves us nothing but condemnation, it is impossible that we should not be greatly offended.[104]

Calvin's acceptance of paradox, however ambivalent, signified not only his appreciation of the mystery at the center of faith but also his insistence on the limits of human rationality and his openness to all the contradictory realities of human experience. "There are some," he observed, "who would like in their disputes always to draw conclusions in the fashion of the philosophers, that everything should be put in order so that there should be no diversity at all and there should be agreement everywhere; but such people have never known what it is to be touched by God and to endure his judgments. And why? God treats us so fiercely that everything becomes obscure. And in fact there are also incongruous things in us: sometimes we desire to live and sometimes we desire to die."[105] For Calvin, too, there were more things in heaven and earth than are dreamt of in philosophy.

10

Power

Calvin was in no respect more a child of his century than in his tendency to conceive of the issues that most troubled him as problems of strength and weakness. A vocabulary of anxiety pervades his discourse, as we have seen; but so does a vocabulary of power and impotence: power as energy, creativity, life, and warmth; impotence as lethargy, dullness, death, and coldness. Because it expressed his sense of powerlessness to control the future, his anxiety was itself closely related to his preoccupation with power. The evils in the world were caused, for him, chiefly by abuses of power. His ethic of self-control was based on a belief that the passions can be subjected to the power of reason; and when he relinquished the conception of the human personality on which that notion was based, he substituted a conception of the personality as a bundle of spiritual energies. He was a humanist because he was convinced of the power of language, and impressed by knowledge less for its truth content than for what it could do. His theology aimed primarily to explain how God's power can remedy the weakness of humanity.

The truism that Calvin perceived God primarily as power points, therefore, to the larger truth that, like Machiavelli in his more limited political world, he saw power as supreme throughout the universe. His thought on this vast subject began, to be sure, with God's power as the infinite source of all power. "What is the power of God?" Calvin asked rhetorically, and immediately replied, "Infinite, a power that we do not conceive of." [1] God's infinite power was implied by Calvin's insistence on his transcendence, his inaccessibility, his remoteness from his creatures.

Power, however, was not, for Calvin, just a philosophical abstraction; his fascination with it had sources deep within himself. Even earthly power awed him: he thought men like himself prone to disorientation in the presence of a ruler. "It would be a rare virtue," he asserted, "for poor little men, when they come into the sight of princes, to keep their presence of mind and not be overwhelmed by worldly splendor. . . . It is a formidable thing to endure the look of princes, for not only dread but even simple respect may confuse good minds. Moreover, what if princes break out in a fury and almost thunder at us?"[2] The prospect of coming into the presence of an omnipotent God was far more disturbing, but in the same way. Since "one does not dare approach a mortal prince, who is only a blackguard," he asked, "how will we come before the majesty of our Creator?"[3] God's presence overwhelms us; when he speaks too, it is "as if we heard him thunder from heaven."[4]

Calvin would never have denied that God is love, and he sometimes suggested that God's love is his primary attribute. "If we seek the cause by which he was once led to create all things and is now moved to preserve them," he wrote, "we shall find that it is his goodness alone."[5] But God's love, to be effective, required that he also be powerful. This, I suspect, was why Calvin paid less attention to God as creator than to God as governor of the world, which, because he created it, is where we experience his love. Calvin did not ignore the creation. He criticized the Platonists, who, unable to conceive of creation *ex nihilo*, made God no more than architect of the world.[6] "God," he remarked, "has more power over men than a mortal man over the clay; for although the potter may be a maker of pots, he is not the creator of the clay."[7] But Calvin's emphasis was on God's governance; indeed, his creation of the world interested him chiefly because it pointed to his control over it. "This word creator,' " he argued, "means that he did everything in such a way that all sovereign power and empire remain his."[8] The entire world "is in his hand and he governs it as he wills."[9]

His most vivid experiences with power on earth were associated with politics and the weather, and he drew on both to depict the power of God. He often compared God explicitly to a secular ruler. If we are slow in responding to God's goodness, he suggested, "he must show us what right [*droit*] he has over us, as when a prince, seeing that his vassal is slow to do his duty, sends his officer to summon him."[10] Calvin often invoked, too, in this connection, the feudal conception of "honor." "It would be better for heaven and earth to be thrown into the abyss together," he wrote, "than that the honor which Christ has been given by God his father should be diminished."[11]

But, ambivalent about all secular rule, Calvin was more inclined to discern God's power in nature, especially in the weather. By his nod alone, he wrote, God can "sometimes shake heaven with thunderbolts, burn everything with lightnings, kindle the air with flashes; sometimes disturb it with various sorts of storms, and then at his pleasure clear them away in a moment; compel the sea, which by its height seems to threaten the earth with continual destruction, to hang as if in mid-air; sometimes arouse it in a dreadful way with the tumultuous force of winds; sometimes with waves quieted, make it calm again."[12] In thunder God is telling us, "I must come to you in a dreadful manner and admonish you in a way that will make you feel, in spite of your murmuring [*en despit de vos dents*], that you cannot escape the incomprehensible majesty in me."[13] Thunder is unique in its capacity to "excite dread in the minds of men."[14] Better than anything else it suggests "the immensity of God's power," by which "we are astounded and overwhelmed in ecstasy."[15]

A major consequence of Calvin's concern to protect God's power was his tendency to minimize "secondary causes." He did not reject the *fact* that God works through them,[16] but, again less concerned with truth than consequences, he discouraged attention to the regularities of nature as likely to reduce the sense of God's power. His objection to the cult of saints was similar; the papists, he complained, "divide up God's power so that any of their petty saints may claim some part of it for themselves."[17] That men call themselves "fathers" bothered him for much the same reason. "The honor of being called 'father' belongs to God alone," he told his congregation, "and it cannot be transferred to men unless it pleases him to bestow it on them."[18]

Calvin attacked natural philosophy, therefore, for its preoccupation with secondary causes. He did not share the belief of some later Calvinists that the study of nature would intensify the sense of God's wisdom and power;[19] he agreed, rather, with humanists such as Petrarch, who had accused the natural scientists of his time of diverting attention from God and the human condition to less urgent matters. Calvin acknowledged, to be sure, that nature exhibits uniformities and that these should be contemplated with "wonder, reflection, and an effort to understand."[20] "Although there is no help except from God," he asserted, "he has ordinary ways by which he extends his grace and strength toward us. When these fail, so that there appears to be no help under heaven, then he acts directly."[21] Indeed, he denied that what can be explained naturally should be interpreted as a miracle, for example the mixture of water and blood that had flowed from Christ's side. It is natural, he insisted, "for coagulated blood to lose its color and resemble water."[22]

But he was too skeptical about human knowledge to allow such naturalism to intrude often into his thought,[23] especially in view of the tendency of science, as he believed, to weaken faith by ignoring God's power. Aristotle himself, though he had "excelled in genius and learning," obscured God's providence with "many erroneous speculations."[24] "Nothing more hinders and prevents us from embracing the promises of God," Calvin argued, "than when we ponder what can be done naturally and what is probable."[25] We must constantly bear in mind instead that, although every inanimate object "has by nature been endowed with its own properties, it does not exercise its own power except in so far as it is directed by God's ever-present hand." Natural entities are "nothing but instruments to which God continually imparts as much effectiveness as he wills, and according to his own purpose bends and turns them to either one action or another." God's governance "is not restricted to the order of nature, which he easily changes whenever it seems right."[26]

His hostility to astrology came partly from his distrust of secondary causation. At times he would admit only that the heavenly bodies serve to mark time, and the variation from year to year in the length of the seasons, which are regulated by the sun, shows that they do even this unreliably.[27] He was sufficiently a man of his time to recognize some influence of stars and planets over human existence. They can also teach us about "famine, barrenness, plagues, abundant harvests, and things of that kind." But, like other humanists, he distinguished sharply between events controlled by nature and those things for which human beings are responsible. "We should always take into consideration," he insisted, "the relationship of the stars to these lower regions," but human affairs "are not ruled by them, as lying and boastful astrologers think."[28] "That there are winter and summer is natural and ordinary," he observed, "but that one people should make war on another is not part of the usual order, is not natural but comes from the ambition and avarice of men."[29] He disapproved of the respect of his contemporaries for astrologers, especially princes, who "listen to and honor them as gods."[30] Even when astrology can help, Calvin argued, it is unreliable because "to lead men away from perversely looking to the stars, God rules earthly things according to his will quite otherwise than can be predicted from the stars."[31]

In addition to its practical weaknesses, astrology, as ancient history showed, had been destructive of both religion and morality. "When the opinion held sway that all events depended on the stars," Calvin noted, "the fear of God disappeared, and nothing was ascribed to his judgments; faith, prayer to God, and the whole exercise of piety were extinguished."[32] As a manifestation of the "preposterous curiosity" of human beings about the future, astrology also expresses anxiety, that is, lack of trust in God.[33] It promised, indeed, nothing but a wretched slavery. "Nothing would be more miserable than man," he wrote, "if he were exposed to every movement of the sky, air, earth, and waters."[34]

His attack on secondary causes was paralleled by his tendency to minimize uniformities and continuities in both nature and human affairs; he was uneasy that human beings might try to subordinate the infinite possibilities latent in God's will to human expectations based on generalization about the nature of things. The notion of dependable regularity in nature seemed to him to imply some limit on the inventiveness of the Deity. But in unexpected changes, as "when the heavens are hidden by clouds, when the air is now tranquil and now agitated by winds, when storms suddenly arise and rain follows, God vividly reveals his manifold wisdom and power."[35] The surprises built into nature testify to God's sovereignty:

If the sun always rose and set uniformly, if time during the year was symmetrical and unchanging, if days in winter were not short nor those of summer long, then we might infer a fixed order of nature; and thus God would be, so to speak, driven from his throne. But since the days of winter do differ from those of summer, and even spring does not always have the same weather but is sometimes turbulent and snowy and sometimes as hot as summer; and since summers are so varied, since no year is like another, since climate changes from hour to hour and moment to moment and heaven puts on a new face:

when we discern all these things, God is rousing us up, lest we be benumbed
in our understanding and erect nature into a kind of god and the true God is
deprived of his due honor.[36]

The rotation of the heavens was for Calvin not proof of the order of nature
but "such a miracle that we should be ravished in astonishment by it"; and
the marvelous suspension of the earth, surrounded on all sides by air so that
"it does not fall into the abyss," was "a thing so admirable that men must
here be confused by it." He rejoiced in the "almost innumerable" variety of
animals, each with its own "suitable and proper food."[37] We should glorify
God for his infinite rather than his intelligible wisdom.[38]

He was especially impressed by the most violent phenomena of nature
because these best display God's power: the sweep of clouds across the sky,
the unnatural mixture of fire and water in lightning and rain (a work possible
only for God), the unpredictable gusting of winds.[39] It invigorated him to
know that, although the air may now be tranquil, "in half an hour the winds
may rise and contend with one another in mid air."[40] But nothing impressed
him as "more terrifying" than tempestuous waters that threaten, by the violence of the waves, "to overwhelm the whole earth."[41]

He also celebrated the evidence of God's power in biological nature,
where it is revealed in the productivity of agriculture and the ferocity of wild
beasts.[42] It is evident in human physiology, notably in sexual reproduction
and childbirth, which Calvin also thought miraculous, though "held cheap
through constant repetition." "If ingratitude did not veil our eyes with insensibility," he observed, "we would be ravished with astonishment at
every childbirth in the world."[43]

In human society, too, God's power is displayed in variety, as with differences among individuals. "Our Lord makes some more keen than others," Calvin explained, "so that they have the industry to achieve what they
undertake, they finish what they decide on, they conduct all their affairs
prudently and understand a great many things quickly; others are slow and
sluggish, so that you have to hit them with great hammer blows when you
want to teach them something. Such diversity as there is among men shows
clearly that if we have some power of judging and discriminating well, it is a
special gift of God, and that we must not attribute such a thing to nature."[44]

God is also responsible for the unexpectedness of history. A radical historicism is implicit in this view; Calvin is with Guicciardini rather than Machiavelli in his conviction that regularities rule history no more than nature.
Even in his dealings with the wicked, he declared, "God is above the whole
common order of nature, so that he can act in a manner that is strange and
new to us."[45] He not only "forms everyone's disposition from birth," he
also makes the dispositions of individuals changeable: "we sometimes see
the rudest men endued with much acuteness, so that they display an unusual
wisdom in some action; and others who excel in understanding lack judgment and discretion" because God "changes their affections as he
pleases."[46] He "often deliberately *changes the law of nature* so that we may

know that what he freely confers is exclusively determined by his will."[47] On all these matters Calvin reveals a large capacity for wonder. He also marveled at the arts of civilization, God's gifts to mankind:

How is it possible? How can gold be discovered in the earth? Here is water, and people make salt of it. How does that happen? Well, God has given this industry to men. There is some metal mixed with the earth, it has no color, it even seems useless. Then how can one discover it? How can it be refined so that it can be used as a precious metal that can be a means of trading among men? How can it be done? As for the other arts, there is no trade so low or so common or so vulgar that at first glance we are not astonished at how it can be done. Even when we look at how wheat is sown: how can it be believed, we ask, how does one make wine and other such things?[48]

His sense of God's power over the world found formal expression in his doctrine of providence, which attributed "counsel and deliberate purpose" to God's use of his power.[49] "There is no erratic power or action or motion in creatures," he wrote, "but they are governed by God's secret plan in such a way that nothing happens except what is knowingly and willingly decreed by him."[50] God "sustains the world by his energy, he governs everything, however remote, so that not even a sparrow falls to the ground without his decree."[51] He rules "not only what happens to things but he also subjects the designs and impulses of men to his will."[52] He controls even the wicked, though they "may be in an uproar and driven blindly," so that they serve his glory. "When we observe how the wicked throw everything into confusion," therefore, "let us not think that God has allowed them to rush forward as they please, but we should be fully persuaded that their furious attacks are under control."[53]

This excluded any role for chance or fortune, commonly invoked, as by Machiavelli, to express the unpredictability of human affairs. In confused times such as his own, Calvin thought, people were especially likely to believe in the rule of fortune; sometimes he equated this refusal to acknowledge God's power over events with "Epicureanism":

It is a very bad temptation for the faithful, when things in the world are confused and it seems that God no longer engages with them but that fortune governs and rules. This has been the cause of those diabolical proverbs that everything is ruled by chance, that things happen blindly, and that God plays with men like tennis balls, that there is no reason or measure, or indeed that everything is governed by some secret necessity and that God does not bother to think of us. These are blasphemies that have always ruled. And why? Because the human mind is bewildered when we try to grasp confused things that surpass our judgment and reason.[54]

"How many of us are there," Calvin asked, "who do not believe that men are whirled and twisted about by blind and indiscriminate fortune?"[55] Against this view, citing Augustine and Basil the Great, he maintained that

" 'fortune' and 'chance' are pagan terms with whose meaning pious minds ought not be occupied"; for "if every success is God's blessing and calamity and adversity his curse, there is no place in human affairs for fortune or chance. . . . God's hand alone is the judge and governor of fortune, good or bad, and it does not rush about with heedless force, but with most orderly justice deals out good as well as ill to us."[56] He preferred even a naturalistic determinism to the invocation of fortune.[57]

But God's purpose remains, for the most part, incomprehensible even to believers. There are times, Calvin recognized, when we must simply "concede to God that he may have reasons for his plan that are hidden from us."[58] God's "wonderful method of governing the universe is rightly called an abyss [in Scripture], because when it is hidden from us, we ought reverently to adore it."[59] As a practical matter, therefore, Calvin's providence is not far from Machiavelli's fortune, as he came close to admitting: "Since the order, reason, end, and necessity of those things that happen for the most part lie hidden in God's purpose and are not apprehended by human opinion, those things which it is certain take place by God's will, *are* in a sense fortuitous."[60]

Nevertheless Calvin thought it possible to "seek illumination from heaven" for some understanding of the workings of providence,[61] and he was prepared to say a good deal on the subject. In the first place, providence reveals something supremely important about God himself. It shows us that the "virtue" of Calvin's God, like that of Machiavelli's prince, is displayed in "motion or action."[62] "Those who admit that God is creator of the world and yet claim that he sits idle in heaven, careless of the world," Calvin declared, "impiously deprive him of his power. . . . they leave him only the shadow of power, manifested only in its effects."[63] Here too he was siding with the humanists who praised the active life. He rejected categorically the notion—he chiefly meant Aristotle's unmoved mover—that God is "idle" [*otiosa*]; on the contrary, God's power is, "as the Scriptures teach, effective and active."[64]

Aristotle's conception of an idle God was as mistaken, for Calvin, as the belief of "the Epicureans" that, because God is indifferent to what happens in the world, men may "follow their impulses and enjoy pleasures as long as life lasts."[65] God's power, for him, "is not shut up in heaven but shows itself in helping men," for whom "his care never falters."[66] Only the "secret providence of God, which watches out for the protection of the human race," can explain why human beings have failed totally to destroy one another.[67] God nourishes them, he cares for them, he guides them along life's way to ends he has appointed. He "does not place men haphazardly on earth, to go wherever they please, but directs everyone by his secret purpose."[68] Those he loves, even when they wander in uncertainty, "yet keep on the right path because God directs their steps."[69] But God equally guides the wicked: "The hearts and minds of men are divinely ruled, so that even our worst enemies, when they rage against us, are moved not only by their own violent impulses but also by the secret instigation and purpose of God."[70]

Calvin inferred from this that all history, pagan as well as sacred, is instructive and useful for those who can recognize the hand of God behind events. Here his doctrine of providence reinforced a humanist's confidence in the value of history. "It is not enough," he declared, "to have our eyes open and to note well and mark what God does during our own lives, but we must profit from ancient histories. In fact this is why our Lord has wanted us to have some notable judgments left in writing, so that the memory of them would remain for ever. And we should not only profit from what is contained in Holy Scripture, but when we hear what is spoken by the histories written by the pagans, we should also have the prudence to apply to ourselves what God has done."[71]

Humanist influence is also at work in Calvin's interest in political history, although here he had especially to deny any role to fortune. "When we see various changes in the world, the downfall of kingdoms, the alteration of territories, the destruction of cities, the overthrowing of nations," he asserted, "we foolishly imagine that fate or fortune controls these events."[72] On the contrary: God makes his providence "especially visible in kingdoms"; and although he "rules over the smallest details in the governance of the human race and the whole world, his special providence shines forth in the empires of this world."[73] Political history teaches the humbling lesson that, "just as the life of every individual has its limits, so God has determined how it should be with the empires of all the earth: the life and death of every kingdom and nation are in the hand and subject to the will of God."[74] The rise and fall of the great men who ruled the Assyrians, Chaldeans, Persians, and Medes, of Alexander and the most pompous Roman emperors, also seemed to Calvin the most striking illustrations of the power of providence. "If a poor man is afflicted by some calamity," he pointed out, "we hardly notice, for we are all accustomed to these things. But when a prince who seems to be raised on high is cast down, we are more touched and must acknowledge the providence of God, unless we are very stupid."[75]

Warfare was for Calvin the realm in which the ways of providence were particularly mysterious, just it had seemed to others particularly ruled by fortune. When men expect peace, "suddenly war will break out from an unexpected direction," by God's command, "as though he assembled soldiers by the call of a trumpet."[76] Once begun, wars are decided not by the virtue, wisdom, or skill of generals, but by God. This is why "inferior or cowardly troops sometimes win, while those more skillful or better equipped struggle in vain."[77] Mysterious waves of terror, a sure sign of divine intervention, can cause experienced armies to flee from unimpressive enemies.[78]

Calvin sometimes treated the workings of providence in politics simply as a matter of God's control over events. At other times, looking deeper, he saw in it the expression of God's justice. Like earthly princes, and again unlike the Epicurean deity, God does "not indulge in pleasure or take his ease, but governs the world, diffuses his power through heaven and earth, judges men, renders to everyone his just reward."[79] If, Calvin asked, "the reprobate prospered with impunity and if the righteous were oppressed and helpless, would not God be like a block of wood or a fiction? For why has he power, unless to exercise justice?"[80] Since justice meant to Calvin chiefly the punishment of the wicked, he tended to conceive of secular history as little more than an awful warning. It displays

> how God has exercised vengeance on all those who devote themselves to cruelty, to rapine, and to other extortions; and, next, how he has punished lecheries and other infections when they have flourished too much; and then how he has punished perjuries; and that he has not been able to endure the pride of men. When we consider all that, should it not serve us well also today? Let us remember well this lesson, that since, from the creation of the world, God has not ceased to warn us that he is judge of the world, we should learn to fear him, and to walk carefully, and that the punishments that he has inflicted on the wicked should be to us so many mirrors and so many bridles to restrain us.[81]

This, then, makes history useful. "If God afflicts somebody," Calvin said, sounding chillingly self-centered, "we ought all to profit from it."[82]

He deplored the inability of all but a few of his contemporaries to think in these terms. "Whenever any adversity occurs," he observed, "its causes are sought in the world, so that almost nobody considers the hand that strikes. When the year's harvest is bad, we consult astrology and attribute it to the conjunction of the stars."[83] Disaster should rather drive us to scrutinize our sins, bring us "to feel we have deserved the wrath of God," and "turn our minds to God and acknowledge him as the judge who summons us, as the accused, before his tribunal."[84] A proper understanding of providence should induce in us a salutary terror: "The dangers and adversities that surround us are God's weapons, nor do they happen to anyone by chance but are directed by his hand. So it happens that he not only incites enemies against us but also ferocious and harmful beasts, that he hardens heaven and earth against us, that he infects the air with deadly pestilence, and finally brings forth catastrophe from all the elements."[85] We must always keep these two principles in mind, that "God is the author of all things that men consider evils," and that "this is because he is a just judge."[86] God's favorite modes of punishment are pestilence, famine, and war.[87]

Occasionally he believed he understood God's punishments. The blood shed by Alexander the Great, he thought, had caused the destruction of his family: Alexander's eighty-year-old mother died by violence, his wife was strangled, his son perished miserably, his brother—a fool, little better than an animal—was slain, and most of his generals died in battle or by treachery.[88] The Turkish conquests had occurred because the inhabitants of Greece and Asia had provoked God's anger by "every kind of foul and monstrous licentiousness" and by "shocking superstitions and impieties."[89]

But for the elect, providence employs suffering not for punishment but for instruction. Calvin did not always sound like Job's friends; he knew that the wicked may go unpunished in this life, and this unpleasant reality tempted him to "remonstrate with God because he does not hurry to free the faithful and applaud their good fortune as if there were no judge in heaven."[90] Indeed this gave him such distress that, on at least one occasion, he lapsed into the language of paganism himself, perhaps because he could not quite bring himself to blame God. It is a peculiar trial for us, he declared, "when *fortuna* favors the reprobate."[91] He also knew that God can treat those he loves "with great rigor, yet not at all because of their sins." God, he explained, sometimes afflicts men "because he wishes to humble them, because he wishes to show his total authority over his creatures and wants them to be like mirrors of patience; again, because he wishes them to feel their weaknesses, to know themselves better when they have perceived within themselves the hidden vices that are uncovered by afflictions, and also to know that they are not so constant as required but have yielded; and when they see how they have stumbled, they may be so much the more stimulated to invoke God."[92] So "there is nothing better than when God sends messages of his wrath, to make us feel his mercy and be displeased with our vices."[93]

There has been some dispute about whether Calvin's providence was a specifically Christian doctrine or a residue of classical paganism,[94] a possibility suggested by his appeal to Virgil to support the identification of God with power.[95] He was, at any rate, concerned to avoid the determinism of the classical doctrine. He distinguished his own position from the "absurd fiction or rather madness" of the Stoics, who, not knowing "that God rules the world with his purpose, justice, and virtue," had "fabricated a labyrinth out of a system of causes so that God himself was bound by the necessity of fate and was violently swept along by the heavenly machinery."[96] God's providence, he insisted, does not operate "as a general principle of confused motion, as if he were commanding a river to flow through its established channels, but is directed toward individual and particular motions."[97]

What is indisputable is the importance Calvin attached to the doctrine for the relief of anxiety. It comforted him to reflect that the power of God holds the universe in place, preserves its order, prevents it from sliding into the abyss. This concern helped him to reject the conventional location of God "in heaven." This was only a figure of speech, he argued, intended to express God's unlimited power over the world, "so that, without restraint, he accomplishes freely whatever he conceives and nothing can prevent him from performing whatever he has decreed."[98] God must have "enough power to do good," because only then can we "safely rest in the protection of him whose will holds subject all the harmful things we may fear, whose authority curbs Satan with all his furies."[99]

He considered the subjective benefits of the doctrine of providence to be boundless. "When the light of divine providence has once shone upon a godly man," he wrote, "he is then relieved and set free not only from the extreme anxiety and fear that were pressing him before, but from every care.

. . . ignorance of providence is the ultimate misery; the highest blessedness lies in knowing it." [100] It gives "incredible freedom from worry about the future." [101] *Nothing*, accordingly, contributes more to faith than this, "for without it everybody would be agitated over the world's being tossed about by chance. So those who try to overturn this article of doctrine, depriving the children of God of true joy and tormenting their minds with a wretched disquiet, create for themselves hell on earth. What more horrible torment can there be than endlessly to tremble in anxiety? We will find no rest until we learn to recline in the providence of God." [102] If we fully believe in the reality of God's power, "no calamities will ever agitate or disturb us." [103] It was particularly comforting, amidst the disorders of his own time, "in which the Christian world is so involved and by whose violence it is so roughly shaken that almost everything seems confused," to remember "that God has a hidden bridle by which he restrains furious beasts so that they cannot break out wherever their mad appetite impels them or surpass the boundaries that the Lord has established." [104]

There are moments, to be sure, when the wicked flourish, "yet God ignores it and does not prevent the blood of the innocent from being shed" and "we cry to him in vain." Calvin explained this variously. God may delay his help because affliction in this life prevents his people from becoming too much attached to it. [105] He may delay his vengeance on the wicked as a kind of rhetorical gesture: "If God immediately cut them down and carried them away like sprouting blades of grain, his power would not be so striking, nor would his goodness be so fully known. So when he permits them to grow to a great height, to swell and blossom, they are finally pulled down by their own weight, or he cuts them down with pruning knives, like fat and swollen ears of wheat." [106] Even in those times when "everything is turned upside down" so that we begin to wonder whether "God still cares about ruling the world," we can be confident of his eventual intervention. For although he "does not bustle about like men nor work in feverish haste, he nevertheless has hidden ways of executing his judgments without moving a finger." [107] God, like a Machiavellian prince, knows how to wait for "the best possible occasion" to accomplish his work. [108]

Calvin advanced the related doctrine of predestination in a more gingerly fashion; it was finally a mystery, to be treated with great caution. He stated it firmly, to be sure. "No one who wishes to be thought religious," he wrote, "dares simply to deny predestination, by which God adopts some to hope of life and sentences others to eternal death." [109] He did not shrink from its harshest implications. "As God by the effectual working of his call to the elect perfects the salvation to which by his eternal plan he has destined them," he wrote, "so he has his judgments against the reprobate, by which he executes his plan for them. What of those, then, whom he created for dishonor in life and destruction in death, to become the instruments of his wrath and examples of his severity? That they may come to their end, he sometimes deprives them of the capacity to hear his word; at other times he blinds and stuns them by the preaching of it." [110] The conclusion of this passage suggests that, for Calvin, predestination is both biblical and a necessary corollary of God's power. It is also proved by experience: we all know that the Gospel has been available to some but not others, and that some reject it.

But here, as so often with Calvin, there is another side to his thought: he hardly dared "simply" to *affirm* predestination. "God's secret election" was an impenetrable mystery to him, and he was intensely opposed to speculation on the subject, which had already made the doctrine "a sea of scandals."[111] He denounced the curiosity that impelled human beings to concern themselves with it, pushing them to exceed their "proper limits" and plunging them "into the depths of the sea."[112] Predestination was an "abyss,"[113] but it was also a "labyrinth from which the mind of man can in no way extricate itself."[114]

The doctrine clearly made him uncomfortable. He thought it "terrible" that, as Scripture compelled him to believe, "only a small number, out of an incalculable multitude, should obtain salvation."[115] He deplored the complacency the doctrine can generate in believers, and he emphasized that election is always unmerited. "The children of Israel," he noted, "differed in no way, by any virtue of their own, from the rest of the world, but God passed by the others to adopt them."[116] He must also have been aware that he was sometimes tempted to believe that *he* could distinguish between the elect and the reprobate,[117] and he knew that this was wrong.[118]

Predestination, for Calvin, can be understood only within the context of faith;[119] then, "treated properly and soberly, no doctrine is more useful."[120] It promotes zeal and industry to live purely,[121] and it stimulates us "to glorify God's judgments and to exclaim with Paul, Oh deep and incomprehensible abyss!"[122] Teaching "that our salvation is grounded only on the goodness of God" and "that we shall always be safe," it evokes gratitude and inspires confidence.[123] This explains why, although earlier editions of the *Institutes* had treated predestination as part of the doctrine of providence, in the final edition Calvin discussed it in connection with salvation. In this context, and only here, is it edifying.

Because God, for Calvin, is identified with power, sin and estrangement from him render human beings powerless. He emphasized, therefore, that sin brings with it lethargy, sloth, indolence, weakness, dullness, coldness, insouciance, all premonitions of death, the ultimate collapse of vitality. Above all he attacked sloth. A "truly wicked slothfulness," he declared, causes human beings "to care for what is carnal and earthly but neglect the eternal salvation of their souls."[124] It interferes with worship; he denounced "the laziness of those to whom it is a burden to submit to any inconvenience to attend divine service" and who "allow nothing to interfere with their convenience and pleasure." Such people "would not sacrifice a hair of their heads for the sake of hearing the gospel and partaking of the sacraments; even when they can hear the churchbells calling them to worship, they prefer to sleep and remain at home."[125] No matter how hard they try, they "drag their legs only with great effort, such is the weakness of nature. . . .

we are so lazy that instead of taking only an instant to move a foot, we need an hour before we can stir; for every step we take forward, we stumble and fall back two. . . . unless someone goads us we will not go forward. The problem, then, is to wake up, to be alert." [126] We must "arouse our hearts and shake off our indolence" to call on God. [127]

Sloth lulls us gradually into sleep, one of Calvin's favorite metaphors for acquiescence to sin. "The devil," he observed, "always has his baubles to put to sleep those he has taken," [128] for "men cannot follow God while asleep." [129] In some sicknesses, he noted, "sleep is fatal. If one disturbs the poor patient by pulling his nose and ears and poking him from every direction, he will be vexed and fretful, for he asks only to rest. But rest would kill him. So it is with sinners, who want to be flattered and to have their consciences put to sleep. If God awakens them and does not allow them to be so stupefied, they will be angered, even though it is for their good." [130] A sinner resembles "a man who is lying asleep in his bed, and a thousand things can be said around him that he will not hear; people will speak, a great deal will be said, but the person asleep knows nothing. But if one made a loud noise, that would awaken him, and then one could not speak softly enough to keep him from hearing everything. So it is with us, for God will show us a great many things that ought to serve for instruction; but we have our eyes closed; he speaks to us but we hear nothing." [131] Even the elect may doze off for a while, "so that one might think that the Spirit given them is wholly extinct and that they no longer know what religion is or the fear of God." [132] Sleep, for Calvin, pointed to death.

Death lurks, as well, in dullness of perception, especially the perception of spiritual realities. Our senses are too "stupid and gross" to take in the wonders God has "offered for our inspection." [133] Our minds "easily contract rust through their sluggishness, which infects and corrupts all knowledge of God until it is entirely destroyed." [134] "Who among us," Calvin asked, "does not unconcernedly pass over with deaf ears, not only the many varied songs of birds, which should inspire us to glorify God, but the very voice of God, which resounds clearly and distinctly in the teaching of the law and the Gospels? Nor is it only for a day that a dull stupor occupies our minds, but it goes on and on until he grants us that vision of himself which alone alters the hearts of men." [135] Indeed, we cultivate dullness precisely when the most passionate commitment is essential; we put ourselves spiritually to sleep, persuaded that we can expect to live for many years and that "thirty years, or even a smaller number, are an eternity." [136]

Above all, death is foreshadowed by coldness. There is hardly a term in Calvin's vocabulary more pejorative than "frigid." He condemned Scholastic theology for its coldness: "Nothing is more common in the world," he remarked, "than to approach the teaching of godliness by way of frigid speculations. This is how theology has been corrupted by the sophists of the Sorbonne." [137] He sometimes professed to be disappointed in this respect by his own followers, charging that, whereas Christians are "negligent and cold and even glacial," idolators, Turks, even papists are filled with ardor. [138] He called on his followers to respond to God with "a burning affection," to be "set on fire" with praise for him, to be "inflamed with desire." [139] The depths of Calvin's hell, had he tried to describe it, would have much resembled Dante's. Yet he thought the fires of hell strictly metaphorical. He considered fire to be cleansing rather than destructive. [140]

He was much concerned, as a physician of souls, to combat human indolence, drowsiness, dullness, coldness, the various signs that we are, in life, already half dead. This concern helps to explain some of his regulations for church order, for example the scheduling of times and places for worship. "Why," he asked, "do we choose the most suitable hours and a particular place to assemble, why does the bell sound and we arrange all things? It is because we would scarcely have the ardor to give ourselves up to God if we were not drawn to it." We must make use of "every means possible to us to bring ourselves to correct this coldness and laziness to which we are so strongly inclined." [141] But God's devices are not only more drastic but also, for this purpose, more effective. He makes us suffer "to awaken us from our indolence": [142]

[God cannot allow] the kingdom of Christ to flourish more perfectly [than it does] lest we fall asleep, to which we are too much inclined. If the church were at peace and the Gospel received without contradiction, and if there were no kings or princes who were not opposed to it, we would promptly become accustomed to our ease and Jesus Christ would reign as a consequence of our belief and not by his power. God therefore wishes that the kingdom of Jesus Christ should be placed in the midst of his enemies in order that we might be kept on a short rein. [143]

Our lives must be vexed, for "if we were left in peace, we would fall asleep, we would no longer have any feeling about anything; but if things go badly, we are forced to think of God, to raise our minds on high, and to consider the judgment that is being prepared, though it has not yet appeared." [144] So, if we are lethargic, God first "threatens us to awaken us; and if his threats are coldly received, he takes up arms and chastises the torpor of men." [145] The Stoics aspired to rise above fear and hope; Calvin aimed to cultivate both as stimulants to action.

But the only decisive antidote to human powerlessness is the transfusion of spiritual energies from an omnipotent God to his helpless human creatures. Calvin described the result as "quickening" [*vivificatio*]. "We can only be like dead men," he declared, "until God brings us to life [*nous vivifie*]." [146] For this purpose Christ's power is "perpetually available to believers," [147] and the power of the Holy Spirit, "persistently boiling away and burning up our vicious and inordinate desires, enflames our hearts with the love of God and with zealous devotion," finally giving us "the power to accomplish what we desire." [148] "God," Calvin asserted, employing one of Machiavelli's favorite words, "always gives us strength [*vertu*]." [149]

These incidental references to Dante and Machiavelli are reminders of the traditional use of a vocabulary of energy in medieval and Renaissance spirituality. Coldness and sloth had been a large component of *acedia*, that affliction of the monasteries which, by the thirteenth century, was spreading among the laity.[150] As early as the ninth century, Rabanus Maurus had included among the symptoms of this ailment "somnolence, laziness in good deeds . . . [and] lukewarmness in work."[151] Bishop Antoninus of Florence had defined *acedia* a century before Calvin as "a certain spiritual coldness or lack of spiritual love and divine fervor, through which the soul is not moved—or is moved with difficulty—to do some good work."[152] Humanists had also picked up this language. Petrarch blamed Cola di Rienzo for his lethargy,[153] and, in the *Secretum*, himself; and Erasmus believed that sin comes "from nothing else but from the coldness and drowsiness of our faith."[154] (Luther, however, condemned Erasmus because "in theology he writes so coldly, stupidly, and dully.")[155] Calvin was again in a goodly and venerable company, but none before him, perhaps, had used this language with such understanding of its larger ramifications.

11

Drama

That the sixteenth century was one of the great periods in the history of the theater is well known, but the larger cultural significance of its theatricality is less commonly recognized. It expressed the uncertainties of a period of rapid change in which the possibilities of human existence were expanding, human identity had become problematic, and the modes of human behavior could no longer be taken for granted. Rooted in both the classics and the Bible, a dramatic vision of existence was as serious an element in the mentality of Calvin's contemporaries as their preoccupation with power.

The vision of the world as a stage on which all human beings are players had been transmitted by the Latin orators and essayists to the humanists of the Renaissance.[1] In antiquity the human drama had often been conceived as tragedy, but for Christendom it had to be a (divine) comedy. "In the vast theater of heaven and earth," as Ford Lewis Battles has summarized the great Christian epic of salvation, "the divine playwright stages the ongoing drama of creation, alienation, return, and forgiveness for the teeming audience of humanity itself."[2] The theatrical metaphor for the human scene pervaded sixteenth-century discourse. Erasmus had used it to express his sense of the variety of the human condition. "Wherever I turn my eyes," he wrote, "I see all things changed, I stand before another stage and I behold a different play, nay, even a different world."[3] Calvin shared this theatrical vision of human existence. He often described the universe as "a glorious theater" in which, as spectators, we admire God's works.[4] We can also watch in it the unfolding drama of historical existence, in which God wishes us "to attend not only to the last hundred years or so but to the time since the creation of the world."[5] Human beings are the audience in God's theater of the world.

But they are also its actors. Like Shakespeare, Calvin saw high drama in the lives of the great. "Kings," he remarked, "are placed, as it were, in a theater, and the eyes of all are turned on them."[6] The Roman emperors had been "kings in the tragic mode" because, "having been thrown down from their lofty position," they were "dragged to a shameful death."[7] But there was also drama in the actions of humbler folk. From Strasbourg he had watched developments in Geneva as a dramatic performance whose "catastrophe" he could not clearly understand,[8] and he continued to view the struggle for control of the city as a "tragic tumult" whose last act remained unfinished.[9] It was also a comedy. His enemy Ami Perrin was a "comic Caesar" who had "put on the socks" and, "now bolder, boasts among his actors after his own Thrasonic fashion."[10]

He viewed his own career in dramatic terms. "I am not ignorant," he wrote Melanchthon in 1552, "of the position in his theater to which God has elevated me";[11] and a few years later, picking up Melanchthon's own theatrical language, he emphasized the superiority of his role to that of the political superstars of the age. "Let this [church] be my theater," he wrote, "and, content with its approval, though the whole world should hiss me, my courage will never fail. I am far from envying silly and noisy declaimers when they enjoy their small laurel of glory in a dark corner for a little while. What is worthy of applause or odious to the world is not unknown to me."[12]

But, although Calvin shared the theatrical perspective of his age, he was sometimes uncomfortable with it. The ambiguity of "play" suggests what troubled him. "Play," as with children, can express what is most authentic and spontaneous in human existence. But role playing, whether in society or on the stage, is different. In society we play roles that may require hiding the true self to meet the expectations of others or to deceive them. Acting on the stage also involves the substitution of an artificial for an authentic self; it does not express the natural vitality and freedom of human being but hides behind a mask, assumes a *persona*—another term borrowed from the theater.[13]

Perceptions of this kind contributed to what Jonas Barish has called "the anti-theatrical prejudice," which played a counterpoint to the theatricality of the Renaissance. It associated acting on the stage with all the sinful practices by which human beings pretend to be what they are not in order to deceive and exploit; it reached a climax with the abolition of the theater in Puritan England. Suspicion of the theater also developed in Calvin's Geneva, and although he did not wholly share it,[14] he sometimes gave vigorous expression to the anti-theatrical prejudice. Theaters, he proclaimed, "resound with lying fictions. . . . and the unlearned are carried away when they are persuaded that what they see represented in the theaters is true."[15] He attacked the papacy for its "fantastical" theatricality. "When the unprincipled men who occupy pulpits under the papacy speak with weeping," he charged, "although they produce not a syllable from God's Word but add some spectacle or fantasy by producing the image of the cross or some such things, like actors on the stage they touch the feelings of the people and cause them to weep."[16]

The charge of "fantasy" gives another clue to what troubled Calvin. He generally opposed "new things,"[17] and theatrical performances smacked of the presumption he associated with all human "invention." At times he suggests Plato. "Poets have invented whatever pleases them," he charged, "and thus they have filled the world with the grossest and foulest errors. Since all theaters resound with these lying fictions, the minds of the crowd have been imbued with this sort of madness, for we know that human nature is always prone to vanity. But when the devil lights the fire, we see how furiously both the learned and unlearned are carried away. So it happens when they are persuaded that what they saw represented in the theaters is true."[18] This also suggests fear that stage performances might arouse the passions.

But Calvin was chiefly motivated in such pronouncements by the same concern for personal integrity that found expression in his loathing of hypocrisy; he yearned for "the profession of the tongue" always to express "the true sentiment of the heart."[19] This ranked higher among his priorities than outward obedience to the law. The virtue that most distinguished his beloved David, Calvin emphasized, had been not his perfection but his honesty [*sinceritas*].[20] Calvin's personal emblem was a hand offering a heart, accompanied by the words *Prompte et sincere*.

This detestation of hypocrisy found expression in his animus against the theater. "Hypocrisy," he knew, had originated as a theatrical term. "In profane writers," he pointed out, "hypocrite was the name for the stage performer who acted out fictitious roles in the theater and in festivals." A hypocrite is thus one who "plays" at being what he is not. He trivializes his existence, which is, after all, "not a farce" or "only a game."[21] Before God "purity of will alone will be demanded of us," and hypocrisy will be confounded.[22]

The antidote to the hypocritical role playing that Calvin associated with theatricality is self-examination; indeed, for Calvin a hypocrite is not so much a man who pretends to be what he is not as one who observes his neighbor but not himself.[23] To please God we must "learn seriously and inwardly to scrutinize ourselves lest any hypocrisy lurk within."[24] He recognized the difficulty of the task; to "search all our feelings honestly," we must "diligently inquire into all the winding recesses with which human minds are filled and perplexed," and even then we may be deceived "by empty imagination."[25] The human heart, he wrote, "has so many crannies where vanity hides, so many holes where falsehood lurks, is so decked out with deceiving hypocrisy, that it often dupes itself."[26] Given its difficulties, Calvin thought self-examination best performed privately, "for when we seek God in troops and one jostles another [one might imagine here an audience in a theater], it is often done without feeling." But solitude makes it possible "for men to compose and examine themselves deeply and seriously and to converse freely with themselves."[27]

If self-examination is to tell us the objective truth about ourselves, it must be conducted in the light of God's law; mere comparison of ourselves with other human beings is useless, "since a one-eyed man among the blind appears to see well, a swarthy man among blacks considers himself white."[28] But the law is like a mirror. "If a man is smudged," Calvin remarked, "everybody will make fun of him but he won't see a thing; but when he comes to the mirror and sees that his face is all smeared, he will hide and go wash himself." [29] He described in detail what we will learn from proper self-examination: "First, by comparing the righteousness of the law with our life we learn how far we are from conforming to God's will. And for this reason we are unworthy to hold our place among his creatures, still less to be accounted his children. Secondly, in considering our powers we learn that they are not only too weak to fulfill the law, but utterly nonexistent." [30] A Christian, for Calvin, must constantly examine himself to discover "his calamity, poverty, nakedness, and disgrace." [31] The law "shows us our filth in order to confound us so that we may be ashamed of our foulness." [32]

The first consequence of self-examination carried out in the light of God's demands must thus be a terrible dismay. "If anyone examines himself," Calvin asked, "what will he find but cause for despair?" [33] But if God's grace is present, the result will be a peace of mind, impossible for a "double heart," than which "nothing is more desirable." The only alternative is that terrible anxiety Calvin understood so well. "Whoever despises this remedy," he proclaimed, "will fear not only mortal men but a shadow or breath of wind." [34] Self-examination, by which human beings can put an end to the "playing" of hypocrisy, is thus essential to lifting the most fearful burden of existence.

But there was a paradox in Calvin's call for self-examination as the means for recovering an authentic self. This was implicit in his insistence on the outcome of the exercise. "The rigor of the examination," he proclaimed, "should proceed until we are cast down into complete consternation, in this way preparing us to receive the grace of Christ." [35] "Once we have carefully examined all that is in us," he proclaimed, "we will find nothing but corruption and damnable vice." [36] We are to engage in this search, then, not in a spirit of openness to whatever it might disclose, but for an ulterior motive: with, in the literal sense, a prejudice. For Calvin, "The *only* way to please God is to be severe in censuring ourselves." [37] By leaving the result closed, Calvin was himself prescribing a role: the role of repentant sinner, to be played self-consciously and self-critically. He noted in himself the usefulness of "outward signs of repentance" to stimulate actual repentance, as "the marks of our guilt move us the more to recognize ourselves as guilty sinners." [38] In short, the distinction between role and reality in this crucial aspect of human existence is made problematic. Instead of restoring the integrity of the self, Calvin splits it into observer and observed, audience and actor, neither capable of natural and spontaneous behavior but only of self-conscious and studied behavior. He was driven back to theatricality even by his effort to escape it.

That he did not escape it is evident in an aspect of his doctrine of providence, which assigns to God the responsibilities not only of playwright and impresario of the performance enacted on the stage of the world but also of casting director. He most often used the term "calling" (*vocatio, vocation*) for the choosing of the elect, and also for the summons of specific individuals to the ministry. But occasionally he used it, as did Luther, to signify God's assignment of human beings to their stations in the occupational or family structures of society.[39] In this usage the conception, like that of providence, could give comfort in a changing world. It was deeply reassuring, in a time of increasing social mobility, for peasants who had moved into towns, young men whose occupations differed from those of their fathers, exiles, all overwhelmed by a sense of arbitrariness, absurdity, rootlessness and danger, to know that God himself had assigned them these new roles.

Calvin intended that it should be. He commended the calling on the ground that it provides a remedy for the anxiety accompanying activity in society, citing Christ's reflections on the lilies of the field. "In this whole speech," he explained, "Christ is reproving the excessive anxiety about food and clothing that causes men to tear themselves apart with worry, and he also prescribes a cure for this disease. We know that men who come into this world are obligated to assume some responsibility. But Christ condemns excessive care on two counts: that men wear themselves out and torment themselves in vain when they are busier than their calling requires or permits, and that they take more upon themselves than they should, relying too much on their own efforts and neglecting to call on God." The elect "may not be immune from toil and care," but they are not deeply anxious because of the guidance, stability, and security provided them by the consciousness of their calling.[40]

By the same token the doctrine of the calling is a remedy for ambition: those who are ignorant of their callings rashly trespass on the tasks of others and, slaves to ambition, soon find themselves wandering in a "labyrinth."[41] But worldly ambition is precluded by recognizing that all callings are equal before God. It is "a singular consolation" to know that "no task is so sordid and base, provided you acknowledge that it is your calling, that it will not shine and be reckoned very precious in God's sight."[42] Most important of all, perhaps, is the ability of the doctrine to give human beings the courage and energy to do what needs to be done. "Strength will never be wanting to God's servants," Calvin promised, "when they are encouraged by the knowledge that God himself is the source of their calling. When they are thus lifted up, God supplies them with such invincible strength and courage that they are formidable to all the world."[43]

But for Calvin, unlike Erasmus, one's calling has no necessary correspondence to one's talents or "nature."[44] Here as elsewhere he preferred to dispense with nature—in this case human nature—as mediator between God and the world: for Calvin, God gives directly to the elect whatever is needed to play the parts he has assigned. In this understanding of the calling, one does not play oneself but, like an actor on the stage, whatever roles one is assigned. This conception had, I think, deep roots in the experience that brought Calvin to Geneva. He had felt unqualified to help Farel in Geneva, and he was never comfortable in the active roles he believed God had assigned him. A major reminiscence is buried in his account of Jeremiah's attempt to evade God's call. Jeremiah had rejected it, Calvin reported, "because its difficulty terrified him. . . . he believed himself quite unequal to undertaking so strenuous an office." God had nevertheless forgiven Jeremiah for his timidity because, Calvin believed, "it proceeded from a proper feeling." He praised Jeremiah for having "thought himself not strong enough to undertake the prophetic office, and wishing to be excused and another chosen with more courage and better qualifications."[45]

He was less interested in occupational than in spiritual roles, and he gave some thought to how most effectively to play the role of Christian, even to the display of affect appropriate to it. To the question, perhaps addressed to him by a member of his congregation, whether true repentance requires weeping, he replied judiciously that faithful men may confess their sins "with dry eyes" but that, in the case of more serious sins, it would be "too dull and slothful not to be wounded with grief and sorrow and not to shed tears."[46] When we examine ourselves in the light of the law, in what might be called the first act in the drama of our own salvation, we ought to experience "anxiety and trepidation of mind," to be "frightened by the awareness of eternal death," and to feel "despondent, confused, and despairing in mind."[47]

Calvin also identified role models, especially in Scripture, for the emulation of Christians, hoping that "examples of virtue for men to copy" would "stimulate the idle and sluggish, the dawdlers in the race," and "prompt them by shame to discharge their responsibilities."[48] David was an example of such obvious virtues as steadfastness in suffering; other figures gave Calvin more trouble. A particularly difficult case was Abraham's grief at the death of Sarah. Here Calvin presented himself as a kind of drama critic not quite able to make up his mind about a performance. He sensed a lapse of decorum in Abraham's distress, perhaps recalling his own disturbingly violent grief at the death of Idelette de Bure a few years earlier. "What purpose could there be," he imagined that a critic more severe than himself might ask, "in approaching the body in order to lament over it? Was not the death of his wife sufficiently sad and bitter to call forth enough grief?" Calvin's response was equivocal; everything, he suggested, depended on Abraham's intention. He had done wrong "if he came to his dead wife in order to stimulate even more weeping and to pierce his heart with fresh wounds." But he was blameless if he wept only privately and in moderation, "for to feel no grief in the contemplation of death is barbarism and insensibility."[49]

Having learned their roles, the elect are ready to participate in the drama of the Christian life. This had, for Calvin, two basic plots. In the first, like Erasmus in the *Enchiridion militis christianae*, he depicted the Christian as a soldier, the Christian life as a struggle culminating in victory. In the second the Christian life was treated as a journey or pilgrimage. Both plots were variants on the theme of development or progress toward a goal. He combined them in the prayer that concluded his exegetical lectures on Daniel: "Grant, Almighty God, since thou proposest to us no other end than that of constant warfare during our whole life and subjectest us to many cares until we arrive at the goal of this transitory struggle: grant, I pray thee, that we may never grow fatigued. May we be ever armed and equipped for battle; and, whatever the trials by which thou dost prove us, may we never be found deficient."[50] Both plots also reflected the circumstances of his own troubled life, at once embattled and homeless.

For Calvin, earthly existence is a perpetual warfare. The reprobate, "born sons of wrath," are at war with God; the elect, under God's command, must face other enemies.[51] First among them is Satan, who, "the very embodiment of rash boldness, of military prowess, of crafty wiles, of untiring zeal and haste, of every conceivable weapon, and of skill in the knowledge of war, relentlessly threatens us."[52] The saints must also contend with hypocrites, evildoers, those who scorn the Gospel.[53] The struggle is full of danger. Unclean spirits "exercise believers in combat, ambush them, invade their peace, attack them, often weary them, rout them, terrify them, and sometimes wound them."[54] The conflict never ceases in this life; at best the elect can hope only for "time to recover their strength."[55]

But such external foes are the least of the Christian's enemies. "The principal combat we must wage," for Calvin, "is against ourselves and against our vices; this is where we must exert ourselves."[56] The difficulties here are even greater: "However much believers sweat, they scarcely do half their duty; indeed they almost fail under the burden."[57] This struggle too is endless; "in the saints, until they are divested of mortal bodies, there is always sin."[58]

The basic sin to be contended against is rebelliousness against God's decrees. Even though they "find it strange and it seems contrary to all reason and equity," Christians must nevertheless bow their heads and say, "Lord, however deep are the abysses of your judgments, we do not presume to reject them."[59] The saints must be patient under affliction, saying, "Lord, we are in your hand, it is not for us to impose a law on you, to summon you now, to tell you to do this or that; but since you have told us that you will end our suffering, indeed happily and desirably, Lord let us wait patiently for what you have promised."[60] Above all, the saints must not complain; to "murmur," as Calvin put it, is the first symptom of rebellion.[61] "When a man can subject himself in all humility and reverence to God and renounce himself," Calvin proclaimed, "when your Creator prevails over you and has entire mastery, that is a good beginning."[62]

The acceptance of God's commands by the Christian soldier is especially difficult because the battle "consists less in inflicting harm on others than in patiently bearing it."[63] He fights by bearing the cross, and for this he must overcome his natural reluctance to suffer. Thus conflict, as a metaphor for the Christian life, merged, for Calvin, with a conception of the Christian life as acquiescence in suffering. He thought human beings "more endangered by prosperity than by adversity, for they are pleased by their successes and intoxicated by their own happiness."[64] They must learn to accept poverty, famine, disease, and exile—with some of which Calvin was well acquainted—indeed death itself, as disciplines that "bring us to a sense of our duty."[65] Through adversity "God tests his own, he examines them by afflictions, he puts them like gold in the furnace, not only to be purged but also to be known." This, for Calvin, was "the foundation of our philosophy." [66]

Because suffering has these salutary uses, God, as Calvin observed in connection with Job's loss of children and property, intends his people really to *feel* their afflictions, receiving them as "medicines." [67] This suggests another impulse in Calvin's rejection of Stoicism. "True patience," he observed, "is not the stubborn endurance of adversities (as the Stoics maintain in praising as virtue an unyielding hardness), but willing submission to God because we trust in his grace." He thought it "obstinacy rather than patience" and "opposition to God" to "scorn calamities under color of fortitude." [68]

His esteem for suffering brought Calvin close, at times, to the sects whose members identified the Christian life with the submission of a faithful minority to persecution. "We cannot fight for Christ," he exclaimed, "except on the understanding that the greater part of the world rises up in hostility against us and pursues us even unto death." Only too often "the good, in their zeal for righteousness, excite the hatred of the wicked. Christians in particular are almost doomed to suffer the hatred of the majority of men." We must prepare ourselves, "in our shade and leisure, when God indulges our weakness and does not permit the wicked wantonly to harass us," by facing the likelihood of future persecution, so that we may be "ready whenever it is necessary to advance into the arena." [69] As persecution grew in France, Calvin became more concrete. "Our Lord has wanted to afflict his own in many places. Poor people have had their throats cut, there have been many horrible and bloody butcheries, many outrages, tyrannies, and cruelties. Then the poor faithful will be expelled from their homes, and it will be much if they escape with their lives. Their goods will be seized, their wives and children will be like poor vagabonds, fleeing here and there, always in danger, like a bird on a branch." [70]

But even rebellion is not the only or even the most formidable adversary of the elect. Sinfulness, as long as the Christian opposes it, is not fatal; salvation is by faith alone, not by righteousness. The worst adversary of the Christian is therefore not sin but doubt, of which anxiety is the immediate consequence. Doubt and anxiety are thus the most terrible adversaries of every Christian, even the most faithful. "Every one of us knows only too well, from his own experience," Calvin insisted, "our difficulty in believing." [71] "Everyone's weakness certainly witnesses to the many doubts that steal upon us." [72] The saints "frequently stagger in unbelief." [73] "Faith is never without its combats," for the devil constantly suggests "many occasions for incredulity." [74] Calvin bore witness to the terrors of doubt. "As soon as we begin to call into doubt the promises of God," he reported, "our minds are distracted by various thoughts, we are terrified and continuously disquieted by the magnitude and variety of our dangers, until finally we are so stupefied that we no longer have any sense of the grace of God." [75] Each of these pronouncements reflects his own most agonizing experiences.

But his own experience also taught him that doubt is regularly contested by faith, although faith never, in this life, gains more than a precarious victory. If God, he confessed, perhaps recalling again the death of his wife,

> lets us remain long in grief and be almost consumed by it, we cannot but feel, humanly speaking, as if he had forgotten us. When the anxiety this provokes seizes the mind of a man, it plunges him in profound unbelief, so that he no longer hopes for any remedy. But if faith comes to his aid, he who thought God hostile or alien to him beholds in the mirror of its promise God's hidden and distant grace. [Christians] oscillate between these two emotions: between the occasions when Satan, by displaying the signs of God's wrath, drives them to despair and ruin, and those occasions when faith, recalling them to its promises, teaches them to wait patiently and rest in God until he again shows his fatherly face. . . . Faith does not obtain the victory at the first encounter but, exercised by many trials, [only] finally emerges the victor.[76]

This disturbing "oscillation" means also, however, that the "fears and cares" of the elect regularly give way to a "secret joy" sent from above.[77]

The outcome of the struggle with doubt is thus not itself doubtful. Doubt "does not mortally wound believers with its weapons but merely harasses them, or at most so injures them that the wound is curable," for "the root of faith can never be torn from the godly breast but clings so fast to the inmost parts that its light is never so extinguishd or snuffed out that it does not at least lurk as it were beneath the ashes."[78] The resistance believers oppose to their moments of doubt is itself a sign that all will be well.[79] We should therefore "not be unduly disturbed when God withdraws his word from us."[80] However enfeebled, faith must recover, for "God remains faithful and never deceives or deserts his own."[81] Calvin's confidence on this crucial matter was an illustration of the power of the doctrine of predestination to console the faithful.

Indeed, although doubt and anxiety are the work of the devil, the struggle against them contributes positively to the Christian life. It is essential to faith that "we have been in trepidation, anxious and disquieted, miserably harassed."[82] Doubt "exercises" faith by preventing it from degenerating into complacency.[83] An untroubled faith would, as Calvin knew, again from his own experience, be neither possible nor desirable. Nevertheless, "moderation" should prevail; the salutary "*solicitude*" of the faithful should not be confused with the terrible "*angoisse*" of unbelief.[84] "We should not tremble," he advised, "in such a way that we are turned about anxiously here and there and do not see the harbor to which we may direct our course."[85]

Calvin's other major plot represented the Christian life as a journey or pilgrimage, movement toward a goal, a conception also familiar to Erasmus.[86] It was not, for Calvin, just a figure of speech, but suffused with his feelings as an exile for whom there could be no return home, only a relentless movement forward. He compared the church to a tent. Because the children of God have "no fixed abode on earth" and must carry their shelter with them, they must be ready to move on whenever God commands.[87] "Our life is like a journey," he declared, "and it is not God's will that we should march along casually as we please, but he sets the goal before us, and also directs us on the right way to it."[88] The journey is no less arduous than military combat: "no one moves easily forward," and most are so weak that, "wavering and limping and even creeping along the ground, they move at a feeble pace" and "groan with weariness."[89] Calvin's conception of the Christian life as a journey is also notable for its single-mindedness. "We must take heed," he warned, "that we do not turn our thoughts or mind to any other activity but, on the contrary, endeavor to be free from every distraction and apply ourselves exclusively to God's calling."[90] We are allowed to love this life, but only if we "travel in it like strangers, always intent on our goal."[91]

Just as the militant Christian can depend, with God's help, on victory, so the Christian pilgrim can be sure that, however slowly, he will reach his goal. As Christians pass through the world, "the supporting hand of God everywhere and forever keeps them," and those whom God "effectively teaches he also strengthens, lest they grow weary in the middle of the journey."[92] Accordingly,

> let each of us proceed according to the measure of his puny capacity and set out upon the journey. No one shall start so inauspiciously as not daily to make some headway, though it be but slight. Therefore let us not cease so to act that we may make unceasing progress in the way of the Lord. And let us not despair at the slightness of our success; for even though attainment may not correspond to desire, when today outstrips yesterday the effort is not lost. Only let us look toward our mark with sincere simplicity and aspire to our goal, not fondly flattering ourselves nor excusing our own evil deeds, but with continuous effort striving toward this end: that we may surpass ourselves in goodness until we attain to goodness itself.[93]

Thus, whether dramatized as warfare or as pilgrimage, the Christian life acquires both unity and internal structure as it moves, through a succession of ardent and strenuous moments, from beginning to glorious denouement. Progressively realizing the divinely appointed purposes of human existence, it develops an increasingly close, confident, and loving relationship with God (faith), which is expressed in an increasingly spontaneous and joyful conformity to God's will (sanctification) and in wholehearted glorification of God and appreciation of his works. Progress and growth, nourished by the energy and strength of the spirit, are finally, for Calvin, the essence of the Christian life. "We must make progress," he proclaimed, "until death."[94]

This sense of the responsibility of the Christian to "progress" was also closely related, as it stimulated a concern to make profitable use of time, to Calvin's anxiety. For him "not only years but every day must be called to account so that each one may make progress. But there are few who require of themselves an accounting of time past, or who concern themselves with future time. So we rightly must pay the penalty of our idleness by spending most of our lives, like children, on the rudiments."[95] We must constantly evaluate the progress we have made in conformity to God's will. Calvin imagined himself—any Christian—doing so: "How? A year has already passed, three years, ten, twenty years since God revealed himself to me; and how have I profited since that time? I have not advanced as far as is required during the time since God received me into his house, during which he has never allowed me to go astray but has given me the grace to persevere."[96] The tension—and paradox—in this attitude to existence was nicely expressed by his near-contemporary, Saint Teresa, another over-achiever: "If we find ourselves unable to get profit out of a single hour, we are impeded from doing so for four. I have a great deal of experience of this."[97]

Calvin was especially concerned with advancement through education. He thought "doubly mad" those "who do not deign to learn because they think they know enough already." Only those who "continue to make progress by constant learning" are truly learned.[98] Moses, he noted, had still been open to God's instruction forty years after he had promulgated the law; David had always been ready to learn.[99] "Since Christians should make progress as long as they live," he urged, "it is certain that no one is so knowledgeable that he can do without teaching. Thus docility is no small part of our wisdom."[100] This hints at the anti-dogmatic principle of Erasmus; Calvin's position suggests the impossibility of a completed theology.

He had in mind, of course, again like Erasmus, the kind of knowledge that engages the whole personality and expresses itself in life; in short, the knowledge of faith, which is perfected in love. "The true growth of Christians," he declared, "is when they progress in knowledge and understanding, and then in love. For the more we make progress in knowledge, the more love should increase in us."[101] This is finally the significance of the obligation to make "daily progress toward believing."[102] With the increase of faith, "we must wish what is best in us to be better."[103] Calvin emphasized, again, that this advance would be neither rapid nor complete. Holiness is not achieved "in one moment or one day or one year; but through continual and sometimes even slow advances, God wipes out in his elect the corruptions of the flesh, cleanses them of guilt, and consecrates them to himself as temples, renewing all their minds to true purity, that they may repent all their lives and know that this warfare will end only at death."[104] In this life progress is open-ended; even those most advanced in growth toward "the full stature of Christ" are for Calvin, so to speak, only adolescents, unevenly developed, awkward, prone to humiliating regressions, yet always yearning for full maturity.[105] This position implied the continuing, if diminishing, imperfection of the elect and the need for tolerating impurity; it provided an antidote to his anxiety in the presence of disorder, even in the church.

But if we do what we must and, as Calvin tells us, remain open to the movements of the spirit and "do not cease to marvel," our faith, "weak as its beginnings may have been, will gradually advance more and more."[106] God's image will be progressively restored in us,[107] and we will experience an ever clearer and more vivid sense of "God's face, peaceful and calm and gracious toward us." We will have seen him, in the beginning, "afar off, but clearly enough to know we are not at all deceived." And "the more we advance, as we ought to continue to advance with steady progress, the nearer and surer sight of him we obtain, which, as it continues, grows even more familiar to us." [108] So the Christian life, for Calvin as for so many before him, culminates in the *visio Dei*.

V

A PROGRAM FOR
THE TIMES

12

Society

Like other Renaissance humanists, Calvin believed that his own time was caught up in a spiritual and moral crisis whose resolution required his own most ardent efforts. To set the world right—oh cursed spite, as he must often have felt—was what he was most insistently "called" to do; God sends prophets and teachers, he proclaimed, "to bring the world to order." [1] Calvin did not conceive of his task in life as the exposition of a "theology" for the ages. He had more urgent matters to attend to.

He implied this in glossing a conversation in which the prophet Isaiah revealed to Hezekiah, the pious king of Judah, the disasters that would befall his family in the next generation. Its wealth would be carried away by the king of Babylon, Isaiah had predicted, and Hezekiah's sons would become eunuchs in that ruler's palace. Hezekiah had reacted to this news with remarkable equanimity. "The word of the Lord which you have spoken is good," he told Isaiah. But, as the text reports, Hezekiah thought this only because the prophecy implied that "peace and security" would continue during his own lifetime. At this point, instead of rebuking the king for his self-centeredness, Calvin applauded the wisdom of his response. "Truly," Calvin reflected, "we ought to labor most for our own time and take it most into account. The future should not be overlooked, but what is present and urgent requires our attention more. For we who live at the same time are bound together by God with a stronger bond [than that which binds us to others] in order that, by consulting together, we may assist each other as much as we can." [2] In his sense of responsibility for the world we may discern the influence of the humanistic ideal of civic life. "It is a beautiful thing to philosophize in retirement far from intercourse with men," he wrote ironically in connection with the monastic *vita contemplativa*, "but it is not the part of Christian meekness, as if in hatred of the human race, to flee to the desert and the wilderness and at the same time to forsake those duties which the Lord has especially commanded." [3]

Calvin's program for dealing with the problems of his own age was based on his conception of God as *"legislateur et roy"* of the universe.[4] It was crucial for him "that God governs us." "When our Lord Jesus Christ appeared," Calvin declared, "he acquired possession of the whole world; and his kingdom was extended from one end of it to the other, especially with the proclamation of the Gospel. . . . God has consecrated the entire earth through the precious blood of his Son to the end that we may inhabit it *and live under his reign.*"[5] This meant that religious reform pointed also to the reform of the secular realm. "We must not only grieve for the offenses committed by unbelievers," Calvin warned, "but also recognize that we remain unworthy to look upon heaven until there is harmony and unanimity in religion, till God is purely worshipped by all, and *all the world is reformed.*"[6] Believers "truly worship God by the righteousness they maintain within their society."[7]

Calvin had often condemned the world for its "disorder"; conversely, he identified the restoration of order with the sovereignty of God. "No order can be said to prevail in the world," he declared, "until God erects his throne and rules among men."[8] But as a reformer in a time of crisis, he now meant by "order" not conformity to the abstract and indifferent principles of the cosmos but a practical order secured by obedience to a God who knows and wills what is best for his creatures. God, in this conception, intended even the heavenly bodies for the use of human beings. They provide light; they mark time.[9] "The sun is our servant," Calvin declared, "the moon our handmaid; the stars also were created to serve us."[10]

This utilitarianism is basic to Calvin's program for a society that exists to serve fundamental human needs; without society human existence would differ little "from that of cattle and beasts of prey."[11] Calvin regularly evaluated human arrangements for their utility. In this perspective marriage is good because it "preserves respectability and checks lascivious wanderings,"[12] and monogamy is better than polygamy because "there can be no conjugal harmony where there is rivalry among wives."[13] Small households are preferable to large because they are quieter.[14]

The same principle also gave to Calvin's social ethic a degree of flexibility not always associated with Calvinism. You should act rightly yourself, Calvin thought, but "not put pressure on others to follow your example, as if it were a rule." Everyone should examine "what his own vocation demands and what pertains to his own duty, and avoid rashly dictating what others should do. For it would be too rigidly imperious to prescribe to others as a rule what we follow as right and consonant with our own duty."[15] His flexibility, indeed, sometimes suggests the opportunism of Renaissance politics. He found biblical support for the notion that "we are not to hasten but should wait patiently and with peaceful minds for the right time [*opportunitas*]" to act.[16] God himself is in this sense an opportunist: he "has his own appointed time and knows the seasons [*opportunitates*] in which it is suitable both to punish the wicked and to assist the good."[17]

Calvin was never much attracted to Christian folly, however much he professed to distrust "the wisdom of the world,"[18] and this flexibility inclined him to a kind of bourgeois realism that he thought authorized by Scripture. A Christian, he argued, "does not knowingly and intentionally allow himself to be imposed on; he does not relinquish his prudence and judgment so that he can be more easily cheated, nor does he forget the difference between black and white." [19] He was persuaded, on the authority of Solomon, that God, "who has set the limits to our life, has at the same time entrusted to us its care; he has provided means and helps to preserve it; he has also made us able to foresee dangers; that they may not overwhelm us unaware, he has offered precautions and remedies. . . . the Lord has inspired in men the arts of taking counsel and caution, by which to comply with his providence in the preservation of life itself. . . . folly and prudence are instruments of the divine dispensation." [20]

Prudence, the virtue of taking precautions against future danger, was at least as attractive to this anxious man as to other humanists. [21] Although he warned against excessive confidence in human ability to anticipate the future, [22] Calvin thought of their ignorance of it as a kind of divine challenge to the ingenuity of human beings; God, he suggested, is "pleased to hide all future events from us so that, treating them as uncertain, we may provide remedies against them." [23] He recommended "comparison of past events" for teaching prudence. [24] Christ, he noted, had taught "careful provision of the things necessary for passing through life" in the parable of the wise and foolish virgins. [25] He minimized the tension between prudence and faith; [26] God "always guides us with the spirit of prudence." [27]

It is hardly surprising, then, that the possibility of an imprudent interpretation of the beatitudes made Calvin uneasy, and he glossed them with some care. We should not resist evil, he agreed, but this does not mean that we should not try to avert it. Because turning the other cheek may only incite greater wrath in an enemy, we should heed the *intent* of the injunction to do so, which is to reduce conflict. The patience shown in yielding up one's coat to him who has already taken one's cloak is commendable, but this does not bar taking a good case before the magistrate. We should give to him who asks but not be prodigal. We should lend without hoping to receive, but this does not prohibit interest; the commandment is intended only to encourage spontaneity in giving. [28] Calvin similarly "interpreted" other commandments. "Sell all ye have" is "not to be applied too exactly," nor should the example of the lilies of the field inhibit all care, but only such as stems from lack of faith. "Judge not" applies only to judgments inspired by malice. [29]

He commended various prudential strategies for survival in a wicked world. Distrust of other human beings seemed to him inevitable. "There are ways to discriminate among people," he urged, "which it would be imprudent and foolish to overlook," and "God permits us to be on our guard against unknown persons." [30] He rejected revenge but upheld the right of self-defense. [31] He also favored careful preparation for travel: "When anyone begins a trip, he inquires how far he can go in one day, he avoids weariness and provides against it as well as he can, and after having decided on

the length of his journey he looks for an inn; he also asks about the route."
Such carefulness differentiates human beings from animals.[32]

Calvin was aware, as well, that Christians sometimes find themselves in situations in which measures normally prohibited are necessary, and he did not hesitate to recommend them. He accepted trickery in the conduct of war, "for wars are not conducted only by smiting: those are considered the best generals who accomplish more by art and counsel than by force."[33] David's employment of Abner suggested to him that the saints may sometimes exploit the wicked.[34] He also agreed that emergencies can justify extraordinary measures. Probably troubled by it himself, he advanced a kind of *raison d' église* to defend the illegal preaching of the apostles: "in times of disorder it is necessary to attempt much that is contrary to established custom, especially when religion and the worship of God must be defended."[35] "Our calling is not always confined to its ordinary duties," Calvin noted, "because God sometimes imposes on his servants new and unusual roles [*personas*]."[36]

In spite of his devotion to inwardness, he was remarkably sensitive to appearances. "A filthy and torn garment disgraces a man," he observed, "while a clean and decorous one wins him much favor."[37] He could sound like a middle-class Castiglione: "As the clothes a man wears or his carriage and gestures sometimes spoil, sometimes enhance the impression he conveys, so *decorum* adorns all his actions."[38] His concern for public decency was also reflected in his refusal to believe that Isaiah had literally walked naked at the Lord's command. "It must not be thought," he warned, "that the prophet exposed himself completely without covering those parts which would be considered disgraceful."[39] Its importance to society made reputation even more important than appearance. "It should always be a concern of the Christian man," he urged, "to arrange his life for the edification of his neighbors."[40] But he also noted the worldly benefits of reputation. When it is bad, one has "difficulty in obtaining what one might want from his neighbor"; one also experiences "delays and reproaches on many sides."[41]

Calvin's shift, in thinking about society, from cosmic idealism to practicality is notable in his attitude to hierarchy. He did not reject it; he thought hierarchy useful for some purposes and under some conditions. He attributed to God the elevation of "princes, aristocrats, nobles, and all the ranks of magistrates and rulers,"[42] since "it is necessary that there should be some order among us."[43] But he did not see in hierarchy a manifestation of Order itself; it was simply one possible mode of social organization. It pertains only to the *"police exterieur."*[44] But before God and in principle all human beings are equal. Spiritually "there is no distinction or difference between man and woman, servant and master, poor and rich, great and small."[45]

Although he was inclined for practical reasons to accept existing social distinctions, he did not necessarily admire them. He loathed slavery. He rejoiced that it had disappeared from all of Europe except Spain, where he attributed its survival to the influence of barbarous Africans and Turks. It was better to hire servants than to own slaves.[46] Nevertheless, since the Old Testament patriarchs had practiced slavery and the apostles had tolerated it, Calvin could not condemn it absolutely.[47]

Though accepting social hierarchy in practice, he tacitly undermined it by emphasizing the vices of those at the top, as in his treatment of noble birth, whose origins he discerned in the "giants" of Genesis:

> Under the magnificent title of heroes, they cruelly exercised dominion and acquired power and fame for themselves by injuring and oppressing their brethren. And this was the first nobility of the world. Lest anyone take too much satisfaction in a long line of ancestors, this nobility, I repeat, raised itself on high by despising and insulting others. A famous name is not in itself to be condemned, since it is necessary for those whom the Lord has ornamented with special talents to be raised above others, and it is useful that there should be distinction of ranks in the world. But ambition is always vicious, especially when joined with a tyrannical ferocity and the powerful scorn the weak; the evil then is intolerable. It is much worse, however, when wicked men are honored for their crimes and the more audacious one is in doing harm, the more insolently he boasts of the empty smoke of titles.[48]

"Honor, wealth, and rank," Calvin observed, "are almost always accompanied by pride, so that it is difficult to subdue with a voluntary humility those who are filled with arrogance and scarcely acknowledge that they are men." Indeed, he noted that great men, whose elevation had originally been a reward for their courage and initiative, tended, once raised on high, to lose these virtues as a result of their ambition, "than which nothing is more servile." Earthly honors bind men, he thought, like "golden fetters, so that they cannot do their duty." A great personage, "if he is wise, will be suspicious of his greatness, lest it be an obstacle to him."[49] He also attacked other vices of the great, among them what seemed to him the mindless and wasteful frenzy of hunting. "When a hunter pursues game," he observed, "he expends much more labor than any workman or farmer. We see that even kings and great courtiers, when they hunt, are so blinded that they perceive no danger nor feel weariness."[50] Waste on the part of the great, the more conspicuous the more reprehensible, particularly offended him. He thought them "commonly ruled by greed for superfluous and excessively expensive luxuries."[51]

His reserve toward social distinction is also reflected in the respect with which he treated the "mechanic" arts; he celebrated them, along with the liberal arts, as gifts of God that display "the power of human acuteness."[52] "Artisans of every sort who serve the needs of men," he proclaimed, "are ministers of God and have the same aim as other ministers: namely the conservation of the human race."[53] God alone is their "author and teacher."[54]

Sometimes he argued, partly perhaps to shame the upper classes, that the poor and humble are better off than the great, morally and in other respects. "In almost every age," he asserted, "the common people, although driven by wildness and barbarity, are less impious than the nobles or courtiers or

other crafty men who think they excel others in talent and prudence."[55] The
poor and humble, he professed to believe, are more likely to be happy than
the rich. They are "free from envy, tumults and strife."[56] They receive as
much enjoyment from their own humbler fare: "Peasants and artisans value
their pork and beef, their cheeses and curds, their onions and cabbages, no
less than most of the rich do their sumptuous fare."[57] Although Christ's
disciples "may not have had splendid fortunes, they lived no less happily at
home, working with their hands, than the richest man alive." Humble folk
also have closer families. "Men of lower rank, used to a quiet and modest
life," he thought, "suffer more when separated from their wives and children than those who are driven by ambition, or those whom good fortune
carries hither and yon."[58] They are also friendlier and more hospitable; "an
invitation from a poor man is easier and more frank" because the poor "do
not fear dishonor if they do not entertain their guests splendidly, for they
adhere more closely to the ancient custom of mutual communication."[59]
Some of these sentiments may suggest a closer acquaintance with books,
especially of Stoic provenance, than with the realities of lower-class life.

Calvin also suggested the superior sanctity of the lowly, the greater likelihood of their being numbered among the elect, and the doubtful prospects
for salvation of the great and powerful. "By its nature wealth does not prevent us from following God," he remarked, "but human nature is so depraved, it is almost certain that those who are well off will choke on their
riches."[60] Christ had first "gathered a church for himself from the common
people."[61] Unlike those apologists for the Counter Reformation who emphasized Christ's descent from David the King,[62] Calvin stressed Christ's
humble origins. "God adorned his Son more with the wretched appearance
of a beggar," he insisted, "than if he had glistened with all the regalia of
kings."[63] He made a point of Christ's employment since childhood as a
workman. He even thought Christ illiterate.[64]

His practicality also revealed itself in an awareness of the realities of
urban society and a mercantile economy. He knew that "today Venice or
Antwerp could not be ruined without great injury to many nations,"[65] and
he had noticed that "nothing strengthens or more rapidly enriches a region
than those great and navigable rivers by which every kind of merchandise
can easily be imported and exported."[66] Such minor events of urban life as
impulse buying had attracted his attention. "We know," he remarked, without moralizing about a propensity he had probably noted in himself, "that a
person who enters a shop full of various kinds of beautiful merchandise,
even with no intention of buying anything, nevertheless changes his mind,
caught by attractive things."[67]

Like other humanists, he defended wealth. "Riches in themselves and by
their nature," he proclaimed, "are not at all to be condemned; and it is even
a great blasphemy against God to disapprove of riches, implying that a man
who possesses them is thereby wholly corrupted. For where do riches come
from, if not from God?" He also thought material inequality inevitable and
not necessarily undesirable. The "varying mixture of rich and poor," after

all, is determined by providence.[68] It is not wrong for the poor to eat "coarse bread and a scanty diet" while the rich live "more abundantly, according to their circumstances," as long as they do so "temperately, not failing others," and taking care of the poor.[69]

Accordingly, Calvin rejected a literal interpretation of Christ's advice to the rich young man to sell all he had and give to the poor. We must, he thought, use common sense here. Christ had intended only to force the young man to recognize his "hidden vice." "A farmer who must live by his labor and support his children would sin by selling his little farm unless he had to," Calvin pointed out; "to hold what God has placed in our hands is more virtuous than to destroy everything, as long as we support our family simply and give something to the poor."[70] He was particularly opposed to "plundering the rich" in order to "deal humanely with the poor."[71] This position shaped his interpretation of the story of Lazarus and Dives. It was not intended, he argued, as a criticism of wealth as such, because it ends with Lazarus in the bosom of Abraham, a rich man. It teaches, rather, "that God, by his grace and infinite goodness, calls rich and poor alike to salvation."[72] Heaven is open "to all who have either used their wealth properly or endured poverty patiently."[73] God, "by incorporating us into the body of his son, makes us again lords of the world, so that we may legitimately enjoy as our own everything that he gives so abundantly."[74]

Calvin thought private property fundamental to social order. "It pertains to the maintenance of human society," he argued, "that each person should possess what is his own; that some should acquire property by purchase, to others it should come by hereditary right, to others by title of gift; that each should increase his means by ingenuity or physical strength or other gifts. In short, political order requires that each should hold what is his own."[75] The advocacy of communism by sectarian groups threatened, he believed, to "overthrow all order" and "turn all the world into a forest of brigands where, without reckoning or paying, each takes for himself what he can get."[76] He thought Scripture so clearly opposed to communism "that no one can be ignorant on the subject." He denied that the apostolic church had practiced it.[77]

He took money for granted as "a medium for reciprocal communication among men, principally used for buying and selling merchandise."[78] Though he had reservations about it, he also thought well of commerce, even defending Joseph for taking the flocks and lands of the penniless Egyptians in return for Pharaoh's grain. "No one," he argued, "freely parts with what he owns."[79] Maritime commerce, in spite of its abuses, he considered of "no small utility to men."[80] The commercial mentality of his age is vividly reflected in the economic metaphor he employed for characterizing the lives of the saints. "Those who expend usefully what God has deposited with them," he observed, "are said to trade. For the life of the godly is aptly compared to business, since they ought to deal with one another in order to maintain their fellowship; and the industry by which each person carries out the injunction laid on him, and his very calling, the capacity of doing right, and his other gifts, are regarded as merchandise, since their purpose and use is to facilitate intercommunication among men."[81] He praised merchants for service to the community: they "not only work hard but also expose themselves to many inconveniences and dangers."[82]

He saw the value, accordingly, of the formal arrangements that facilitate commercial transactions. Among these were precise and dependable contracts, so important for reducing the anxieties of doing business.[83] Another was the taking of interest. Calvin took pains to dissociate Christ's injunction to "lend, expecting nothing in return" from ordinary business loans.[84] He took issue with the conventional view that "all usury is to be condemned without exception"; where the rich are concerned, he insisted, "usury is freely permitted." His attitude to it, to be sure, was tinged with distaste:

> Only those exactions are condemned as unjust in which the creditor, losing sight of equity, burdens and oppresses his debtor. I should, indeed, be unwilling to take usury under my patronage, and I wish the name itself were banished from the world; but I do not dare to pronounce upon so important a point more than God's words convey. It is abundantly clear that the ancient people were prohibited from usury, but we must need confess that this was a part of their political constitution. Hence it follows that usury is not now unlawful, except insofar as it contravenes equity and brotherly union.[85]

Calvin's ambivalence and inconsistency on social and economic matters was partly a result of his effort, as so often elsewhere, to balance between extremes. He sought to avoid either endorsing or condemning loans at interest. He could not argue that riches pose no danger to the Christian life, but he wanted also to dissociate himself from those who thought poverty itself a virtue:

> Many place angelical perfection in poverty, as if the cultivation of piety and obedience to God were impossible without the divestment of wealth. Few indeed imitate Crates the Theban, who threw his treasures into the sea because he did not think he would be saved unless these were sacrificed. And many fanatics refuse rich men the hope of salvation, as if poverty were the only gate to heaven, although it sometimes involves men with greater disadvantages than riches. But Augustine reminds us that rich and poor share the same heritage. . . . On the other hand, we must beware of the opposite evil, lest riches hinder or so burden us that we advance less readily toward the kingdom of heaven.[86]

He thought middling rank and wealth preferable to either extreme. "How much more useful and desirable for us," he exclaimed, "is a moderate fortune, which is at least more peaceful and neither exposed to storms of envy nor liable to dark suspicions."[87]

Middle-class attitudes also shaped his esteem for work; his doctrine of the calling meant that we should invest our God-given energies primarily in our work. Christ taught, he believed, "that men were created for activity," that they are not to "sink into laziness." [88] "We are born to work," he informed his congregation: "God does not intend us to be lazy when we are living in this world, for he has given men hands and feet, he has given them industry." It may be that "the work in which men now engage is a punishment for sin," but work is itself a need of human nature. Adam, before the Fall, was "placed in a garden in order to tend it." A human being who does not work is like "a block of useless wood." [89]

He detested idleness, which, as misuse of time, made him anxious. "When we see what a short interval of life is allotted to us," he argued, "we ought to be ashamed of languishing in idleness." [90] There was "nothing more disgraceful," in his opinion, "than a lazy good-for-nothing who is of no use either to himself or to others but seems to have been born only to eat and drink." [91] He was indignant at the notion that the apostles were unemployed and even more that anyone should consider them to have been mendicants. "Those who think that they abandoned their possessions and came to Christ naked and empty-handed are talking nonsense," he declared, "but they are truly even more foolish who identify perfection with begging." [92]

Yet, recognizing that even work can be carried to excess, Calvin again strove for a middle ground. Work too had to be kept under control, for "men torment and weaken themselves in vain when they busy themselves more than their calling permits or requires." [93] He may have been thinking of himself in remarking that "a great many people are their own executioners through working constantly and without measure." [94] Control is also needed to make work efficient and useful. "We know," he remarked, "how perversely men bustle about unless a definite regimen is prescribed to them so that they do not run around in circles." [95]

His doctrine of the calling contributed in various ways to the efficiency of work, notably as it promoted the division of labor. He suggested this in what was also a warning to himself, distracted as he was by his many and diverse duties. "Let God's servants learn to measure their capacities carefully," he warned, "lest they grow weak by ambitiously embracing too many occupations." "The propensity to engage in too many things" is "a common malady" that shows disregard for individual talents and limitations. "Individuals," he pointed out, conveniently forgetting his dissociation elsewhere of calling from natural talent, "are only endowed with a limited measure of gifts," and these should determine "the distribution of duties." [96]

But Calvin was also concerned lest the division of labor be too rigid to serve changing needs. This required him to grapple with Paul's injunction that "everyone remain in the situation to which he was called." It was important, Calvin thought, that a tailor be allowed "to learn another trade, or a merchant to shift to agriculture." Paul "only meant to correct the thoughtless eagerness that impels some to change their situation without sufficient reason, moved by superstition or some other influence." [97]

Calvin's esteem for work was accompanied by exhortations to frugality. God, he often repeated, "has commended frugality and temperance to us and prohibited luxuriating wantonly in abundance." He insisted that "the rich, whether through inheritance or their own industry, should bear in mind that what is left over is meant not for intemperance or luxury but for relieving the needs of brethren." [98] Christians must "learn both to avoid squandering their resources in unnecessary expenditure and to be liberal when appropriate." [99] He offered an example, a reflection, perhaps, of the housing shortage in Geneva, its population swollen by refugees: "If someone with a large household uses a large house, he cannot be blamed; but when men, swollen with ambition, make superfluous additions to their houses so that they may live more comfortably, and when one person alone occupies a habitation that would be enough for several families, this would be empty display and must be condemned. Such people act as if they should be able to eject others and alone enjoy a house and home, and as if others should live in the open air or go elsewhere to find a place to live." [100]

His esteem for frugality shaped his vision of Christ as "a singular example of a thrifty and frugal life." [101] This notion made for some imaginative readings of Scripture, as when Calvin considered the "great feast" in the house of Levi, with its "copiousness and elegance of food." Christ's presence at this event compelled him to recognize "that Christ was not so austere as not sometimes to allow himself to be entertained by the rich, as long as there was no extravagance." Nevertheless, Calvin insisted, "There is no doubt that, since he was himself a singular example of continence, he would have exhorted his own guests to a frugal and restrained diet, and he would never have tolerated a wasteful and profligate extravagance." [102] He dealt with the alabaster flask of ointment brought to Christ by the penitent woman in the village of Nain with something close to casuistry. In this case, he suggested, we must look to the intention of the action:

> The wretched sinner showed in this way that she owed everything to him. He did not at all wish for luxury, he was not allured by sweet smells, he did not approve of ornate worship, but he only needed the fervor by which she showed her repentance. That she fell to the ground at Christ's feet and lay there prostrate revealed her shame and humility. She expressed by the ointment that she offered herself and all she had to Christ as a sacrifice. We should imitate her in all these things; but the extravagance of the ointment was a unique action on which it would be wrong to base a rule. [103]

Ignoring its implications for the value of work, he also imposed the ideal of frugality on the story of Martha and Mary. Christ, he suggested, had reproved Martha for having "gone too far" in her hospitality. He "preferred to be treated frugally and with modest fare, rather than to subject a holy matron to do so much work." [104]

Calvin was equally frugal about time. His biblical commentaries often suggest his awareness of its passage. "I pass on quickly," he may explain in the course of a lecture, "before the time stops me." [105] He approved of birthday celebrations chiefly because they give us an opportunity to consider "how the time God has given us has been wasted in wickedness and uselessness." [106]

But always fundamental to Calvin's social thought was his concern for community. He was concerned with work and the use of both wealth and time chiefly because he saw them as scarce resources for meeting community needs.

> God has joined and united us together so that we might have a community, for men should not be separate. It is true that our Lord had ordained *la police* so that each may have his household, his family, his wife, his children, so that each one will have his station, but in such a way that no one may be exempted from the community so that he can say, I will live for myself alone. That would be to live worse than a beast. What then? We should know that God has obligated us to one another to help each other; and at least, when we see anyone in need, although we cannot do him the good we would like, that we treat him humanly. . . . It is too great a cruelty on our part if we see a poor and afflicted man and do not try to help him but rather turn away from him.[107]

He employed the traditional organic metaphor for society, in which, as he wrote, no member has "power for itself nor applies it to its own private use, but each pours it out to the fellow members"; what chiefly matters is "the common advantage of the whole body."[108] Occasionally he identified this community, like a Stoic, with the whole human race. All people, he could maintain, are "bound together as by a sacred chain," which "should be embraced in one feeling of love."[109] But this sublime conception generally yielded, for him, to a more practical view of community based on neighborhood. "All the blessings we enjoy," he proclaimed, "have been entrusted to us by the Lord on this condition, that they should be dispensed for the good of our neighbors."[110] Neighborhoods, furthermore, were themselves based on households, and when he discussed social relationships at this level, he preferred a metaphor from the world of work with connotations rather different from those of a body. "Society," he declared, "consists of groups that are like yokes, in which there is a mutual obligation of parties." He counted six status categories in the household, linked by three sorts of yoke: the yoke of marriage uniting husband and wife, the yoke binding parents and children, and the yoke connecting masters and servants.[111] When he thought about society in this way, his objection to treating human beings like beasts disappeared. "God," he declared, "has put men, as one would do with beasts, under a yoke, so to speak; the brute beasts should teach us what we must do."[112]

As the metaphor of the yoke suggests, he was profoundly aware of the economic dimension of human community. He had understood its importance since his youth; even for the Stoics, he pointed out, it had been "axiomatic that men have been begotten for the sake of their fellows to share one another's toil, to take counsel together, to share themselves and their possessions, insofar as it is for the public good."[113] Human interdependence was expressed in the division of labor, by which human beings had developed "arts and crafts, so that one will be a baker, another an agricultural worker, another a shoemaker, another a clothier." But this arrangement had, for Calvin, a social as well as an economic purpose. God had intended the division of labor to reinforce community by making human beings dependent on each other.[114]

Thus, if Calvinism contributed through the doctrine of predestination to "a feeling of unprecedented inner loneliness of the single individual," as Max Weber believed,[115] this was contrary to Calvin's intention. He insisted on the primacy of community over individual, functionally but in the end also spiritually. He thought individuals "too tenacious of their rights, too zealous for their own convenience to the detriment of others." Christ, he pointed out, had taught his followers "not to force their rights all the way." We must "be ready to settle even at a loss rather than pursue our rights relentlessly." Anyone who "neglects the common interest for his private interest not only shows himself lacking in the true understanding of piety but also improperly seeks his own advantage."[116]

The charge was obviously directed against the rich; for Calvin, wealth was given by God to meet the needs of community, notably those of its neediest members. It was, for him, only common sense "that the hungry are defrauded of their rights if their hunger is not relieved."[117] We are all, he wrote, "stewards of everything God has conferred on us by which we are able to help our neighbor, and are required to render account of our stewardship."[118] The rich "must one day give a reckoning of their vast wealth, that they may carefully and faithfully apply their abundance to good uses approved by God."[119]

Again Calvin aimed to be practical; he insisted on *effective* provision for the needs of the poor. "Praise for benevolence," he argued, "should not be based on indiscriminate giving but on succoring the poor, and expenditure on proper and legitimate uses."[120] A truly "provident man [*homo providus*]" will also calculate, on the basis of his other obligations, how much he can afford to give to others. He should not, by his generosity, "cheat his children or his household, nor impoverish his own family."[121] Calvin was aware that the danger of extremism in this area was slight, but the point reflects, once more, his practicality.[122]

His practicality, his common sense, and his flexibility in the context of changing economic and social needs are all evident in his reflections on the Fifteenth Psalm, a *locus classicus* for the discussion of a variety of unjust economic practices broadly considered usurious. He was prepared to condemn any economic transaction "in which fairness is not respected *on both sides.*" Any exchange "in which one party wickedly aims to profit by the loss of the other, whatever we call this," he declared, "is blameworthy." He admonished his readers "against trying to cheat and deceive; let them not imagine anything to be lawful that is grievous and harmful to others." This general principle allowed him to distinguish between the permissible and impermissible. "It is a principle of justice common to all peoples and times that we should not oppress miserable and needy men, from which it follows that the profit gained without injuring anyone by him who lends his money at interest is not to be considered unlawful.'' He concluded by an appeal to the Golden Rule, which should make ''lengthy disputation unnecessary.'' [123] The basis of a Christian society, for Calvin, is a constant awareness, deeply rooted in the heart, of human community in Christ.

13

Polity

One of the worst abominations of classical antiquity, Calvin thought, had been the cynical exploitation of religion by rulers for purposes of social control. "We will not find, among either the Greeks or Latins," he declared, "any of the upper classes and the major rulers sharing the errors of the people. They feigned religion to keep the others obedient. They participated in great processions, they pretended no small reverence; but privately, among their intimates, they laughed at all these absurdities."[1] Calvin, as we have seen, was also incensed by the abuse of the piety of the people in his own time, when "clever men" among the rulers of Europe were inventing "many things in religion by which to inspire common folk with reverence and to strike them with terror."[2] He may have been deploring what Machiavelli recommended; but both recognized the political uses of religion.

Calvin proposed to abolish this "mixture" of the wickedness of men with heavenly things by distinguishing sharply between the "spiritual" realm of "piety and reverencing God," and the "temporal" or "political" realm responsible for "laying down laws" and "the duties of humanity and citizenship that must be maintained among men." When he made this distinction he sounded much like Luther on the two "regiments," a distinction he associated with the dualistic conception of human being that sometimes attracted him. "There are in man, so to speak," Calvin wrote, "two worlds, over which different kings and different laws have authority." One "resides in the inner mind," the other "regulates only outward behavior." They "must always be examined separately."[3] They must also be kept separate. "Pious kings," Calvin wrote, "leave to the church her jurisdiction, and to priests the duties assigned them by the Lord."[4] The clergy, on the other hand, must exercise no civil authority. Calvin was proud that in Geneva he and Farel had restored "the power of the sword and other parts of civil jurisdiction that bishops and priests had wrested from the magistrate."[5]

This was necessary because, for Calvin, the civil magistrate played a far more positive role in the divinely ordained scheme of things than for Luther.

Because Christ, as Calvin proclaimed, is king over the whole earth, God's glory, although it "glows in every part of the world, especially shines forth when legitimate government flourishes among mortals."[6] The power of princes exists to promote God's glory; hence the maintenance of a practical order in society—*la police*—is "a holy thing in this world."[7] A true king, as he informed Francis I in the epistle to the first edition of the *Institutes,* must "recognize himself as a minister of God in governing his kingdom."[8] Civil authority is therefore "a calling, not only holy and lawful before God, but also the most sacred and by far the most honorable of all callings in the whole life of mortal men."[9] Indeed not only princes but all magistrates were, for Calvin, ministers of God, his vicars, "not rightly inaugurated in their duties unless they consecrate themselves to God and reverence his majesty."[10] In serving him, they must be guided by his Word "as the certain rule of all government and administration"; and they must finally "render an account of their office to him as supreme judge."[11]

More specifically, rulers represent "God's tribunal on earth." Their first responsibility is the administration of justice as lesser judges, subordinate to the Supreme Judge, to whom they are accountable.[12] In this capacity they must "bridle" the wicked "lest they break loose," and they must "draw the sword" against those who disrupt the social order.[13] For this, rulers require "the power and greatness necessary to punish evil," without which "the world would be full of robberies and murders."[14]

This conception of civil government was traditional; rulers had long been expected to suppress wickedness and vice. But social discipline seemed particularly urgent to Calvin: chaos would everywhere result, he believed, if government were relaxed, for "we know how great is the wantonness of human nature."[15] Without government and laws, he declared, "it would be far better for us to be wild beasts wandering in the forests, for we know how ferocious are human passions. Unless, therefore, there is some restraint, the condition of wild beasts would be better than ours." Beasts, after all, "can dispense with a governor because they do not tear apart their own kind."[16] When crime is left unpunished, "it pollutes the whole country." This dreadful thought touched off old anxieties and memories of ancient myths; pollution, Calvin warned, incites the wrath of God "against a whole people, but chiefly in the person of the king."[17] Even tyranny is preferable to anarchy; when "the judgment-seats have been pulled down, everyone insults everybody else, cruelty flourishes, and licentiousness rages without control."[18] Where "no one yields to others, everyone tests how much he can get away with. The result is freedom to plunger and ravage, deception and killing."[19] Like Machiavelli, Calvin ridiculed idealistic philosophical discourse about politics for its lack of realism about human nature.[20]

Dealing with the wickedness of mankind requires initiative, diligence, and self- discipline on the part of rulers. "Princes are not raised to honor by God so that they may settle into indolence or indulge their passions," Calvin declared; "the office of a prince is a laborious burden if he discharges it rightly."[21] A ruler must also be severe. "No one will be fit to govern a people," he insisted, "unless he has learned to be rigorous when necessary. Licentiousness cannot be avoided under an effeminate and slothful prince, or even under a prince who is too easy-going and negligent."[22] A prince who fails to punish evildoers makes himself their accomplice.[23] But he parted company with Machiavelli in his conviction that a ruler should also be a good and pious man. Scripture, he pointed out, warns "kings and those eminent in wealth or power on earth to submit reverently to God's Word and not think themselves exempt from the laws of the community, or absolved because of their greatness, for God does not respect persons."[24] A ruler's virtues should also set an example to his successors.[25]

All of this implied the subordination of the ruler to God's law, but Calvin insisted on more than this. He was convinced that "men cannot dwell together without laws" and that "without laws human existence would be a barbarity worse than solitude."[26] But God wishes all in authority to rule not only by law but by a "fixed law," for "when laws are variable, many persons inevitably suffer injury, and no private right will be secure unless the law is universal. Where laws can be made and remade, caprice replaces justice."[27] As this position implies, judges—the point is not made explicit but it certainly includes the prince who is chief magistrate in any polity— "should be limited by specific laws lest, left to themselves, they should be influenced this way or that by favoritism or malice."[28] With this high view of law it is hardly surprising that Calvin took a benign view of the recourse of Christians to courts of law, citing in this connection the willingness of Paul to submit to the judgment of the Roman authorities in Judea. "Whenever a similar need occurs," he argued, "we should not scruple to seek help from laws and the political order," for "God, who has instituted courts of law, allows his own their legitimate use."[29]

Just as rulers are required to maintain order, subjects are obligated to obey them. "It is our duty," Calvin declared, "to show ourselves compliant and obedient to whomever he sets over the places where we live."[30] Nor should obedience be rendered grudgingly: "Subjects should not be held in subjection to princes and governors only by terror, as persons are accustomed to yield to an armed enemy who will promptly take vengeance on them if they resist, but because the obedience rendered to them is rendered to God, from whom their power comes."[31]

Because the wickedness of a ruler does not end the need of the community for political discipline, it cannot excuse disobedience. Calvin believed, like Luther, that even wicked rulers have been appointed by God, though "in his anger, to punish our ingratitude."[32] Although, "blinded with pride," such rulers "despise the rest of the world as if their splendor and dignity distinguished them from the common condition of men."[33] Resistance to them is equivalent to "resisting God himself."[34] Calvin condemned it categorically. "Whoever rises insolently in rebellion against the magistrate and those with authority or office," he charged, "seeks anarchy." Rebellion "aims at the disruption of order, yes, and what is more, strikes at humanity itself."[35] The very thought of rebellion is "not only foolish and useless but altogether criminal."[36] This again sounds much like Luther.

But underlying this conservative and thoroughly traditional position were very untraditional assumptions about politics. Calvin accepted the political absolutism dominant in his time, but he was no apologist for it. He accepted it on practical grounds, not because the absolute monarchy of God over the universe established it as the perfect kind of government. He accepted it only as the most effective form of government for most states and for the time being. But he opposed abstract speculation about ideal polities. It would be "an idle pastime," he wrote, "for men in private life to dispute over what would be the best kind of government in the place where they live." This question "admits of no simple solution but requires deliberation, since the nature of the discussion depends largely upon the circumstances." It is difficult to decide in general what form of government "excels in *usefulness*, since [the available alternatives] contend on such equal terms." This is why, "if you fix your eyes not on one city alone, but look around and glance at the world as a whole, or at least cast your sight upon regions farther off, divine providence has wisely arranged that various countries should be ruled by various kinds of government. For as elements cohere only in unequal proportion, so countries are best held together according to their own particular inequality." Again Calvin suggests Machiavelli.[37]

Once more his primary criterion was utility. He opposed "long discourse concerning the best kind of laws" on the ground that "every nation is left free to make such laws as it foresees to be profitable for itself," subject only to "the perpetual rule of love."[38] Though all laws should aim at equity, utility points to their diversity, which "is perfectly adapted to maintain the observance of God's law."[39] It also calls for flexibility, as he noted in criticizing the protest of Leo the Great against the famous decree of Chalcedon that appeared to undermine the Roman primacy. "We know," he wrote, "that *politia* admits, nay even requires, various change according to the varying condition of the times."[40]

He also preferred, while acknowledging that it was not appropriate for all political bodies, what Walter Ullmann has called the "ascending theme" in politics.[41] He favored a republic, and he articulated his republicanism with clarity and force in the last chapter of the *Institutes*. That this chapter might have antagonized some readers, notably in France, and that it hardly seems essential to the work as a whole suggests the depth of his republicanism. It may also hint at his awareness of affinities between civic humanism and evangelical Christianity.[42]

His republican sympathies underlie his outrage at "tyranny," which offended him on various counts. A tyrant is, in the first place, by definition a ruler out of control, self-control being one of the virtues indispensable to "ministers of divine justice."[43] Calvin was outraged by the excesses of tyrants:

> When tyranny has lost its concern for justice, there are no limits to its wickedness; and lamentations do not soften it but aggravate its cruelty. And flatterers excite it by saying that the shortest way to control subjects and keep them quiet is so to oppress them that they do not even dare to open their mouths,

and if they complain or murmur that they should be more harshly treated so that they may be hardened to servitude and, as it were calloused to bondage. Tyrants therefore do not rest from their injuries and contumelies until the wretched people have altogether given up.[44]

The pope, as we have noted earlier, was for Calvin a prime example of tyranny: "He exempts himself from all judgments and wishes to rule in such a tyrannical fashion that he regards his own whim as law."[45]

From the standpoint of subjects, tyranny is a violation of human dignity; full humanity requires liberty, which—Calvin quoted Sophocles on the point—is lost by anyone under the rule of a tyrant.[46] Under tyranny "many thousands of men are subject to one" and "suffer many humiliations."[47] and only a degraded people could "prefer the yoke of tyranny to the inconveniences of change."[48] "There is nothing that men endure with more distress," Calvin observed with sympathy, "than to have a yoke laid on them, nor do they willingly submit to the despotic rule of the powerful. . . . There is no doubt that God has struck with the spirit of cowardice those who, like asses, willingly offer their shoulders for burdens."[49] Tyrants are hated "by the whole world," so that, "when they are dead or ruined, everybody rejoices and expresses feelings he had previously dissembled through fear." Tyranny is a perversion of order; its overthrow can thus be called a *restitutio*. God himself, Calvin thought, cannot endure tyrants; he listens in sympathy to the "secret groans" of those who live under them.[50] Even when he attacked rebellion against a tyrant, as consistency required him to do, he gave off a double message. "A man of most excellent disposition," he wrote, "finds it utterly senseless to bear an unjust and excessively imperious domination, if only he can in some way throw it off. And this is the common judgment of human reason: the mark of a servile and abject person is to bear it with patience; that of an honorable and freeborn man to shake it off. . . . But the Lord condemns this excessive haughtiness and enjoins upon his own people a patience disgraceful in men's eyes."[51] What is explicit here is belied by Calvin's detestation of tyrants.[52]

He also detested world empires, and indeed all large aggregations of political power. Because "no one person is competent to rule the whole earth," he believed, the notion of universal empire is "utterly absurd."[53] "The more these monarchies grow," he remarked of Daniel's four kingdoms, "the more licentiousness increases in the world, as practical experience readily teaches. Thus how great is the folly and madness of almost all who want kings to be extremely powerful, as though one wanted a river to flow very rapidly! For the swifter, the deeper, and the wider a river is, the more destructively it will inundate the whole neighborhood."[54] He shared the civic humanists' hatred of the Roman Empire for subverting the republic,[55] and he drew from Augustine the characterization of "almost all large kingdoms" as "great robberies."[56] Such views were closely related to the actual pluralism of contemporary Europe.[57]

It is well known that Calvin also provided, in a manner consistent with his doctrine of the calling and the needs of practical order, for resistance to ungodly rulers and unlawful commands. "We must obey princes and others who are in authority," he asserted, "but only insofar as they do not deny to God, the supreme king, father, and lord, what is due him."[58] Passive disobedience to "the impious and wicked edicts of kings" is therefore permissible to all subjects;[59] Calvin pointed, as an example, to the refusal of the Hebrew midwives to obey Pharaoh's order to kill the male infants of Hebrew mothers. Those who obey the wicked commands of men, he commented, "display by their cowardice an inexcusable contempt for God."[60] The obligation of obedience to rulers "is never to lead us away from obedience to him to whose will the desires of all kings ought to be subject, to whose decrees all their commands ought to yield, to whose majesty their scepters ought to be submitted."[61]

Moreover, Calvin provided for active resistance to public authority in accordance with the principle that a ruler "must be brought to order" who "exalts himself to the point that he diminishes the honor and right of God" and "goes beyond the limits of his office."[62] But this responsibility cannot rightly be assumed by anybody; it is a function of vocation. To private persons, "no command has been given except to obey and suffer"; but lesser magistrates should "apply themselves with the highest diligence to prevent freedom (whose guardians they have been appointed) from being in any respect diminished, far less be violated. If they are not sufficiently alert and careful, they are faithless to their country."[63] "I am so far from forbidding them to withstand the fierce licentiousness of kings in accordance with their duty," he asserted, "that, if they wink at kings who violently fall upon and assault the lowly common folk, I declare that their dissimulation involves nefarious perfidy, because they dishonestly betray the freedom of the people, of which they know that they have been appointed protectors by God's ordinance." He cited both ancient and contemporary precedent for such intervention.[64] Because these subordinate officials are, in such matters, directly responsible to God rather than to their immediate superiors, Calvin's position was also subversive of hierarchy.

This was the ordinary—the "orderly"—form of political revolution. But knowing something of the past and sure that history is ruled by providence, Calvin also recognized the possibility of another kind. As had happened with Moses, he observed, God sometimes "raises up open avengers from among his servants and arms them with his command to punish a wicked government and deliver his people, oppressed in unjust ways, from miserable calamity." God may also "direct to this end the rage of men who intend one thing but perform another"; thus the Persian conquest of Babylon had liberated the people of Israel. "However these deeds of men are judged in themselves," Calvin observed, "the Lord accomplished his work through them, both when he broke the bloody scepters of arrogant kings and when he overturned intolerable governments. Let the princes hear and be afraid."[65]

Both these examples again suggest God's aversion to tyranny and Calvin's preference for a republic. As kings are rarely "endowed with enough

keenness and prudence to know how much is enough" and are always likely
to rule "immoderately," it is "safer and more bearable for a number to
exercise government, so that they may help one another and teach and admonish one another; and if one asserts himself unfairly, there may be a number of censors and masters to restrain his willfulness." A republic, in short,
is more *moderate* than other forms of polity; and because "no kind of government is more happy than one where freedom is regulated with becoming
moderation and is properly established on a durable basis," so also Calvin
"reckoned most happy those permitted to enjoy this state."[66]

His emphasis on the obligation of governments to implement God's will
in the world also consecrated the *vita activa* and further allied him with civic
humanism. "No kind of life is more praiseworthy to God," he believed,
"than that which is useful to the society of man."[67] Since God requires that
the world be ruled, it would be "deplorable" if careers in politics were "not
only scorned but stubbornly rejected."[68]

Calvin's political theory was not original, and it is least interesting, perhaps, when he tries to make it consistent, as in his effort to distinguish two
realms of governance in the manner of Luther. He is most instructive where
the unresolved tensions in his thought make themselves felt. In fact, the
political realm was not, for Calvin, only an "order of repression." When he
thought of it in this way, he used such terms as *administratio* or—in the
vernacular—*police*. Another less precise term in his political vocabulary
suggests his more positive conception: *"status,"* a word that did not yet
quite refer specifically to politics.[69] In Calvin's usage it still combined a narrowly political with a more comprehensive social content, which is suggested in a model of a "rightly ordered state" that he discovered in
Scripture. The state, he learned there, included "first grain and other things
necessary for nourishment, then military strength, third skill in ruling a people and other aspects of political government, fourth the prophetic office,
and fifth the mechanical arts." A "well-regulated commonwealth [*statum
reipublicae bene constitutum*]" is one in which "the various orders of judges
and senators, soldiers, captains, artisans and doctors [i.e., ministers] aid
each other by their mutual relationships and join together to promote the
general welfare of all the people."[70] This model suggests that in practice a
ruler presides over a complex network of associations and is responsible for
far more than punishing the wicked. The administration of "justice" means,
in addition to punishment, protecting the weak and helpless (especially wid-
ows, orphans, and strangers), and ensuring that all receive their due.[71]

The most sensitive problem that this larger conception of political responsibility created for Calvin concerned the responsibilities of government
in connection with the church. On this matter his distinction between the
two realms tended to blur.[72] He may have had reservations about the distinction; he once characterized it as only an "accommodation" on the part
of Christ "to the common understanding."[73]

He included the clergy among those over whom the jurisdiction of the
civil magistrate extended, citing ancient practice; the fathers had not disap-

proved "of princes interposing their authority in ecclesiastical matters, provided it was done to preserve the order of the church and not disrupt it, and to establish discipline, not dissolve it. For since the church does not have the power to coerce and ought not seek it, it is the duty of godly kings and princes to sustain religion by laws, edicts, and judgments."[74] The Ecclesiastical Ordinances required a minister to "swear and promise to be subject to the laws and magistracy" of Geneva "as far as my office allows" and "to guard and maintain the honor and welfare of the Seigneury and the City, to take pains, so far as is possible, that the people continue in beneficial peace and unity under the government of the Seigneury, and to consent in no wise to those who would violate it."[75]

Rulers also have obligations to the church. They must "defend the worship of God and execute vengeance on its profane despisers, or those who seek to reduce it to nothing, or who adulterate true doctrine with their own errors and so dissipate the unity of the faith and disturb the peace of the church."[76] They are also to "remove superstitions and put an end to all wicked idolatry, to advance the kingdom of Christ and maintain purity of doctrine, to purify scandals and cleanse the filth that corrupts piety and impairs the luster of the divine majesty."[77] These injunctions were basic to Calvin's rejection of religious toleration, which he equated with permissiveness toward pollution.[78] Rulers, in short, have major responsibilities in the realm of the spirit.

Harro Höpfl has attributed this change to Calvin's practical experience in Geneva,[79] and I have no doubt that the problems Calvin encountered in dealing with the Genevan town council required some modification of his original views, although he never repudiated them. But the change also found support, I think, in his deep attachment to a traditional paternalistic model of politics that may have been reinforced by more personal impulses. For Calvin, fatherhood was not a private and biological phenomenon. It embodied an authority that was religious and political as well as familial. Every human being looks up at once to God the Father and the spiritual fathers who represent him, to the father of his country or his city fathers, and to the father who sired him. This paternal chain from heaven to earth means that no father is strictly secular, and thus that there can be no ultimate separation of realms. The conception suggests something like a tacit indictment of his own father.

Lurking behind it is also the ancient association, at once classical and Germanic, of fatherhood and priesthood. Calvin more than once revealed its influence; it was not only for practical reasons that "all families of the pious should be organized like so many little churches."[80] Progeny "are given to mortals on this condition, that every man should aim, by instructing his children, with all his power, to pass on the name of God. Therefore fathers of families are ordered to be assiduous zealously to recall to their children the benefits of God."[81]

Calvin's stipulations for the spiritual administration of the family thus have implications for all authority. "Anyone," he declared, "who is in-

cluded among the children of God, who is entrusted to exercise authority
over others and wishes to rule over wife, children, and servants in the household, is unworthy if he does not take care to give a place to Christ. Therefore
let each of the faithful strive to organize his household as an image of the
church. All the godly ought to exert themselves so that every kind of superstition is prohibited in their homes. They are not to have godless families but
retain them in the fear of the Lord."[82] A father, in short, has priestly duties
within the household:

> Certainly God does not make known his will to us in order that knowledge of it
> should perish with us, but that we might be witnesses to posterity, and that
> posterity should pass on what was received from our hands, so to speak, into
> the hands of their descendants. Therefore it is incumbent on fathers zealously
> to communicate to their own children what they have learned from God. In
> this way the truth of God must be propagated among us, so that no one may
> savor it privately but that each may edify others according to his own calling
> and mode of faith.[83]

Calvin also held that a father should display, in his own sphere, the energies requisite for the *vita activa civile* of a good ruler. So, "if a godly man
has deviant children, or a wife who misbehaves, or worthless and dishonest
servants, let him not close his eyes nor allow his household to be polluted by
his own sloth."[84]

If the family resembles a church, perhaps *is* in some sense an *"eccle-
siola,"* a polity, for Calvin, should be like a family; and a ruler should display a father's feelings and exercise a father's duties in his realm. He noted
with approval the pagan precept that "a good king holds the place of a
father," interpreting it to mean that "royal power cannot be separated from
paternal affection" and that "those who wish to be considered legitimate
princes and to prove themselves ministers of God must show that they are
fathers to their people."[85] The analogy of the family was often on his mind
when he thought about politics. Just as every father should "organize his
household so that it is an image of the church," he declared, "it is much
more requisite for a prince not to allow the name of God to be profaned in his
domain, as far as he can avoid it."[86] Sound doctrine "is more necessary for
[rulers] than for the common people. For not only does the duty of the fathers of families lie on each of them, but the Lord has also set them over the
whole people."[87] Even lesser magistrates must, "when they punish crimes,
so temper their rigor that they do not put aside the feeling of humanity but
are merciful without being lax or remiss: in short they should be fathers to
those they condemn."[88]

The assignment of major spiritual duties to political rulers was, therefore,
built into Calvin's very mode of thought, and he could describe these duties
in such sweeping terms that the distinction between political and spiritual
responsibility was all but obliterated. "Civil government," he wrote, "has
as its appointed end, so long as we live among men, to cherish and protect

the external worship of God, to defend sound and pious doctrine and the position of the church, to adjust our life to the society of men, to form our social behavior to civil righteousness, to reconcile us with one another, and to promote general peace and tranquility." This explains its importance:

> The function [of civil government] among men is no less than that of bread, water, sun, and air; indeed its place of honor is far more excellent. For it does not merely see to it, as all these serve to do, that men breathe, eat, drink, and are kept warm, even though it surely embraces all these activities when it provides for their living together. It does not, I repeat, look to this only, but also prevents idolatry, sacrilege against God's name, blasphemies against his truth, and other public offenses against religion from arising and spreading among the people. . . . In short it provides that a public manifestation of religion may exist among Christians, and that humanity be maintained among men.[89]

That Calvin himself was troubled about what he proposed in this passage is suggested by its immediate sequel. "Let no man be disturbed," he continued in one of those moves with which he characteristically accompanied pronouncements about which he felt unsure, "that I now commit to civil government the duty of rightly establishing religion which I seem above to have put outside of human decision." He was not, he argued, allowing men "to make laws according to their own decision concerning religion and the worship of God."[90] He appealed, in support of his position, first of all to "secular writers," that is, to classical authority. "All have confessed," he wrote, "that no government can be happily established unless piety is the first concern; and that those laws are preposterous which neglect God's right and provide only for men. Since, therefore, among all philosophers religion takes first place, and since this fact has always been observed by universal consent of all nations, let Christian princes and magistrates be ashamed of their negligence if they do not apply themselves to this concern."[91] It is also obvious that the argument hardly solves the practical questions raised by the assignment of spiritual responsibilities to political rulers. If anything, it points, as we will see in the next chapter, to the subordination of polity to church.

14

Church

Because, for Calvin, the improvement of society and government depended finally on the improvement of human beings, the crucial arena for the reformation was the church, for only the church, through the grace of the Holy Spirit, could reform the human heart. But, chiefly concerned with its effectiveness in the world, he gave little attention to the church as a subject of theological reflection; his program for the church was again thoroughly practical. From the beginning, to be sure, he had specified in his credal statements the marks of the "true" church. With Farel he insisted on its unity in the Geneva Confession of 1536 and also required the gospel to be "purely and faithfully preached, proclaimed, heard, and kept" and the sacraments "properly administered." His catechism of 1537 distinguished between a visible and an invisible church, the latter limited to the elect.[1]

This distinction, however, served largely to relieve him from explicit discussion of the invisible church implicit in the doctrine of predestination; he was chiefly concerned with the visible church for whose affairs he was responsible. The last book of the *Institutes*, which deals directly with the church, mainly treats ecclesiastical organization and practice rather than ecclesiology. In spite of his conviction that "the true dignity of the church is internal,"[2] he entitled this section "The External Means or Aids by which God Invites Us into the Society of Christ and Holds Us Therein."

But the strong feeling that infused the conventional parental imagery with which he discussed the church suggests the depth of his concern for it and hints again at his experience with his own father. The pope, as head of the papal church, had been, he wrote, "such a father as the poets describe Saturn to have been, one who devours his children."[3] The church, he thought, should rather be a loving mother who bears, nourishes, and preserves her spiritual children. "There is no other way to enter into life," he wrote, "but that this mother should conceive us in her womb, give us birth, feed us at her breast, and lastly keep us under her care and guidance until, putting off mortal flesh, we become like the angels."[4] He proposed, then, to

214

reject the pope, the better to love and be cherished by the church. But this was no easy matter. He could not simply repudiate that part of himself which came from this bad father, whose teachings had been, in any event, a powerful force for order. It is scarcely remarkable that Calvin, made so anxious by disorder, was unable to purge himself of attitudes that were, in him, sometimes more rigid than those of the papal church, and that he who had so vigorously denounced the "tyranny" of Rome was sometimes perceived as the tyrant of Geneva.

Like other humanists, Calvin professed to value the unity of the church.[5] "Always, both by word and deed," he wrote to Sadoleto, "I have protested how eager I was for unity."[6] It distressed him that, when "fraternal agreement" should "flourish among all the children of God," the church exhibited "only the broken pieces of a torn body."[7] He believed, like Erasmus, that "agreement is a singular good, since there is nothing better or more desirable than peace";[8] and he routinely denounced schismatics, heretics, and all "who yearn to divide churches."[9]

But he thought it futile to insist on an institutional unity that was neither attainable, given the political realities of his time, nor, as papal tyranny had demonstrated, always desirable. When the champions of Rome cited the centralized Jewish priesthood and the empire of the Romans as models for the organization of the church, he boldly repudiated the very notion of unity as essential to perfection. "There is no reason," he wrote, "why what has been useful in one nation should be extended to the whole earth." The Romans had once been able to unite so many peoples, as the papacy had done later, not because of any divine mandate but only because the condition of the world at that time made unity temporarily desirable. "Now, when true religion is spread over the whole earth," he asked, "who cannot see the utter absurdity of giving the rule of East and West to one man?"[10]

The "only bond of holy unity" in the church, for Calvin, was Christ. "He who departs from him," he wrote, "disturbs and violates unity, while out of him there is nothing but sacrilegious conspiracy."[11] The essential unity of the church, in short, is spiritual. The church universal in this world is simply a congeries of local churches sharing a common faith but otherwise differing according to varying local needs:

> The church universal is a multitude gathered from all nations; it is divided and dispersed in separate places, but it agrees on the one truth of divine doctrine and is bound by the bond of the same religion. Under it are thus included individual churches, disposed in towns and villages according to human need, so that each rightly has the name and authority of the church. . . . In this way we preserve for the universal church its unity, which devilish spirits have always tried to sunder; and we do not defraud of their authority those lawful assemblies that have been set up in accordance with local needs.[12]

Notable in this conception, first formulated in the 1539 edition of the *Institutes* but preserved unchanged in the final version of 1559, is its emphasis not only on "individual churches" but their identification with "towns and villages." For Calvin, although *the* church might in some abstract sense be a unity, *a* church remained, for him, in spite of his experience with territorial Protestantism, always a specific community, local and personal. This localized conception of the church, like that of Savonarola in Florence, was widespread in the towns of the later Middle Ages. It corresponded to one kind of polity in an increasingly fragmented Europe, but not to the territorial monarchies of the future. Later Calvinism would have to adjust to this new kind of polity.

When Calvin laid down regulations for "the church," then, he had in mind chiefly a church based on a town such as Geneva. It was in such a church, for him, that Christians receive instruction in the faith and grow together in the Christian life. A church, he insisted, must be a practical community, and first of all a community in faith, which is not "a particular thing for one man alone but is for the profit and instruction of the whole church";[13] he thought nothing "more odious or execrable" than for an individual "to make up his own mind about what he should believe."[14] Only in particular churches, too, can Christians mutually aid and comfort one another. No Christian "has power for himself or applies it to his own private use," Calvin insisted, "but each pours it out to his fellow members: God does not extend his hand to us so that each may follow his own course but that we may assist others and help them to advance."[15] It is also in particular churches that Christians worship together; worship is an expression of obedience not only to God but also to the community of faith; this is why no individual is free "to contrive any sort of worship he pleases."[16] Prayer, from this perspective, must be in the vernacular because only then is it a "sharing" [*communicatio*] among all the faithful.[17] Calvin rejected, as expressing "pride, dislike, or rivalry," the notion that "private reading and meditation" make public worship unnecessary.[18] All Christians, without exception, must join in the common worship; even "young women, who are not so well educated as men, will fail in their duty unless they are active with the rest of the church in praising God."[19]

His insistence on the church as a functioning community was closely related to his rejection of what he called "Nicodemism," the posture of those of his contemporaries who, like Nicodemus, "came to Jesus by night but remained openly among his enemies." Calvin was persuaded that they shared Protestant beliefs but declined to break openly with the papal church and to join the community of true Christians. They hoped, Calvin charged, that "by wearing this mask" they could "mock God with impunity."[20] "The inward worship of the heart," he charged, "does not suffice unless it is accompanied by outward profession among men."[21]

He was particularly attached to the Lord's Supper, which he interpreted as "the bond of charity" that united the faithful community. "Communion," for him, was literally a function of community, by which "we are joined in one body and one substance with our head."[22] "As the bread that is there sanctified for the common use of us all is made of many grains so mixed together that one cannot be discerned from the other," he wrote, "so ought we to be united among ourselves in one indissoluble freindship."[23] But he also argued for communion in both kinds as a recognition of the full community of the faithful.[24] The close connection between the sacrament and the spiritual unity of the church explains why the Lord's Supper is restricted to those who have made peace with each other. It also helps to explain Calvin's unsuccessful advocacy of communion at every service in the Genevan church.[25] The way in which the sacrament was celebrated in the Roman church offended his sense of community. Private masses, in which "one person withdraws and gulps alone and there is no sharing among the faithful," seemed to him a mockery of communion.[26] He compared the almost inaudible "muttering" of the celebrant of a mass to the spell of a sorcerer.[27]

"Some form of organization is necessary in all human society," Calvin believed, "to foster the common peace and maintain concord." But it "ought especially to be observed in churches, which are best sustained when all things are under a well-ordered constitution and which, without concord, become no churches at all."[28] Indeed, "if no society, indeed no household that has even a small family, can be kept in a proper state without discipline, discipline is much more necessary in the church, whose condition should be most orderly of all."[29] Without regulation "everything will be confused and there will be much dissension and taking offence."[30] The church, too, needs *la police*.

This meant first of all the need of churches for a leadership analogous to leadership in the secular world.[31] "The office of pastor," to be sure, as Calvin insisted, "is distinct from that of prince; they are so different that they cannot come together in one man."[32] But in both cases leaders should be chosen in accordance with "the nature of things," which dictates that "those who excel in talent, or wisdom, or other gifts should also be superior in authority." The absence of leadership also invites disaster in both realms.[33] The leaders in the two realms, furthermore, should collaborate as agents of social control. "As the magistrate ought by punishment and physical restraint to cleanse the church of offenses," Calvin wrote, "so the minister of the word should help the magistrate in order that fewer may sin. Their responsibilities should be so joined that each helps rather than impedes the other."[34] Ideally, then, minister and magistrate seem to be the parallel officers of a body at once ecclesiastical and political.

But this parallelism was no more stable in Calvin's thought than it had been in the Middle Ages, though immediately for a rather different reason. The coincidence of church membership with residence in the town made the Genevan church a "mixture" of righteous and wicked, a situation that, however he could reconcile himself to it doctrinally, aroused his deepest anxieties and drove him toward clerical supremacy. He yearned for a pure church, a visible and exclusive community of saints, however small. He decried those who thought too much about the size of the church. "We are always wanting a multitude," he observed, "and evaluating in that way the condition of the church. It would be more desirable for us to be few and for the glory of God to shine in us all."[35] "For us," he asserted, there can be brotherhood only "among the children of God."[36] This suggested a separatist model of the church; a part of Calvin was closer to Anabaptism than he would have cared to admit.

This impulse, nevertheless, explains his effort to convert Geneva into a visible community of saints. He felt strongly about this; toleration of the least impurity would lead to the infection of the whole:

> Vices must not be permitted in a people who profess Christianity; they must be punished even among those who are only passing through. Why is that? When blasphemies are condemned among us, if we hear a passer-by blaspheme or mock God and this should be endured and kept secret, would it not be a kind of profanation that would infect everything to tolerate such blasphemies so that they become fashionable and nothing were done to repress them? . . . If we allow debauched persons and ruffians to bring in their corrupt ways and introduce more evil than we already have, if we permit the profligate and corrupt to come here to practice their lewdness, will we not necessarily become debauched and totally corrupt with them?[37]

His zeal was intensified by a dread that the Protestant attack on the disciplines of the old church might release anarchy. "Neither people nor prince," he lamented early in his ministry, "distinguishes between the yoke of Christ and the tyranny of the pope."[38] Many, "having shaken off the yoke of Christ, will not endure any discipline; they want to overturn all order, though boldly claiming the name of reformation."[39]

To maintain discipline within the community, Calvin established for Geneva a "consistory" of "elders" that met privately "so that their deliberations, in the absence of the crowd, might be more orderly."[40] The elders, he explained in an endeavor to preserve the notion of parallel governance, are to a church what its council is to a city.[41] But the parallelism is misleading; Calvin's elders in fact assumed a major responsibility that had previously belonged to the council. In addition, all church members were obligated to reprove and correct the behavior of others. Calvin was aware of the dangers here; nothing was easier, in such matters, "than to exceed proper limits." He knew that malice was all too likely to be the source of censure, and he stipulated that, "whenever we must criticize vices, we should remember to begin with ourselves, so that, recalling our own weaknesses, we are temperate toward others." We must be sure of the facts and slow to judge.[42] Sometimes, indeed, Calvin seemed to distrust all judgments except of oneself; he knew that self-righteousness is a common source of the condemnation of others.;[43] In principle, nevertheless, he insisted on a universal obligation to reprove sinners. "If there are people who profess Christianity but nevertheless conduct themselves badly and are a scandal," he declared, "we must not excuse them but directly condemn them."[44]

He valued the Eucharist, as a rite of community but also because those who proposed to receive it were required to give notice in advance; this gave the clergy opportunities to admonish, instruct, and console those for whose spiritual welfare they were responsible.[45] Although he condemned much pertaining to the confessional in the old church, he did not want it abolished without the substitution of some other discipline. "A church," he wrote, "cannot be called well-ordered and regulated unless in it the Holy Supper of our Lord is always attended and celebrated, and this under such good supervision that no one dare to present himself unless devoutly and with genuine reverence."[46] But high standards for receiving the sacrament are in some tension with frequent communion; this may be why he finally allowed it to take place only at intervals.

His ultimate device for keeping the church pure was excommunication, of which exclusion from communion is the immediate and most visible consequence. He set great store by it as "a holy and lawful discipline taken from the word of God,"[47] by which the church excludes "manifest adulterers, fornicators, thieves, robbers, seditious persons, perjurers, false witnesses, and the rest of this sort, as well as the insolent who, when duly admonished of their lighter vices, mock God and his judgment."[48] Excommunication warns the sinner to repent and put his life in order, and it reduces the likelihood of his corrupting others. But above all, by purifying the church of its "foul and decaying members," it guards against "mixture," thereby serving the needs of metaphysical as well as practical order and paying tribute to the honor and majesty of God.[49] Believers have an obligation, Calvin insisted, "to restore it to its former completeness,"[50] and he would have preferred himself, he wrote, to die a hundred deaths rather than "suffer to be overthrown what I know is taken from the word of God."[51]

The anxiety that all disorder produced in Calvin also inclined him to favor authoritarian modes of control. This found expression in a clericalism doubtless sharpened by the hostility he encountered among the laity of Geneva but remarkable in one so critical of the clergy in the old church. God had made the clergy responsible for order in the church. "Each of us," he informed his congregation, "must submit to that order [*police*] which God has established in his church. . . . That is why he wanted ministers. . . . And let us not murmur because we are not all granted such a privilege, for it is his will that his body, that is his church, should be governed in this way."[52] The ministers, for Calvin, are "the chief sinew by which believers are held together in one body." Through them God "dispenses and distributes his gifts to the church. . . . Neither the light and heat of the sun, nor food and drink, are so necessary to nourish and sustain the present life as the apostolic and pastoral office is necessary to preserve the church on earth."[53] Though he did not directly challenge the doctrine, Calvin did not subscribe to Luther's priesthood of all believers.[54]

He justified his clericalism in various ways. Sometimes he was simply pragmatic. Priestly authority was needed, he thought, as "a necessary bridle for the good of the church."[55] He also appealed to the paternal authority of the priesthood. To the church in Geneva, in the course of negotiating the terms of his return in 1539, he wrote sternly from Strasbourg, "Those who hold the position of minister of the Word, since the governing of your souls has been committed to them, are to be acknowledged in the relation of parents to you, and valued and honored for the service they perform among you through the Lord's calling."[56] He employed, too, the famous medieval image that represented the clergy as the "soul" of the church (though in Calvin's version sometimes also the heart!), the laity as merely its body.[57] Calvin repeatedly affirmed the authority of clergy over laity. This was why God had smitten the well-meaning Uzzah, who had put out his hand to prevent the Ark from falling; in doing so, he had usurped a responsibility restricted to priests who were "standing near and ready to perform it."[58] By the same token the Genevan clergy, in their contest with the lay town council to control the church, contended "with bold and invincible zeal" for a "sacred power that ought to be inviolable."[59]

Calvin's clericalism was based above all on God's appointment. Pastors have been "called," as he had been, by a God whose calling they cannot reject "without being rebels against him."[60] He divided this calling into two parts: an internal and general calling by the Holy Spirit, which guarantees "that we receive the proffered office, not with ambition or avarice nor with any other selfish desire, but with a sincere fear of God and desire to build up the church," and an external call to preside over a particular congregation.[61] It is essential, he argued, for a minister to be certain of his calling; only his certainty can justify an appeal, such as evidently seemed to Calvin inevitable in a ministerial career, "to the tribunal of God" against his opponents.[62]

The authority of the clergy was commensurate, for him, with the magnitude, the weight, and the difficulty of their duties. Too few who entered the ministry, he thought, took its responsibilities seriously enough:

> Today hardly one in a hundred considers how difficult and arduous it is faithfully to discharge the office of pastor. Hence many are led into it as something trivial and not serious; and afterwards experience teaches them, too late, how foolishly they aspired to the unknown. Others think themselves endowed with great skill and diligence and promise themselves great things from their talent, learning, and judgment; but afterwards they experience too late how limited their equipment is, for their powers fail them at the outset. Others, while knowing there will be many serious battles, have no fear, as though they were born for contention, and put on an iron front. Still others who want to be ministers are mercenaries. We know indeed that all God's servants are wretched in the eyes of the world and common sense, for they must make war on the passions of all and thus displease men in order to please God.[63]

The burdens of the minister's calling seemed to Calvin virtually infinite, and an infinite source of anxiety. "Whatever may be the opinion of others," he wrote early in his own ministry, "we do not think that our tasks are confined within such narrow limits that, once the sermon has been preached, our task is finished and we have only to rest. It is necessary to give the most direct and most vigilant attention to those whose blood will be required of us, since, if it is lost, it will be by our negligence."[64] He brooded over the "horrible punishment" in store for clergy "if, by their fault, the truth perishes that is the image of divine glory, the light of the world, the salvation of men."[65] At the same time he sympathized with ministers who, under such burdens, grew discouraged.[66]

He knew from his own experience that Protestant clergy, as they struggled with numerous obstacles to their ministries, were sheep among wolves, in danger from every direction, needing the wisdom of the serpent to survive.[67] Any minister who performs his duties faithfully, he observed, will "be loaded with much abuse and called contentious, morose, a disturber of the peace."[68] Ministers, he complained, are uniquely "exposed to slanders and insults," "wicked men find many occasions to censure them," and "as soon as any charge is made against them, it is believed as surely and firmly as if it had been already proved."[69]

Two responsibilities of the ministry were, for Calvin, especially intimidating. One was the obligation to reprove sinners. Pastors must "admonish, exhort, and deprecate"; the laity must "listen to them as to God himself."[70] Calvin called for preaching that would "remove the excuses and pretences with which hypocrites cover themselves" and "drag them from their hiding places."[71] "No wonder [the ministers] have so many enemies," he exclaimed, "since it is their duty to censure the vices of all, to oppose all wicked desires, and to repress by their severity whoever seems to go astray."[72] The task was dangerous, especially when it required censuring the powerful, for not even the mightiest layman was immune from the moral surveillance of the ministers. Nevertheless, none are "fit to guide the church" unless, like Jeremiah, they "possess such constancy that they fear no one and are not intimidated by the power of anyone, so that they have the courage to attack the highest and greatest."[73] A pastor "must dare to reprove, freely and with intrepid spirit, both kings and queens," Calvin insisted, "for the word of God is not to be limited to the people or to humble men, but subjects to itself all, from the least to the greatest."[74]

The clergy had also to be able to face persecution. Calvin worried about this in connection with the endangered Calvinists of France. Before the peril to his followers became acute, he was satisfied with a rather theoretical compromise. "We must take the moderate line," he argued; "no one should desert his post out of fear, or treacherously betray his flock, or give an example of cowardice; and yet no one should rashly throw himself away. If the whole church should be under attack or part of it condemned to death, it would be wicked for the pastor to take flight, whose duty is to protect the members of his church with his own life. Yet it could happen that his absence would better serve the church by calming the fury of its enemies."[75] But as civil war in France came closer, he took a firmer line. Ministers must not falter in the face of danger, he warned: "If swords threaten them from one direction and fires are lit in another, if they are faced with the pillaging of their goods, if exile confronts them, they must nevertheless continue on their course."[76] This followed from the integrity he had identified as the basic qualification of a minister, because, as he said, "learning and eloquence and every other excellence can be feigned."[77] Integrity would enable a pastor to hold out to the end.

If the clergy are authorized to command, the laity are obligated to obey, lest they be "bears" rather than sheep.[78] Calvin was incensed by lay resistance to a clerical control so benign and well intentioned, so different from the tyranny of the Roman priesthood. It was scarcely to be endured, he felt, that those who had "calmly endured the harsh tyranny of the pope" and "calmly swallowed the most cruel insults of the monks" now tended "to fly into a passion against the paternal and wholesome rebukes of their pastors."[79] "Foul and horrible would be the waste," he exclaimed, "if it were permissible to reject promiscuously what the officers of the church establish."[80] Sensitive, perhaps, to the mixed response of his Genevan congregation to his own sermons, he was especially insistent that the laity listen attentively and with docility to the sermons of ministers; the laity must "reverently receive whatever upright teachers proclaim in God's name, when they are discharging their office, *for they are not to be looked upon as men.*"[81] "We do not come to the sermon," he proclaimed, "to say whether the doctrine is good and holy. God would be much obliged to us for pronouncing his word worthy of reception! He does not intend us to be his judges."[82] "Ministers of God" should "cite the opponents of their teaching before God's tribunal to receive certain condemnation."[83]

The laity are also obliged to support the ministers materially, though the example of the Roman church was a reminder that the clergy should not demand more than they need.[84] On this matter, too, Calvin sounded somewhat aggrieved. "It is shameful," he exclaimed, "to cheat those by whom our souls are fed of their bodily nourishment; it would be unworthy to refuse to those from whom we receive heavenly blessings their earthly compensation. But it is now and has always been the nature of the world to stuff the maws of the ministers of Satan, while grudgingly supplying food to godly pastors."[85]

There is clearly much evidence to support the notion of a severe and authoritarian Calvin. But, as always, there was another side to him, even as a churchman. He could also be flexible, politic, accommodating to circumstance, considerate of human weakness and need, and above all practical. Even on theological questions he was sometimes less concerned to enforce agreement with himself than to reduce controversy and division, and he recognized that even in principle some variety in the church is both inevitable and tolerable. One side of him continued to echo the evangelical fundamentalism of Erasmus:

> Not all the articles of true doctrine are of the same sort. Some are so necessary to know that they should be certain and unquestioned by all men as the proper principles of religion. Such are: God is one; Christ is God and the Son of God; our salvation rests in God's mercy; and the like. Among the churches

other articles of doctrine are disputed which still do not break the unity of faith. Suppose that one church believes—short of unbridled contention and opinionated stubbornness—that souls upon leaving bodies fly to heaven; while another, not daring to define the place, is convinced nevertheless that they live in the Lord. What churches would disagree on this one point? Does this not sufficiently indicate that a difference of opinion over these nonessential matters should in no wise be the basis of schism among Christians? First and foremost, we should agree on all points. But since all men are somewhat beclouded with ignorance, either we must leave no church remaining, or we must condone delusion in those matters which can go unknown without harm to the sum of religion and without loss of salvation.[86]

That he may have often had to remind himself of the need for flexibility does not reduce the seriousness of his commitment to it.

But his flexibility is more evident in other matters, notably ecclesiastical polity. His basic principle was that nothing is binding on consciences but what is specified by Scripture. The details of ecclesiastical polity and cult can therefore vary according to local custom and need. In regard to *"la police,"* we are "left at liberty."[87] The essential criterion in such matters, as he put it, is convenience:

The established custom of the region, or humanity itself and the rule of modesty, dictate what is to be done or avoided. In them a man commits no crime if, out of imprudence or forgetfulness, he departs from them, although if out of contempt, this willfulness is to be disapproved. Similarly, the days themselves, the hours, the structure of the places of worship, what psalms are to be sung on what day, are matters of no importance. But it is *convenient* to have definite days and stated hours, and a place suitable to receive all, if there is any concern for the preservation of peace. For confusion in such details would become the seed of great contentions if every man were allowed, as he pleased, to change matters affecting public order! For it will never happen that the same thing will please all if matters are regarded as indifferent and left to individual choice.[88]

This made possible considerable latitude. "Let there be no ambition, no obstinacy, no arrogance or contempt for other churches," Calvin proclaimed, "but, on the contrary, let there be striving for edification, let there be moderation and common sense; and then nothing about variety in usages will call for blame."[89] In effect, this recognized that much in the visible church is spiritually indifferent, including its institutional structures. "Each church," Calvin declared, "is free to establish whatever form of organization is suitable and useful for itself, for God has prescribed nothing specific about this."[90] Calvin could accordingly accept episcopacy as a mode of organization, though by no means its theological justification. Bishops, he believed, had emerged in the early church to serve practical and administrative needs: "to report on business, to request opinions, to preside over others in counseling, admonishing, and exhorting, to govern the whole action by [their] authority, and to carry out what was decreed by common decision."[91] There was no reason why they should not continue to perform these tasks. "The minds and behavior of men" make it necessary, as he well knew, for one minister to preside over the others, at least locally.[92] He took a similar view of church law, since it is never to be considered "necessary for salvation and thus binding consciences by scruples; nor is it to be associated with the worship of God, and piety thus be lodged in it."[93]

The rule of convenience, as we have seen, applied particularly, for Calvin, to the common worship; on this important matter the freedom he denied to individuals he readily allowed to churches. The preface to his first French catechism was deeply Erasmian in its acceptance of variety as a condition of unity and peace in the church:

> If we are zealous for union and peace, let us press for unity of doctrine and above all of mind, rather than insisting obstinately on perfect conformity in ceremonies. It would be highly unworthy of us to seek, in things that God has left free for the larger purpose of edification, after a servile conformity that does not edify. Certainly, when we come before that highest tribunal to render an account of our lives, it will not be a question of ceremonies, nor will conformity in externals be examined, but the proper use of our liberty, which will be judged legitimate only if it has promoted edification. All our concern, vigilance, diligence, and zeal should be applied to edification, which we can attain only by a serious fear of God, a sincere piety, and an unfeigned sanctity of life.[94]

He was somewhat more cautious as the years passed, but he continued to favor flexibility on such matters. "The church permitted itself freedom from the beginning to have slightly different rites," he pointed out fifteen years later. "Therefore we need not be too finicky about things that are not so necessary, provided that external displays do not pollute the simple institution of Christ."[95] "We must especially beware," he warned, "lest the consensus of the faithful be torn over external observances and the bond of charity be broken." We must not "attempt to coerce others, but leave everyone his liberty. . . . For although calling on God ranks first in spiritual worship, the means for doing it, adjusted to the crude understandings of men, may properly include things ceremonial and indifferent, although their observance should not be too urgently pressed."[96] "As the circumstances of the times demand," he wrote, "we are at liberty to change what men have invented."[97] In worship too he was prepared, after all, to tolerate human invention.

He was usually content, therefore, to recommend general principles of worship that individual churches might apply in accordance with their various and changing needs. He aimed, broadly, to promote "reverence for sacred things," the "modesty and gravity which ought to be seen in all honorable acts," and the avoidance of "all confusion, barbarity, obstinacy, turbulence and dissension."[98] But he also believed, without insisting on them for everyone, that particular gestures or actions are aids to worship. Although he thought "bending the knee" unimportant, he liked to kneel, on the ground that it prepares the mind to engage seriously in prayer, is a reminder of our inability to stand before God, and pleases God as a symbolic act.[99] He also approved of fasting, a disciplinary and penitential practice that, as we have seen, he thought Protestants practiced too little.[100]

The forms of worship were far less important to him than that it should be from the heart; this was not a thing indifferent. The praise of God should proceed, he insisted, "from a pure and sincere disposition of the heart."[101] It should also involve the whole person. David's dance before the Ark exemplifies what it means to worship God fully; we should, like David, "exercise ourselves and employ all our senses, and our feet, and our hands, and our arms, and all the rest, so that everything is put in the service of God and magnifies him." He was too aware of historical and cultural differences, however, to recommend David's exuberant piety to the church in Geneva. David's dance, he observed, "was expedient for the time, but we must always keep the difference in mind." Nevertheless, he insisted, God wants us to respond to him "not coldly and perfunctorily" but always with "a burning affection that breaks out impulsively and impetuously."[102]

He thought music especially helpful for the release of religious feeling. God himself, he declared, "omits no sweet melody, no sad and grave strain to draw us to himself, though we lie like stones."[103] He disapproved of musical instruments in church services, including organs, because they "only amuse people in their vanities."[104] He also distinguished sharply between sacred and secular music. "There is a great difference," he observed, "between the music one makes to entertain men at table and in their homes, and the psalms which are sung in the church in the presence of God and his angels."[105] He excluded from worship all music "composed only for sweetness and delight of the ear." Even with sacred music he thought it necessary to be "very careful that our ears not be more attentive to the melody than our minds to the spiritual meaning of the words."[106] But Calvin's caution here expresses his sensitivity to the power of music, and therefore of its potential value to the church. He thought the singing of psalms "very expedient for the church's edification"; by it "the hearts of all are roused and incited to offer with one accord similar prayers and render similar praises and thanks to God."[107] Psalm singing "lends dignity and grace to sacred actions and has the greatest value in kindling our hearts to a true zeal and eagerness to pray," and intensifies a congregation's sense of community.[108]

Prayer, both public and private, is another aspect of worship, for Calvin, that should engage the whole personality; if our prayers are "cold," we should be "ashamed and dismayed."[109] He thought of prayer as comforting and even therapeutic. We pray, he observed, when we are thankful or "in torment" and "troubles press upon us"; then, like sons, we "unburden all our feelings in the bosom of our father." The result is a sense of "peculiar peace and tranquility."[110]

Just as Calvin's authoritarianism was qualified by his republicanism when he discussed secular polity, so a sense of the dignity of the lay estate

was in tension with his clericalism. He believed, indeed, that full engage-
ment with lay responsibilities should be a prerequisite for those who "rule in
the church." The clergy should not, from this standpoint, constitute a separate caste; and from time to time he also emphasized that "the authority of
pastors is especially to be contained within boundaries that must not be
transgressed."[111] They are limited first of all by a mandate to preach only
the Gospel that is implicit in God's call; they are to "invent nothing themselves, nor teach whatever they please, but faithfully transmit [only] what
God has committed to them."[112] Unlike secular rulers, to whom God has
given power, pomp, and splendor, pastors are also "ministers and helpers"
of their congregations, to whom "Christ gives nothing more than that they
should be servants and completely abstain from dominion."[113] This also
means that the laity have an obligation to examine critically what their pastors tell them. "All who serve in the ministry, from the greatest to the
least," Calvin asserted, "belong to *us,* so that we are free not to embrace
their teaching until they show that it is from Christ." We are all obligated
"to consider what is the truth"; nor should we "receive everything that
people tell us in passing without knowing why or how, but we should inquire
diligently into the truth of what we are told." It is thus "the common situation of every pastor to be judged by the church."[114]

This is why ministers should, at least in principle, be elected by the
whole membership of the church. Fearing that the election of a pastor might
"go wrong through fickleness, evil intentions, or disorder," Calvin proposed
that it should be supervised by other ministers. The consent and approval of
the people is always necessary, he explained, "but pastors should rule so
that their authority, like a bridle, holds in check the violence of the people,
lest they exceed their limits."[115] He tended, in church as well as state, to
prefer an ascending theme of authority, but it made him anxious enough to
require checks and balances.[116] In actuality, as Höpfl has pointed out, pastors in Geneva were not chosen in this way; they were nominated by the
company of pastors and appointed by the town council.[117] This suggests the
limits either of Calvin's authority in Geneva or of his enthusiasm for so dem-
ocratic an ecclesiastical polity in a community he trusted so little.

Still another tension in his program for the church arose from his awareness, along with the needs of community, of the individuality of Christian
experience. Even when Christians sit together as a body to hear the Gospel,
he declared, God "speaks to individuals," each of whom is "to apply to
himself whatever God promises to his church collectively."[118] Christ wants
"each one to run with all speed for himself, unhindered and free from every
tie."[119] Calvin's insistence that theology is not a monopoly of specialists
tended in the same direction. For him, neither "acuteness of understanding"
nor "liberal education in the schools" helps anyone to "grasp spiritual
teaching."[120] He attacked the papacy for "shutting theology up in the
study" and treating its people like "brute beasts, without [the capacity of]
discriminating between black and white." Nothing can be "less consistent
with holy and Christian order" he argued, "than excluding the body of the

people from the common doctrine, as if they were a herd of pigs." God does not address "only a few theologians but communicates with all the people, even the most ignorant," so that "all, from the humblest to the greatest, may be united in the same obedience of faith."[121] "Many poor ignorant people today, though unlearned and inexperienced in speaking," therefore, "teach Christ more faithfully than all the theologians of the pope with their lofty speculations."[122] Indeed, teachers themselves are still learners. "No one can ever be a good minister of God's Word," Calvin declared, "unless he is first of all a student"; and even as a teacher, a minister "should not sit down and command others but should walk along with them as companions."[123] Conversely, "everyone, according to the measure of his faith, ought to communicate to his brethren what he has received"; learners should also be teachers.[124]

As "God's school,"[125] Calvin's church was more like a humanist academy than a school of theology, and he imagined God now, looking over the shoulders of his pupils, watching "their gestures, walking, words, and everything else."[126] Scripture, in this context, was a textbook through which God propounded his teachings to his children.[127] When a biblical text was embarrassingly obvious, "saying nothing that each of us does not already know," Calvin explained it as pedagogical repetition. "Isn't it necessary," he asked, "for God as schoolmaster to repeat our lesson several times?"[128] God also teaches through his ministers; for Calvin, "preaching" and "teaching" were virtually synonymous. We have "a sure testimony of God's presence," Calvin declared, "whenever true and faithful teachers rise to speak."[129] That Protestant preaching was truly *teaching* seemed to him a major difference between Protestant and papal churches.[130] Conversely, Calvin thought *teachableness* incumbent on all in the church. God requires all of us, he argued, to be "fools in our own estimation, and, like children," to be "docile."[131] If a minister, as sometimes happened, had nothing to teach his congregation, it should display its "piety and obedience toward God" by nevertheless remaining "teachable."[132] Like all teachers, Calvin also complained about the slowness and forgetfulness of most of the church's students in "a subject that properly demands a whole lifetime, indeed a hundred lives."[133]

He gave much attention to what makes teaching effective in the church. It must be practical: rightly done "it is not only free from all fallacies but does not make men giddy with futile questions, does not indulge foolish curiosity, and does not encourage the itch to know more than is proper; it aims at lasting edification."[134] It must also be presented with fervor. Human beings cannot simply be "told what is right"; they must be "pricked by exhortation and summoned to the judgment seat of God so that they may not sleep in their errors."[135] It was especially necessary today for "the servants of God to exhort more vehemently to rouse hypocrites and the obstinate from their torpor."[136] An effective teacher, in short, requires *zeal,* about which Calvin had no reservations when he was sure that it came from God.

"Doctrine without zeal," he declared, "is either a sword in the hand of a lunatic, or lies cold and useless, or serves a perverse ostentation."[137]

But what is to be taught is always the Gospel, and the purpose of expounding it "to lead men to faith and hold them fast in perseverance with continuing profit."[138] Calvin recommended an order of instruction whose principles were essentially psychological. It begins with a full account of the misery and wickedness of mankind, setting forth "faithfully from the law, the prophets, and the Gospel how dreadful is God's vengeance."[139] Then, after giving full attention to the problem, we advance to its solution. For because God "does not at all want to leave us like lost folk, after we have been properly mortified," and also because "he wants to shed his grace and mercy, his life and salvation upon all," the disclosure of God's wrath is followed by the proclamation of "hope to those who have transgressed."[140] Preaching, then, like the church, is "a mother" who conceives and gives birth to faith.[141]

But the efficacy of this double message requires the collaboration with the teacher/preacher of the Holy Spirit. The sermon performs God's work outwardly; inwardly the Spirit "illuminates our minds" and "renews our hearts."[142] Preaching "accomplishes nothing by itself; but since it is an instrument divinely empowered for our salvation, an instrument made effective by the Spirit, let us not separate what God has joined together. Faith comes from hearing, but illumination in faith comes only to those to whom the Lord has revealed his power inwardly."[143] "Doctrine is cold," Calvin declared, "unless it is given divine efficacy."[144] Effective instruction depends on the power of the Holy Spirit.

The humanity that pervades Calvin's perception of pastoral responsibility also found expression in his awareness of the *inconvenience* of the strictness he often required. A good pastor, he thought, succeeded in preserving a middle position between excessive severity and excessive softness, but too many failed. On the one hand, "pretending zeal, some are always fulminating and forget that they are men; they show no sign of friendliness but exude only bitterness. . . . Terrifying sinners so inhumanely, without any sign of anguish or sympathy, they make God's Word seem insulting and distasteful." On the other hand, some flatter their congregations, "ignore the most serious iniquities," and "mislead and destroy miserable men by their blandishments."[145] He may have suspected that he tended more to the first mistake than to the second. "By nature," he remarked in what sounds like another personal confession, "we are almost all too irritable, and Satan pushes us to an inhumane rigor under the pretext of strictness. As a result wretched men, denied forgiveness, are swallowed up by grief and despair."[146] Too much rigor was a great danger to the church. As he wrote against the Anabaptists, "Whenever, under the pretext of zeal for perfection, we cannot bear any imperfection either in the body or the members of the church, the devil is inflaming us with pride and seducing us through hypocrisy to abandon the flock of Jesus Christ."[147] He also recognized a connection between self-knowledge and sympathy, between blindness to the defects in oneself and severity to others. "Men who truly fear God and sincerely and firmly endeavor to train disciples for his service, because they are more severe on themselves than on others, are not such exacting masters; because they know their own infirmity, they forgive the weak more readily."[148]

He recalled too, from time to time, that ultimately only God can judge.[149] When these considerations ruled his mind, his understanding of the church was no longer exclusive but comprehensive. Practical considerations pointed in the same direction; the attempt to enforce purity in the church, he recognized, results in schisms and sects.[150] These reflections led him to denounce the compulsion to purify the church that was so powerful an impulse within himself. "Many seriously err," he asserted, "who, when they see evil persons mixed with good, think that they will be polluted by contagion unless they straightway separate from the whole flock."[151] Such moralists, far from promoting order—his language now is both familiar and surprising—"mix up and confuse everything with their inconsiderate zeal."[152] They lack faith that the church will survive "notwithstanding the vices and stains that may inhere in the common life of men."[153] As we know it on earth, the church must always be "mixture," beyond our sorting out, of "permanent citizens" and "transients." In this life we must "endure evils impossible to correct until the ripeness of time brings purification."[154] "It never has been otherwise or will be until the end of the world."[155]

But Calvin could also be less grudging. He knew well enough that the problem of "mixture" was deeper than the mingling of reprobate and elect in the church, that every Christian, even among the elect, is also a mixture of good and evil. "We all have many vices, many weaknesses and corruptions," he confessed; "our faith is not at all as perfect as it should be." But "however much our wings droop and we limp along and sometimes even fall, if nevertheless we move towards God and always struggle to advance in the service of our God, he receives and accepts us, although there is much to reprove." The church, the Scriptures, the sacraments, have been given, not because of the purity of human beings, but because of their imperfection.[156]

15

Conclusion

Montaigne, Calvin's near-contemporary, offered, in one of his most characteristic pronouncements, advice on the representation of the human condition that Calvin himself might have relished. "In view of the natural instability of our conduct and opinions," Montaigne wrote, "it has often seemed to me that even good authors are wrong to insist on fashioning a consistent and solid fabric out of us. They choose one general characteristic and go and arrange and interpret all a man's actions to fit their picture; and if they cannot twist them enough, they go and set them down to dissimulation."[1] Montaigne's awareness of the inconstancy and unpredictability of human beings may have been peculiarly appropriate to his own century; but for both psychological and cultural reasons it also has a larger validity, at any rate for inhabitants of the West since antiquity. So does his warning against reductionism in the interpretation of other human beings. I have tried in this book to keep both of his stipulations in mind.

The result has been the identification of two Calvins, coexisting uncomfortably within the same historical personage. No set of antitheses can adequately characterize them, though various conventional dichotomies used by cultural historians may help to suggest their significance. One of these Calvins was a philosopher, a rationalist and a schoolman in the high Scholastic tradition represented by Thomas Aquinas, a man of fixed principles, and a conservative. For this Calvin, Christianity tended toward static orthodoxy, and a Christian was a person endowed with certain *status*. This philosophical Calvin, peculiarly sensitive to the contradictions and dilemmas of an eclectic culture and singularly intolerant of what we now call "cognitive dissonance," craved desperately for intelligibility, order, certainty. Distrusting freedom, he struggled to control both himself and the world. He represented Troeltsch's church type (a conception with psychological and cultural as well as sociological and ecclesiological implications), and he placed the community above the individual. This Calvin was chiefly driven by a terror that took shape for him in the metaphor of the abyss.

The other Calvin was a rhetorician and humanist, a skeptical fideist in the manner of the followers of William of Ockham, flexible to the point of opportunism, and a revolutionary in spite of himself. This Calvin did not seek, because he neither trusted nor needed, what passes on earth for intelligibility and order; instead, he was inclined to celebrate the paradoxes and mystery at the heart of existence. He also asserted the primacy of experience and practice over theory, and he had a considerable tolerance for individual freedom. Christianity, for this Calvin, was dynamic and could be appropriated only gradually and imperfectly; a Christian in this context was a person making progress toward the full stature of Christ. Much in this Calvin suggests Troeltsch's sect type (though not, I think, what Troeltsch called "mysticism"). This humanistic Calvin chiefly dreaded what he often described as entrapment in a labyrinth. It is above all in the degree to which the living, historical Calvin combined these two tendencies—was himself full of paradoxes—that he reveals himself as a man of the sixteenth century.

Both these "types" are themselves too complex to be described as "ideal." In addition, as with genuine ideal types, the contrasting attributes of the two Calvins were, as Calvin might have put it, not only combined but promiscuously jumbled together within the historical Calvin, much as they have been variously combined in the whole course of Western civilization. In this respect, therefore, Calvin was not only a singularly representative sixteenth-century personage; because the sixteenth century was passing through a crisis of choice between alternative adaptations to the world that were perennially available in Western culture, he was also Everyman. Abominating "mixture" and unusually sensitive to its presence, he was more heroic than most of us, if not necessarily more successful, in his struggle to come to terms with the tensions in himself.

In Calvin's struggle to *reduce* the incompatible impulses in himself to a comfortable integrity, his more philosophical side was dominant, seeking to reconcile and unite them dialectically. He seems dimly to have recognized this when he claimed, as he often did, that his own position represented a mean between extremes. He preferred, in short, to integrate rather than to choose between contrary pressures.[2] If the historical Calvin, when he recognized the paradoxical quality of the Gospel, sometimes seems, in contrast to Luther, or even Erasmus and Rabelais, merely to be acknowledging dutifully and mechanically an awkward truth that did not naturally belong to his mental world, this was because the philosophical Calvin was looking doubtfully over his shoulder and inhibiting his appreciation of it. If, then, we ask what "Calvinism," or at least Calvin's own "Calvinism," consisted in, we must begin by recognizing that it was composite. It was the product of impulses and needs of varying provenance that defied systematization. The composite character of his thought doomed the philosophical side of his mind, though without destroying it, to failure.

The situation was rather different for the rhetorical Calvin, who had a considerable tolerance for ambiguity and incongruity: in a word, for the "mixture" so repugnant to the philosophical Calvin. The thought of the rhetorical Calvin, concerned to balance rather than to reconcile partial and incompatible insights and demands, was profoundly political. This Calvin suggests a kind of theological analogue to Machiavelli, the champion of the mixed constitution. Unable to escape the wars within himself, this Calvin could only strive for some practical equilibrium among contending forces. What Hanna Pitkin has concluded about Machiavelli applies also to Calvin, who was equally a child of his century: his thought sought to "hold in tension seemingly incompatible truths," and in this way he was "a better teacher than many a more consistent theorist, because he refused to abandon for very long any of the aspects of the truth he saw."[3]

Like other humanists, this Calvin was also inclined to consider human communication less an exchange of timeless truths than an instrument for the decorous achievement of particular goals within society, a conception that had often pushed humanists into political life. This Calvin provided his followers with guidance not for transcending but for living with the anomalies and contradictions of the human condition. Christian faith, in this perspective, provides the strength to accept, endure, and even relish them.

This humanistic side of Calvin was also the source of what was most original in him. There was little novelty in his theology; he would have rejected any suggestion that even what he had taken from Luther was new. In fact Calvin loathed novelty; like the other Reformers, he aimed only to aid in the restoration of what had been lost, as he believed, under the auspices of the papacy. His identification by posterity with a body of thought known as "Calvinism" would have given him particular trouble. But the adequate restatement of "mere Christianity" that he sought in the special circumstances of his own time required, as any humanist understood, decorous adaptation to a new audience and new historical conditions. This adaptation was the only innovation Calvin could have endured. Yet his awareness of the need for accommodation to the times was so strong that it drove him to what, for the times, was a new way of looking at theological discourse. The Gospel, conceived only as a set of timeless truths was, for this Calvin, powerless; it had to be adapted to the world. This Calvin, perhaps equally with Erasmus, thus points to the liberal, perhaps even the liberation, Christianity of the future, though not—for the other Calvin was always looking over his shoulder—in its most radical versions.

Recognition of the composite nature of Calvin's thought is also useful in reflecting on the old question whether Calvin was essentially "medieval"— the "iast of the Schoolmen"—or whether he was somehow a man of the "modern" world. Both these terms have become problematic, though perhaps for different reasons: "medieval" because we now recognize a complexity in medieval culture as great as (and much like) the complexity of Calvin himself; "modern" because of the difficulty of achieving clarity about the characteristics of the contemporary world. Nevertheless, it would hardly do justice to Calvin, and would certainly serve no useful purpose, to leave it that, as a man of his time, he was both medieval and modern. My own view is that the philosophical Calvin, though there is plenty of evidence of his survival into the modern world, was more typical of the medieval past; the humanistic Calvin, who reflects a larger skepticism, relativism, and pragmatism than were generally possible in the Middle Ages, is far closer to the secular culture of the modern world. This judgment too, of course, reflects an effort at balance.[4] The historical Calvin was much like Copernicus: unable to abandon traditional modes of thought, partly because of temperament but above all because he depended on them to make sense of the world; yet he undeniably was fumbling toward a new culture.

Recognition of the composite and political quality of Calvin's thought is essential for explaining both the success of the movement that came eventually to bear his name in his own time and its durability in later centuries under quite different conditions; without this quality it seems to me unlikely that Calvinism would have been more than a local and minor sect, without a future or the capacity to expand. Doubtless, as Michael Walzer has argued against Max Weber, Calvinism, for some social groups, relieved rather than intensified anxiety;[5] but it was not unique in its capacity for this. It had other practical virtues. For those with no taste for revolution, its ambiguity made hard choices unnecessary, and a traumatic break with the past avoidable. Calvinism could be made to sanction change while at the same time appealing to the most conservative of human instincts. Because it balanced, however precariously, the antithetical impulses of its age, it could attract the proponents both of liberty and of order, and men and women of many nations and diverse social groups. It could also satisfy those who shared some, if not all, of Calvin's needs, or in whom those needs were mixed in different proportions: at the same time, for example, Scotsmen and a broad spectrum of Protestants inside as well as outside the Anglican establishment.

But the mixture of the two Calvins in the Calvin of history also implies— and this too is a paradox—not their equality but a triumph in principle of rhetoric over philosophy, for while philosophy has traditionally excluded rhetoric, rhetoric, intrinsically as impure as life itself, has generally been willing to appropriate, for the sake of utility, bits and pieces of philosophy. A similar triumph is also evident in the program Calvin devised for meeting the practical needs of his time. This program was a mixture of elements from both his cultures, in which however a flexible common sense was dominant; only occasional, vague hints from the philosophical side of himself entered into it to reassure some of his more traditional followers. Calvin may have yearned for a pure church and the identification of society with the Kingdom of God, but in the end he settled for mixtures.

Later Calvinists inherited from him this unstable mixture, which, though different in other respects, was in this one not altogether unlike the Christianity of the later Middle Ages. As a precarious balance among antithetical and shifting impulses, Calvinism was vulnerable, in much the same way as the later medieval church, to radical disruption. There has recently been much debate about whether later Calvinists, beginning with Beza, continued or significantly altered the teaching of Calvin. The existence of two rather different Calvins suggests that this way of describing the relationship between Calvin and his successors misses the essential point. Later Calvinists were legitimate heirs of the philosophical and systematic Calvin, but they rejected, in a significantly less "modern" climate, the rhetorical and political qualities that had held Calvin's own Calvinism together, substituting for this purpose a tense dogmatism that could also be traced back to Calvin. But although dogmatic Calvinism succeeded in containing for nearly two centuries the antithetical impulses of the original Calvinism, in a larger sense it was untrue to the historical Calvin. By the eighteenth century a Calvinism that had lost its political dimension was breaking up and tending eventually toward the polar extremes of evangelical pietism and deistic rationalism, both of which, nevertheless, can also plausibly claim Calvin as spiritual father.

This account of the relationship between the historical Calvin and historical Calvinism may not endear Calvin to purists of either stamp. For some Calvinists, the conception of Calvin as a tidy and systematic thinker, which is not altogether wrong, continues to enhance his authority and their own security; for others, this conception makes him easy to dismiss as irrelevant to the messy real world, in which mixture is a condition of creativity, indeed of life itself. But the more complex Calvin I have described in this book is not so easy to dismiss. Like other great figures of his century, he was peculiarly sensitive to the subtleties and contradictions of the human condition and can tell us much about it. He could also be singularly practical about coping with its difficulties. And for those simply interested in our collective past he can, through the power of his rhetoric, be profoundly illuminating about a critical moment in the development of Western culture.

NOTES

Introduction

1. See among others, in addition to Max Weber, "Die protestantische Ethik und der Geist des Kapitalismus," *Archiv für Sozialwissenschaft und Sozialpolitik,* XX–XXI (1904–1905); Perry Miller, *The New England Mind: The Seventeenth Century* (New York, 1939); David Little, *Religion, Order, and Law: A Study in Pre-Revolutionary England* (New York, 1969); Michael Walzer, *The Revolution of the Saints: A Study in the Origins of Radical Politics* (Cambridge, Mass., 1965); R. Hooykaas, *Religion and the Rise of Modern Science* (Edinburgh and London, 1972); and, in what comes close to a parody of the conception, the first chapter in W. Stanford Reid, ed., *John Calvin: His Influence in the Western World* (Grand Rapids, Mich., 1982).

2. It is reasonable to assert, with Michael Mullett, that "if the word Calvinist is to have any meaning, it must mean a Christian acting in conformity with the Christian religion as interpreted by John Calvin" (*Radical Religious Movements in Early Modern Europe* [London, 1980], p. 37), but this is contrary to conventional usage, which is rarely much concerned with reasonableness. On the varieties of Calvinism, Menna Prestwich, ed., *International Calvinism, 1541–1715* (Oxford, 1985) is useful.

3. I have omitted Luther from this list, with some hesitation, after reading G. R. Elton, "Commemorating Luther," *Journal of Ecclesiastical History,* 35 (1984), 614–619.

4. The late M. Howard Rienstra, director of the H. H. Meeter Center for Calvin Studies at Calvin College, reported to me that its holdings include some 3,000 books and 12,000 articles on Calvin.

5. Even Alexandre Ganoczy, in one of the freshest among recent studies of Calvin, reflects something of this attitude; for Ganoczy, Calvin "belongs to the history of the church" because he "was essentially a religious man and a man of the church." To lose sight of this primary fact, Ganoczy observed, would be "to reduce the study to sociological, psychological, philosophical, and political phenomena" (*Le jeune Calvin; Genèse et évolution de sa vocation reformatrice* [Wiesbaden, 1966], p. 5). This suggests an odd conception of reductionism as well as a curiously disembodied understanding of the term "religious."

6. On the substitution of this Calvin for the living Calvin of history, see Basil Hall, "The Calvin Legend," pp. 1–18, and "Calvin against the Calvinists," pp. 19–37, in G. E. Duffield, ed., *John Calvin* [*Courtenay Studies in Reformation Theology,* 1] (Appleford, Abingdon, 1966).

7. On the inescapable limitations of sixteenth-century discourse, I remain deeply indebted to Lucien Febvre's *Le problème de l'incroyance au XVIe siècle: La religion de Rabelais* (Paris, 1942).

8. The canonization of Calvin began as early as Beza's *Life,* a work that, from an author who had known Calvin so long and so closely, is curiously lifeless and lacking in human insight. Beza was sensitive to the charge that, after accusing Catholics of idolatry, he had made Calvin into a "god." But his response seems rather to support than to refute this charge. He explained that his aim had been "to commemorate the labors of holy men on behalf of religion, together with their words and actions, through the knowledge of which the good become better while the wicked are reproved" (*Joannis Calvini Vita,* CO XXI, 119–120). Calvin suggested his own view of this sort of composition in a letter to Melanchthon, June 28, 1545, CO XII, 99. "In the church," he wrote with particular reference to Luther, "we must always be on our guard lest we pay too great a deference to men. For it is all over with her when a single individual, be he whosoever you please, has more authority than all the rest."

9. Thomas Forsyth Torrance confided to his readers that he had accommodated himself to the disconcerting discovery "that Calvin's own theological position was very different from the hardened system that has long passed under the name of Calvinism" and that there is a temptation "to eliminate certain elements of his thought as inconsistent with his main position" by trying "to handle these apparent contradictions as sympathetically as possible, on *the assumption that Calvin could not have been as self-contradictory as he would at first appear"* (*Calvin's Doctrine of Man* [London, 1952], pp. 7–8; italics added). Cf. Benjamin Charles Milner, Jr., *Calvin's Doctrine of the Church* [*Studies in the History of Christian Thought,* 5] (Leiden, 1970), pp. 1–5, which simply assumes the existence of (and therefore inevitably finds) a unifying principle in Calvin's ecclesiology. The gratuitousness of such assumptions has also been noted by Harro Höpfl, *The Christian Polity of John Calvin* (Cambridge, 1982), p. 3. On the deadening consequences, see B. Girardin, *Rhétorique et théologique: Calvin, le Commentaire de l'Epitre aux Romains Théologique Historique,* 54] (Paris, 1979), p. 77. That historical theology is not the only discipline to suffer from unexamined assumptions is suggested by Hans Kellner, "Triangular Anxieties: The Present State of European Intellectual History," in Dominick LaCapra and Steven L. Kaplan, eds., *Modern European Intellectual History* (Ithaca, N.Y., 1982), pp. 116–117. The "assumption of unity," Kellner observes, "has been just as tyrannical for historians," especially intellectual historians.

10. William Monter, *Calvin's Geneva* (New York, 1967), p. 98. Cf. George S. Hendry in *Theology Today,* XLI (1984), 98: "Calvin presented his thought calmly and judiciously, with conviction but without passion." I cite these passages only as evidence of the persistence of a received version of a figure who was infinitely more complex and interesting than this perception of him implies.

11. Various negative portraits of Calvin are reviewed by Richard Stauffer in the first chapter of *L'Humanité de Calvin* (Neuchâtel, 1964).

12. Karl Barth, for example, makes of Calvin "from a philosophical point of view a classical Platonist" (*Church Dogmatics,* trans. G. T Thompson et al. [Edinburgh, 1932–69], I, pt. 2, p. 728); Gerd Babelotsky, in contrast, though identifying Platonic elements in Calvin's thought, refrains from classifying him as a Platonist (*Pla-*

tonischer Bilder und Gedankengänge in Calvins Lehre vom Menschen [Wiesbaden, 1977]). On the question of Calvin's Stoicism, see André Malan Hugo's introduction to Ford Lewis Battles and André Malan Hugo, eds., *Calvin's Commentary on Seneca's De Clementia* (Leiden, 1969), pp. 46–47, 60–62. Cf. generally the reservations about efforts to understand Calvin in terms of particular schools of philosophy in Charles Partee, *Calvin and Classical Philosophy* [*Studies in the History of Christian Thought,* 14] (Leiden, 1977).

13. Cf. Beatrice Gottlieb's introduction to her excellent translation of Lucien Febvre, *The Problem of Unbelief in the Sixteenth Century* (Cambridge, Mass., 1983), p. xxiv.

14. Cf. Dominick LaCapra, "Rethinking Intellectual History and Reading Texts," *Modern European Intellectual History,* 55.

15. Fredson Bowers, ed., *Pragmatism* (Cambridge, Mass., 1975), p. 24.

16. In addition to Oberman's own *The Harvest of Medieval Theology: Gabriel Biel and Late Medieval Nominalism* (Cambridge, Mass., 1963) and *Werden und Wertung der Reformation: Vom Wegestreit zum Glaubenskampf* (Tübingen, 1977), see among other works E. Jane Dempsey Douglass, *Justification in Late Medieval Preaching: a Study of John Geiler of Keisersberg* (Leiden, 1966); David Curtis Steinmetz, *Misericordia Dei: The Theology of Johannes von Staupitz in its Late Medieval Setting* (Leiden, 1968); Steven E. Ozment, *Homo Spiritualis: A Comparative Study of the Anthropology of Johannes Tauler, Jean Gerson and Martin Luther in the Context of their Theological Thought* (Leiden, 1969) [*Studies in Medieval and Reformation Thought,* 1, 4, 6, respectively]; and James S. Preus, *From Shadow to Promise: Old Testament Interpretation from Augustine to Luther* (Cambridge, Mass., 1969).

17. Hans Baron, "Calvinist Republicanism and its Historical Roots," *Church History,* VIII (1939), 30–41; Walzer, *Revolution of the Saints,* pp. 23–24; Hugh R. Trevor-Roper, *Religion, the Reformation, and Social Change* (London, 1967), p. 26; Robert M. Kingdon, "Social Welfare in Calvin's Geneva," *American Historical Review,* 76 (1971), 50–69, and "The Control of Morals in Calvin's Geneva," in Lawrence P. Buck and Jonathan W. Zophy, eds., *The Social History of the Reformation* (Columbus, Ohio, 1972), pp. 3–16.

18. Höpfl, *Christian Polity of Calvin;* Suzanne Selinger, *Calvin Against Himself: An Inquiry in Intellectual History* (Hamden, Conn., 1984).

19. The most familiar portrait of the mature Calvin suggests this; cf. the sensitive description of it in Ganoczy, *Jeune Calvin,* p. 1. Others have looked for development in Calvin and failed to find it; I am inclined to attach considerable significance to the finding by Francis Montgomery Higman, *The Style of John Calvin in His French Polemical Treatises* (London, 1967), pp. 115–118, that Calvin's expository style underwent little change during his lifetime; it only became more polished. Susan Elizabeth Schreiner, "The Theater of His Glory: Nature and the Natural Order in the Thought of John Calvin," Ph.D. diss., Duke University, 1983, pp. xix–xx, found no important changes in his thought about nature. T. H. L. Parker, *John Calvin: A Biography* (London, 1975), pp. 73–74, noted that in spite of its being vastly expanded, the second edition of the *Institutes* contained little that was new, although Calvin's general consistency did not prevent his changing his mind on details (cf. Höpfl, *Christian Polity of Calvin,* p. 67).

20. I respect Höpfl's warning, in *Christian Polity of Calvin,* p. 3, against amassing quotations that are "contextless and random, taken from works of unequal level and from different periods"; but I have not found it fruitful, for my purposes, to make

such discriminations as he has found necessary for his own work. It has been precisely the accumulation of evidence "from works of unequal level and from different periods" that underlies my sense of the continuity of Calvin's fundamental concerns.

21. Febvre, *Problème de l'incroyance,* p. 11.

22. From the preface to the English translation of his *L'Homme devant la mort* (*The Hour of Our Death,* trans. Helen Weaver [New York, 1981], p. xvii).

23. Sixteenth-century thinkers are increasingly interpreted as complex bundles of contradictory impulses; cf. Hanna F. Pitkin's stimulating *Fortune is a Woman: Gender and Politics in the Thought of Niccolo Machiavelli* (Berkeley, 1984); Stephen Greenblatt, *Renaissance Self-Fashioning: More to Shakespeare* (Chicago, 1980), a work to which I am generally indebted; and Richard L. Regosin, "Recent Trends in Montaigne Scholarship: A Post-Structuralist Perspective," *Renaissance Quarterly,* XXXVII (1984), 34–54.

24. Cf. the conclusion of the first chapter of the *Institutes,* in which he speaks of "the right order of teaching."

25. A less systematic Calvin is, however, now beginning to emerge; cf. E. David Willis, "Rhetoric and Responsibility in Calvin's Theology," in Alexander J. McKelway and E. David Willis, eds., *The Context of Contemporary Theology: Essays in Honor of Paul Lehmann* (Atlanta, 1974), pp. 43–63.

26. Cf. Richard Stauffer, "Le discours à la première personne dans les sermons de Calvin," *Regards contemporains sur Jean Calvin* (Paris, 1965), pp. 206–238. The problem with Calvin's occasional "I" is not altogether different from that posed by Montaigne's more regular use of the first person; cf. Regosin, "Montaigne Scholarship," 34.

27. Selinger, *Calvin against Himself,* esp. pp. 72–84, seems to me in important respects right about this.

28. Comm. Ps., pref.

29. Quoted by Ernst Cassirer, *Essay on Man: An Introduction to a Philosophy of Human Culture* (New Haven, 1962), p. 180.

Chapter 1

1. On the general point I am indebted to Paula Fredricksen, "Paul and Augustine: Conversion Narratives, Orthodox Traditions, and the Retrospective Self," *Journal of Theological Studies,* N.S., 37 (1986). See Peter Brown, *Augustine of Hippo* (Berkeley, 1967), for the actual continuities between Augustine's pagan and Christian lives and the gradualness of his conversion.

2. The most balanced discussion of this subject is Ganoczy, *Jeune Calvin,* pp. 6–14, 276–304. Ganoczy views Calvin's conversion not as a discrete event but as a process, perhaps never completed. Among recent works that still treat Calvin's conversion as a specific event, the fullest is Paul Sprenger, *Das Rätsel um die Bekehrung Calvins* (Neukirchen, 1960); see also Ford Lewis Battles, *Calculus Fidei: Some Ruminations on the Structure of the Theology of John Calvin* (Grand Rapids, Mich., 1978), pp. 5–14, and Parker, *Calvin,* pp. 22, 162–165, which dates the conversion remarkably early. For useful remarks on the numerous "conversions" among the followers of Erasmus, cf. James Kittelson, *Wolfgang Capito: From Humanist to Reformer* (Leiden, 1975), pp. 110–111.

3. I quote in the translation of Parker, *Calvin,* p. 163.

4. See Ganoczy, *Jeune Calvin,* pp. 17–20, for a protest against the anachronistic use of this term and its absence from Calvin's vocabulary.

5. Cf. Comm. Acts 9:5, where he concludes that "we now have Paul tamed but not yet a disciple of Christ."

6. *Traité des scandales* (1550), in Albert-Marie Schmidt, ed., *Oeuvres de Jean Calvin* (Paris, 1934), II, 251.

7. Comm. Jer. 31:18.

8. Dedication to Comm. Sen. 13; on these matters Selinger, *Calvin Against Himself*, pp. 85–88, is often perceptive, though I do not fully agree with her interpretation.

9. Letter to Nicolas Duchemin, May 14, 1528, in CO X, 8. Ganoczy's refusal to see anything in this letter but "un Picard fier et reservé" who "cachera toujours sa douleur" (*Jeune Calvin*, p. 54) seems to carry ecumenical generosity too far. Calvin did not "always hide his grief"; see below p. 23. As Ganoczy suggests (p. 55), this letter makes it seem unlikely, as argued by Abel Lefranc, *La jeunesse de Calvin* (Paris, 1888), that his father's excommunication "left wounds in the soul of the future Reformer" (p. 55). I am inclined to agree with Hall, "Calvin Against the Calvinists," p. 21, that the data regarding Calvin's earliest years are insufficient to support the suggestion that his conception of a distant, omnipotent, and arbitrary deity had its origins in his relations with his father, as Oskar Pfister argued, *Das Christentum und die Angst: eine religionspsychologische, historische und religionshygienische Untersuchungen* (Zurich, 1944). However, it seems to me that Calvin's relations with his own father may have nourished his perception of the pope as a bad father (cf. pp. 215–216 below).

10. Serm. No. 43 on 2 Sam., 376. I cite in Hanns Rückert, ed., *Predigten über das 2 Buch Samuelis* (Neukirchen, 1961), I.

11. See Ganoczy, *Jeune Calvin*, pp. 34–43, on this chapter in Calvin's life, although Ganoczy tends to minimize the influence of Paris on his thought.

12. The basic study of this development is Augustin Renaudet, *Préréforme et l'humanisme à Paris pendant les premières guerres de l'Italie (1494–1517)* (Paris, 1916; rev. ed. 1953). On Lefèvre see also Georges Bedouelles, *Lefèvre d'Etaples et l'intelligence des écritures* (Geneva, 1977), and Philip Edgcumbe Hughes, *Lefèvre: Pioneer of Ecclesiastical Renewal in France* (Grand Rapids, Mich., 1984).

13. No. 1033 in P. S. and H. M. Allen, eds., *Opus Epistolarum Des. Erasmi Roterodami* (Oxford, 1906–1958), IV, 103.

14. In the preface to his commentaries on the Gospels, quoted by Bedouelle, *Lefèvre*, p. vii; see also p. 16.

15. See generally Febvre, *Problème de l'incroyance*, and Michael Screech, *Rabelais* (Ithaca, 1980), a chapter-by-chapter commentary on *Gargantua et Pantagruel* that identifies its Erasmianism.

16. *Traité des scandales*, pp. 223–224. Rabelais responded in 1552 in Book IV, ch. xxxii of his great work, describing "the demoniacal and Calvinist impostors of Geneva" as "formless, ill-favored monsters fashioned in spite of nature."

17. The point has been made with particular vigor by Trevor-Roper, *Religion, the Reformation and Social Change*, p. 26: "Calvin, far more than is generally admitted, was the heir of Erasmus: the heir in a more intolerant age, it is true, the heir who has to fight for his legacy, and whose character is changed by the struggle, but still, in essentials, the heir. If we follow his career, or read his works, we are constantly reminded of Erasmus. Calvin was nurtured on Erasmian teaching. He published his great work in the last city of Erasmus [Basel]. Some of his writings are almost plagiarisms of Erasmus. Like Erasmus, unlike Luther, Calvin believed in a reformed

visible Church: the hierarchy was not to be destroyed but purified, made more efficient, more dynamic."

18. This has been increasingly recognized, beginning with Quirinus Breen, *John Calvin: a Study in French Humanism* (Chicago, 1931), and "John Calvin and the Rhetorical Tradition," *Church History,* XXVI (1957), 3–21. See also Josef Bohatec, *Budé und Calvin: Studien zur Gedankenwelt des französischen Frühhumanismus* (Graz, 1950); Charles Trinkaus, "Renaissance Problems in Calvin's Theology," *Studies in the Renaissance,* I (1954), 54–80, and "The Religious Thought of the Italian Humanists and the Reformers: Anticipation or Autonomy?" in Charles Trinkaus and Heiko A. Oberman, eds., *The Pursuit of Holiness* (Leiden, 1973), pp. 352–357; Roy W. Battenhouse, "The Doctrine of Man in Calvin and Renaissance Platonism," *Journal of the History of Ideas,* IX (1948), 447–471; François Wendel, *Calvin et l'humanisme* (Paris, 1976); Partee, *Calvin and Classical Philosophy,* esp. p. 8. Resistance to the notion of the mature Calvin as a humanist, as in Parker, *Calvin,* p. 18, seems to be possible only if P. O. Kristeller's basic *Renaissance Thought: The Classic, Scholastic and Humanist Strains* (New York, 1961) is ignored.

19. On Calvin's classical learning, see Ford Lewis Battles, "The Sources of Calvin's Seneca Commentary," in G. E. Duffield, *Calvin* (Appleford, Abingdon, 1966), pp. 38–66.

20. Comm. Sen., 6–7.

21. Letter to François Daniel, 1532, CO X, 21.

22. Charles Garside, Jr., "The Origins of Calvin's Theology of Music, 1536–43," *Transactions of the American Philosophical Society,* 69 (1979), quotes his letter of 1557 to Conrad Hubert to this effect.

23. In his preliminary statement describing "the subject matter of the present work."

24. Cf. *Inst.,* IV, vii, 27, where he charged that contemporary popes had "never grasped anything of Christ except what they had learned in the school of Lucian."

25. *Projet d'ordonnances ecclésiastiques,* CO X, 21.

26. The most comprehensive account of these matters is the first volume of Charles Borgeaud, *Histoire de l'Université de Genève* (Geneva, 1900–1934). Much of the detail in this curriculum was borrowed immediately from the scheme of Jacob Sturm, the great humanist educator of Strasbourg.

27. Cop's address is included in CO IX, 873–876; Engl. trans. Dale Cooper and Ford Lewis Battles, *The Hartford Quarterly,* VI (1965), 76–85, and in an appendix to Battles's translation of the 1536 *Institutes* (Atlanta, 1975), 462–471.

28. See, on the central importance of exile as a major theme in the culture of the age, Randolph Starn, *Contrary Commonwealth: The Theme of Exile in Medieval and Renaissance Italy* (Berkeley, 1982); A. Bartlett Giamatti, *Exile and Change in Renaissance Literature* (New Haven, 1982); and Thomas M. Greene, *The Light in Troy: Imitation and Discovery in Renaissance Poetry* (New Haven, 1982), pp. 28–53.

29. Cf. his attacks on those he called "Nicodemites," especially in his *Excuse à Messieurs les Nicodémites* (1544), but also in other works, for example Comm. John 7:50: "There are many in the present day who plead that they resemble Nicodemus and hope that, by assuming this mask [of conformity to the papal church] they will mock God with impunity." On the general subject, cf. Carlo Ginzburg, *Il Nicodemismo: Simulazione e dissimulazione nell'Europa del '500* (Turin, 1970); and for the religious exiles' feelings of superiority, Donald R. Kelley, *François Hotman: A Revolutionary's Ordeal* (Princeton, 1973), p. 45.

30. Comm. Josh. 2:4.

31. Comm. Jer. 9:2.

32. IV, vii, 17. Screech, *Rabelais,* pp. 84–85, makes a point of Rabelais's royalist (as contrasted with clerical) Gallicanism.

33. Cf. Robert M. Kingdon, *Geneva and the Coming of the Wars of Religion in France* (Geneva, 1956), pp. 2–11.

34. Especially on the eve of the outbreak of the Wars of Religion; cf. the epistle to his commentary on Daniel (1561) and his first sermon on II Samuel, pp. 6–7.

35. Comm. Gen. 12:1; cf. Comm. Deut. 28:64.

36. Comm. Jer. 49:24.

37. As quoted by the elder Seneca and cited by Starn, *Contrary Commonwealth,* pp. 24–25. Calvin was by no means alone among Frenchmen lamenting exile; Kelley, *Hotman,* p. 50, quotes a poem by Theodore Beza: "Goodbye, France, goodbye: / The place which first took shape / Before my eyes, / The place which first listened / To my cries."

38. Letter to a French Seigneur, Oct. 18, 1548, CO XIII, 63–64; see also Comm. Gen. 12:1.

39. Serm. No. 104 on Job, 541.

40. Letter to Martin Dorp, May 1515, *Opus Epistolarum Erasmi,* II, 92.

41. Letter of 1540, CO XI, 56.

42. Cf. Lucien Richard, *The Spirituality of Calvin* (Atlanta, 1974), p. 97. Höpfl, *Christian Polity of Calvin,* p. 20, sees here "an elegant play upon words."

43. *Institutio principis christiani* (1516), *Christiani matrimonii institutio* (1526), and *Declamatio de pueris statim ac liberaliter instituendis* (1529).

44. Cf. John T. McNeill's introduction to the *Institutes,* p. xxxii.

45. In this interpretation I have been much influenced by Ganoczy, *Jeune Calvin,* esp. pp. 97 and 253; Ganoczy notes the absence from the work of the word *"reformatio."* M. Howard Rienstra has demonstrated, in an unpublished paper made available to me, that as late as 1543, in his *Supplex Exhortatio ad invictissimum Caesarem Carolum Quintum et illustrissimos principes aliosque ordinis,* Calvin still preferred *restitutio* and *restituere* to *reformatio*; Rienstra suggests that Calvin may have changed under Anabaptist pressure in later years.

46. See especially Ganoczy, *Jeune Calvin,* pp. 138–150. Richard Stauffer, "Calvin," *International Calvinism,* p. 19, points out that Calvin's organization of topics follows that of Luther's Short Catechism.

47. "If they are compared, you know yourself how much Luther excels," he wrote to Farel (Feb. 28, 1539, CO XI, 24).

48. This occurs within a carefully balanced statement in a letter to Bullinger, Nov. 25, 1544, CO XI, 774.

49. Jan. 12, 1538, CO X, 139.

50. Letter to Pierre Viret, May 19, 1540, CO XI, 36; cf. Comm. Dan. 8:22–23.

51. Letter to Bucer, Jan. 12, 1538, CO X, 138.

52. Comm. Ps., pref., 25–26.

53. *Vita Calvini,* CO XXI, 125.

54. Cf. Stauffer, *L'Humanité de Calvin,* ch. 2.

55. Comm. Ps., pref. 25–26.

56. Comm. Titus, ep.

57. Letter to Bucer, Oct. 15, 1541, CO XI, 297.

58. Letter to the ministers of Neuchâtel, Sept. 26, 1558, CO XVII, 351–352.

59. A good introduction to the situation is Monter, *Calvin's Geneva.* On the

power of Bern in this period, see Thomas A. Brady, Jr., *Turning Swiss* (Cambridge, 1985), p. 13.

60. Cf. Ganoczy, *Jeune Calvin*, pp. 49, 119. That Calvin did not object to this may suggest his eagerness to take a responsible place in the Genevan church.

61. Letter to Farel, April 1539, CO X, 339.

62. Cf. Willem Balke, *Calvin and the Anabaptist Radicals,* trans. William J. Heynen (Grand Rapids, Mich., 1981), pp. 73–96.

63. Letter to Louis du Tillet from Strasbourg, July 10, 1538, CO X, 221.

64. Emile Doumergue, *Jean Calvin: Les hommes et les choses de son temps* (Lausanne, 1899–1928), I, pp. 297–299, in discussing the first of his extant letters to Bucer, dated Sept. 4, 1532, speculates that there may have been earlier letters.

65. On Calvin in this milieu, Girardin, *Rhétorique et théologique* is stimulating.

66. Erasmus, too, had chosen Romans for his first Paraphrase. The audience for biblical commentaries in Strasbourg was large. Kittelson, *Capito,* p. 209 quotes from Capito's preface to the published edition of his own lectures on Habbakuk (1526), for which it had been assumed that the audience would be small: "But because it seems proper to turn away no one, in a short time the listeners were there in throngs, many more than we had guessed there would be, in fact so many that my upper room holds them only painfully."

67. Cf. Girardin, *Rhétorique et théologique,* pp. 104–118; and Balke, *Calvin and the Radicals,* pp. 123–153.

68. This is suggested by Salo W. Baron, "John Calvin," *Encyclopaedia Judaica* (Jerusalem, 1972), V, 66–68. This episode may be reflected in Calvin's *Ad quaestiones et obiecta Judaei cuiusdam Responsio,* first published in 1597 and included in CO IX, 653–674.

69. Letter to Farel, Apr. 20, 1539, CO X, 337.

70. Comm. Ps., pref., 25–28.

71. Letter of July 1538, CO X, 219.

72. May 10, 1551, CO XIV, 121–122; Calvin expressed essentially the same sentiments to Farel in a letter of June 15, CO XIV, 132–134.

73. Letter to Bullinger, June 26, 1548, CO XII, 729. For an example of Calvin's rebukes, see his letter to Bucer, Jan. 12, 1538. Calvin thought Bucer too likely "to soften down his expressions so as to give offense to as few persons as possible" (CO X, 137–144).

74. Comm. Rom. (1540), ep.

75. CO IX, 891–894.

76. *Consilia ad disciplinam ecclesiasticam caelibatum in ministro non ita requirendum esse,* CO X, 228.

77. Letter to Farel, May 19, 1539, CO X, 348. On Calvin's indifference to a "fine figure," cf. p. 137 below.

78. Cf. T. H. L. Parker, *The Oracles of God: An Introduction to the Preaching of John Calvin* (London, 1962), p. 31. On Calvin's marriage in general, see also Stauffer, *L'Humanité de Calvin.*

79. Parker, *Calvin,* p. 102, speaks only of the premature birth of a son in 1542; but see Calvin's letters to Farel, May 30, 1544, CO XI, 719, reporting the birth of a daughter, and Aug. 21, 1547, for another infant boy, CO XII, 580. For what may have been still another child who died at birth, see his letter to M. de Falais, Apr. 1546, CO XII, 322.

80. On the general point, see Kelley, *Hotman,* pp. x, 47–48. Kelley, pp. 42–43, quotes letters to Calvin in which Hotman wrote him that "since the day I found true

religion, I have loved no one, not even my father, more than you," and assured Calvin of his "filial love."

81. Quoted from his *Réponse aux injures de Balduin* (1562) by Stauffer, *L'Humanité de Calvin,* p. 43.

82. Letter to Viret, Apr. 7, 1549, CO XIII, 212–231; Viret's reply spoke both of Calvin's "characteristic softness" and his strength in restraining his grief (232–233). On Calvin's need for "self-control" in grief, see p. 182 below. The next year Calvin dedicated his commentary on II Thessalonians to the physician Benedict Textor in appreciation for his careful attendance on Calvin's wife.

83. Letter to Richard Vauville, Nov. 1555, CO XV, 867.

84. Serm. I Tim., 255.

85. Letter to Farel, Mar. 29, 1540, CO XI, 30. He used the same language in a letter to Viret, May 19, 1540, CO XI, 36.

86. Letter of April 1539, CO X, 339.

87. Letter to Farel, Oct. 27, 1540, CO XI, 90–92; he wrote a similar letter to Viret on Mar. 1, 1541, CO XI, 167–169.

88. Letter to Bucer from Geneva, Oct. 15, 1541, CO XI, 299.

89. Comm. II Thess. 3:6–10.

90. Letter to Farel, Sept. 16, 1541, CO XI, 281.

91. Letter to Myconius, Mar. 14, 1542, CO XI, 379.

92. Letter to Viret, Mar. 27, 1547, CO XII, 505.

93. Letter to Farel, May 30, 1543, CO XI, 719.

94. Text in CO XI, 546, n. 8.

95. Text in CO XII, 564.

96. Calvin to Viret, Mar. 27, 1547, CO XII, 505.

97. As in his letters to members of the Budé family, for example, June 19, 1547, to M. de Budé, CO, XII, 542–543.

98. Comm. Is. 16:4.

99. See Monter, *Geneva,* p. 82. It seems likely that living costs were indeed increasing; this was the period of what would be known as the great price rise. In view of these complaints, Calvin's praise of the city fathers for their hospitality to foreigners (Comm. John, ep.) was hortatory if not ironic. That year (1551) had seen an effort to bar all new residents from admission to political life for twenty-five years.

100. Comm. I Tim. 6:14.

101. Comm. Matt. 26:10.

102. Letter to the faithful in France, Jul. 24, 1547, CO XII, 562.

103. Letter of Oct. 15, 1541, CO XI, 299.

104. Letters of Feb. 16, 1543, CO XI, 515, and Nov. 28, 1552, CO XIV, 415. See also the extended but general complaints in his letter to Farel, Dec. 28, 1547, CO XII, 542–543; and Comm. Ps., pref.

105. Comm. Ex. 6:10; cf. Comm. Is. 25:1.

106. Comm. II Cor. 7:5; cf. Comm. Acts 15:22.

107. Cf. Comm. Matt. 10:16.

108. Comm. Jer. 15:10.

109. Comm. I Tim. 5:19.

110. Comm. Jer. 17:16.

111. Letter to Viret, Jan. 24, 1551, CO XIV, 27.

112. Letter to Blaurer, Feb. 14, 1552, CO XIV, 474.

113. Letter to Christopher Fabri, Jan. 13, 1553, CO XIV, 455.

114. Letter to Bullinger, Nov. 26, 1553, CO XIV, 673–674.

115. Cf. his letter to Farel, Aug. 20, 1553, CO XIV, 589–590. His letter to Sulzer, Sept. 8, 1553, CO XIV, 614–615, suggests the effect on him of the capital executions of his own followers; he thought it appropriate that the saints should display no less zeal than their enemies. My own view is that Calvin's defense of the execution of Servetus was itself suspiciously "defensive"; cf. the evidence presented by Mario Turchetti, *Concordia o tolleranza? François Bauduin (1520–1573) e i 'Moyenneurs'* (Geneva, 1984), 363–376. For an unusually balanced discussion of the affair, see Hall, "Calvin Legend," 9–11.

116. Monter, *Geneva,* pp. 75–88, provides a clear and succinct account of the entire episode. Calvin treated this crisis most fully in a letter to Bullinger, June 15, 1555, CO XV, 676–685.

117. Letter of Feb. 3, 1557, CO XVI, 406.

118. Letter to Francesco Dryander, May 18, 1547, CO XII, 524–525.

119. Cf. Comms. Is. 14:31 and Jer. 5:15, 13:21. In none of these passages did he suggest that the danger was spiritual as well as political.

120. Letter to Farel and Viret, Jul. 25, 1541, CO XI, 257.

121. Letter of Oct. 1549, CO XIII, 438.

122. Letters to Farel, Mar. 15, 1539, CO X:ii, 328, and June, 1540, CO XI, 52; to Bullinger, Sept. 7, 1553, CO XIV, 610; to William Cecil, Jan. 29, 1559, CO XVII, 419–420. He was also capable of thanking the Duchess of Somerset profusely—and perhaps ironically—for the gift of a ring (June 15, 1549, CO XIII, 300–302), and complaining of its small value to Farel (Jul. 9, 1549, CO XIII, 325).

123. CO XIV, 37.

124. On his audience, see Kingdon, *Geneva,* pp. 14–15. See also T. H. L. Parker, *Calvin's New Testament Commentaries* (London, 1971), for much of what follows.

125. Girardin, *Rhétorique et théologique,* pp. 299–312, analyzes this dialogue.

126. Letter to Dryander, Mar. 7, 1550, CO XIII, 536. See also Calvin's account of how this worked in the epistle to Edward VI of his revised Isaiah commentary.

127. At the conclusion of lectures 123 and 32 on Jeremiah.

128. CO XX, 299. On Calvin as preacher, see Stauffer, "Calvin méconnu"; Parker, *Calvin,* pp. 89–96; Ford Lewis Battles, "The Future of Calviniana," in Peter de Klerk, ed., *Renaissance, Reformation, Resurgence* (Grand Rapids, Mich., 1976), p. 145; David C. Steinmetz, "The Theology of Calvin and Calvinism," in Steven Ozment, ed., *Reformation Europe: A Guide to Research* (St. Louis, 1982), pp. 212–214. Not all Calvin's sermons have yet been published; many, indeed, have disappeared. Early in the nineteenth century the pastor in charge of the Bibliothèque de Genève where they were stored sold most of the volumes of Calvin's manuscript sermons "by weight," that is, presumably as waste paper; and although some were eventually recovered, about a thousand were permanently lost.

129. Parker, *Calvin,* p. 88.

130. See his letters to M. de Falais, May 26 and Sept. 10, 1547, CO XII, 530, 586–587, for examples of Calvin's mixture of practicality and tact in such business.

131. *Le catéchisme français,* CO V, 319.

132. Letter to Christophe Libertet, Sept. 11, 1535, CO X, 51.

133. This was *in* a letter, Feb. 17, 1551, CO XIV, 51. It is not clear whether he was thanking or reproaching Bullinger, who was very different in temperament from Farel and Bucer, for Bullinger's "generous indulgence" in allowing him to be silent.

134. CO XX, 299.

135. Letter to Blaurer, Feb. 14, 1552, CO XIV, 474.

136. Serm. No. 17 on Job, 212.

137. Letter to Mme. de Coligny, Aug. 5, 1563, CO XX, 129.

138. Serm. No. 72 on Job, 130. His *je* here referred to Everyman but certainly included himself. A few weeks earlier he had remarked in passing, "Il est vray qu'on vivra cinquante ou soixante ans" (Serm. No. 30 on Job, 387). Calvin was then about forty-five.

139. Letter of Feb. 8, 1564, CO XX, 252–224. Calvin repeated much of this detail in a letter to Bullinger on Apr. 6, CO XX, 282–283.

Chapter 2

1. For more general discussion of the age, see my "Anxiety and the Formation of Early Modern Culture," in Barbara C. Malament, ed., *After the Reformation: Essays in Honor of J. H. Hexter* (Philadelphia, 1980), pp. 215–46.

2. Letter to Farel, Oct. 1540, CO XI, 84.

3. *Inst.,* III, xiv, 6.

4. Comm. Josh. 2:1.

5. Comm. Josh. 24:29.

6. Comm. Ps. 29:5.

7. Cf. Hans Blumenberg, *The Legitimacy of the Modern Age,* trans. Robert M. Wallace (Cambridge, Mass., 1983), 149–51.

8. Comm. Ps. 18:8.

9. Comm. Jer. 19:12–13.

10. Comm. Jer. 31:35–36; cf. Serm. No. 11 on Job, 435. Schreiner, "Theater of His Glory," 29–31, discusses Calvin's threatening water imagery.

11. Serms. No. 34 and 96 on Job, 420 and 434–435.

12. Comms. Jer. 5:22, Ps. 33:7.

13. Comm. Jer. 31:35–36.

14. Comm. Is. 51:16.

15. Comm. Jer. 5:25.

16. Serm. No. 79 on Job, 220.

17. Comm. Ps. 30:6.

18. Comm. Ps. 57:2.

19. Comm. Jer. 18:1–6.

20. As in Serm. No. 38 on Job, 477: "les choses sont confusés comme en obscurité."

21. Cf. *Traité des scandales*, p. 163: "les distinctions éclaircissent beaucoup toutes les matières dont on a traiter."

22. Higman, *Style of Calvin*, p. 156.

23. Comm. Ps. 81:14.

24. Comm. Jer. 17:5–6.

25. Cf. Ganoczy, *Jeune Calvin*, pp. 200–208, on the importance of "*solus*" in Calvin's vocabulary, and Jonas Barish, *The Antitheatrical Prejudice* (Berkeley, 1981), p. 87, on the anxiety generally aroused in the period by "mixture."

26. Cf. Starn, *Contrary Commonwealth*, p. 2, on the traditional view of an exile, going back to Isidore of Seville, "as one who crossed over or lived outside some home boundary."

27. Comm. Ps. 74:16; see also Comm. Acts 17:26.

28. Comm. I Cor. 2:3, 7:25.

29. Comm. Josh. 2:14.

30. Serm. No. 81 on Job, 246. He took up the theme again in serm. No. 91, 375.

31. Comm. Jer. 22:14; he justified his criticism on the ground that such windows reflected luxury and intemperance and were neither useful nor fitting, but he did not explain why he thought this.

32. Comm. Deut. 22:5.

33. Serm. No. 11 on I Cor., 713–714.

34. Serm. No. 23 on Job, 285–286.

35. Serm. No. 143 on Deut., 234.

36. Cf. Higman, *Style of Calvin*, p. 88. Calvin had recognized and perhaps been encouraged by the use of antithesis in Scripture; cf. Comm. Dan. 9:18.

37. Comm. Luke 16:36.

38. *Inst.*, III, iii, 12.

39. Comm. John 3:21.

40. Comm. Ps. 51:1.

41. Comm. Ps. 106:35; see also Comm. Ps. 119:115, 119.

42. Comm. Acts 15:9; Comm. Luke 2:22; Comm. Ps. 19:12; *Inst.*, III, xii, 4: Comm. Gal., 6:8; *Inst.*, xiii, 3.

43. Serm. No. 18 on Job, 227.

44. Comms. Heb., pref.; Phil. 3:15; Acts 21:26.

45. Cf. Stephen Greenblatt, "Filthy Rites," *University Publishing*, 8 (Fall, 1979), 5–6, contrasting Luther's and More's uses of this imagery. Beza used it too; cf. Kelley, *Hotman*, p. 67; for Rabelais see Screech, *Rabelais*, pp. 50–52, 459–460.

46. He may have picked up the last of these from his legal studies; in law a *casus perplexus* was a case characterized by maximum uncertainty (Screech, *Rabelais*, pp. 257, 264–265).

47. Comm. Ps. 90:10.

48. Comm. Ps. 30:6.

49. Comm. Is. 61:2.

50. Comm. Gal. 6:7.

51. Comm. Jer. 20:14–16.

52. Comm. Ps. 119:30.

53. Comm. Dan. 12:1.

54. Comm. Ps. 91:13.

55. Comm. Jer. 12:13.

56. Comm. Deut. 32:24.

57. Comm. Is. 59:10.

58. Comm. Jer. 30:10; cf. 23:5–6.

59. Comm. Jer. 38:25–26; for possible Ciceronian influence here, cf. Comm. Deut. 28:64.

60. Comm. Ex. 1:9; cf. Comm. Is. 30:1.

61. Comm. Is. 9:12.

62. Serm. No. 48 on Job, 601.

63. Comm. Is. 13:5.

64. Comm. Ex. 1:9.

65. Comm. II Cor. 9:11.

66. Comm. I Tim. 6:7

67. Serm. No. 100 on Job, 489.

68. *Inst.*, III, xx, 44.

69. Comm. Gen. 50:22.

70. Comm. Josh. 1:5.

71. Comm. I Tim. 3:15.

72. Comm. I Cor. 7:36.

73. Comm. Acts 1:8. On curiosity as a vice, see Blumenberg, *Legitimacy of the Modern Age*, pp. 229–453.

74. Comms. Dan. 1:4, Luke 16:27 and 30. Calvin was thus an early representative of the Protestant attack on popular occultism; cf. Keith Thomas, *Religion and the Decline of Magic: Studies in Popular Beliefs in Sixteenth and Seventeenth Century England* (London, 1971), pp. 51–112.

75. Comm. I John 4:4.

76. Comm. Is. 13:1.

77. Comm. Rom. 8:38; cf. Comm. Acts 23:11 on Paul's anxiety "about the future."

78. Comm. I Cor. 7:32; cf. Serm. No. 1 on II Sam., 1, on how "God sometimes grieves us doubly when we expect to rejoice," for he may "give us some occasion to feel his grace" and then an "opposite occasion of being troubled and tormented."

79. Comm. Luke 12:29.

80. Comm. Matt. 6:27.

81. Comms. Rom. 1:13, Is. 18:4.

82. Comms. II Tim. 4:6, Deut. 32:48.

83. Comm. Gen. 50:2.

84. Comm. Acts 2:24; cf. Serm. No. 98 on Job, 468: "la mort est une malediction, et comme une corruption de nature, comme un changement de l'ordre de Dieu."

85. Comm. Heb. 2:15.

86. Cf. Alberto Tenenti, *Il senso della morte e l'amore della vita nel Rinascimento* (Florence, 1957), pp. 278–316.

87. Comm. Ps. 30:6.

88. Comm. Ez. 5:18; cf. Comm. Deut. 28:64.

89. *Inst.*, I, xvii, 10; cf. Serm. No. 104 on Job, 540–541.

90. Comm. Phil. 1:23; this again is an Erasmian theme, as in the colloquy *Funus*.

91. *Inst.*, III, ix, 5.

92. *Inst.*, II, viii, 3.

93. Comm. Is. 57:20.

94. *Responsio ad Sadoleti epistolam*, CO V, 412, in the translation of John C. Olin (New York, 1966).

95. Comm. Is. 10:3.

96. Comm. Ps. 32:4.

97. Serm. No. 51 on Job, 633. Calvin's motive here seems to be to excuse God for appearing to have treated Job unjustly. For hints of the pre-Christian source of this attitude, see Hans Blumenberg, *Work on Myth*, Robert M. Wallace, trans. (Cambridge, Mass., 1985).

98. *Supplex Exhortatio ad Caesarem de restituenda ecclesia*, CO VI, 486.

99. *Inst.*, III, iv, 27; see also Comm. Rom. 4:14 and 5:1.

100. *Inst.*, IV, x, 2.

101. *Inst*, III, iv, 17; for another strong passage, see Serm. No. 38 on II Sam., 331–332.

102. Serm No. 44 on Deut., 412–413.

103. Cf. Steven E. Ozment, *The Reformation in the Cities: The Appeal of Protestantism to Sixteenth-Century Germany and Switzerland* (New Haven, 1975).

104. Comm. I Cor. 13:5.

105. Serm. No. 68 on Job, 80–81.

106. Comm. I Cor. 7:33.

107. *Inst.*, II, vii, 11.

108. Comm. Dan. 10–12.

109. Comm. Gen. 19:19.

110. Comm. Ps. 56:4.

111. Cf. Gerald May, *Care of Mind, Care of Spirit: Psychiatric Dimensions of Spiritual Direction* (San Francisco, 1982), p. 20.

112. Serm. No. 41 on II Sam., 362–363; Serm. No. 4 on Job, 63–64.

113. Comm. Gen. 24:21.

114. Comm. Matt. 8:25.

115. Comm. Matt. 6:26.

116. Comm. Jer. 38:20–22.

117. Comm. Luke 1:73.

118. Comm. Ps. 4:9; italics added.

119. For the philosophical background of the conception, see Blumenberg, *Legitimacy of the Modern Age*, pp. 81–85. It is also biblical; in the Septuagint, for example (Gen. 1:2), it signifies formlessness, and in the New Testament (Luke 8:31, Rom. 10:7, Rev. 9:1) the abode of demons or the dead.

120. Quoted in Paolo Simoncelli, *Evangelismo italiano del Cinquecento: Questione religiosa e nicodemismo politico* (Rome, 1979), p. 7.

121. Serm. No. 9 on Job, 128. Rabelais also employed the term positively: Gargantua's letter to Pantagruel declares that he wanted to make of his son an *"abysme de science"*; cf. Screech, *Rabelais*, p. 67, on the antiquity of this phrase.

122. *Inst.*, I, xvii, 2.

123. Serm. No. 73 on Job, 150.

124. Serm. No. 41 on Deut., 383.

125. CO XX, 299.

126. Comm. I Tim. 6:7; Serm. No. 26 on Job, 324.

127. Serm. No. 37 on II Sam., 320; Serm. No. 96 on Job, 435.

128. Serm. No. 48 on Job, 600.

129. Comm. Jer. 9:22.

130. Cf. Mary Douglas, *Purity and Danger: An Analysis of Concepts of Pollution and Taboo* (London, 1966).

131. Comm. I Peter 1:14, 18; cf. *Inst.*, I, vi, 1.

132. Comm. Ps. 30:6.

133. Serm. No. 8 on I Cor., 680.

134. Comm. Is. 59:10; see also Comm. Acts 23:11 for the use of *"ango"* in the sense of "to make anxious."

135. For these characterizations and for Calvin's basic independence, I am indebted to Jeanne Rutenburg. Calvin had little interest, for example, in the ark as a type of the church, though he was aware of this association and even attributed it, erroneously, to Scripture (Comm. I Pet. 3:21).

136. Comm. Ps. 71:5; cf. Ps. 22:10 for another hint of the claustrophobic sensations provoked in him by fetal confinement in the womb.

137. *Inst.*, II, x, 10; cf. *Traité des scandales*, p. 193, on Noah: "ce saint Patriarche étant forclos du ciel et de l'air, ne trouve vie sinon au sépulcre, et ne peut respirer sinon en lieu où il crève et soit étouffé de puantise." Calvin's comparison of the Genevan church to Noah's ark in a letter to Bullinger, Feb. 23, 1554 (CO XIV, 673–674) is revealing in light of these associations.

138. Note, however, Comm. Ps. 86:9, where he seems to suggest that a labyrinth

may exit into the abyss, a mixture of metaphors perhaps stemming from the ambiguous genealogy of "abyss."

Chapter 3

1. Serm. No. 44 on Deut., 414.
2. Cf. Brown, *Augustine*, pp. 288–89, 343.
3. Comm. Ezek. 9:3–4.
4. Serm. No. 93 on Job, 400.
5. Comm. Jer. 31:22; Serm. No. 52 on Job, 646.
6. Comm. Gen. 20:9.
7. Comm. Titus 3:3.
8. Comm. John 8:7. Calvin may have begun early to correct others. Beza reported that well before his break with Rome, he had been "a strict censor of everything vicious in his companions: (*Vita Calvini*, CO XXI, 121).
9. Comm. Acts 6:14. Höpfl, *Christian Polity of Calvin*, pp. 35–38, is good on the general point.
10. Comm. Jer. 20:8–9.
11. *Inst.*, III, x, 4.
12. For example, Serm. No. 9 on I Cor., 689–690, on freedom to eat the food of an unbeliever, which Calvin found too permissive.
13. Comm. Jer. 30:9.
14. Comm. Is. 3:24.
15. Comm. Acts 28:6.
16. Comm. Ps. 94:4; Serm. No. 2 on II Sam., 17.
17. Serm. No. 10 on Job, 130.
18. Comm. Jer. 12:1
19. Comm. Jer. 32:16–18.
20. Comm. Phil. 3:1.
21. Comm. II Tim. 4:2.
22. Comm. Acts 6:11.
23. Comm. Matt. 23:1.
24. Calvin was here in agreement with Thomas More. In *Utopia* Raphael Hythloday describes a Utopian convert who, "as soon as he was baptized, in spite of our advice to the contrary, spoke publicly of Christ's religion with more zeal than discretion" (ed. Edward Surtz [New Haven, 1964], p. 132).
25. Bucer had referred to it as Calvin's *ingenium irritabile* (Doumergue, *Calvin*, II, pp. 296, 404).
26. Comms. Ex. 5:20, Gen. 50:1.
27. *Inst.*, III, vii, 4.
28. Comm. Matt. 20:24.
29. Comm. Gal. 5:26. Conversely, "humility is the mother and root of all virtue" (Serm. No. 80 on Job, 234).
30. Comm. John 4:9.
31. On changing emphases in moral theology, cf. Lester K. Little, "Pride Goes Before Avarice: Social Change and the Vices in Latin Christendom," *American Historical Review*, 76 (1971), 16–49.
32. Comms. Dan. 1:8, Deut. 6:10.

33. Serm. No. 4 on Job, 68.

34. Comms. Gen. 18:27, Luke 16:19–31.

35. Comm. Gen. 41:40.

36. Comm. Matt. 6:19.

37. Serm. No. 39 on Deut., 352; Comm. Heb. 10:24.

38. Serm. No. 4 on I Cor., 625; Comm. Jer. 2:36.

39. Cf. Serm. No. 3 on II Sam., 26, and Serm. No. 38 on Deut., 343.

40. Serm. No. 38 on Deut., 341; Serm. No. 32 on II Sam., 284.

41. Comm. John 8:11.

42. Comm. Matt. 1:19.

43. As in Comm. Gen. 16:1, where he criticized Sarai for arranging matters between Abram and Hagar.

44. Comm. Gen. 9:20.

45. Comm. Is. 56:12.

46. Comm. Lev. 10:9.

47. Comm. Dan. 5:2.

48. Comm. II Tim. 2:22; Serm. No. 52 on Job, 652.

49. Serm. No. 12 on I Cor., 733; see also Serm. No. 19 on III Sam., 164.

50. Comm. Is. 3:17.

51. Serm. No. 19 on II Sam., 165.

52. Comm. Jer. 2:33.

53. Serm. No. 32 on II Sam., 281.

54. Letter to Nicolas Parent, Dec. 14, 1540, CO XI, 131.

55. Comm. Is. 3:17.

56. Serm. No. 3 on II Sam., 23.

57. Comm. Is. 3:24.

58. Comm. Is. 3:17.

59. Comm. Is. 47:2.

60. Comm. Gen. 24:64.

61. Comm. Is. 3:17.

62. Comm. Titus 2:3.

63. Comm. I Tim. 5:5.

64. Comm. II Tim. 3:6.

65. Serm. No. 48 on Job, 601.

66. Cf. Nancy S. Struever, *The Language of History in the Renaissance: Rhetoric and Historical Consciousness in Florentine Humanism* (Princeton, 1970), p. 80.

67. *Harmonia ex tribus Evangelistis composita*, ep.

68. Comm. Is. 8:7.

69. Comm. Jer. 37:18.

70. Comms. Jer. 22:15, 42: 1–3; Dan. 11:26.

71. Comms. Ps. 29:9, Luke 1:52, Jer. 22:15, Dan. 11:6, Gen. 47:23; Serm. No. 34 on II Sam., 298.

72. Comm. Is. 19:4.

73. Comm. Hos. 1:3–4.

74. Comm. Dan. 3:13, 4:28–32.

75. Comm. Dan. 4:25.

76. Comm. Ezek. 4:4–8.

77. Serm. No. 3 on II Sam., 25.

78. Comm. Dan. 6:3–5.

79. Serm. No. 32 on II Sam., 283.

80. Comm. Is. 22:17.
81. Comm Ps. 94:10.
82. Comm. Is. 3:13.
83. Comm. Matt. 28:15.
84. Serm. No. 13 on I Cor., 744–745.
85. Serm. No. 84 on Job, 286.
86. Serm. No. 39 on Deut., 354.
87. Comm. Is. 5:8.
88. Comm. Is. 23:15.
89. Comm. Matt. 5:8.
90. Serm. No. 39 on Deut., 348; Comm. Lev. 19:35.
91. Comm. Ps. 15:5.
92. Comm. I Cor., theme.
93. Comm. Is. 23:8. See Serm. No. 30 on II Sam., 268, for Venetian greed.
94. Comm. Jer. 48:45.
95. Comm. Matt. 7:13.
96. Comm. John 7:48.
97. Comm. Gen. 14:1.
98. Serms. No. 5 and 6 on II Sam., 42 and 46, preached shortly after the massacre of Wassy.
99. Comm. Ps. 76:3.
100. Serm. No. 30 on II Sam., 267; Comm. Dan. 11:24.
101. Comm. Ezek. 6:11; Serm. No. 3 on II Sam., 21.
102. Comm. Is. 13:17.
103. Comm. Gen. 14:1; Serm. No. 3 on II Sam., 21.
104. Comm. Ps. 72:7.
105. Serm. No. 12 on Job, 161.
106. Comm. Jer. 22:14.
107. Comm. Is. 5:11.
108. Serm. No. 2 on Job, 40; cf. Greenblatt, *Renaissance Self-Fashioning*, p. 12, on Thomas More's sense of the moral ambiguity of dinner parties.
109. Comm. Dan. 1:8. The "worldly asceticism" Max Weber discerned in Calvinism may have been devised to resolve this dilemma.
110. Cf. Charles Trinkaus, "Humanist Treatises on the Status of the Religious," *Studies in the Renaissance*, XI (1964), 35.
111. Comm. II Cor. 6:11.
112. Comm. Lam. 1:2.
113. Comm. Jer. 9:5.
114. Lionel Trilling, *Sincerity and Authenticity* (Cambridge, Mass., 1972), sees this as a special problem of the sixteenth century.
115. Comm. Ps. 28:3.
116. Comm. Sen. 52–53. Calvin is here quoting Cicero, Ep. Att., 7.1.6.
117. Comm. Gen. 50:1. For Erasmus on hypocrites, cf. James Tracy, *Erasmus: The Growth of a Mind* (Geneva, 1972), p. 49.
118. Comms. Ps. 12:3, 28:3.
119. Comm. Ps. 123:3.
120. *Inst.*, IV, v, 13.
121. Comm. Jer. 27:16.
122. *Inst.*, IV, v, 19; Comm. Num. 12:1.
123. *Inst.*, IV, v, 18.

124. Comm. Act 19:23–24.
125. Comm. Is. 60:9.
126. Is. 49:23.
127. Comm. Jer. 44:17.
128. *Traité des scandales*, pp. 278–279.
129. Comm. I Cor. 7:7.
130. *Inst.*, IV, vii, 19.
131. *Inst.*, IV, vii, 25.
132. Cf. Serm. No. 12 on II Sam., 104.
133. *Inst.*, IV, xi, 12, although he also observed that Valla was "little conversant with ecclesiastical affairs." Calvin denounced other papal arguments from history in *Admonitio paterna Pauli III. Romani Pontificis ad Invictissimum Caesarem Carolum V*, CO VII, 272.
134. Comm. Matt. 24:1.
135. Comm. Dan., ep.
136. Comm. Jer. 29:24–27.
137. Comm. Jer. 27:16.
138. Comm. Jer. 18:18.
139. Comm. II Thess. 3:11.
140. Comm. Acts 15:5.
141. *Acta Synodi Tridentinae cum Antidoto*, CO VII, 422.
142. Comm. II Cor. 10:12.
143. Comm. Jer. 5:30–31.
144. *Supplex exhortatio*, CO VI, 473.
145. *Inst.*, III, v, 1.
146. Comm. Jer. 6:20; for Erasmus on hypocrisy, see his letter to Volz, Aug. 14, 1518, *Opus epistolarum*, III, 373.
147. Comm. Gen. 50.2.
148. Comm. Is. 49:18.
149. Comm. Is. 58:10.
150. Comm. Dan. 4:27.
151. Comm. Is. 58:4.
152. Comm. I Tim. 4:2.
153. Comm. Jer. 21:1–4.
154. Comm. Jer. 6:20.
155. *Inst.*, I, iv, 4.
156. *Inst.*, IV, xviii, 18.
157. Comm. Jer. 4:28.
158. Comm. Matt. 9:12.
159. Comm. Dan. 11:33–34.
160. Comm. I Cor. 11:30.
161. Comm. I Tim. 5:24.
162. Comm. Dan. 3:2–7.
163. Comm. Dan. 1:4.
164. *Inst.*, IV, xi, 14.
165. *Inst.*, IV, vii, 24.
166. *Inst.*, IV, vii, 27.
167. Comm. Ezek. 3:16–17.
168. *Inst.*, IV, ii, 7–9.
169. Comm. Is. 30:1; see also Serm. No. 13 on I Cor., 744.

170. Serm No. 12 on II Sam., 102; No. 6 on II Sam., 49–50.

171. *Inst.*, III, vii, 7.

172. Comm. Phil. 2:22; Serm. No. 2 on Job, 43–44; No. 3 on Job, 54.

173. *Inst.*, III, iv, 19.

174. Comm. Matt. 5:45.

175. Comm. Luke 18:8.

176. Comm. Ps. 127:1.

177. Serm. No. 18 on I Cor., 808.

178. *Traité des scandales*, p. 225; Comm. Jer. 38:15. For the vagueness of "atheism" in the sixteenth century, see Fébvre, *Probléme de l'incroyance*, pp. 138–144.

179. Comm. I Tim. 1:19.

180. Comm. Gal. 4:29.

181. Comm. Is. 9:10.

182. Letter to Somerset, Oct. 22, 1548, CO XIII, 80. In Serm. No. 27 on II Sam., 237, he compared the disorders of his own time to those in David's.

183. Comm. I Cor. 11:30.

184. Comm. Is. 9:10.

185. Serm. No. 81 on Job, 247.

Chapter 4

1. These lines reflect the influence of Johann Huizinga's classic *Waning of the Middle Ages*, originally published as *Herfstij der Middeleeuwen: Studie over Levens—en Gedachten-formen der Veertiende en Vijftiende Eeuw in Frankrijk en de Nederlanden* (Haarlem, 1919).

2. For what follows I am indebted to unpublished papers of F. Edward Cranz, especially "New Dimensions of Thought in Anselm and Abelard as against Augustine and Boethius."

3. *De anima*, III, 7 431 a1.

4. Cf. John W. Baldwin, *Masters, Princes and Merchants: the Social Views of Peter the Chanter and his Circle* (Princeton, 1970), I, p. 82. For sixteenth-century views of language there are useful remarks in Screech, *Rabelais*, pp. 387–388, 416; and Girardin, *Rhétorique et théologique*, p. 152.

5. Cf. M. D. Chenu, *Nature, Man, and Society in the Twelfth Century: Essays on New Theological Perspectives in the Latin West*, ed. Jerome Taylor and Lester K. Little (Chicago, 1968), p. 107.

6. On the cultural significance of seeing and hearing I owe much to Erich Auerbach's classic *Mimesis: the Representation of Reality in Western Literature*, trans. Willard R. Trask (Princeton, 1953), esp. chs. 1 and 2.

7. Especially in the opening lines of *Metaphysics*, I, i.

8. *Biblia Sacra cum glossa ordinaria, et Nicolai Lyrani expositionibus, literali et morali* (Lyon, 1545), V, 242, *re* John 20:29.

9. Quoted by Michael Baxandall, *Painting and Experience in Fifteenth Century Italy* (Oxford, 1972), p. 41.

10. *Timaeus* 47a.

11. *De senectute*, ch. 21.

12. See pp. 98–99 below.

13. Comm. Jer. 7:8.

14. Comm. Acts 24:10.

15. Comm. Ps. 36:2.

16. Comm. Is. 41:20; italics added.

17. Serm. No 5 on I Cor., 641–642; cf. Higman, *Style of Calvin*, pp. 134–135.

18. *Inst.*, I, xiv, 1.

19. Serm. No. 8 on I Cor., 677. The cosmological conservatism of Geneva was pointed out long ago by Quirinus Breen, *Calvin*, pp. 155–156; see the bibliography on this subject in Schreiner, "Theater of His Glory," xiv, n. 2.

20. Comm. Gen. 1:16.

21. Comm. Is. 48:13.

22. Comm. Ps. 148:3.

23. Comm. Jer. 51:15–16.

24. Comm. Ps. 148:3.

25. *Inst.*, I, v, 5.

26. Comm. Acts 17:18.

27. Comm. Ezek. 1:11.

28. Comm. Ps. 89:3. Sensing a problem here, he immediately explained that by "heavens" he meant "not only what is visible" but "what is above the whole structure of the world; for the truth of God is placed above the elements of the world in the glory of God's heavenly kingdom."

29. Serm. No. 96 on Job, 434–435.

30. Cf. above, p. 86, for his dread that the waters might indeed cover the earth.

31. Comm. Jer. 50:36; he also attacked its immoderate application; cf. Doumergue, *Calvin*, I, pp. 32–34.

32. Comm. Jer. 10:1–2; see pp. 167–168 below, for his attack on this pagan term.

33. Comm. James 5:7; cf. Comms. John 12:31 and 5:7. Cf. Schreiner, "Theater of His Glory," 142–49.

34. Comm. Ps. 145:10.

35. One support for this may have been the Greek of the New Testament, in which the "world" that God so loved that he gave his only son (John 3:16) is *kosmos*.

36. Comm. Is. 40:26; see also *Inst.*, I, xv, 3.

37. Comm. Ezek. 7:12.

38. Comm. Gen. 4:14; he also found this principle implicit in the creation of Eve (Comm. Gen. 2:18).

39. Comm. Is. 30:1.

40. Serm. No. 36 on Deut., 313. The same principle dictates the subjection of animals to human beings (Comm. Hosea 2:18).

41. Comm. Is. 24:2.

42. Comm. Is. 2:3.

43. Comm. Matt. 24:45.

44. Comm. I Thess. 4:11.

45. Comm. I Tim. 5:14.

46. *Inst.*, III, x, 6.

47. Comm. Ps. 147:19.

48. Comm. Gen. 26:10.

49. *Inst.*, II, ii, 22.

50. *Inst.*, I, v, 7.

51. Comm. Lev. 18:6. On Calvin and natural law, see John T. McNeill, "Natural Law in the Teaching of the Reformers," *Journal of Religion* XXVI (1946), 168–182.

52. Serm. No. 30 on II Sam., 263.

53. Comm. Jer. 6:4–5. On the just war, see also *Inst.*, IV, xx, 11.

54. Comm. Jer. 18:20.

55. Serm. No. 92 on Job, 386.

56. Serm. No. 39 on Deut., 349.

57. Comm. Ps. 119:52

58. *Inst.*, III, xiv, 2.

59. Comm. Matt. 6:21.

60. Serm. No. 13 on I Cor., 740. There is, then, some precedent in Calvin himself for the ambivalence about the innocence of children often present among his followers; cf. Philip Greven, *The Protestant Temperament: Patterns of Child-Rearing, Religious Experience, and the Self in Early America* (New York, 1977), pp. 28–31.

61. Comm. Dan. 6:8–9.

62. Comm. Gen. 2:18.

63. Comm. Is. 34:12.

64. Serm. No. 12 on I Cor., 724; Comm. I Cor. 11:7. Calvin did not doubt that woman was created in God's image, but he argued that God is "principalement glorifié, quand un homme, c'est à dire un mesle sera nay" (Serm. No. 11 on Job, 146–147). He pointed out, however, that only a female can give birth to a male; men are therefore not to glory in their superiority.

65. Serm. No. 12 on I Cor., 730.

66. Comm. I Tim. 2:13.

67. Comm. I Cor. 11:7.

68. Comm. I Cor. 14:34. This commentary was first published in 1546, well before the accession of Mary and Elizabeth in England or Catherine de'Medici in France, as well as some years before his encounter with John Knox, author of the notorious *First Blast of the Trumpet against the Monstrous Regiment of Women* (1558). Calvin reported in a letter to Bullinger, Apr. 28, 1554, what he had said to Knox on this matter.

69. Comm. Acts 18:26.

70. Cf. Serm. No. 12 on I Cor., 734.

71. Comm. I Cor. 11:7; Serm. No 12 on I Cor., 730.

72. Comm. I Tim. 5:14.

73. Serm. No. 16 on II Sam., 138.

74. Serm. No. 38 on Deut., 345.

75. Comm. Gen. 34:1.

76. Comm. Titus 2:4.

77. Comm. Gen. 29:27. Yet he did not altogether blame Jacob; cf. p. 137 below.

78. Comm. Gen. 29:27.

79. Comm. Lam. 3:27.

80. Comm. I Tim. 5:8; cf. his admiration, in Serm. No. 2 on Job, 44, for Job's durable authority over his adult sons.

81. Cf. *Inst.*, II, viii, 35.

82. Comm. Gen. 9:22; see also Comms. I Tim. 5:4, Ex. 20:12.

83. Comm. II Cor. 13:2.

84. Comm. I Cor. 4:22.

85. Comm. Gen. 34:1.

86. Comm. I Cor. 7:37.

87. Comm. Jer. 29:3–6.

88. Comm. I Cor. 7:37.

89. Comm. Acts 17:27; cf. *Inst.*, I, v, 3.

90. For his most systematic discussion of philosophical anthropology, see *Inst.*, I,

xv, 6; this is not one of his clearer passages. Karl Barth, in *Church Dogmatics,* III, pt. 2, p. 384, has noted in Calvin (as in the other great figures of the Reformation) what he considers a defective (because Hellenic rather than biblical) anthropology. The point ignores the question of what might have been possible in the eclectic culture of the sixteenth century.

91. *De anima,* I 402 a1. Calvin recognized the difficulties of the subject, but he nevertheless described its treatment by "the philosophers" as "true, not only enjoyable but also profitable to learn, and skillfully assembled" (*Inst.,* I, xv, 6).

92. Comm. Heb. 4:12.

93. Comm. Ps. 103:14.

94. He carefully reviewed the various meanings of "soul" in Scripture in his treatise against the Anabaptists but made little effort to harmonize them (*Contre les Anabaptistes,* CO VII, 114).

95. *Inst.,* I, xv, 6; Serm. No. 12 on Job, 162.

96. For example, Serm. No. 39 on Job, 483; Comms. Ps. 3:1–2, I Thess. 5:23.

97. As in Comm. Ps. 69:1.

98. Comms. Ps. 119:80, Phil. 4:7; Serm. No. 43 on Job, 542.

99. As in Comms. Luke 1:46, Heb. 4:12, I Cor. 2:11.

100. Cf. Comms. John 13:21, Heb. 4:12, and Ps. 139:7, and, for a particularly convoluted passage, I Thess. 5:23.

101. Comm. Ezek., 3:24.

102. *Inst.,* II, xiv, 1.

103. Serm. No. 39 on Job, 480; Serm. No. 17 on Job, 210; Comm. Luke 16:22.

104. Comm. I Thess. 5:23; cf. Comm. Matt. 16:26, 6:11.

105. *Inst.,* I, xv, 3. Charles Trinkaus, *"In Our Image and Likeness": Humanity and Divinity in Italian Humanist Thought* (Chicago, 1970), has much that is useful for understanding Calvin's interest in this matter.

106. Serm. No. 41 on II Sam., 359.

107. Comm. Acts 17:22.

108. *Inst.,* I, xv, 7

109. Inst., II ii, 12.

110. Serm. No. 94 on Job, 411.

111. *Inst.,* I, v, 5.

112. Serm. No. 30 on II Sam., 264.

113. Serm. No. 39 on Job, 489–490.

114. Comm. Jer. 51:19.

115. Cf. Serms. No. 10 on I Cor., 708–709, and No. 36 on Job, 488.

116. Serm. No. 38 on Job, 478.

117. Comm. Luke 24:41.

118. Serm. No. 11 on Job, 149; Comm. John 11:33.

119. Serm. No. 28 on Job, 354; Comm. Matt. 6:10.

120. Serm. No. 39 on Job, 483–483.

121. *Inst.,* III, x, 3.

122. Serms. No. 38 on Deut., 337; No. 13 on Job, 170.

123. Serm. No. 39 on Job, 482–482.

124. Comm. Gen. 9:23.

125. Comm. John 5:28.

126. Comm. Gen. 1:26; cf. *Inst.,* I, xv, 3.

127. Comm. Ps. 8:8–10.

128. Comm. Ps. 89:3.

129. Comm. Num. 11:28; Serm. No. 48 on Job, 594–595.

130. Comm. John 17:12.

131. Comm. Num. 16:1.

132. The text is in John Dillenberger, ed., *John Calvin: Selections from His Writings* (New York, 1971), p. 43.

133. Cf. Greene, *Light in Troy*, pp. 29–32.

134. *Inst.*, ep. On Hildebrand, cf. Gerhart B. Ladner, "Reformatio," in Samuel H. Miller and G. Ernest Wright, eds., *Ecumenical Dialogue at Harvard: The Roman Catholic-Protestant Colloquium* (Cambridge, Mass., 1964), p. 177. Calvin vigorously denounced what he considered Hildebrand's novelties in *Admonitio Pauli III cum Scholiis*, CO VII, 253–288.

135. Comm. Ep. John 2:8.

136. Comm. Is. 2:4; cf. Serm. No. 68 on Job, 80. Cop's discourse had sounded the same Erasmian note: "What is better than peace, than tranquility!"

137. Comm. Acts 23:10.

138. Serm. No. 30 on II Sam., 260.

139. Comm. Dan. 2:31–35; cf. Comm. Heb. 6:2 for a more theoretical statement.

140. Comm. Dan. 4:34.

141. Comm. Dan. 7:23–24.

142. Comm. Is. 37:26.

143. Comm. Is. 37:26; for the civic humanism implicit in this passage, see Hans Baron, *The Crisis of the Early Italian Renaissance: Civic Humanism and Republican Liberty in an Age of Classicism and Tyranny* (Princeton, 1955).

144. Comm. Deut. 34:7.

145. Comm. Is. 37:36; this again suggests Machiavelli.

146. Comm. Gen. 29:4.

147. Comm. Heb. 13:2; see also Comm. Gen. 18:2, and cf. Erasmus's colloquy *Diversoria*.

148. Comm. Gen. 26:8; cf. Serm. No. 91 on Job, 373, where Calvin insisted on a continuous moral decline since the time of Job.

149. Comm. Dan. 2:46, 5:10–11.

150. Calvin generally sided with those Fathers who identified reform with return rather than those who associated it with progress; see Gerhart B. Ladner, *The Idea of Reform: Its Impact on Christian Thought and Action in the Age of the Fathers* (Cambridge, Mass., 1959), pp. 133–136, 142–147, 156–160.

151. Comm. Acts 17:26.

152. Comm. Gen. 10:8. Cf. *Traité des scandales*, pp. 186–205, for a general review of these cycles in the history of the church.

153. Comms. Rom. 11:2, Matt. 24:34.

154. *Supplex exhortatio*, CO VI, 497.

155. Comm. Acts 4:34.

156. Comm. Acts 14:23; *Inst.*, IV, iii, 9, ix, 1, xiii, 10, xviii, 9.

157. *Traité des scandales*, pp. 281–282; Comm. John 1:1.

158. Parker, *Calvin's New Testament Commentaries*.

159. *Inst.*, IV, xiv, 26; III, iii, 8. On the general point, cf. Luchesius Smits, *Saint Augustin dans l' oeuvre de Jean Calvin* (Louvain, 1957).

160. *Inst.*, I, xiii, 11.

161. Comm. Acts 15:2.

162. *Inst.*, IV, iv, 3.

163. *Inst.*, IV, vii, 12, 17.

164. *Inst.*, IV, xi, 14.
165. Comm. II Tim. 2:2.
166. Comm. Rom. 11:22.
167. *Inst.*, III, iv, 39.
168. *Inst.*, IV, vii, 18.
169. *Supplex exhortatio*, CO VI, 498; cf. *Inst.*, III, iv, 7.
170. Comm. Is. 14:29.
171. Comm. Gen. 4:26.
172. *Responsio ad Sadoleti epistolam*, CO V, 394.
173. Comm. Ps. 172:1.

Chapter 5

1. Comm. Dan. 5:25–28.
2. Letter to Jodocus Jonas, May 10, 1521, *Opus Epistolarum*, IV, 486–493.
3. ". . . que de ceulx les prieres n'ont jamais este esconduites qui ont mediocrite requis" (*Gargantua et Pantagruel*, IV, prologue); cf. Screech, *Rabelais*, pp. 118–119, 254, 329.
4. *Inst.*, I, xii, 1.
5. Comm. II Cor. 10:5.
6. Comm. I Cor. 13:4–5.
7. Serm. No. 31 on Deut., 257.
8. Comm. Matt. 14:28; see also Comm. Jer. 1:6–7.
9. Comm. Ex. 11:8.
10. Comm. Acts 13:10.
11. Comm. Is., ep.
12. *Inst.*, III, iii, 14.
13. Comm. John 11:33.
14. Comm. Deut. 8:17.
15. Comm. Ps. 69:4.
16. Comm. Jude 10.
17. Comm. Titus 2:6.
18. Comm. Dan. 2:22.
19. Comm. Ps. 14:2.
20. Comm. Ps. 36:4. Cf. Serm. no. 26 on Job, 319, on virtue as subjection to reason.
21. Com. Eph. 5:28.
22. Comm. Ezek. 11:19–20.
23. Comm. Dan. 9:14; Serm. No. 3 on I Cor., 611.
24. Serm. No. 7 on Job, 94; Serm. No. 18 on II Sam., 156.
25. Serm. No. 6 on II Sam., 46.
26. Comm. Is. 6:11.
27. Comm. Acts 15:10.
28. Comm. Ezek. 11:19–20.
29. Comm. Jer. 20:14–16.
30. Serm. No. 51 on Job, 642.
31. Comm. Is. 37:17, a text that hardly seems to support his gloss; cf. Comm. Ps. 37:7 for another strange reading.
32. Serm. No. 47 on Job, 590.
33. Serm. No. 39 on Deut., 351.

34. Letter of Oct. 24, 1538, CO X, 273.
35. Comm. Ps. 112:5.
36. Comm. Heb. 9:5.
37. Comm. Lam. 3:19.
38. Comm. Matt. 5:25.
39. Comm. Gen. 11:4.
40. Comm. Num. 11:4.
41. *Inst.*, III, iii, 17.
42. Comm. Matt. 4:1.
43. Comm. Dan. 10:3.
44. Serm. No. 9 on II Sam., 75.
45. Comm. Jer. 51:60–64.
46. Comm. Ps. 69:4.
47. Serm. No. 17 on II Sam., 146.
48. *Inst.*, IV, xii, 1.
49. Comm. Ps. 104:15.
50. Comm. Acts 26:25.
51. Comm. Ps. 22:31; cf. Comm. II Tim. 3:15.
52. Comm. Is. 2:3.
53. Comm. Sen., 260–261.
54. Comm. Col. 3:20.
55. Comm. Heb. 6:9.
56. Comm. I Cor. 3:2.
57. Comm. I Cor. 3:12.
58. Comm. Jer. 39:3–4.
59. Quintilian, *Institutio oratoria*, II, viii, 66.
60. Serm. No. 31 on Job, 385.
61. *Harmonia ex tribus Evangelistis composita*, ep.
62. Comm. Is. 58:5; on imitation in humanism, cf. Greene, *Light in Troy*, pp. 81–103.
63. Comm. Gen. 42:17.
64. Comm. I Cor. 7:36.
65. Comm. Ps. 12:1–2.
66. Comm. Dan., ep.
67. Serm. No. 31 on Job, 385.
68. Comm. Rom. 4:23.
69. Comm. Gen. 18:18.
70. Comm. Gen. 18:27.
71. Serm. No. 1 on I Cor., 581–582; cf. Serm. No. 6 on Job, 83, on Abraham.
72. Comm. Ps. 36:2; cf. *Inst.*, III, iii, 7.
73. Comm. Ps. 14:4.
74. Comm. Rom. 4:23.
75. Comm. Ex. 3:1; Serm. No. 30 on Deut., 237.
76. Cf. Serms. No. 1 on Job, 21–22; No. 2, 33.
77. Cf. Comm. Ps. 26:1, 32:3; on David as model penitent in the sixteenth century, cf. Greenblatt, *Renaissance Self-Fashioning*, p. 118. Calvin could also point to David as an example to avoid; cf. Serm. No. 16 on II Sam., 137–138.
78. Comm. Jer. 37:20.
79. Ep. Dan. lxvi.
80. *Inst.*, II, i, 6.

81. Comm. Jer., after lect. 86. For the text, lacking in CO, see the Amsterdam edition of 1667.

82. Comm. Matt. 16:24.

83. Comm. I John, 3:16.

84. Comm. Matt. 21:12; also Comm. John 2:17. Calvin saw danger in the possibility that the laity might imitate Christ's cleansing of the temple, that is, by taking initiatives to reform the church. This responsibility belonged, for Calvin, only to those duly "called" to the task; its assumption by others would have increased rather than decreased the disorder in the world.

85. Comm. Matt. 16:24.

86. Comm. John 13:21.

87. Comm. I Cor. 11:1.

88. Comm. Gen. 19:24.

89. Comm. Gen. 6:22.

90. Comm. Gen 44:2. Honesty compelled Calvin to admit, however, the possibility that the workmanship on this silver cup might have made it more valuable than a golden one.

91. Serm. No. 2 on II Sam., 10.

92. Serm. No. 7 on II Sam., 54–56; Comm. Gen. 16:11.

93. Serms. No. 7 on Job, 54–56, and No. 14 on II Sam,. 119.

94. Comm. Ex. 1:18.

95. Comm. Josh. 2:4.

96. Comm. Ex. 2:1.

97. Serm. No. 2 on II Sam., 145; cf. Comm. Ps. 88:5, 10.

98. Serm. No. 30 on Job, 369.

99. Serm. No. 18 on Job, 221.

100. Serm. No. 14 on Job, 178.

101. Serm. No. 26 on Job, 324–325.

102. Serm. No. 11 on Job, 145.

103. Serm. No. 11 on Job, 150–151.

104. Serm. No. 16 on Job, 198.

105. Letter to Viret, Nov. 14, 1546, CO XII.

106. Comm. Gen. 39:1.

107. Serm. No. 8 on II Sam., 68.

108. Comm. II Cor. 11:3.

109. Comm. I Tim., ep.

110. Comm. Deut. 28:21; Comm. Is. 35:1.

111. *Inst.*, II, viii, 38.

112. Comm. Is. 22:17.

113. Comm. Is. 2:16.

114. Comm. Dan. 11:45.

Chapter 6

1. Comm. II Tim. 3:14.

2. Letter to Lelio Socino, 1551, CO XIV, 230.

3. Comm. Gen. 4:20; Comm. Is. 19:3. Calvin objected to the occult sciences on the ground that they had a different origin.

4. Letter to Bucer, Feb. 1549, CO XX, 530–531.

5. Serm. No. 103 on Job, 522–523; cf. *Inst.*, II, ii, 16.

6. Comm. I Cor. 15:33, citing Paul's example; Comm. Titus 1:12, citing Basil.

7. Cf. Wendel, *Calvin et l'humanisme*, p. 75.

8. Comm. Ps. 104:29.

9. Comm. Gen. 37:25.

10. Comm. Matt. 7:16.

11. Comm. John 2:12.

12. Serm. No. 41 on Deut., 378.

13. Letter to a Seigneur of Piedmont, Feb. 25, 1554, CO XV, 42.

14. Comm. Jer. 26:3.

15. Comm. II Tim. 1:13.

16. Serm. No. 78 on Job, 208.

17. *Inst.*, III, ii, 5.

18. Comm. Jer. 27:10; Comm. Gal. 1:8. On the general point, cf. R. T. Kendall, *Calvin and English Calvinism to 1649* (Oxford, 1980), p. 19, and T. H. L. Parker, *Calvin's Doctrine of the Knowledge of God* (rev. ed., Edinhburgh, 1969), p. 132.

19. Comm. Jer. 31:34.

20. *Inst.*, III, ii, 12.

21. *Traité des scandales*, pp. 170–171. Radically ambivalent, Calvin, to be sure, immediately contradicted himself: "Ce n'est point une fable pour rire, ni un monstre qu'on doive avoir en horreur, mais un mystère pour adorer."

22. *Inst.*, I, vi, 1.

23. Comm. Is. 45:19.

24. Comm. Gen. 2:8.

25. Comm. Gal. 4:22.

26. Comm. Is. 30:8.

27. Serm. No. 42 on Deut., 384.

28. Comm. Jer. 29:9.

29. Comm. Ps. 27:1.

30. Serm. No. 44 on Deut., 412; cf. Serm. No. 45, 420: "Car il n'y a plus de doute, quand nostre Seigneur a parlé."

31. Comm. Jer. 23:17–18, 26:3.

32. This tendency was noted as early as 1538 by his old friend Louis du Tillet in a letter of Dec. 1, 1538.

33. Comm. I Cor. 15:33.

34. Serm. No. 6 on II Sam., 50.

35. *Inst.*, I, vii, 5; cf. Comm. Matt. 11:25.

36. Comm. Dan. 8:20–25.

37. Quoted by Marjorie O'Rourke Boyle, *Rhetoric and Reform: Erasmus' Civil Dispute with Luther* (Cambridge, Mass., 1983), p. 53. Cf. Greenblatt, *Renaissance Self-Fashioning*, pp. 61, 69, 11, on the need for certainty in More and Tyndale.

38. Cf. Screech, *Rabelais*, pp. 134–135.

39. *Inst.*, III, ii, 15; the Platonic language here is also worth noting.

40. Girardin, *Rhétorique et Théologique*, esp. pp. 253–265; much of what Girardin here calls "rhetoric" seems to me, more precisely, dialectic. For Calvin's knowledge of Scholasticism, see Armand La Vallee, "Calvin's Criticism of Scholastic Theology," Ph.D. diss., Harvard University, 1967. Higman, *Style of Calvin*, has much of importance about Calvin's argumentation but ignores its debt to Scholasticism; cf. pp. 17–20, 44, 88, 94.

41. *Inst.*, I, xvi, 9.

42. *Inst.*, II, iv, 1.

43. Comm. Jer. 31:31–32; cf. Comm. II Tim. 1:13 for another example.

44. Cf. Salvatore I. Camporeale, *Lorenzo Valla: umanesimo e teologia* (Florence, 1972), pp. 149–171.

45. Cf. Higman, *Style of Calvin*, pp. 71–72, on Calvin's use of antithesis.

46. Cf. Comm. I John 2:3 for a complicated example.

47. Comm. Phil. 1:6. Cf. Higman, *Style of Calvin*, p. 104, on Calvin's "rhetorical logic."

48. *Inst.*, I, xv, 6.

49. *Inst.*, IV, xvii, 24.

50. Comm. Dan. 9:14.

51. Comm. Ps. 19:3. I am touching here on a much-disputed question, especially between Emil Brunner, for whom Calvin left a large place for the knowledge of God from nature, and Karl Barth, for whom he left little or none. Schreiner, "Theater of His Glory," ix–xv, provides a useful review of this controversy. For me it is futile because of Calvin's ambivalence; he can be cited on both sides of the issue. For one of Calvin's more balanced statements, see Serm. No. 43 on Job, 531–532.

52. Cf. *Inst.*, I, xi, 1.

53. Comm. Ezek. 8:7–11.

54. Comm. Ps. 107:6.

55. Comm. Ps. 50:14–15; cf. Comms. Jer. 11:1–5 and Ps. 28:2.

56. Comm. John 19:8.

57. Comm. Dan. 5:13–16; cf. Comm. Ezek. 8:7–11.

58. Comm. Is. 57:1; cf. Serm. No. 34 on Job, 419.

59. *Inst.*, I, v, 1.

60. Comm. Rom. 1:19.

61. *Inst.*, I, xiv, 20.

62. Serm. No. 96 on Job, 434.

63. *Praefationes bibliis Gallicis Pietri Roberti Olivetani*, CO IX, 793, 795.

64. *Inst.*, I, v, 3.

65. Comm. Jer. 10:10.

66. *Inst.*, I, v, 4.

67. Comm. Acts 17:28.

68. Comm. Ps. 19:1.

69. Comm. Ps. 68:32.

70. Comm. Jer. 10:1–2. These passages are far more enthusiastic than his more balanced treatment of the subject in *Inst.*, II, ii, 18–22, but they seem to me to reflect one side of his contradictory views.

71. Comm. Dan 3, 28.

72. Comms. Gen. 23:3; Jer. 34:4–5; Serm. No. 100 on Job, 493.

73. Serm. No. 2 on Job, 158.

74. Serm. No. 46 on Job, 572.

75. Comm. Rom. 1:20.

76. Comm. Ps. 135:5.

77. Comm. Ps. 83:19; cf. *Inst.*, I, iii, 1, where he quotes Cicero on the point. See also Comm. Jer. 50, 7.

78. Comm. Is. 14:14.

79. Serm. No. 34 on Job, 426.

80. Serm. on John 1:1–5, 470–471, 473, 475.

81. Cf. Serm. No. 134 on Job, 203: "De toute éternité, devant que le monde fût

créé, toutes choses lui ont été présentes, il n'a point augmenté en sagesse, il n'est point aussi diminué de rien, mais il a tout connu."

82. Comm. Ps. 69:28.

83. Serm. on John 1:1–5, 470–471; cf. Comms. Ps. 106:45, and Jer. 49:20.

84. Comm. Ps. 90:2.

85. Comm. Lam. 5:19.

86. Comm. Ps. 90:2.

87. Comm. Rom. 1:18; Serm No. 31 on Job, 482, treats God's "repentance" in the same way.

88. Comm. Gen. 6:6. Cf. Erasmus in the preface to *De libero arbitrio*: although in Scripture, "God is angry, grieves, is indignant, rages, threatens, hates, and again has mercy, repents, changes his mind, not that such changes take place in the nature of God, but that to speak thus is suited to our infirmity and slowness" (quoted from the translation of E. Gordon Rupp, *Luther and Erasmus: Free Will and Salvation* [London, 1969], p. 41).

89. Serm. No. 32 on Deut., 267.

90. Serm. No. 30 on Job, 371.

91. Comm. Is. 23:9; see also Comm. Jer. 50:44, and Serms. on Job 7, 102, and 9, 540.

92. Comm. Ps. 37:1.

93. Comm. Ps. 145:17.

94. Comm. Deut. 32:51.

95. Comm. Josh. 6:21.

96. Serm. No. 13 on II Sam., 106; see also his justification for the killing of David's Moabite captives, Serm. No. 27 on II Sam., 236–237.

97. Comm. Num. 31:14.

98. Serm. No. 81 on Job, 249–250.

99. Comm. Josh. 7:24.

100. Comm. Josh. 10:18, 10:40; cf. Comm. Ex. 11:2 and Serm. No. 17 on II Sam., 142–146, for other examples of this position.

101. Comm. Luke 1:52; cf. Comm. Ps. 94:15 on the harmony and order of God's plan.

102. Comm. Gen. 45:8, 42:1.

103. Comm. Is. 57:1. Calvin was probably thinking of the Schmalkaldic War.

104. *Inst.*, I, xviii, 3; italics added.

105. Gordon Leff, *Gregory of Rimini: Tradition and Innovation in Fourteenth Century Thought* (New York, 1961), pp. 21–22; cf. F. Edward Cranz, "Philosophy," *Renaissance News*, XIX (1967), p. 88.

106. Cf. Blumenberg, *Modern Age*, pp. 170–171: "The *gloria dei* as the embodiment of the final purpose of the world and of man served not only to formulate the mythical figure [of God] more abstractly but also to adapt it to the Aristotelian idea of the exclusive self-reference of the unmoved mover as the thought having itself as its sole object." See also, on the general point, pp. 174–175, 486, 567–568 of this work.

107. *Instruction et confession de foy dont on use en l'église de Genéve*, CO XXII, 33.

108. Comm. Ps. 97:7.

109. Serms. No. 101 and 19 on Job, 502 and 241–242.

110. Comm. Dan. 4:35.

111. Comm. Ezek. 10:11–12.

112. Comm. Ps. 115:3.

113. Comm. Jer. 31:31–32; cf. *Inst.*, III, xxiv, 17.

114. Comm. Jer. 46:14; cf. Comm. Seneca, 38–39, 336–337; Comm. Dan. 9:18–19; Comm. Acts 7:1; Comm. I cor. 2:13; Serm. No. 35 on Job, 431.

115. On this attitude, see Erich Auerbach, *Literary Language and Its Public in Late Latin Antiquity and in the Middle Ages* (Princeton, 1965), pp. 25–67.

116. *Inst.*, I, viii, 1.

117. Comm. I Cor. 1:17.

118. *Inst.*, I, viii, 11.

119. Comm II Cor. 11:6.

120. Comm. I Cor. 1:17.

121. Comm. I Cor. 2:4.

Chapter 7

1. Quoted by Eugenio Garin, *L'umanesimo italiano: filosofia e vita civile nel Rinascimento* (Bari, 1964), p. 38.

2. Quoted by Jerrold E. Seigel, *Rhetoric and Philosophy in Renaissance Humanism: Ciceronian Elements in Early Quatrocento Thought and Their Historical Setting* (Princeton, 1968), 76–77.

3. *Inst.*, I, viii, 1. For his knowledge of ancient rhetoric, see Battles's introduction to Comm. Sen., 76–84.

4. Comm. I Cor. 12:12.

5. Comm. Matt. 27:45.

6. Comm. Gen. 22:11.

7. Comm. Sen., 91.

8. *Inst. oratoria*, I, vi, 45.

9. Serm. No. 13 on I Cor., 744.

10. *Inst.*, IV, xix, 1.

11. Comm. Gen 14:1; cf. Smits, *Augustin dans l'oeuvre de Calvin*, p. 249.

12. Comms Jer. 5:15, 9:5.

13. Serm. No. 56 on Job, 705.

14. Comm. Jer. 5:15.

15. Comm. Ezek. 1:24. Cf. Pontano: "Speech is the administrator of all those things which, conceived in the mind and activated by thinking, are dragged forth into the public world" (quoted by Charles Trinkaus, *The Scope of Renaissance Humanism* [Ann Arbor, 1983], p. 366).

16. Comm. Jer. 18:11.

17. Comm. Ps. 45:2.

18. Comm. I Cor. 2:11; Comm. Matt. 12:34; Serm. No. 33 on Deut., 275; Serm. No. 40 on Deut., 369; Comm. John 1:1.

19. Comm. Ps. 81:5. In Comm. Ezek. 2:3 he observed that "those in exile inevitably contract many faults of language."

20. Comm. I Cor. 3:2.

21. Comm. Matt. 3:7.

22. see below, 142–143.

23. Serm. No. 78 on Job, 206. Consolation was a traditional concern of rhetoricians.

24. Comm. Lam. 1:2.

25. Serm. No. 62 on Job, 5.

26. *De vera participatione carnis et sanguinis christi in sacra coena*, CO IX, 514.

27. Comms. Ex. 4:11, I Cor. 1:17.

28. Comm. Ex. 31:18.

29. Cf. Ronald Levao, *Renaissance Minds and their Fictions: Cusanus, Sidney, Shakespeare* (Berkeley, 1985).

30. On this aspect of humanism see Salvatore Camporeale, "Lorenzo Valla tra Medioevo e Rinascimento: Encomion s. Thomae—1457," *Memorie Domenicane*, n.s., 7 (1976), 1–141; and "Umanesimo e teologia tra '400 e '500," *Memorie Domenicane*, n.s., 8–9 (1977–1978), 412–436.

31. Cf. Theodor E. Mommsen, "Petrarch's Conception of the 'Dark Ages,'" *Speculum*, XVII (1942), 226–242.

32. Cf. Greene, *Light in Troy*, pp. 81–104.

33. Comm. I Cor. 14:5.

34. Cf. *Inst.*, IV, xix, 36.

35. Smits, *Augustin dans l'oeuvre de Calvin*, pp. 191–202; Parker, *Calvin's New Testament Commentaries*, pp. 147–150; Battles, Comm. Sen., 63–71, 118–124; François Wendel, *Calvin: The Origins and Development of his Religious Thought*, trans. Philip Mairet (London, 1963), p. 31.

36. Cf. Girardin, *Rhétorique et théologique*, pp. 176–180.

37. Cf. Comm. John 11:1, on the identification of the village of Lazarus and his sisters as a "*castellum.*"

38. Comm. Dan. 7:7, concerning a mistake in listing the provinces of the Empire.

39. Comm. Dan. 5:1.

40. *Inst.*, IV, xvi, 12.

41. Comm. Rom., ep. On the general point, see Smits, *Augustin dans l'oeuvre de Calvin*, p. 249.

42. *Inst.*, IV, xix, 12.

43. Comm. Is. 14:12.

44. Cf. with Eusebius's commendation of Theophilus in Erasmus's *Convivium religiosum*: "You explain the matter very well by comparing passages, an excellent method of biblical study" (*The Colloquies of Erasmus*, trans. Craig R. Thompson [Chicago, 1965], p. 61). For Calvin's indebtedness to the humanism of Erasmus, see more generally Boyle, *Rhetoric and Reform*, pp. 43–46, on Erasmus's *Ratio verae theologiae*, which he followed closely.

45. An exception, as Jeanne Rutenburg has pointed out to me, was his Jewish sources, whose authors, with the exception of Josephus, he tended to lump together as "the Jews."

46. Smits, *Augustin dans l'oeuvre de Calvin*, pp. 237–239, 250–251, 186–190.

47. Comm. Gen. 11:1. He would have known of Berosus through Josephus; an account of the period after the flood attributed to Berosus (but in fact invented by the fifteenth-century humanist Annius of Viterbo) had also been included in a collection of "lost works," probably known to Calvin, entitled *Antiquitatum variarum volumina XVII cum commentariis* (Rome, 1498, and frequently reprinted).

48. Cf. n. 40 above.

49. *Antidotum*, CO VII, 416, 111. Calvin often noted errors in the Vulgate, as in *Inst.*, III, ii, 38; III, iv, 9; III, xv, 4; but as Parker observes, *Calvin's New Testament Commentaries*, pp. 143–145, he used the vulgate himself, preferring it to the New Testament of Erasmus. In Comm. Acts 26:28 he cited a reading of Valla. He was reticent about his own indebtedness to Erasmus, but he made extensive use of Erasmus's *Annotationes*; cf. Parker, pp. 129–142.

50. Serm. on John 1:1–5, 465.

51. *Antidotum*, CO VII, 414.

52. Cf. Hans-Joachim Kraus, "Calvin's Exegetical Principles," *Interpretation*, XXI (1977), 8.

53. *Commentarius in harmoniam evangelicam*, ep.; but cf. Comm. Rom., ep., where he criticized Bucer's verbosity.

54. Letter to Viret, May 19, 1540, CO XI, 6.

55. Comm. Rom., ep.

56. Comm. Rom., ep.

57. Cf. Parker, *Calvin's New Testament Commentaries*, p. 88.

58. Comm. Romans, ep. For his reservations about the Fathers, see p. 148 below.

59. Cf. Ford Lewis Battles, "The Future of Calviniana," in Peter de Klerk, ed., *Renaissance—Reformation —Resurgence*, (Grand Rapids, Mich., 1976), p. 143. Calvin wrote a preface for a proposed French edition of Chrysostom, in CO IX, 831–838. For earlier humanist interest in Chrysostom, cf. Charles L. Stinger, *The Renaissance in Rome* (Bloomington, Ind., 1985), pp. 169–170, 223–234.

60. Comm. I Cor. 3:15. Jerome is significantly absent from Calvin's list; for his scorn for Jerome, see Comm. Ezek., 4:4–8. Calvin may have been repelled by Jerome because of his association with the Vulgate, but he may also have deplored the Renaissance cult of Jerome as ascetic desert saint; cf. Eugene F. Rice, Jr., *Saint Jerome in the Renaissance* (Baltimore, 1985). For Calvin's use of Bernard, see Jill Raitt, "Calvin's Use of Bernard of Clairvaux," *Archiv für Reformationsgeschichte*, 72 (1981), 98–121.

61. Comm. Ps. 89:9.

62. Comm. Matt. 13:55.

63. Comms. II Cor. 12:8, Dan. 7:7, Gen. 31:5.

64. Comm. Gen., argumentum. In Comm. Jer. 36:1–2 he reflected on the advantages of written over oral testimony.

65. Comms. Jer. 35:1–7, 5:3; Is. 22:9.

66. Comm. I Tim. 5:23.

67. Comm. John 8:3.

68. Comms. Jer. 5:3, Is. 53:1.

69. Comm. II Cor 4:6.

70. Comm. Ps. 89:9; cf. Comm. Jude 14.

71. Comm. Rom., ep.

72. Comm. Matt. 4:5.

73. Comm. Gen. 10:1.

74. *Inst.*, IV, ix, 14. This may also reflect his reserve about the Book of Revelation; cf. Parker, *Calvin's New Testament Commentaries*, pp. 76–77. Again he may have been following Erasmus, who omitted only this from his New Testament parapharases.

75. Comm. Matt. 2:1.

76. Comm. Matt. 27:45.

77. Comm. Is. 58:5.

78. Comm. Is. 15:2–3.

79. Comm. Is. 58:5.

80. Comm. I Cor. 11:12.

81. Serm. No. 32 on II Sam., 280–281; cf. Serm. No. 10 on II Sam., 86.

82. Serm. No. 18 on II Sam., 155.

83. Comm. John, argumentum.

84. Comm. Matt. 4:5.

85. Comm. Matt. 2:1.

86. Comm. Matt. 6:24. Calvin applied the same principle to the Pentateuch.

87. Comm. Luke 8:19; cf. Comm. Dan. 7:12, for similar problems in the Hebrew Scriptures.

88. *Traité des scandales*, pp. 165–166; this observation is embedded, however, in a passage otherwise ambivalent on the point.

89. Cf. Comm. Is. 5:1; the "noble and sonorous" song of Isaiah beginning "let me sing for my beloved" moved him to remark generally that "the greatest art goes into the composition of poetry."

90. Comm. Phil. 3:1; this may suggest that he generally associated jesting with coarseness.

91. Comm. Is. 51:19.

92. Serm. No. 41 on II Sam., 359.

93. As in Serm. on John 1, 1–5, 478.

94. Comm. Gal. 4:22.

95. *Inst.*, II, v, 19.

96. Comm. II Cor. 3:6–7.

97. Comm. Gal. 4:22; cf. Comm. II Cor. 3:6.

98. Comm. Matt. 13:10.

99. Comm. Matt. 3:16; cf. *Inst.*, IV, xvii, 20–21.

100. Comms. Matt. 25:41, II Thess. 1:7. Again he was following Erasmus; cf. Febvre, *Problème de l'incroyance*, p. 255.

101. Comm. Jer. 49:3; see also Comms. Jer. 46:3–5 and Is. 34:4.

102. Comm. Acts 26:23.

103. Comm. Jer. 31:15–16; cf. Comm. Matt. 2:18.

104. Comm. Jer. 50:19.

105. Serm. on John 1:1–5, 467–468.

106. Comm. Gal. 4:19.

107. Comm. Luke 2:48.

108. Comm. Josh. 2:7.

109. Comm. Ex. 6:10.

110. Serm. No. 34 on Job, 423; on the general point, cf. Battles, "God was Accomodating Himself," 19–38.

111. *Inst.*, IV, vii, 5; Serm. on John 1:1–5.

112. Serm. No. 4 on Job, 63.

113. Here he followed an ancient tradition eventually resurrected by Vico; cf. the introduction by Thomas Goddard Bergin and Max Harold Fisch to *The New Science of Giambattista Vico* (Ithaca, 1968), pp. xxxix–xli.

114. Comm. Gen. 2:10, 6:14; see also Comms. Gen. 1:14 and 3:1, Ex. 7:8.

115. Comm. Ps. 19:4; cf. Comm. Ps. 135:7, 114:5.

116. Comm. Ps. 149:2; *Inst.*, IV, iii, 4.

117. Comm. Matt. 18:16.

118. *Inst.*, III, xviii, 9.

119. Comm. Matt. 12:5.

120. Comm. Matt 7:16.

121. Serm. No. 85 on Job, 294–295.

122. Serm. No. 43 on Deut., 396.

123. Serm. No. 42 on Deut., 387; cf. Serm. No. 16 on II Sam., 134–135, and *Inst.*, I, 13, 1.

124. Serm. No. 16 on II Sam., 135–136.

125. *Inst.*, II, vi, 4.

126. Comm. John 1:1. On Valla, cf. Donald R. Kelley, *Foundations of Modern Historical Scholarship: Language, Law, and History in the French Renaissance* (New York, 1970), p. 28, citing *Dialecticae disputationes*, I, 9; for Erasmus, cf. Boyle, *Language and Method*, pp. 3–31.

127. Comm. I John 2:22. but cf. Serm. No. 45 on Deut., 429, and *Inst.*, IV, viii, 7, which represent Christ as only perfecting a knowledge more obscurely available elsewhere.

128. *Inst.*, IV, xiv, 3; cf. Serm. No. 1 on I Cor., 585–586.

129. Comm. I Pet. 1:3; cf *Inst.*, II, ii, 1.

130. "John Calvin and the Rhetorical Tradition," *Church History*, XXVI (1957), 3–21.

131. *Inst.*, III, vi, 1. On *perspicua brevitas* as rhetoric, cf. Quintilian, IV, i, 34: "We shall also find it a useful device for wakening the attention of our audience to create the impression that we shall not keep them long and intend to stick closely to the point."

132. Comm. Ps., pref.

133. Serm. No. 56 on Job, 697.

134. Comm. Gen. 19:24; for Erasmus, see Boyle, *Language and Method*, p. 11.

135. Parker, *Calvin's New Testament Commentaries*, p. 33.

136. Comm. Rom. 12:6.

137. Comm. I Tim. 3:2. On the general point see Rodolphe Peter, "Rhétorique et prédication selon Calvin," *Revue d'histoire et de philosophie religieuses*, LV (1975), 249–272.

138. Comm. I Cor. 1:17.

139. Comm. Matt. 13:5.

140. Serm. No. 95 on Job, 419–420, 424.

141. Serms. No. 95 on Job, 424; No. 49, 609.

Chapter 8

1. *Church Dogmatics*, III, pt. 2, 384.

2. For Calvin's most systematic review of philosophical anthropology, see *Inst.*, II, ii, 2.

3. Comm. John 12:40; cf. Comms. Deut. 29:4, Rom. 2:15.

4. Comm. Eph. 1:16; cf. Comm. Matt. 14:24.

5. Comm. Is. 51:7; cf. Comm. I Thess. 3:13, where he identifies heart with "conscience" and "inwardness."

6. Serm. No. 45 on Deut., 422.

7. Comm. Ps 26:2; italics added.

8. Comm. Rom. 7:14.

9. Comm. Rom. 8:10.

10. Comm. John 1:14.

11 Comm. John 3:6; on Calvin's view of Catholic teaching, see also *Supplex exhortatio*, CO VI, 483.

12. Comm. Gal. 5:19.

13. Comm. II Cor. 7:15.

14. *Inst.*, II, vii, 10.

15. Comm. Gen. 6:3.

16. Comm. Rom. 12:2.

17. *Inst.*, I, xv, 6.

18. *Inst.*, II, ii, 26.

19. *Inst.*, II, ii, 14.

20. Comm. I Cor. 4:5.

21. Comm. Jer. 17:9–10.

22. Comm. Acts 8:2. He was already cool to Stoicism in his Seneca commentary; see esp. 358–368.

23. Comm. I Pet., 1:6. On the propriety of grieving, see Serm. No. 3 on II Sam., 26.

24. *Inst.*, III, viii, 9.

25. Comm. Matt. 26:37.

26. Comm. Ex. 32:19; cf. Comms. Phil. 2:27, Gen. 45:1, Luke 6:8.

27. Comm. Deut. 22:6.

28. Comm. Ps. 143:6.

29. Comm. Rom. 9:3.

30. Comm. II Cor. 2:4.

31. Serm. No. 58 on Job, 728.

32. Comm. Ex. 4:3.

33. Serm. No. 39 on Job, 481, 488; see also Comm. Ps. 139:15.

34. Comms. I Tim. 5:23, John 4:32, Col 2:23.

35. Comm. Matt. 3:4.

36. Serm. No. 10 on I Cor., 698; cf. Serm. No. 90 on Job, 476– 477.

37. Serm. No. 10 on I Cor., 698.

38. Comm. Ezek. 5:5–6.

39. Comm. Matt. 13:46, italics added; Augustine's distinction is developed in *De doctrina christiana*, iii–v.

40. Comm. Ps. 104:31.

41. *Inst.*, III, x, 1, 3.

42. Comm. Gen. 1:30.

43. *Inst.*, III, x, 2.

44. *Inst.*, I, xi, 12.

45. Epistle to the Geneva Service Book of 1542, CO VI, 170; cf. Comm. Gen. 4:20.

46. Comm. I Tim. 4:3.

47. Serm. No. 39 on II Sam., p. 347.

48. Comm. Gen. 43:33; cf. *Inst.*, III, x, 2.

49. Comm. John 2:8. Here again he was in agreement with Erasmus; cf. *Convivium religiosum, Colloquies*, 62–63.

50. Comm. Ps. 104:15; he opposed making the danger of drunkenness "a pretext for a new cult based on abstinence" (Comm. Luke 1:15).

51. Comm. Luke 14:12.

52. Comm. Gen. 21:8; cf. the colloquium *Convivium religiosum*.

53. Cf. Comm. Gen. 3:6.

54. *Inst.*, II, iii, 4.

55. *Inst.*, IV, xiii, 3; cf. his rejection of virginity as virtuous, Comm. I Cor. 7:7.

56. Comm. I Cor. 7:7.

57. *Inst.*, II, viii, 43; cf. Comm. Matt. 19:10–12.

58. *Inst.*, II, viii, 43; but cf. *Traité des scandales*, pp. 277–278, which gives only second place to this motive for marriage.

59. Comm. I Cor. 7:9.

60. Comm. Luke 1:23.

61. *Inst.*, IV, xii, 24.

62. Comm. I Cor., 7:6.

63. Comm. Jer. 3:4.

64. Comm. Dan. 11, 38–39.

65. Comm. Gen. 29:18; for another example of his interest in sexual attraction see Comm. Gen. 12:11, where he was concerned to reconcile the account of Sarai's beauty with her advanced age.

66. Comm. Deut. 24:5; Calvin went beyond the Scriptural text in insisting on the mutuality of sexual pleasure: "imo ultro concedit, ut maritus et uxor se oblectent."

67. Comm. Matt. 21:16.

68. Serm. No. 71 on Job, 116.

69. Comm. I Tim. 2:15.

70. Comm. Is. 49:15.

71. Comm. I Tim. 5:11; cf. *Inst.*, IV, xiii, 19.

72. Comm. I Cor. 7:36.

73. Comm. Josh. 15:14–63.

74. Comm. Lev. 21:13.

75. Comm. Matt. 19:9. This also pointed to the abolition of the double standard in Geneva. A few years after Calvin's return from Strasbourg, the company of pastors formulated "ordinances on marriage" that include the following provision: "Although in former times the rights of the wife have not been equal to those of the husband in a divorce case, and since according to the testimony of the apostle the obligation is mutual and reciprocal as regards the marriage bed [*la cohabitation du lict*], in which the wife is no more subject to the husband than the husband to the wife, if a man is convicted of adultery and the wife asks to be separated from him, it should be granted her, if they cannot be reconciled by good advice" (Jean-François Bergier and Robert M. Kingdon, eds., *Registres de la Compagnie des Pasteurs de Genéve au temps de Calvin*, [Geneva, 1962–1964], I, p. 35). Cf. I, p. 41, where, in connection with an actual case, Calvin is reported to have said that "adultery is a sufficient cause for divorce as much for the wife as for the husband; however much the husband may be superior to the wife, in this there is nevertheless equality." He cited I Cor. 7:3–4. On the general point I am indebted to Jane Dempsey Douglass, *Women, Freedom, and Calvin* (Philadelphia, 1985).

76. Serm. No. 11 on Job, 148.

77. Comm. Gen. 2:18; cf. Comm. I Cor. 7, 1.

78. Comm. John 1:13.

79. Comm. I Cor. 11:7.

80. Comm. I Cor. 11:3.

81. Cf. Jane Dempsey Douglass, "Christian Freedom: What Calvin Learned at the School of Women," *Church History*, 53 (1984), 155–173, which treats Calvin's thought in the general context of the sixteenth-century *querelle des femmes*.

82. Comm. Deut. 31:12.

83. *Traité des scandales*, p. 244.

84. Comm. Mark 16:1; cf. Comm. John 20:1.

85. Douglass, *Women*, pp. 22, 55.

86. Serm. No. 42 on Job, 529. On this issue he made one of his rare attacks on

Erasmus, who, he charged, had "worked too hard to excuse such gross insanity." He also implied that Erasmus had known better, which suggested that his fault had been moral rather than intellectual (Comm. Rom. 5:14).

87. Comm. Matt. 6:22. This was, at the very least, a mistake in exegesis, Calvin thought, because "Christ in this place is not speaking of any *faculty* with which we are endowed, but of how we should conduct ourselves."

88. Serm. No. 57 on Job, 710: on the *facere quod in se est*, see Oberman, *Harvest of Medieval Theology*, pp. 132–134.

89. Comm. Rom. 12:1.

90. Comm. I Peter, 1:14.

91. Comm. Ps. 51;7; *Inst.*, II i, 8–9.

92. *Inst.*, III, xiv, 9.

93. Comm. Gen. 3:6.

94. Serm. No. 33 on Deut, 279–280.

95. *Inst.*, II, ii, 25.

96. Serm. No. 46 on Job, 569–570.

97. *Inst.*, II, vi, 1.

98. Comm. Ezek. 11:19–20.

99. Comm. Ps. 19:13.

100. Serm. No. 2 on I Cor., 603. See also Comm. Is. 1:3.

101. Serm. No. 32 on Deut., 262; cf. *Inst.*, IV, xv, 10. Calvin refused, however, to speculate, as Augustine had done, on the means by which this seed of Adam was transmitted. "Lest we be driven into that labyrinth," he said, "it is sufficient to hold that Adam, after his defection, was despoiled of every gift with which he had been endowed, so that reason, which before shone in him, was extinguished, and will, which before had been shaped in obedience to God, became stubborn, mind and heart were corrupted, and thereafter he begat children like himself" (Comm. Ps. 51:7).

102. Cf. Comm. I Cor. 6:11.

103. Comm. I John 5:16.

104. *Inst.*, III, xviii, 10; cf. Comm. Gen. 3:6.

105. Comm. Is. 8:7.

106. Comm. Phil. 4:5.

107. Comm. Ps. 119:174. Calvin describes the movement from faithlessness to particular sins among the Jews in Comm. Heb. 3:18.

108. Serms. No. 11 on II Sam., 90, and No. 88 on Job, 231.

109. *Inst.*, III, xii, 1.

110. Cf. Comm. Ps. 69:20.

111. Comm. Jer. 32:19.

112. Serm. No. 88 on Job, 338.

113. *Inst.*, III, xiii, 2; cf. Comm. Dan. 4:17, 37.

114. Comm. Jer. 9:23–24; for Montaigne, see Maurice Rat, ed. *Essais* (Paris, 1958), II, p. 178.

115. This is the view of Torrance, *Calvin's Doctrine of Man*, pp. 35–82. Stauffer, "Calvin méconnu," p. 199, correctly notes Calvin's insistence on the persistence of God's image.

116. *Inst.*, II, v, 19.

117. Serm. No. 2 on I Cor., 605.

118. Comm. Matt. 12:43.

119. *Inst.*, I, xv, 4; Comm. Gen. 1:26.

120. Comm. Ex. 20:13; cf. Comm. James 3:9.

121. Serm. No. 62 on Job, 9.

122. *Inst.*, III, vii, 6.

123. Serm. on John 1:1–5, 480.

124. For extended treatment of this theme, see Trinkaus, *In Our Image and Likeness*.

125. Comm. Gen. 50:3.

126. Comm. Is. 8:11.

127. Jer. 9:13–15; see also Jer. 7:25–26.

128. Comm. I Cor. 11:21; *Supplex exhortatio*, CO VI, 497.

129. *Inst.*, III, xiv, 9; this is also a major theme of his sermons on Job.

130. Comm. Gen. 7:6; cf. *Rhetorica*, II, xiii, 1–14 (1389a–1390b).

131. Serm. No. 17 on Job, 211.

132. Serm. No. 57 on Job, 716–717.

133. Comm. Gen. 7:6.

134. Comm. Ex. 7:6. This was one of his last works, published the year of his death.

135. Comm. Jer. 2:30, a work published only a year before his death.

136. Comm. Ps. 95:9; cf. Comm. Ps. 49:14.

137. Comm. Dan. 3:3–7.

138. Comm. Jer. 6:21.

139. Serm. No. 15 on I Cor., 766, in connection with the confessional.

140. Comm. Sen. 4–5. A similar passage had appeared in the discourse of Nicolas Cop. For Lorenzo Valla on the point, see *De vero bono,* in Giorgio Radetti, ed., *Scritti filosofici e religiosi* (Florence, 1953), p. 5.

141. *Inst.*, III, xiv, 4.

142. *Inst.*, III, xiv, 3.

143. As generally in Comms. Ps. 9:2, I John 5:12.

144. Comm. Dan. 7:6; cf. Comm. Dan. 2:31–35.

145. Comm. Sen. 32–35. He elaborated on the point in Comm. Dan. 7:19–20.

146. Comm. Dan. 7:7.

147. Comm. Dan. 7:23–24.

148. Comm. Dan. 7:19–20. For humanist republicanism, cf. Baron, *Crisis of the Early Italian Renaissance.*

149. Comm. Dan. 2:44–45.

150. Comm. Dan. 2:40–43, 7:23–24.

151. Comm. Dan. 11:38–39.

152. Comm. Dan. 11:36, referring to *Pro Flacco*, 69.

153. Comm. Dan. 11:36.

154. Comm. Gal. 5:22.

155. *Inst.*, I, xv, 7, 8.

156. Comm. Gen. 3:6.

157. Comm. II Cor. 12:10.

158. Comm. Gal. 5:26.

159. Comm. Dan. 11:33–34.

160. Comm. Ps. 49:1.

161. Comm. Is. 32:5.

162. Comm. Is. 53:11; cf. Petrarch: "What is the use of knowing what virtue is if it is not loved when known? . . . It is better to will the good than to know the truth" (*De*

sui ipsius et multorum ignorantia, trans. Hans Nachod, in Ernst Cassirer et al., eds., *The Renaissance Philosophy of Man* (Chicago, 1948), pp. 104–105.

163. Comm. Ps. 73:1.

164. Comm. Ps. 73:1.

165. Comm. John 4:20; *Traité des scandales*, p. 175. Cf. Comm. Ps. 105:25. Calvin thought that even Augustine had "tormented himself with subtleties" (Comm. I John 3:2).

166. Comm. Ps. 78:8, John 4:20.

167. *Inst.*, IX, xiii, 17; see also IV, iii, 4, where Calvin denies that even institutions divinely ordained for the apostolic church are perpetually binding.

168. Cf. Turchetti, *Concordia o tolleranza?*, pp. 463–467.

169. *I: st.*, II, iv, 39.

170. Comms. John 4:20, Jer. 14:20.

Chapter 9

1. For the notion of a Renaissance "crisis of knowing," see Alisdair Macintyre, "Epistemological Crises, Dramatic Narrative and the Philosophy of Science," *Monist*, 61 (1977), 453–472. For its later stages, see Barbara Shapiro, *Probability and Certainty in Seventeenth-Century England: A Study of the Relationships Between Natural Science, Religion, History, Law, and Literature* (Princeton, 1983).

2. Quoted by Thomas Tentler, *Sin and Confession on the Eve of the Reformation* (Princeton, 1977), p. 147.

3. Quoted by D. P. Walker, *The Ancient Theology: Studies in Christian Platonism from the Fifteenth to the Eighteenth Century* (Ithaca, 1972), p. 59.

4. *Gargantua et Pantagruel*, III, xxxvi; the translation is that of J. M. Cohen (London, 1955). On the skepticism of Rabelais, see Screech, *Rabelais*, pp. 134, 255, and cf. Regosin, "Montaigne Scholarship," 43.

5. Quoted by Jerrold E. Seigel, *Rhetoric and Philosophy in Renaissance Humanism* (Princeton, 1968), p. 74.

6. *Discorsi*, I, 47.

7. *Ricordi*, Ser. C, 6.

8. Charles G. Nauert, Jr., *Agrippa and the Crisis of Renaissance Thought* (Urbana, 1965), p. 49.

9. Quoted by Raymond Klibansky, *Saturn and Melancholy: Studies in the History of Natural Philosophy, Religion, and Art* (New York, 1964), p. 363.

10. Quoted by Richard Yanowitz, "Tudor Attitudes Towards the Power of Language," Ph.D. diss., University of Calfornia, Berkeley, 1978, p. 113.

11. In his letter to Pico della Mirandola, in Quirinus Breen, "Melanchthon's Reply to G. Pico della Mirandola," *Journal of the History of Ideas*, 13 (1952), 417.

12. Quoted by Carlos G. Noreña, *Juan Luis Vives* (The Hague, 1970), p. 238.

13. *Loci communes*, Wilhelm Pauck, ed., *Melanchthon and Bucer*, (London, 1969), p. 99.

14. Cf. Guicciardini, *Ricordi*, Ser. C, 10: "Let no one trust so entirely to natural prudence as to persuade himself that it will suffice to guide him without help from experience. For there is no man, however prudent, who has beem employed in affairs, but has had cause to know that experience leads us to many results we never could have reached by the force of natural intelligence only."

15. Cf. *Inst. oratoria*, II, xvii, 30; see also Quentin Skinner, *The Foundations of Modern Political Thought* (Cambridge, 1978), I, pp. 218–219.

16. *De disciplinis*, in *Obras completas* (Madrid, 1948), p. 614.

17. Quirinus Breen, "Melanchthon's Reply to G. Pico della Mirandola," *Journal of the History of Ideas*, 13 (1952), 417–418.

18. Macintyre cites this example in "Epistemological Crises," 459.

19. *De ignorantia*, 104; italics added.

20. Jean Gerson, *Selections*, ed. Steven E. Ozment (Leiden, 1969), p. 29.

21. *De ignorantia*, 78.

22. *Hyperaspistes*, LB X, 1284A, quoted by Boyle, *Rhetoric and Reform*, p. 46.

23. Trinkaus notes his concern with epistemological problems in "Renaissance Problems in Calvin's Theology," 66–68.

24. *Inst*; ep.

25. For what follows see, in general, Edward A. Dowey, *The Knowledge of God in Calvin's Theology* (New York, 1952), and T. H. L. Parker, *Calvin's Doctrine of the Knowledge of God* (Edinburgh, 1969).

26. Comm. Luke 24:16.

27. Comms. Gen. 3:6, Ps. 119:73. Calvin seems to use "reason" here in a very general sense to signify all the powers of the mind. Cf. *Inst.*, I, xv, 6.

28. Comm. Jer. 5:15.

29. Serm. No. 57 on Job, 717; *Inst.*, III v, 10, in connection with Purgatory; Comms. Dan 2:23, John 10:8.

30. Comm. I Cor. 3:15; Calvin mentioned Cyprian, Ambrose, Augustine, Gregory, and Bernard.

31. Comm. Jer. 11:13.

32. Comm. I Peter 1:18.

33. Comm. Eph. 4:17.

34. *Inst.*, II, ii, 13 and I, V, 12; cf. Serm. No. 101 on Job, 503.

35. Comm. John 1:5.

36. Comm. Is. 6:4.

37. Comms. I Cor. 1:22–23, Matt. 11:25.

38. Serm. on John 1:1–5, 475; cf. Comm. I Tim. 3:15.

39. Comm. John 4:36. Even Plato, who had come closest to the truth, "could not even dimly sense" how human beings could be united with God (*Inst.*, III, xxv, 2.).

40. Serm. No. 58 on Job, 727; cf. Comm. Ps. 105:16 for his doubt of the capacity of the mind to grasp the order of nature.

41. *Inst.*, I, v, 12.

42. Serm. No. 96 on Job, 433; see also Serm. No. 19, 246.

43. Comm. John 13:17.

44. *Inst.*, II, xxiii, 8.

45. *Inst.*, I, v, 12.

46. Diogenes Laertius, *Lives of the Philosophers*, 9, 51.

47. Comm. Ezek. 10:11–12.

48. Comm. Ps. 115:3.

49. Comm. Jer. 31:31–32; cf. *Inst.* III, xxiv, 17.

50. *Inst.*, II, ii, 13.

51. Comms. Ps. 119:23, Is. 26:3.

52. *Inst.*, II, ii, 24.

53. Comm. Rom. 1:22; cf. *Inst.*, I, v, 12.

54. *Inst.*, II, ii, 18.

55. Comm. Ps. 29:9; on Plato, cf. Comm. Rom. 1:23.

56. Comm. Acts 17:16.

57. Comm. I Cor. 1:21; cf. *Inst.*, I, v, 11, for philosophy in antiquity.

58. *Inst.*, I, v, 12.

59. Comm. Col. 2:8; cf. Quintilian, II, xvii, 39: "The orator knows that what he states is no more than probable." See also Aristotle, *Rhetoric*, I, ii, 15 (1357a–b).

60. *Inst.*, IV, xviii, 1. He made against Pseudo-Dionysius the same charges that he made against the Scholastics; cf. Comm. Acts 17:34 and *Inst.*, I, xiv, 4.

61. *Inst.*, ep.

62. Comm. Matt. 6:23.

63. Comm. Jer. 51:19.

64. Serm. No. 26 on Job, 330.

65. *Responsio ad Sadoleti epistolam*, CO V, 395–396.

66. *Inst.*, I, xvii, 2, and III, iv, 1; Comm. Num. 23:1.

67. *Inst.*, III, xii, 1.

68. *Inst.*, III, iv, 1.

69. *Responsio ad Sadoleti epistolam*, CO V, 405.

70. Comm. II Cor. 12:4. Among matters on which he discouraged speculation were the order of angels (*Inst.*, I, xiv, 8, 12) and the perpetual virginity of Mary (Comm. Matt. 1:25).

71. Serms. No. 102 on Job, 513; no. 43 on Job, 534–536; No. 42 on Deut., 391; see also Comm. Deut. 18:9. On the larger implications of "curiosity," see Blumenberg, *Legitimacy of the Modern Age*, pp. 229–453.

72. *Inst.*, I, xiii, 5.

73. Comm. I Tim. 6:4.

74. Comm. Ps. 119:98.

75. *Inst.*, III, ii, 1 and 8.

76. *Inst*, I, ii, 2.

77. *Inst.*, III, vi, 4.

78. Comm. Acts 17:29; Serm. No. 15 on II Sam., 127; Serm. No. 85 on Job, 298.

79. Comm. Dan. 12:2.

80. Comms. Is. 42:1 and 58:2, Gen. 28:13, Luke 11:27, Acts 8:6.

81. Comms. Gen. 15:4, Ezek. 11:24–25.

82. *Inst.*, I, xi, 5–7; cf. Comms. Gal. 3:1, Jer. 51:18.

83. Comm. Ps. 19:1. On the importance of oral communication in urban culture and therefore for the Reformation, cf. Michael Mullett, *Radical Religious movements*, pp. 25–28.

84. Comm. Acts 6:2.

85. Comm. Ps. 119:98.

86. Comm. Ps. 66:5; cf. Comm. Zech. 2:9.

87. Serm. No. 21 on Job, 263.

88. Comm. Zech. 2:9.

89. *Inst.*, I, i, 1.

90. Cf. E. David Willis, "Rhetoric and Responsibility," 52–53.

91. Comm. I Cor. 8:1.

92. Serm. No. 102 on Job, 513–515.

93. Serm No. 103 on Job, 521–522; cf. Comm. I Thess. 5:21. On Calvin's tendency generally to represent the particular truths he espoused as the mean between two equally erroneous extremes, cf. Battles, *Calculus Fidei*, pp. 32–38.

94. Serm. No. 103 on Job, 526; *Inst.*, III, xxi, 3.

95. Serm. No. 57 on Job, 711.

96. *Inst.*, I, v, 9.

97. *Inst.*, III, vi, 4.

98. Serm. No. 57 on Job, 709, and Comm. Phil. 1:10, citing II Tim. 3:16, a text Calvin often used in this connection; cf. Serm. No. 5 on I Cor., 641.

99. Parker, *Knowledge of God*, pp. 15–16, calls attention to this change, though he gives it a somewhat different interpretation.

100. Cf. John Dillenberger, *Contours of Faith: Changing Forms of Christian Thought* (Nashville and New York, 1969), p. 39; "Calvin can be said to be the least systematic of the systematic theologians. He wished to be a biblical theologian *par excellence* and his *Institutes* are like a wheel without a rim, a hub full of spokes. Every theological point is hammered out along the spoke from the hub towards its end, and some spokes are longer than others. There is no rim which connects the ends of the spokes, hence no system in the sense in which we use it. The rim would be most unsymmetrical, analogically most unsystematic."

101. *Inst.*, III, vi, 1. He was ambivalent enough to add, however, that when the Holy Spirit "lays down [a methodical plan] anywhere, he sufficiently hints that it is not to be neglected by us," but he did not offer examples of such "method." Perhaps this was an example of balancing between extremes.

102. Comm. Ps. 148:3.

103. *Traité des scandales*, pp. 169–170; cf. Serm. No. 101 on Job, 506–507, and Comm. Is. 53:1: ". . . est stultitia, quoniam exsuperat omnes humanos sensus."

104. *Traité des scandales*, pp. 157, 163–164, 182–183. See also Comms. John 18:38, Luke 2:12, Rom. 3:5; I Cor. 1:21. Calvin's ambivalence persisted nevertheless; cf. his letter of 1552 to Lelio Socino: "Certainly I, if anyone, have always abhorred paradoxes."

105. Serm. No. 50 on Job, 627.

Chapter 10

1. Serm. No. 81 on Job, 246.

2. Comm. Matt. 10:17–18. This may be a reminiscence of his attendance at the German Diets during his exile in Strasbourg.

3. Serm. No. 44 on Job, 552.

4. Serm. No. 43 on Deut., 397–398.

5. *Inst.*, I, v, 6.

6. Comm. John 1:3. This did not prevent him from using similar language himself; cf. *Inst.*, I, v, 2, and Comm. Gen. 2:2.

7. Comm. Jer. 18:1–6; cf. Serms. No. 80 on Job, 236, and No. 13 on I Cor., 740–741.

8. Serm. No. 7 on Job, 100.

9. Comm. Ps. 121:1.

10. Serm. No. 7 on Job, 96. On the general point cf. Bohatec, *Budé und Calvin*, pp. 325–345.

11. *Traité des scandales*, p. 217. Cf. Serms. No. 31 and 32 on Deut., 257 and 259. In his deathbed farewell to the Seigneurs of Geneva, he asserted that God "wills us to do him *homage*, recognizing that we depend entirely on him."

12. *Inst.*, I, v, 6. Calvin was aware that the association of thunder with divine communication was an ancient *topos*; cf. Serm. No. 96 on Job, 438–439. For Erasmus on the terror aroused by storms see the colloquy *Naufragium*, but, in contrast to Calvin, Erasmus associated such phenomena with the devil; on this point see Tracy,

Erasmus, pp. 99–100. Here Rabelais, who has Pantagruel encounter God in a storm (*Gargantua et Pantagruel*, IV, xviii–xxiv), is closer to Calvin.

13. Serm. No. 96 on Job, 439.

14. Comm. Ps. 77:16–18.

15. Comm. Ps. 145:2.

16. Cf. *Inst.*, I, xvi, 5, where he acknowledged that the natural order is generally regular.

17. Comm. Dan. 2:47; cf. Serm. No. 45 on Deut., 421.

18. Serm. No. 36 on Deut., 312.

19. Wendel, *Calvin et l'humanisme*, p. 82, rightly contrasts Calvin with Melanchthon, who had a keen interest in the natural sciences.

20. Comms. Ps. 54:3, Acts 2:11.

21. Comm. Ps. 54:3.

22. Comm. John 19:34.

23. Cf. Comm. Ps. 40:6.

24. Comms. Gen. 19:24, Ps. 107:43.

25. Comm. Jer. 51:53; see also Comm. Ps. 105:16.

26. *Inst.* I, xvi, 2 and 3; Comm. Is. 41:18–19.

27. Comm. Jer. 10:1–2.

28. Comm. Is. 19:12. On Calvin's little treatise of 1549, *Contre de l'astrologie iudiciaire*, see Wayne Shumaker, *The Occult Sciences in the Renaissance: A Study in Intellectual Patterns* (Berkeley, 1972), pp. 44–46.

29. Comm. Jer. 10:1–2; see also Comm. Acts 19:19.

30. Comm. Is. 19:12.

31. Comm. Acts 11:28.

32. Comm. Jer. 10:1–2; cf. *Inst.*, I, xvi, 3.

33. Comm. Deut. 18:16.

34. *Inst.*, I, xvi, 3.

35. Comm. Jer. 51:15–16.

36. Comm. Dan. 2:21.

37. Comm. Ps. 104:27.

38. Serm. No. 95 on Job, 429–430.

39. Comm. Ps. 135:7.

40. Comm. Jer. 49:36.

41. Comm. Jer. 5:22.

42. Comms. Gen 47:13, Dan. 6:24, Num. 21:6.

43. Comm. Ps. 22:10.

44. Serm. No. 101 on Job, 503.

45. Serm. No. 81 on Job, 248.

46. Comm. Dan. 1:9.

47. Comm. Gen. 48:17; italics added.

48. Serm. No. 101 on Job, 504–505.

49. Comm. Ps. 135:6.

50. *Inst.*, I, xvi, 3.

51. Comm. Ezek. 10:17.

52. Comm. Deut. 2:24.

53. Comm. Is. 7:19.

54. Serm. No. 91 on Job, 371; cf. *Inst.*, I, xvii, 1.

55. *Inst.* I, xvi, 8; cf. Comm. Is. 13:1

56. *Inst.*, I, xvi, 8–10.

57. Comm. Dan. 2:21.

58. *Inst.*, II, xi, 14.

59. *Inst.* I, xvii, 2; see also Comm. Matt. 11:26.

60. *Inst.* I, xvi, 8–10; italics added. As early as his Seneca commentary, Calvin had recognized that the difference between attributing events to "fortune" and to an incomprehensible God was little more than verbal (32–33).

61. Comm. 73:16.

62. Comm. Ezek. 1:24.

63. Comm. Ps. 135:6.

64. Comm. Is. 44:26.

65. Comm. Is. 22:13.

66. Comm. Ps. 9:9.

67. Comm. Gen. 33:4.

68. Comm. Is. 13:3.

69. Comm. Luke 2:1.

70. Comms. Is. 13:3, Jer. 42:11–12.

71. Serm. No. 73 on Job, 145–6.

72. Comm. Acts 17:26.

73. Comm. Dan. 5:18–20.

74. Comm. Jer. 27:6–7; cf. Comm. Acts 17:26 on providential rule over their size.

75. Serm. No. 48 on Job, 593–596; for the Romans, see also Comm. Is. 22:21.

76. Comm. Is. 5:26.

77. Comm. Dan. 8:20–25.

78. Comm. Ps. 44:10.

79. Comm. Jer. 38:16.

80. Comm. Jer. 51:56.

81. Serm. No. 73 on Job, 145–146.

82. Serm. No. 78 on Job, 213.

83. Comm. Jer. 14:1.

84. Comm. Ps. 6:2.

85. Comm. Deut. 32:24.

86. Comm. Jer. 25:20.

87. Comm. Jer. 24:10 and 27:8; cf. Comm. Is. 5:10 and 24:5.

88. Comm. Dan. 7:6; see Comm. Dan. 2:31–235 for the destruction of the Roman Empire.

89. Comm. Is. 36:20.

90. Comm. Ps. 92:6; for a similar invocation of fortune, Comm. Ps. 37:7.

91. Comm. Ps. 37:7.

92. Serms. No. 78 on Job, 205, and No. 59, 97.

93. Serm. No. 35 on II Sam., 303.

94. Barth, *Church Dogmatics*, III, pt. 3, pp. 30–31, thought it not Christian. Blumenberg, *Legitimacy of the Modern Age*, p. 37, emphasizes the philosophical origins of the doctrine in general, though without reference to Calvin, contrasting it with the eschatology of the New Testament, which it replaced.

95. Comm. Acts 17:18.

96. Comm. Acts 17:18; see also *Inst.*, I, xvi, 8.

97. *Inst.* I, xvi, 3.

98. Comm. Ps. 115:3.

99. *Inst. I, xvi, 3*.

100. *Inst.* I, xvii, 11.

101. *Inst.* I, xvii, 7.

102. Comm. Ps. 107:42; cf. *Inst.*, I, xvi, 9.

103. Comm. Is. 40:12; cf. Comm. Ps. 62:12.

104. Comm. Is. 7:19.

105. Comm. Ps. 9:13.

106. Comm. Is. 18:5.

107. Comm. Is. 18:4.

108. Comm. Ps. 105:23.

109. *Inst.* III, xxi, 5.

110. *Inst.* III, xxiv, 12; see also Comms. Matt. 13:14 and Acts 24:25.

111. Comm. Is. 53:1; *Traité des scandales*, p. 212. Höpfl, *Christian Polity of Calvin*, p. 243, n. 5, remarks on Calvin's embarrassment at being drawn into a defense of the doctrine.

112. Comm. Rom. 9:14. Again he agreed with Rabelais; cf. *Gargantua et Pantagruel*, IV, prologue.

113. Serm. No. 40 on Job, 502.

114. Serm. No. 44 on Deut., 410; see also Comm. Rom. 9:14 and *Inst.*, III, xxi, 1.

115. Comm. Rom. 9:27.

116. Comm. Ps. 147:9.

117. In Comm. Ps. 69:3, Calvin seems to recognize this possibility in principle. Barth, *Church Dogmatics*, II, pt. 2, p. 40, notes this with disapproval but recognizes that Calvin knew better.

118. Comm. Jer. 17:17–18 and 20:12.

119. *Inst.* III, xxiv, 5; cf. Dillenberger, *Contours of Faith*, p. 145.

120. Comm. Eph. 1:4.

121. Comm. Is. 41:8.

122. Comm. Matt. 23:24.

123. Comm. Luke 10:20; *Inst.* III, xxiv, 6.

124. Comm. Matt. 16:2.

125. Comm. Ps. 84:7.

126. Serm. No. 44 on Deut., 413–414.

127. Comm. Is. 22:11.

128. Serm. No. 3 on I Cor., 610.

129. Serm. No. 44 on Deut. 413–414.

130. Serm. No. 33 on II Sam., 287.

131. Serm. No. 48 on Job, 604

132. Serm. No. 37 on II Sam., 322.

133. Serm. on John 1:1–5, 477.

134. Comm. Is. 44:21.

135. Comm. Matt. 26:75.

136. Comm. Ps. 90:3.

137. Comm. I John 2:3.

138. Comm. Is. 44:14.

139. Serm. No. 16 on II Sam., 133; Comm. Is. 42:2; Serm. No. 70 on Job., 102–103.

140. Comm. II Peter 3:10.

141. Serm. No. 16 on II Sam., 134.

142. Comm. Dan 9, 18.

143. Serm. No. 12 on II Sam., 105.

144. Serm. No. 91 on Job, 372.

145. Comm. Dan. 9:13; see also Comm. Ezek. 9:2.

146. Serm. No. 70 on Job, 109. On this conception, cf. the perceptive article of Margaret R. Miles, "Theology, Anthropology, and the Human Body in Calvin's *Institutes of the Christian Religion*," *Harvard Theological Review*, 74 (1981), 303–323.

147. *Inst.*, II, x, 4.

148. *Inst.*, III, i, 3; Serm. No. 44 on Deut., 409–410.

149. Serm. No. 88 on Job., 342; cf. Serm. No. 15 on II Sam., 126.

150. Siegfried Wenzel, *The Sin of Sloth: "Acedia" in Medieval Thought and Literature* (Chapel Hill, 1967), p. 68, a work on which much of this paragraph is based.

151. Quoted by Wenzel, *The Sin of Sloth*, pp. 36–37, from *De ecclesiastica disciplina*.

152. Quoted by Wenzel, *The Sin of sloth*, p. 165.

153. *Epistolae familiares*, XIII, 6 (1352).

154. *De libero arbitrio*.

155. Quoted from *Praelectio in psalmum* by Marjorie O'Rourke Boyle, "For Peasants, Psalms: Erasmus' *editio princeps* of Hayms (1533)," *Medieval Studies*, XLIV (1982), 465.

Chapter 11

1. On the history of this venerable trope, see Ernst Robert Curtius, *European Literature and the Latin Middle Ages*, trans. Willard R. Trask (New York, 1953), pp. 138–144.

2. "God Was Accommodating," 2–3.

3. Quoted by Myron P. Gilmore from the dialogue *Ciceronianus*, in *Humanists and Jurists: Six Studies in the Renaissance* (Cambridge, Mass., 1963), 103–104.

4. As in *Inst.*, I, vi, 2; see also I, v, 8, and II, vi, 1.

5. Serm. No. 31 on Job, 387.

6. Comm. Jer. 38:25–26.

7. Comm. Is. 22:21.

8. Letter to Farel, Mar. 29, 1540, CO XI, 30; "catastrophe," in its primary meaning, is a technical term for the denouement of a tragedy.

9. Letter to Farel, Dec. 28, 1547, CO XII, 642–643, citing Terence.

10. Letters to Viret, Mar. 27, 1548, and to Farel, Nov. 27, CO XIII, 103, 109. Thraso was a braggart in Terence's *Eunuch*.

11. Letter of Nov. 28, 1552, CO XIV, 415.

12. Letter of Aug. 23, 1555, CO XV, 738.

13. Cf. Barish, *Antitheatrical Prejudice*, p. 155; Barish notes that the Oxford English Dictionary "supplies similar coordinates for the verbs *play* and *act*, which may (in general) mean *either* 'to sustain a feigned character, make a pretence, act deceitfully'—i.e., engage in mimicry or hypocrisy—*or*, more neutrally, 'to pursue a course of action,' 'to perform a function'—to go about one's business in a normal manner. A man who has 'played his part' has done what was expected of him; he has fulfilled the obligations contracted by performing similar actions in the past. But most men play their parts somewhat inexpertly; they fail to coincide exactly with their assumed roles."

14. In fact he rebuked a ministerial colleague who had almost caused a riot in Geneva by trying to prevent a staging of the acts of the apostles (Parker, *Calvin*, pp. 100–101). He used theatrical language in describing this event: "Our plays were al-

most converted into tragedy," he wrote Farel on Jul. 4, 1546, CO XIII, 355; see also his letter of June 3, 1546, CO XII, 347–348. Cf. Monter, *Calvin's Geneva*, p. 109, for another example of Calvin's approval of a dramatic performance. He may have been influenced by Jean Sturm, who had staged plays for pedagogical purposes in his school in Strasbourg; cf. Miriam U. Chrisman, *Lay Culture, Learned Culture: Books and Social Change in Strasbourg, 1480–1599* (New Haven, 1982), p. 198.

15. Comm. Dan. 3:3–7.

16. Comm. Jer. 9:17–18; cf. Comm. Is. 60:9. See Chapter 4, p. 80, for Calvin's disapproval of fantasy.

17. As in Serm. No. 44 on Deut., 412.

18. Comm. Dan. 3:3–7.

19. Comm. Ps. 116:10.

20. Comm. Ps. 18:23.

21. Serm. No. 105 on Job, 554.

22. *Inst.*, III, xii, 4.

23. Comm. Jer. 40:1–4.

24. Comm. Ex. 10:16; cf. Comm. John 13:22.

25. Comm. Ex. 9:30.

26. *Inst.*, III, ii, 10.

27. Comms. Jer. 26:3, Ps. 4:5, Ps. 77:6.

28. Comm. Gal. 6:4.

29. Serm. No. 41 on Deut., 382; cf. *Inst.*, II, vii, 7.

30. *Inst.*, II, viii, 3.

31. *Inst.*, II, ii, 10; see also III, xvii, 3.

32. Serm. No. 41 on Deut., 382.

33. Comm. Jer. 9:23–24.

34. Comm. Gen. 50:15.

35. *Inst.*, III, xii, 5.

36. Serm. No. 41 on Deut., 378.

37. Comm. Jer. 8:4–5.

38. Comm. Is. 22:12.

39. Cf. *Inst.*, III, ix, 4.

40. Comms. Matt. 6:25–30, and Luke 12:22–28. In one respect Calvin's doctrine of the calling does not fit the theatrical model. Whereas actors on the stage play many roles, a stable social order, he believed, requires human beings to play only one occupational role during their lives. He was prepared, however, to relax this limitation for sufficient cause (see Chapter 12, p. 199).

41. Comm. Ps. 131:1.

42. *Inst.*, III, x, 6.

43. Comms. I Tim. 6:12, Jer. 1:17; for a negative corollary, cf. Serm. No. 43 on II Sam., 374.

44. On this contrast, see Richard M. Douglas, "Talent and Vocation in Humanist and Protestant Thought," in Theodore K. Rabb and Jerrold E. Seigel, eds., *Action and Conviction in Early Modern Europe: Essays in Memory of E. H. Harbison* (Princeton, 1969), p. 261.

45. Comm. Jer. 1:6. He also compared his own calling to that of Paul, though on different grounds; cf. Comm. Gal. 1:15.

46. Comm. Matt. 26:75.

47. *Inst.*, II, vii, 4, and viii, 3; cf. Comm. Jer. 8:6.

48. *Harmonia ex tribus Evangelistis composita*, ep.

49. Comm. Gen. 23:2, first published five years after his own wife's death.
50. Text in *Proelectiones in librum prophetiarum Daniels* (Amsterdam, 1667), p. 206.
51. Comm. Luke 2:14.
52. *Inst.*, I, xiv, 13; cf. *Inst.*, ep. and Comm. Acts 1:4.
53. Serm. No. 14 on I Cor., 761.
54. *Inst.*, I, xiv, 18.
55. *Inst.*, III, ix, 1; Comm. Acts 12:1.
56. Serm. No. 54 on Job, 679.
57. Comm. I John 5:3.
58. *Inst.*, III, iii, 10.
59. Serm. No. 59 on Job, 98.
60. Serm. No. 27 on Job, 339. On the relation between patience and hope, see also Comms. Lam. 3:31 and Rom. 15:4.
61. *Inst.*, III, ix, 4; cf. Serm. No. 5 on I Cor., 634–635.
62. Serm. No. 98 on Job, 466–467.
63. Comm. II Tim. 2:3.
64. Comm. Is. 32:11.
65. Comms. Jer. 20:6, Ps. 119:67.
66. Serm. No. 5 on Job, 69–70; Comms. Ps. 46:4, Ps. 41:2; *Inst.*, III, ix, 1, and II, ii, 11.
67. Serm. No. 7 on Job, 95; Comm. Ps. 89:31.
68. Comm. Ps. 94:12.
69. Comm. Matt. 5:10.
70. Serm. No. 31 on II Sam., pp. 272–273.
71. Comm. I John 1:1
72. Comm. Ps. 119:116.
73. *Inst.*, IV, i, 29.
74. Serm. No. 55 on Job, 686.
75. Comm. Is. 43:5.
76. Comm. Ps. 22:2; cf. Comms. Gen. 42:9 and Ps. 73:11; *Inst.*, III, ii, 4, 16–18.
77. Comm. Ps. 94:18.
78. *Inst.*, III, ii, 21.
79. Serm. No. 55 on Job, 684–685.
80. Comm. Ps. 77:8.
81. Comm. Ps. 88:15.
82. Comm. Is. 12:2.
83. Serm. No. 55 on Job, 685; Comm. Jer. 14:10; *Inst.*, III, ii, 17, and iii, 10.
84. Serm. No. 6 on I Cor., 648–649.
85. Comm. Is. 7:2.
86. Cf. his letter to Volz, Aug. 14, 1518, *Opus epistolarum*, III, 370.
87. Comms. Jer. 10:20, John 12:25.
88. Comms. Jer. 5:4–5; cf. Comm. Matt. 24:43.
89. *Inst.*, III, vi, 5; Comm. Ps. 71:16.
90. Comm. Phil. 3:13.
91. Comm. John 12:25.
92. Comms. Ps. 119:33, Gen. 4:12.
93. *Inst.*, III, vi, 5.
94. Comm. Eph. 4:15: "proficiendum est usque ad mortem."
95. Comm. Heb. 5:12.

96. Serm. No. 98 on Job, 461.

97. *Life*, in *The Complete Works of Saint Teresa of Jesus*, trans. E. Allison Peers (London, 1950), I, pp. 69–70.

98. Comm. Is. 50:4.

99. Comms. Num. 27:5, Ps. 86:11.

100. Comm. Heb. 8:11; cf. *Inst.*, III, ii, 4.

101. Comm. Phil. 1:19; cf. Comms. I Thess. 4:10 and I John 2:5.

102. Comm. John 2:11. Of the disciples: "Ita qui iam credebant, quatenus ad scopum maiores quotidie faciunt progressus, credere incipiunt."

103. Comm. I Thess. 4:10.

104. *Inst.*, III, iii, 9; cf. Comm. Ps. 65:4.

105. Comm. Eph. 4:14–15.

106. Comms. Luke 2:33, 7:29.

107. *Inst.*, III, iii, 9.

108. *Inst.*, III, ii, 19.

Chapter 12

1. Comm. Jer. 1:9–10.

2. Comm. Is. 39:8.

3. *Inst.*, IV, xiii, 16.

4. Cf. Heiko A. Oberman, "The 'Extra Dimension' in the Theology of Calvin," *Journal of Ecclesiastical History*, XXI (1970), 45–46.

5. Serm. No. 45 on Deut., 426–427; italics added.

6. Serm. No. 30 on Deut., 238; I have altered the order of Calvin's clauses and added italics to bring out what seems to me his meaning.

7. Comm. Matt. 12:7.

8. Comm. Ps. 96:10.

9. Comm. Jer. 10:1–2.

10. Comm. Ezck. 8:16.

11. Comm. Is. 24:2.

12. Comm. I Cor. 7:14.

13. Comm. Dan. 11:37.

14. Comm. Gen. 13:7.

15. Comm. Gen. 14:23.

16. Comm. John 12:1; cf. Comm. Dan. 8:19. Calvin was here adapting the classical adage "Festina lente," a favorite of Erasmus. Cf. Margaret Mann Phillips, *The 'Adages' of Erasmus: A Study with Translations* (Cambridge, 1964), pp. 171–90.

17. Comm. Is. 13:6.

18. Cf. Comm. I Cor. 3:18, where he associates worldly wisdom with self-reliance.

19. Comm. I Cor. 13:7.

20. *Inst.*, I, xvii, 4. He was, however, insufficiently impressed with the book of Proverbs to comment on it.

21. On prudence in general, cf. Eugene F. Rice, *The Renaissance Idea of Wisdom* (Cambridge, Mass., 1958).

22. Comm. John 6:3.

23. *Inst.*, I, xvii, 4.

24. Comm. Is. 19:12.

25. Comm. Matt. 25:2.

26. Comm. Josh. 2:14; see also Comm. Gen. 26:2.

27. Serm. No. 15 on II Sam., 125.

28. Comm. Matt 5:39.

29. Comm. Matt. 5:48, 6:19.

30. Comms. Gen. 12:12, II Cor. 11:14. But cf. Serm. No. 30 on II Sam., 263, where he cautioned against excessive suspicion.

31. Comm. Matt. 5:39.

32. Comm. Jer. 2:24.

33. Comm. Josh. 8:15. The notion of art in war also suggests Machiavelli.

34. Serm. No. 8 on II Sam., 65.

35. Comm. Acts 4:1.

36. Comm. Num. 25:7.

37. Comm. Rom. 13:14.

38. Comm. I Cor. 11:2; italics added.

39. Comm. Is. 20:2; in *Inst.*, III, x, 2, Calvin argued that clothing is intended for propriety and decency as well as necessity.

40. Comm. II Cor. 8:21; cf. Comm. Gen. 26:8.

41. Comm. Ex. 4:18.

42. Comm. Is. 23:9.

43. Serm. No. 11 on I Cor., 720.

44. Serm. No. 11 on I Cor., 720. On the arbitrariness in the subjection of women to men, see also Serm. No. 12, 728.

45. Serm. No. 35 on Deut., 304.

46. Comm. Jer. 34:8–17.

47. Comm. Gen. 12:5.

48. Comm. Gen 6:4; italics added.

49. Comm. John 12:42; cf. Comms. Matt. 27:57 and James 2:5–6.

50. Comm. Jer. 9:5.

51. Comm. James 5:5.

52. *Inst.*, II, ii, xiv. But cf. Comm. Is. 28:29, where he expressed particular esteem for "the learned and exalted sciences such as medicine, jurisprudence, astronomy, geometry, logic, and such like."

53. Comm. Is. 3:4.

54. Comm. Is. 28:29.

55. Comm. Is. 28:14; see also Serm. No. 28 on II Sam., 250.

56. Comm. Gen. 26:14.

57. Comm. Num. 11:5.

58. Comm. Matt. 19:28.

59. Comm. John 2:1. The nostalgia here suggests Erasmus's colloquy *Diversoria*.

60. Comm. Matt. 19:23.

61. Comm. Acts 9:43. This recognition was still mingled with aristocratic disdain; he also observed that "a great crowd of people had received Christ, but they were the crowd, only the dregs of men" (Comm. Acts 13:50).

62. For example, Giovanni Botero, *Discorso della nobiltà*, included in his *Relationi universali* (Venice, 1640), p. 704.

63. Comm. Matt. 21:1.

64. Comm. Matt. 13:53–54.

65. Comm. Is. 23:2.

66. Comm. Is. 8:7.

67. Comm. Matt. 21:12.

68. Comm. Ex. 11:2. For the humanist attitude to wealth, cf. Hans Baron, "Franciscan Poverty and Civic Wealth as Factors in the Rise of Humanistic Thought," *Speculum* 13 (1938), 1–38.

69. Comm. II Cor. 8:15; see also Serm. No. 84 on Job, 287.

70. Comm. Matt. 19:20–22.

71. Comm. Jer. 22:16.

72. Serm. No. 2 on Job, 36.

73. Comm. Luke 6:25; see also Comm. Luke 6:24.

74. Comm. I Tim. 4:5; again Calvin departs from the Augustinian formula *utor non frui*.

75. Comm. Ex. 16:17; cf. Comm. Ezek. 7:12.

76. *Contre la secte des Libertins*, CO VII, 170.

77. Comm. Acts 2:44.

78. Comm. Gen. 23:16. He also knew that "money is the sinews of war" (Comm. Is. 45:2).

79. Comm. Gen. 47:16, 20. The case neverthless gave him trouble, and he came close to reversing himself, citing the Golden Rule: "It is certain that all contracts are wicked in God's sight that are not formed according to the rule of charity."

80. Comm. Is. 2:16. Again, as though he felt he had gone too far, he almost immediately reversed himself by denouncing riches as a source of luxury, effeminacy, and voluptuousness. This, he thought, was commonly seen in "wealthy countries and commercial cities."

81. Comm. Matt. 25:20, on the parable of the talents.

82. Comm. Ps. 15:5; Calvin here distinguished merchants from usurers.

83. Comm. Gen. 29:14.

84. Comm. Luke 6:35.

85. Comm. Ex 22:25. See Comm. Ps. 15:5 for a much stronger denunciation of usury: "It is scarcely possible to find in the world a usurer who is not at the same time an extortioner and addicted to unlawful and dishonorable gain. Accordingly Cato of old justly placed the practice of usury and the killing of men in the same rank of criminality, for the object of this class of people is to suck the blood of other men." The standard work on this and related aspects of Calvin's thought is André Biéler, *La penseé économique et sociale de Calvin* (Geneva, 1959).

86. Comm. Gen. 13:1.

87. Comm. Gen. 26:16.

88. Comm. Matt. 20:1.

89. Serm. No. 35 on Deut., 296; this repeats material in Comms. Gen. 2:15 and Ps. 127:1.

90. Comm. John 9:4.

91. Comm. I Thess. 4:11.

92. Comm. John 19:27. Cf. the condemnation of begging in the *Articles concernant l'organisation de l'église*, CO X, 25.

93. Comm. Matt. 6:25–30.

94. Serm. No. 2 on I Cor., 606.

95. Comm. Num. 4:4.

96. Comm. Ex. 18:13. For an extended discussion of the division of labor, see Serm. No. 13 on I Cor., 739.

97. Comm. I Cor. 7:20.

98. Comm. II Cor. 8:15. This also suggests the conclusion of Erasmus's *Convivium religiosum.*

99. Comm. Ex. 32:2.

100. Comm. Is. 5:8. Calvin often expressed his concern with this problem, the cause of much tension between Genevans and outsiders. Cf. Comm. Is. 16:4: "Let us therefore learn from this passage [on the 'outcasts of Moab'] to be kind and dutiful to fugitives and exiles, and especially to believers, who are banished for their confession of the Word. No duty can be more pleasing or acceptable to God."

101. Comm. Luke 7:44.

102. Comm. Luke 5:29.

103. Comm. Luke 7:44.

104. Comm. Luke 10:38.

105. Comm. Lam. 3:65.

106. Comm. Matt. 14:6.

107. Serm. No. 71. on Job, 115.

108. *Inst.*, III, vii, 5.

109. Comm. Acts 13:36; *Inst.*, II, viii, 55.

110. *Inst.*, III, vii, 5.

111. Comm. Eph. 5:22.

112. Serm. No. 71 on Job, 120; he develops the metaphor at some length here.

113. Comm. Sen., 82–85.

114. Serm. No. 101 on Job, 504; Comm. Rom., ep.

115. *The Protestant Ethic and the Spirit of Capitalism*, trans. Talcott Parsons (London, 1930), p. 104. It should be remembered, however, that Weber was careful not to attribute the "Calvinism" he described to Calvin himself.

116. Comms. Ps. 122:6, Matt. 5:25.

117. Comm. Is. 58:7.

118. *Inst.*, III, vii, 5.

119. Comm. John 6:13.

120. Comm. Ps. 112:9.

121. Comm. Ps. 31:19.

122. It was directed chiefly against the more radical sects; cf. Comm. II Cor. 8:13.

123. Comm. Ps. 15:5; italics added.

Chapter 13

1. Comm. Ezek. 8:12; cf. comm. Dan. 3:2–7.

2. *Inst.*, I, iii, 2; see above pp. 54–55, 63.

3. *Inst.*, III, xix, 15; cf. IV, xx, 1, where he repeated the distinction. It may be important, in view of what follows, to remember that these passages, which first appeared in the 1536 edition of the *Institutes*, were retained in later editions.

4. Letter to Myconius, Mar. 14, 1542, CO XI, 379.

5. *Responsio ad Sadoleti epistolam*, CO V, 389.

6. Comm. Ps. 82:1. On the general point, see the strong statement in Oberman, "Extra Dimension," 46–47.

7. Comm. Is. 49:23; Serm. No. 48 on Job, 599.

8. On the general point, cf. Höpfl, *Christian Polity of Calvin*, pp. 44–49.

9. *Inst.*, IV, xx, 4. This may be rhetorical hyperbole.

10. Comms. Num. 6:16, Deut. 1:16.

11. *Inst.*, II, viii, 46.

12. Comm. Ex. 18:15.

13. Comm. Ex. 2:12; *Inst.*, II, iii, 3.

14. Serm. No. 9 on II Sam., 77; Comm. I Tim. 2:2. Walzer is correct in seeing Calvin's state as "an order of repression" (*Revolution of the Saints*, pp. 30, 42), but it was more than this; see pp. 211–214.

15. Comm. Is. 3:5.

16. Comm. Jer. 30:9; Comm. Is. 34:12.

17. Comm. Gen. 20:9.

18. Comm. Is. 3:5.

19. Comm. Dan. 4:10–16; cf. Serm. No. 12 on I Cor., 731.

20. Comm. Ps. 127:1.

21. Comm. Is. 22:24.

22. Comm. Ps. 72:4; cf. *Inst.*, IV, xx, 10.

23. Serm. No. 9 on II Sam., 77.

24. Comm. Jer. 36:29–30; cf. Comm. Ps. 101:3.

25. Comm. Is. 22:24.

26. Comm. Lam. 5:14; cf. *Inst.*, II, ii, 13, on man as a social and civil being with an innate conception of law.

27. Comms. Dan. 6:8–9; John 19:11.

28. Comm. Deut. 1:16.

29. Comm. Acts 25:11; cf. Comms. Matt. 5:40, I Cor. 6:7, and *Inst.*, IV, xx, 17 and 21.

30. *Inst.*, IV xx, 8; cf. Comm. Acts 23:5.

31. *Inst.*, IV, xx, 22.

32. Comm. Is. 22:21.

33. Comm. Ps. 28:9.

34. *Inst.*, IV, xx, 23.

35. Comm. Acts 23:5.

36. *Inst.*, IV, xx, 8.

37. *Inst.*, IV, xx, 8. Calvin was not altogether consistent; cf. serm. No. 12 on II Sam., 102, where he pointed out that "even pagans" had been taught by God that "kings and princes" were appointed to be shepherds of their people. In Comm. Gen. 49:8 he also observed that when God instituted a government for his people, he chose monarchy. But both passages seem equivocal.

38. *Inst.*, IV, xx, 14, 15.

39. *Inst.*, IV, xx, 16.

40. *Inst.*, IV, vii, 15.

41. *Principles of Government and Politics in the Middle Ages* (Baltimore, 1966).

42. Cf. Hans Baron, "Calvinist Republicanism and its Historical Roots," *Church History*, VIII (1939), 30–41.

43. *Inst.*, IV, xx, 6.

44. Comm. Ex. 5:9. This passage, from the early period of the religious wars in France, seems unlikely to refer only to Pharaoh's treatment of the Israelites.

45. *Inst.*, IV, vii, 21.

46. Comm. Dan. 2:5.

47. Comm. Dan. 5:18–20.

48. Comm. Matt. 2:9.

49. Comm. is 3:12.

50. Comm. Is. 14:7–8.

51. *Inst.*, II, ii, 24.

52. Serm. No. 10 on II Sam., 86.

53. *Inst.*, IV, vi, 8–9.

54. Comm. Dan. 2:39; the image is from Isaiah 8:7; it is also central to Machiavelli's *Prince*.

55. Comm. Dan. 7:25.

56. Comm. Is. 47:10.

57. See Donald R. Kelley, "Civil Science in the Renaissance: Jurisprudence in the French Manner," *History of European Ideas*, 2 (1981), 262–263, for similar attitudes in the nationalism of French jurists.

58. Comm. Acts 4:19.

59. Comm. Jer. 37:18.

60. Comm. Ex. 1:17.

61. *Inst.*, IV, xx, 32.

62. Comm. Act 5:29. For what follows, see Quentin Skinner, *The Foundations of Modern Political Thought* (Cambridge, 1978), II, pp. 189–358.

63. *Inst.*, IV, xx, 8.

64. *Inst.*, IV, xx, 31.

65. *Inst.*, IV, xx, 30, 31.

66. *Inst.*, IV, xx, 8. His preference for republics was obviously not reduced by his belief that the papacy was hostile to them; cf. *Antidotum*, CO VII, 381.

67. Comm. Matt. 25:24.

68. Comm. Is. 3:5.

69. Cf. J. H. Hexter, *The Vision of Politics on the Eve of the Reformation: More, Machiavelli, and Seyssel* (New York, 1973), esp. pp. 154–156.

70. Comm. Is. 3:2, 4; cf. Comm. Ps. 122:3, where he discusses Jerusalem as a "well-ordered city [*urbs bene composita*]" and the broad interpretation he gives to "justice" and "judgment" in Comm. Gen. 18:19.

71. Comm. Jer. 7:5–7. "Strangers" suggests Calvin's interest in refugees.

72. Cf. Höpfl, *Christian Polity of Calvin*, pp. 44–49.

73. Cf. Comm. Matt. 22:21.

74. *Inst.*, IV, xi, 16; Calvin added this to the edition of 1543. For the denial of coercive power to the church, *Inst.*, IV, xi, 3.

75. *Ordonnances écclesiastiques*, CO X, 32.

76. Comm. Dan. 4:1–3. See also Comm. Deut. 13:5 and 19; Comm. Acts, 18: 12–14.

77. Comm. Is. 49:23; see also Comms. I Tim. 2:2 and Ex. 32:29.

78. Serm. No. 35 on Deut., 307.

79. Höpfl, *Christian Polity*, p. 66.

80. Comm. I Cor. 16:19; cf. Comm. Gen. 17:12.

81. Comm. Is. 38:19.

82. Comm. Acts 16:15.

83. Comm. Gen. 18:19.

84. Comm. Acts 10:2; cf. Comm. Gen. 18:6 for Calvin on Abraham's household as an example of sound domestic administration.

85. Comm. Is. 22:21.

86. Comm. Acts 16:15.

87. Comm. Jer. 26:10. His conclusion here suggests the Jesuit institution of the spiritual advisor: "If, then, private persons need to be taught daily, so that they may

govern themselves and their families properly, what should be done by rulers, who are like fathers of the commonweal?''

88. Comm. Josh. 7:19.

89. *Inst.*, IV, xx, 2; cf. Comm. Is. 49:23.

90. *Inst.*, IV, xx, 3.

91. *Inst.*, IV, xx, 9.

Chapter 14

1. *Confession de foy de Genève*, CO IX, 698; *Catéchisme de Genève*, CO VI, 41–42.

2. Comm. Is. 49:18.

3. *Admonitio Pauli III ad Caesarem. Cum Scholüs*, CO VII, 258, 283; cf. Comm. Acts 4:29 on the pope's forfeiture of his paternal authority.

4. *Inst.*, IV, i, 4.

5. Cf. Ganoczy, *Jeune Calvin*, p. 96, and Heiko Oberman, "The Shape of Late Medieval Thought: The Birthpangs of the modern Era," *Archiv für Reformationsgeschichte*, LXIV (1973), 13–33.

6. *Responsio ad Sadoleti epistolam*, CO X, 409.

7. Comm. Ps. 133:1.

8. Comm. Jer. 32:39.

9. Comms. Act 24:14, II Thess. 2:3; *Inst.*, IV, i, 5.

10. *Inst.*, IV, vi, 2, and viii, 12–13; Comms. Matt. 10:2, I Cor. 9:5.

11. *Admonitio Pauli III*, CO VII, 259. He denied the unity of the Roman church on this ground (*Traité des scandales*, p. 246).

12. *Inst.*, IV, i, 9.

13. Serm. No. 73 on Job, 141–142.

14. Comm. Acts 19:23–24.

15. Comm. Dan. 11:33–34; cf. Comm. Rom. 12:6 and *Inst.*, III, vii, 5.

16. Comm. Jer. 7:21–24; *Inst.*, I, xii, 3. Cf. Höpfl, *Christian Polity of Calvin*, pp. 38–41.

17. *Inst.*, III, xx, 33; Comm. I Cor. 14:14–16.

18. *Inst.*, IV, i, 5.

19. Comm. Ps. 148:11.

20. Comm. John 7:50; his most general attack on Nicodemism is *Excuse à Messieurs les Nicodemites*, CO VI, 589–614.

21. Comm. Gen. 12:7. He also denounced Nicodemism from the pulpit; see Serm. No. 3 on I Cor., 616.

22. Letter to Viret, Aug. 23, 1542, CO XI, 431.

23 *Petit traicté de la s. Cène*, CO V, 443; Calvin was drawing here on I Cor. 10:17.

24. Serm. No. 7 on I Cor., 663–664.

25. *Articles concernant l'Eglise et du culte à Genève*, CO X, 7; he took up the matter again in the *Ordonnances ecclésiastiques of 1541*, CO X, 25.

26. Serm. No. 19 on I Cor., 820; cf. Comm. Matt. 26:26 and *Inst.*, IV, xviii, 8.

27. Serm. No. 19 on I Cor., 819–820.

28. *Inst.*, IV, x, 27.

29. *Inst.*, IV, xii, 1.

30. Serm. No. 11 on I Cor., 712.

31. On this analogy cf. Walzer, *Revolution of the Saints*, p. 51, and Höpfl, *Christian Polity of Calvin*, p. 54.

32. *Inst.*, IV, xi, 8.

33. Comms. Gal. 2:9, Jer. 3:5.

34. *Inst.*, IV, xi, 3.

35. Comm. Is. 4:3.

36. Comm. Ps. 133:2. But cf. Serm. No. 13 on II Sam., 114: "nous ne refusions pas toutes amytiés de ceux qui ne seront pas encores réduitz en l'obéissance de Dieu. Car 'il nous faudroit sortir de ce monde' si nous voulions nous séparer du tout de ceux qui ne scavent que c'est de la vraye religion."

37. Serm. No. 35 on Deut. 306–307.

38. Letter to Farel, Mar. 1539, CO X, 331.

39. Comm. Jer. 3:6–8.

40. Comm. Acts 21:18.

41. *Inst.*, IV, xi, 6.

42. Comm. Gal. 6:1; Serms. on Job, No. 15, 193–194; No. 72, 135–136; No. 78, 207.

43. Serms. on Job, No. 18, 223; No. 56, 699.

44. Serm. No. 9 on II Sam., 30.

45. Letter to Farel, May 1540, CO XI, 41. Calvin was then in Strasbourg, where his church was small and such surveillance was more practicable than it might have been elsewhere.

46. *Articles concernant l'organisation de l'Eglise*, CO X, 5–6.

47. Letter to the pastors of Zürich, Nov. 26, 1553, CO XIV, 676.

48. *Inst.*, IV, xii, 4.

49. *Inst.*, IV, xii, 5; cf. Comms. I Tim. 1:20, I Cor. 5:4 and 11.

50. Comm. John 9:22.

51. Letter to the pastors of Zürich, Nov. 26, 1553, CO XIV, 676.

52. Serm. No. 43 on Deut., 405.

53. *Inst.*, IV, iii, 2.

54. Cf. Höpfl, *Christian Polity of Calvin*, pp. 106–107.

55. Comm. John 7:48.

56. June 25, 1539, CO X, 352.

57. Cf. Comm. Jer. 31–14.

58. *Admonitio Pauli III*, CO VII, 266–267; the incident is in II Sam. 6:7. Calvin's explanation, which has no explicit basis in the text, is curiously at odds with his treatment of the episode in Serm. No. 17 on II Sam., 142, in which he represented the death of Uzzah as illustrating that "the judgments of God are a profound abyss."

59. Letter to Myconius, Mar. 14., 1542, CO XI, 379.

60. Comm. Acts. 5:32.

61. *Inst.*, IV, iii, 11; Comm. Jer. 23:21. Calvin, with his usual practicality, also thought it permissible to offer oneself for the ministry in anticipation of a call (Comm. I Tim. 3:1).

62. Comm. Jer. 20:7.

63. Comm. Jer. 17:16.

64. *Le catéchisme français*, CO V, 319.

65. Comm. I Tim. 3:15. For similar anxieties among pre-Reformation clergy, cf. Douglass, *Justification in Late Medieval Theology*, p. 153.

66. Cf. Comm. Is. 49:4.

67. Cf. Comm. Matt. 10:16. Some of this may also echo John Chrysostom, *De sacerdotio*.

68. Comm. Jer. 15:10.

69. Comm. I Tim. 5:19.

70. *Confession de la foy*, CO IX, 699.

71. Comm. Is. 58:2

72. Comm. I Tim. 5:19.

73. Comm. Jer. 34:21.

74. Comm. Jer. 13:18. "Queens" suggests that Calvin had particularly in mind Catherine de' Medici, Mary of Scotland, and perhaps Elizabeth of England.

75. Comm. Matt. 10:23; cf. Comm. Acts 14:5.

76. Comm. Dan. 11:33–34.

77. Comm. Acts 1:24.

78. Comm. Acts 20:20.

79. Comm. II Cor. 11:20.

80. Comm. Deut. 17:12.

81. Comm. Jer. 43:8–10; italics added.

82. Serm. No. 44 on Deut., 413.

83. Comm. II Cor. 4:3.

84 *Inst.*, IV, iv, 6.

85. Comm. Gal. 6:6; see also Comm. II Thess. 3:6.

86. *Inst.*, IV, i, 12.

87. Serm. No. 11 on I Cor., 711.

88. *Inst.*, IV, x, 31; italics added.

89. Comm. I Cor. 14:36.

90. Comm. I Cor. 11:2.

91. *Inst.*, IV, iv, 2. On the general point, cf. Jacques Pannier, *Calvin et l'épisco-pat* (Strasbourg, 1927).

92. Comm. Phil. 1:1.

93. *Inst.*, IV, x, 27.

94. *Catechismus sive Christianae religionis institutio*, CO V, 322.

95. Comm. Acts 8:38.

96. Comm. Matt 9:14.

97. *Supplex exhortatio*, CO VI, 493.

98. *Inst.*, IV, x, 28–29.

99. Comm. Dan. 6:10.

100. Cf. Serm. No. 39 on II Sam., 339–340; see also *Inst.*, IV, xii, 17. He objected only to making it mandatory and "binding on consciences" (*Traité des scandales*, pp. 271–272).

101. Comm. Ps. 50:14.

102. Serm. No. 18 on II Sam., 155–156.

103. Comm. Matt. 11:12.

104. Serm. No. 16 on II Sam., 140; cf. Comm. Ps. 33:2.

105. Quoted by Garside, "Calvin's Theology of Music," 18–19; this work is also generally useful on the point.

106. *Inst.*, III, xx, 32.

107. *Articles concernant l'organisation de l'Eglise*, CO X, 6.

108. *Inst.*, III, xx, 32; cf. Parker, *Calvin*, pp. 87–88.

109. *Articles concernant l'organisation de l'Eglise*, CO X, 12.

110. Comm. Jer. 14:22, 32:16–18; *Inst.*, III, xx, 2; Serm. No. 70 on Job, 102.

111. Comms. I Tim. 3:4, Acts 4:17.

112. Comm. Jer. 1:9–10; see also *Inst.*, IV, viii, 1.

113. Comms. II Cor. 1:24, 4:5; Matt. 20:25.

114. Comm. I Cor. 3:22, 4:3; Serm. No. 26 on Job, 323.

115. *Inst.*, IV, iii, 15; Comm. Acts 6:3. Calvin believed this described the practice of the ancient church; cf. *Inst.*, IV, iv, 10.

116. *Inst.*, IV, iv, 11–12; *Supplex exhortatio*, CO VI, 491.

117. *Christian Polity of Calvin*, p. 92.

118. Comm. Ps. 125:1.

119. Comm. Matt. 24:40.

120. Comm. Is. 29:11–12.

121. Serm. No. 42 on Deut., 384–385; Comm. Acts 15:30; Serm. No. 26 on Job, 322; Comm. John 7:49.

122. Comm. John 1:45.

123. Serm. No. 43 on Deut., 406; Comm. Is. 2:3. See also Serm. No. 78 on Job, 209; and Comm. Dan. 9:1–3.

124. Comm. Ps. 119:171, 22:31; see also Comm. Heb. 5:12 and Serm. No. 59. on Job, 733.

125. Comm. Ps. 119:35; cf. Battles, "God Was Accommodating," 29–30, on the patristic backgrounds of the conception of God as teacher.

126. Comm. Jer. 32:40.

127. *Inst.*, I, vi, 4.

128. Serm. No. 34 on Job 9:7–8, 419.

129. Comm. Jer. 32:33.

130. *Supplex Exhortatio*, CO VI, 490–491.

131. Comm. Ps. 19:7.

132. *Inst.*, IV, iii, 1.

133. Comms. Deut. 6:6, Jer. 9:23–34; see also Comm. Phil. 3:1.

134. Comm. Acts 26:25.

135. Comm. I Thess. 2:12.

136. Jer. 4:21; cf. Comm. Deut. 32:44.

137. Comm. Acts 18:25.

138. *Inst.*, III, xxiii, 13. But cf. III, xxiv, 13, on the problem posed for Calvin by those who listen without benefit.

139. Comm. Jer. 9:17–18.

140. Serm. No. 6 on I Cor., 652.

141. Comm. II Cor. 13:5.

142. Comm. Hos. 2:19–20.

143. Comm. Luke 1:16; see also Comm. Rom. 11:14.

144. Comm. John 17:1.

145. Comm. Dan. 4:20–22; cf. Comm. Ezek. 3:18.

146. Comm. Matt. 18:21; cf. Comm. Gen. 45:3 on Joseph's treatment of his brothers. Calvin was critical of the ancient church for driving sinners to despair (Comm. II Cor. 2:6).

147. *Contre les erreurs des Anabaptistes*, CO VII, 77.

148. Comm. Matt. 23:4.

149. Cf. *Inst.*, IV, xii, 9.

150. Cf. his letter to Farel, Dec. 19, 1539, CO X, 435.

151. Comm. Ps. 26:5.

152. Comm. Matt. 23:1.

153. *Contre les erreurs des Anabaptistes*, CO VII, 68.

154. Comm. Ps. 15:1; see also Comms. Gen. 43:32 and Matt. 13:37.

155. Comm. Dan. 11:33–34.

156. Serm. No. 18 on I Cor., 810.

Conclusion

1. "De l'inconstance de nos actions," *Essais*, II, pp. 1–2; I quote from the translation by Donald Frame. For similar sentiments in Calvin, see p. 133.

2. Cf. p. 159.

3. *Fortune Is a Woman*, p. 285; for Stephen Greenblatt's similar characterization of Thomas More, see *Renaissance Self-Fashioning*, pp. 36–37, and *passim*.

4. In discussing "secularism," everything depends on definition; among treatments of this disputed term, I find particularly satisfying that of Larry Shiner, "The Meanings of Secularization," *International Yearbook for the Sociology of Religion*, 3 (1967), pp. 51–59.

5. *Revolution of the Saints*, pp. 307–316.

BIBLIOGRAPHY

I. Editions, Citations, and Translations

Unless otherwise indicated, I refer to Calvin's work in the Corpus Reformatorum edition, *Ioannis Calvini Opera quae supersunt omnia*, ed. G. Baum, E. Cunitz, and E. Reuss (Brunswick and Berlin, 1863–1900), cited throughout as CO. I have assumed that those wishing to look directly at the texts will be familiar with this edition; accordingly I have not indicated volume or column numbers except in the case of lengthier works. For Calvin's sermons on II Samuel, I cite from the Supplementa Calviniana: Sermons inédits, *Prëdigten über das 2. Buch Samuelis*, ed. Hanns Rückert (Neukirchen, 1961); for his Seneca commentary, *Calvin's Commentary on Seneca's De Clementia*, tr. and ed. Ford Lewis Battles and Andre Malan Hugo (Leiden, 1969); and for his *Traité des scandales* the version in *Oeuvres de Jean Calvin*, ed. Albert-Marie Schmidt (Paris, 1934), II, 143–197.

I have been helped by the translations of Calvin by Benjamin W. Farley, *John Calvin's Sermons on the Ten Commandments* (Grand Rapids, 1980); John W. Fraser, *Concerning Scandals: John Calvin* (Grand Rapids, 1978); John C. Olin, *John Calvin and Jacopo Sadoleto: A Reformation Debate* (New York, 1966); and those included in *Calvin: Theological Treatises*, ed. J. K. S. Reid (London, 1954) [vol. XXII in the Library of Christian Classics]; and in *Calvin's New Testament Commentaries*, ed. David W. Torrance and Thomas F. Torrance (Grand Rapids, 1963–1974). In many cases, however, I have made new translations of my own, especially for Calvin's Old Testament commentaries. Anyone who has compared the Latin of the *Corpus Reformatorum* with the nineteenth-century translations of the Calvin Text Society, will understand why I have done so. With occasional exceptions, however, I have usually followed the excellent translation of the *Institutes* by Ford Lewis Battles in the Library of Christian Classics (London, 1961).

As my work progressed, I found that my translations tended to be increasingly free, but I have taken this as a sign of growing confidence that I understood Calvin's meaning. At any rate the peculiar publication history of his sermons and commentaries suggests how little we can be certain that our texts of these works represent Calvin's exact words. Quotation marks in written reports of oral discourse, as Jack Hexter has noted, do not have quite the same significance as elsewhere.*

II. Works Cited

Ariès, Philippe. *The Hour of Our Death*. Tr. Helen Weaver. New York, 1981.

Auerbach, Erich. *Literary Language and Its Public in Late Latin Antiquity and in the Middle Ages*. Princeton, 1965.

————. *Mimesis: The Representation of Reality in Western Literature*. Tr. Willard R. Trask. Princeton, 1953.

Babelotsky, Gerd. *Platonischer Bilder und Gedankengänge in Calvins Lehre vom Menschen*. Wiesbaden, 1977.

Baldwin, John W. *Masters, Princes and Merchants: The Social Views of Peter the Chanter and His Circle*. Princeton, 1970.

Balke, Willem. *Calvin and the Anabaptist Radicals*. Tr. William J. Heynen. Grand Rapids, 1981.

Barish, Jonas. *The Antitheatrical Prejudice*. Berkeley, 1981.

Baron, Hans. "Calvinist Republicanism and Its Historical Roots." *Church History*, VIII. 1939.

———— *The Crisis of the Early Italian Renaissance: Civic Humanism and Republican Liberty in an Age of Classicism and Tyranny*. Princeton, 1955.

———— "Franciscan Poverty and Civic Wealth as Factors in the Rise of Humanistic Thought." *Speculum*, 13. 1938.

Baron, Salo W. "John Calvin." *Encyclopaedia Judaica*. Jerusalem, 1972.

Barth, Karl. *Church Dogmatics*. Tr. G. T. Thompson et al. Edinburgh, 1932–1969.

Battenhouse, Roy W. "The Doctrine of Man in Calvin and Renaissance Platonism." *Journal of the History of Ideas*, IX. 1948.

Battles, Ford Lewis. *Calculus Fidei: Some Ruminations on the Structure of the Theology of John Calvin*. Grand Rapids, 1978.

————. "The Future of Calviniana." *Renaissance, Reformation, Resurgence*. Ed. Peter de Klerk. Grand Rapids, 1976.

————. "God Was Accommodating Himself to Human Capacity." *Interpretation*, 31. 1977.

————. "The Sources of Calvin's Seneca Commentary." *Calvin*, ed. G. E. Duffield. Appleford, 1966.

Baxandall, Michael. *Painting and Experience in Fifteenth Century Italy*. Oxford, 1972.

Bedouelles, Georges. *Lefèvre d'Étaples et l'intelligence des écritures*. Geneva, 1977.

Bergier, Jean-François, and Kingdon, Robert M., eds. *Registres de la Compagnie des Pasteurs de Genève au temps de Calvin*. Geneva, 1962–1964.

Bergin, Thomas Goddard, and Fisch, Max Harold. *The New Science of Giambattista Vico*. Ithaca, 1968.

Biéler, André. *La pensée économique et sociale de Calvin*. Geneva, 1959.

Blumenberg, Hans. *The Legitimacy of the Modern Age*. Tr. Robert M. Wallace. Cambridge, Mass., 1983.

————. *Work on Myth*. Tr. Robert M. Wallace. Cambridge, Mass., 1985.

*J.H. Hexter, "Quoting the Commons, 1604–1642," *Tudor Rule and Revolution: Essays for G. R. Elton from His American Friends*, ed. DeLloyd J. Guth and John W. McKenna (London, 1982), 369–391.

Bohatec, Josef. *Budé und Calvin: Studien zur Gedankenwelt des französischen Frühhumanismus*. Graz, 1950.

Borgeaud, Charles. *Histoire de l'Université de Genève*. Geneva, 1900–1934.

Botero, Giovanni. *Relationi universali*. Venice, 1640.

Bouwsma, William J. "Anxiety and the Formation of Early Modern Culture." *After the Reformation: Essays in Honor of J. H. Hexter*. Ed. Barbara C. Malament. Philadelphia, 1980.

Boyle, Marjorie O'Rouke. *Erasmus on Language and Method in Theology*. Toronto, 1977.

———. *Rhetoric and Reform: Erasmus' Civil Dispute with Luther*. Cambridge, Mass., 1983.

———. "For Peasants, Psalms: Erasmus' *editio princeps* of Hayms (1533)." *Medieval Studies*, XLIV. 1982.

Brady, Thomas A., Jr. *Turning Swiss*. Cambridge, 1985.

Breen, Quirinus. *John Calvin: A Study in French Humanism*. Chicago, 1931.

———. "John Calvin and the Rhetorical Tradition." *Church History*, XXVI. 1957.

———. "Melanchthon's Reply to G. Pico della Mirandola." *Journal of the History of Ideas*, 13. 1952.

Brown, Peter. *Augustine of Hippo*. Berkeley, 1967.

Camporeale, Salvatore. "Lorenzo Valla tra Medioevo e Rinascimento: Ecomion S. Thomae—1457." *Memorie Domenicane* N.S., 7. 1976.

———. *Lorenzo Valla: umanesimo e teologia*. Florence, 1972.

———. "Umanesimo e teologia tra '400 e '500." *Memorie Domenicane*, N.S., 8–9. 1977–1978.

Cassirer, Ernst. *Essay on Man: An Introduction to a Philosophy of Human Culture*. New Heaven, 1962.

Chenu, M. D. *Nature, Man, and Society in the Twelfth Century: Essays on New Theological Perspectives in the Latin West*. Eds. Jerome Taylor and Lester K. Little. Chicago, 1968.

Chrisman, Miriam U. *Lay Culture, Learned Culture: Books and Social Change in Strasbourg, 1480–1599*. New Haven, 1982.

Cranz, F. Edward. "Philosophy." *Renaissance News*, XIX. 1966.

Curtius, Ernst Robert. *European Literature and the Latin Middle Ages*. Tr. Willard R. Trask. New York, 1953.

Dillenberger, John. *Contours of Faith: Changing Forms of Christian Thought*. Nashville and New York, 1969.

Douglas, Mary. *Purity and Danger: An Analysis of Concepts of Pollution and Taboo*. London, 1966.

Douglas, Richard M. "Talent and Vocation in Humanist and Protestant Thought." *Action and Conviction in Early Modern Europe: Essays in Memory of E. H. Harbison*. Eds. Theodore K. Rabb and Jerrold E. Seigel. Princeton, 1969.

Douglass, E. Jane Dempsey. "Christian Freedom: What Calvin Learned at the School of Women." *Church History*, 53. 1984.

———. *Justification in Late Medieval Preaching: A Study of John Geiler of Keisersberg*. Leiden, 1966.

———. *Women, Freedom, and Calvin*. Philadelphia, 1985.

Doumergue, Émile. *Jean Calvin: Les hommes et les choses de son temps*. Lausanne, 1899–1928.

Dowey, Edward A. *The Knowledge of God in Calvin's Theology*. New York, 1952.

Elton, G. R. "Commemorating Luther." *Journal of Ecclesiastical History*, 35. 1984.

Febvre, Lucien. *Le problème de l'incroyance au XVIe siècle: la religion de Rabelais.* Paris, 1942.

Fredricksen, Paula. "Paul and Augustine: Conversion Narratives, Orthodox Traditions, and the Retrospective Self." *Journal of Theological Studies,* N.S., 37. 1986.

Ganoczy, Alexandre. *Le jeune Calvin: genèse et évolution de sa vocation reformatrice.* Wiesbaden, 1966.

Garin, Eugenio. *L'umanesimo italiano: filosofia e vita civile nel Rinascimento.* Bari, 1964.

Garside, Charles Jr. "The Origins of Calvin's Theology of Music, 1536–43." *Transactions of the American Philosophical Society,* 69. 1979.

Giamatti, A. Bartlett. *Exile and Change in Renaissance Literature.* New Haven, 1982.

Gilmore, Myron P. *Humanists and Jurists: Six Studies in the Renaissance.* Cambridge, Mass., 1963.

Ginzburg, Carlo. *Il Nicodemismo: Simulazione e dissimulazione nell'Europa del '500.* Turin, 1970.

Girardin, B. *Rhétorique et théologique: Calvin. le Commentaire de l'Épitre aux Romains* [Théologique Historique, 54]. Paris, 1979.

Greene, Thomas M. *The Light in Troy: Imitation and Discovery in Renaissance Poetry.* New Haven, 1982.

Greenblatt, Stephen. "Filthy Rites." *University Publishing,* 8. 1979.

———. *Renaissance Self-Fashioning: More to Shakespeare.* Chicago, 1980.

Greven, Philip. *The Protestant Temperament: Patterns of Child-Rearing, Religious Experience, and the Self in Early America.* New York, 1977.

Hall, Basil. "The Calvin Legend." *John Calvin.* Ed. G. E. Duffield. Appleford, Abingdon, 1966.

———. "Calvin against the Calvinists." *John Calvin.* Ed. G.E. Duffield. Appleford, Abingdon, 1966.

Hexter, J. H. "Quoting the Commons, 1604–1642." *Tudor Rule and Revolution: Essays for G. R. Elton from His American Friends.* Ed. DeLloyd J. Guth and John W. McKenna. London, 1982.

———. *The Vision of Politics on the Eve of the Reformation: More, Machiavelli, and Seyssel.* New York, 1973.

Higman, Francis Montgomery. *The Style of John Calvin in His French Polemical Treatises.* London, 1967.

Hooykaas, R. *Religion and the Rise of Modern Science.* Edinburgh and London, 1972.

Höpfl, Harro. *The Christian Polity of John Calvin.* Cambridge, 1982.

Hughes, Philip Edgcumbe. *Lefèvre: Pioneer of Ecclesiastical Renewal in France.* Grand Rapids, 1984.

Kelley, Donald R. "Civil Science in the Renaissance: Jurisprudence in the French Manner." *History, Law and the Human Sciences.* London, 1984.

———. *Foundations of Modern Historical Scholarship: Language, Law, and History in the French Renaissance.* New York, 1970.

———. *François Hotman: A Revolutionary's Ordeal.* Princeton, 1973.

Kellner, Hans. "Triangular Anxieties: The Present State of European Intellectual History." *Modern European Intellectual History.* Eds. Dominick LaCapra and Steven L. Kaplan. Ithaca, 1982.

Kendall, R. T. *Calvin and English Calvinism to 1649.* Oxford, 1980.

Kingdon, Robert M. "Social Welfare in Calvin's Geneva." *American Historical Review*, 76. 1971.

―――. *Geneva and the Coming of the Wars of Religion in France*. Geneva, 1956.

―――. "The Control of Morals in Calvin's Geneva." *The Social History of the Reformation*. Eds. Lawrence P. Buck and Jonathan W. Zophy. Columbus, Ohio, 1972.

Kittelson, James. *Wolfgang Capito: From Humanist to Reformer*. Leiden, 1975.

Klibansky, Raymond. *Saturn and Melancholy: Studies in the History of Natural Philosophy, Religion and Art*. New York, 1964.

Kristeller, P. O. *Renaissance Thought: The Classic, Scholastic and Humanist Strains*. New York, 1961.

LaCapra, Dominick. "Rethinking Intellectual History and Reading Texts." *Modern European Intellectual History*. Eds. Dominick La Capra and Steven L. Kaplan. Ithaca, 1982.

Ladner, Gerhart B. "Reformatio." *Ecumenical Dialogue at Harvard: The Roman Catholic-Protestant Colloquium*. Eds. Samuel H. Miller and G. Ernest Wright. Cambridge, Mass., 1964.

―――. *The Idea of Reform: Its Impact on Christian Thought and Action in the Age of the Fathers*. Cambridge, Mass., 1959.

Leff, Gordon. *Gregory of Rimini: Tradition and Innovation in Fourteenth Century Thought*. New York, 1961.

Lefranc, Abel. *La jeunesse de Calvin*. Paris, 1888.

Levao, Ronald. *Renaissance Minds and Their Fictions: Cusanus, Sidney, Shakespeare*. Berkeley, 1985.

Little, David. *Religion, Order, and Law: A Study in Pre-Revolutionary England*. New York, 1969.

Little, Lester K. "Pride Goes before Avarice: Social Change and the Vices in Latin Christendom." *American Historical Review*, 76. 1971.

Macintyre, Alisdair. "Epistemological Crises, Dramatic Narrative and the Philosophy of Science." *Monist*, 61. 1977.

May, Gerald. *Care of Mind, Care of Spirit: Psychiatric Dimensions of Spiritual Direction*. San Francisco, 1982.

McNeill, John T. "Natural Law in the Teaching of the Reformers." *Journal of Religion*, XXVI. 1946.

Miles, Margaret R. "Theology, Anthropology, and the Human Body in Calvin's *Institutes of the Christian Religion*." *Harvard Theological Review*, 74. 1981.

Miller, Perry. *The New England Mind: The Seventeenth Century*. New York, 1939.

Milner, Benjamin Charles Jr. *Calvin's Doctrine of the Church* [Studies in the History of Christian Thought, 5]. Leiden, 1970.

Mommsen, Theodor E. "Petrarch's Conception of the 'Dark Ages.'"*Speculum*, XVII. 1942.

Monter, William. *Calvin's Geneva*. New York, 1967.

Mullett, Michael. *Radical Religious Movements in Early Modern Europe*. London, 1980.

Nauert, Charles G. Jr. *Agrippa and the Crisis of Renaissance Thought*. Urbana, 1965.

Norena, Carlos G. *Juan Luis Vives*. The Hague, 1970.

Oberman, Heiko A. "The 'Extra Dimension' in the Theology of Calvin," *Journal of Ecclesiastical History*, XXI. 1970.

———. *The Harvest of Medieval Theology: Gabriel Biel and Late Medieval Nominalism*. Cambridge, Mass., 1963.

———. "The Shape of Late Medieval Thought: The Birthpangs of the Modern Era." *Archiv für Reformationsgeschichte*, LXIV. 1973.

———. *Werden und Wertung der Reformation: Vom Wegestreit zum Glaubenskampf*. Tübingen, 1977.

Ozment, Steven E. *Homo Spiritualis: A Comparative Study of the Anthropology of Johannes Tauler, Jean Gerson and Martin Luther in the Context of Their Theological Thought* [Studies in Medieval and Reformation Thought, 6]. Leiden, 1969.

———. *The Reformation in the Cities: The Appeal of Protestantism to Sixteenth-Century Germany and Switzerland*. New Haven, 1975.

Pannier, Jacques. *Calvin et l'épiscopat*. Strasbourg, 1927.

Parker, T.H.L. *Calvin's Doctrine of the Knowledge of God*. Rev. ed., Edinburgh, 1969.

———. *Calvin's New Testament Commentaries*. London, 1971.

———. *John Calvin: A Biography*. London, 1975.

———. *The Oracles of God: An Introduction to the Preaching of John Calvin*. London, 1962.

Partee, Charles. *Calvin and Classical Philosophy* [Studies in the History of Christian Thought, 14]. Leiden, 1977.

Peter, Rodolphe. "Rhétorique et prédication selon Calvin." *Revue d'histoire et de philosophie religieuses*, LV. 1975.

Pfister, Oskar. *Das Christentum und die Angst: eine religionspsychologische, historische und religionshygienische Untersuchungen*. Zürich, 1944.

Phillips, Margaret Mann. *The 'Adages' of Erasmus: A Study with Translations*. Cambridge, 1964.

Pitkin, Hanna F. *Fortune Is a Woman: Gender and Politics in the Thought of Niccolo Machiavelli*. Berkeley, 1984.

Prestwich, Menna, ed. *International Calvinism, 1541–1715*. Oxford, 1985.

Preus, James. S. *From Shadow to Promise: Old Testament Interpretation from Augustine to Luther*. Cambridge, Mass., 1969.

Raitt, Jill. "Calvin's Use of Bernard of Clairvaux." *Archiv für Reformationsgeschichte*, 72. 1981.

Regosin, Richard L. "Recent Trends in Montaigne Scholarship: A Post-Structuralist Perspective." *Renaissance Quarterly*, XXXVII. 1984.

Reid, W. Stanford, ed. *John Calvin: His Influence in the Western World*. Grand Rapids, 1982.

Renaudet, Augustin. *Préréforme et l'humanisme à Paris pendant les premières guerres de l'Italie (1494–1517)*. Paris, 1916; rev. ed. 1953.

Rice, Eugene F. *The Renaissance Idea of Wisdom*. Cambridge, Mass., 1958.

———. *Saint Jerome in the Renaissance*. Baltimore, 1985.

Richard, Lucien. *The Spirituality of Calvin*. Atlanta, 1974.

Screech, Michael. *Rabelais*. Ithaca, 1980

Seigel, Jerrold E. *Rhetoric and Philosophy in Renaissance Humanism: Ciceronian Elements in Early Quattrocento Thought and Their Historical Setting*. Princeton, 1968.

Selinger, Suzanne. *Calvin against Himself: An Inquiry in Intellectual History*. Hamden, Conn., 1984.

Shapiro, Barbara. *Probability and Certainty in Seventeenth-Century England: A*

Study of the Relationships between Natural Science, Religion, History, Law, and Literature. Princeton, 1983.

Shiner, Larry. "The Meanings of Secularization." *International Yearbook for the Sociology of Religion*, 3. 1967.

Shumaker, Wayne. *The Occult Sciences in the Renaissance: A Study in Intellectual Patterns*. Berkeley, 1972.

Simoncelli, Paolo. *Evangelismo italiano del Cinquecento: Questione religiosa e nico-demismo politico*. Rome, 1979.

Skinner, Quentin. *The Foundations of Modern Political Thought*. Cambridge, 1978.

Smits, Luchesius. *Saint Augustin dans l'oeuvre de Jean Calvin*. Louvain, 1957.

Sprenger, Paul. *Das Rätsel um die Bekehrung Calvins*. Neukirchen, 1960.

Starn, Randolph. *Contrary Commonwealth: The Theme of Exile in Medieval and Renaissance Italy*. Berkeley, 1982.

Stauffer, Richard. "Le discours à la première personne dans les sermons de Calvin." *Regards contemporains sur Jean Calvin*. Paris, 1965.

———. *L'Humanité de Calvin*. Neuchatel, 1964.

Steinmetz, David Curtis. *Misericordia Dei: The Theology of Johannes von Staupitz in Its Late Medieval Setting*. Leiden, 1968.

———. "The Theology of Calvin and Calvinism." *Reformation Europe: A Guide to Research*. Ed. Steven Ozment. St. Louis, 1982.

Stinger, Charles L. *The Renaissance in Rome*. Bloomington, 1985.

Struever, Nancy S. *The Language of History in the Renaissance: Rhetoric and Historical Consciousness in Florentine Humanism*. Princeton, 1970.

Tenenti, Alberto. *Il senso della morte e l'amore della vita nel Rinascimento*. Florence, 1957.

Tentler, Thomas. *Sin and Confession on the Eve of the Reformation,*. Princeton, 1977.

Thomas, Keith. *Religion and the Decline of Magic: Studies in Popular Beliefs in Sixteenth and Seventeenth Century England*. London, 1971.

Torrance, Thomas Forsyth. *Calvin's Doctrine of Man*. London, 1952.

Tracy, James. *Erasmus: The Growth of a Mind*. Geneva, 1972.

Trevor-Roper, Hugh R. *Religion, the Reformation, and Social Change*. London, 1967.

Trilling, Lionel. *Sincerity and Authenticity*. Cambridge, Mass., 1972.

Trinkaus, Charles. "Humanist Treatises on the Status of the Religious." *Studies in the Renaissance*, XI. 1964.

———. *'In Our Image and Likeness': Humanity and Divinity in Italian Humanist Thought*. Chicago, 1970.

———. "Renaissance Problems in Calvin's Theology." *Studies in the Renaissance*, I. 1954.

———. "The Religious Thought of the Italian Humanists and the Reformers: Anticipation or Autonomy?" *The Pursuit of Holiness*. Eds. Charles Trinkaus and Heiko A. Oberman. Leiden, 1973.

———. *The Scope of Renaissance Humanism*. Ann Arbor, 1983.

Turchetti, Mario. *Concordia o tolleranza? François Bauduin (1520–1573) e i 'Moyenneurs'*. Geneva, 1984.

Ullmann, Walter. *The Individual and Society in the Middle Ages*. Baltimore, 1966.

———. *Principles of Government and Politics in the Middle Ages*. New York, 1961.

Walker, D. P. *The Ancient Theology: Studies in Christian Platonism from the Fifteenth to the Eighteenth Century*. Ithaca, 1972.

Walzer, Michael. *The Revolution of the Saints: A Study in the Origins of Radical Politics*. Cambridge, Mass., 1965.

Weber, Max. *The Protestant Ethic and the Spirit of Capitalism*. Tr. Talcott Parsons. London, 1930.

Wendel, François. *Calvin et l'humanisme*. Paris, 1976.

————. *Calvin: The Origins and Development of His Religious Thought*. Tr. Philip Mairet. London, 1963.

Wenzel, Siegfried. *The Sin of Sloth: 'Acedia' in Medieval Thought and Literature*. Chapel Hill, 1967.

Willis, E. David. "Rhetoric and Responsibility in Calvin's Theology." *The Context of Contemporary Theology: Essays in Honor of Paul Lehmann*. Eds. Alexander J. McKelway and E. David Willis. Atlanta, 1974.

Index

303